AQUARIUM SYSTEMS

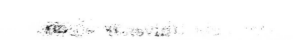

AQUARIUM SYSTEMS

Edited by

A. D. HAWKINS

*Department of Agriculture and Fisheries
for Scotland, Marine Laboratory,
Aberdeen, Scotland*

ACADEMIC PRESS

A Subsidiary of Harcourt Brace Jovanovich, Publishers

London · New York · Toronto · Sydney · San Francisco

ACADEMIC PRESS (LONDON) LTD
24/28 Oval Road
London NW1

United States Edition published by
ACADEMIC PRESS INC.
111 Fifth Avenue
New York, New York 10003

British Library Cataloguing in Publication Data

Aquarium systems.
1. Aquariums
I. Hawkins, A. D.
639.3′4   QH68
ISBN 0–12–333380–6

LCCCN   81–66388

Filmset in Great Britain by Latimer Trend & Company Ltd, Plymouth
Printed in Great Britain by St Edmundsbury Press, Bury St Edmunds, Suffolk

CONTRIBUTORS

P. D. ANTHONY Marine Laboratory, P.O. Box 101, Victoria Road, Aberdeen, Scotland

J. H. S. BLAXTER Dunstaffnage Marine Research Laboratory, P.O. Box 3, Oban, Argyll, Scotland

G. CANSDALE SWS Filtration Ltd, Hartburn, Morpeth, Northumberland, England

C. B. COWEY Institute of Marine Biochemistry, St. Fittick's Road, Aberdeen, Scotland

D. FORD Animal Studies Centre, Freeby Lane, Waltham on the Wold, Melton Mowbray, Leicestershire, England

S. H. GRUBER School of Marine and Atmospheric Science, 4600 Rickenbacker Causeway, Miami, Florida 33149, USA

A. D. HAWKINS Marine Laboratory, P.O. Box 101, Victoria Road, Aberdeen, Scotland

M. M. HELM Fisheries Experiment Station, Benarth Road, Conwy, Gwynedd, North Wales

R. S. KEYES Sea World, San Diego, California, USA

R. LLOYD Fisheries Laboratory, Burnham on Crouch, Essex, England

A. H. McVICAR Marine Laboratory, P.O. Box 101, Victoria Road, Aberdeen, Scotland

R. H. RICHARDS Institute of Aquaculture, University of Stirling, Scotland

D. J. SOLOMON Fisheries Laboratory, Pakefield, Lowestoft, Suffolk, England

J. E. THORPE Freshwater Fisheries Laboratory, Pitlochry, Perthshire, Scotland

P. TYTLER Department of Biology, University of Stirling, Scotland

P. R. WALNE Fisheries Experiment Station, Benarth Road, Conwy, Gwynedd, North Wales

C. S. WARDLE Marine Laboratory, P.O. Box 101, Victoria Road, Aberdeen, Scotland

J. F. WICKINS Fisheries Experiment Station, Benarth Road, Conwy, Gwynedd, North Wales

v

A Tribute to
Peter R. Walne, D.Sc., F.I. Biol.

Peter Walne died on 30 October, 1978 at the age of 52 shortly after completing the manuscript of his contribution to this volume.

He joined the Ministry of Agriculture, Fisheries and Food in 1948, and was appointed to the staff of the Fisheries Experiment Station, Conwy, becoming officer-in-charge in 1968.

Peter's work was in the rearing of oysters, initially developing the techniques pioneered by Dr H. A. Cole in outdoor tanks, and later as knowledge and expertise increased, in closely controlled laboratory conditions. By the early 1960s, a practical system of oyster hatchery operation had been developed, and this was taken up by the shellfish industry. At the time of his death, four private hatcheries in the UK were collectively producing tens of millions of juveniles for home and overseas markets.

In addition to his work with the native oyster, *Ostrea edulis*, Peter realized the potential of hatchery techniques as a way of introducing exotic species to Britain without the risk of importing their associated pests and parasites. It was under his close supervision that the Pacific oyster, *Crassostrea gigas*, was imported from Canada in 1965. This species now provides a valuable fishery in many parts of the UK, supported by hatchery-reared juveniles.

Peter was a prolific writer; his advice on bivalve cultivation and related topics was sought world-wide. He travelled extensively, including visits to work in Canada, Chile, Hong Kong and Israel. At home, he was in demand as a member of various committees and advisory bodies serving science and industry. Peter's scientific prowess and dedication to work were an inspiration to his colleagues and students and many people's careers have been favourably influenced by his guidance.

PREFACE

The research scientist working with living fish faces many problems. The overriding one is the task of collecting and maintaining the live fish in a healthy state, suitable for experimental study. Few laboratories are so well organized that the research worker simply goes along to the aquarium, transfers a fish to his experimental apparatus and starts work. Often it is necessary to construct a small self-contained aquarium before the work can be done. Having selected a suitable species, it is then necessary to obtain the fish, perhaps by going out and catching them. Subsequently, one has to arrive at the best way of keeping them alive and healthy. Then, during experiments, it is common to transfer fish from tank to tank, to anaesthetize them, and to handle them in various ways.

This book was written as a practical guide to fish-keeping in the laboratory. It deals with basic aspects of aquarium construction and design but, in addition, goes much further to consider various methods of fish capture and handling, fish anaesthesia, the application of various surgical procedures, fish diseases and parasites, and the food and feeding of fish in the aquarium. The particular problems of rearing larval fish, of keeping salmonids, sharks and shellfish are also considered. This book does not however contain complete descriptions of existing aquarium systems. The literature is already full of such descriptions.

Such a book had to be a co-operative venture, and is the result of collaboration between quite a large group of authors, each dealing with a different aspect of keeping fish. All the participants are working scientists, with practical experience of the topics they are writing about. Though primarily intended for the research scientist, the book may also prove of interest to those architects and engineers called upon to design aquarium systems. So many of the problems of keeping fish arise from misunderstandings between the many people of different disciplines who become involved in aquarium construction. Hopefully, the book will overcome some of the difficulties.

July 1981   A. D. HAWKINS

ACKNOWLEDGEMENTS

I acknowledge with pleasure the co-operation of the authors who contributed to this book. I am especially grateful to Mr B. B. Parrish of the Marine Laboratory, Aberdeen for his support and encouragement, and to my colleagues Charles Robb, Alastair Johnstone, Paul Anthony, Alan Dunthorn and Kathleen Horner for their help and advice.

CONTENTS

Chapter 1

Aquarium Design

A. D. Hawkins and P. D. Anthony

Marine Laboratory, Aberdeen, Scotland

I. THE AQUARIUM ENVIRONMENT

A. General

Fish come from many different habitats, ranging from regions of great environmental stability, like the deep sea, to very changeable places like the sea-shore, ditches or mud-flats. Some are very conservative in their needs, sensitive to any change in the environment and demanding stable conditions if they are to thrive; others are more adaptable and better able to withstand environmental fluctuations. The fluctuations that the fish encounter may be irregular and unpredictable, but often they are periodic, like daily changes in the light level or seasonal changes in temperature.

All animals are limited in the range of conditions which they can tolerate, and if forced outside these, they will die. The responses that individual organisms may show to environmental changes within their lethal range are of several kinds. One response is an immediate regulatory adaptation to change. Thus, a reduction in salinity may trigger various short-term regulatory mechanisms which enable the fish to maintain a proper balance of internal salts. Fish from environments which show frequent or pronounced changes are usually able to regulate over a much wider range than those which habitually live under relatively constant conditions. Regulation incurs the expenditure of energy and therefore cannot be regarded as an independent process. Its activation in response to an environmental change may restrict the ability of the animal to respond to some other change. It may also limit the level of general activity and the behavioural repertoire of the animal.

On a longer time scale, the organism may acclimate to a set of conditions. That is, it may show long-term morphological and physiological adaptations which are reversible, but fundamental in nature. Thus, the fish may increase the number of its red blood cells in poorly oxygenated water, or may show some reorganization of its metabolism and system of enzymes when exposed to a new temperature. Again, the animal expends energy to maintain and extend its being, but after an initial investment, the heavy running costs of continual regulation are dispensed with, thereby increasing the scope for other activities among which must be included the activation of other regulatory mechanisms. Such a long-term adjustment to environmental change is not only reactive, but can also take place as a developmental or seasonal adaptation which anticipates exposure to a new environment.

Lethal conditions are reached when the level of a particular physical or chemical factor is beyond the capacity of the organism to regulate. An example is the exposure of a fish to an excessively high temperature, or to a high level of a toxic chemical. Lethal levels are generally discovered experimentally for any species by exposing the animal to progressively more extreme conditions and recording their survival times. The tolerance to a particular condition is then expressed as a cumulative mortality curve, from which the median survival time is obtained (i.e. the time during which half the population survive). Alternatively, the concentration level of a particular substance which kills half the population after a given exposure time may be determined.

When fish are to be kept in aquaria, the lethal conditions are not the most important to be considered. The lethal limits simply represent the outermost boundaries of the range of conditions in which the fish can survive. Lethal factors rarely exert a destructive effect at one level and remain entirely harmless below this level. In any case, the objective in a research aquarium is not simply to keep fish alive. Rather, it is to keep fish under conditions to which they are properly acclimated, living well within the range over which they can regulate their physiology and behaviour, preferably close to some optimum where the costs of regulation are minimal.

Within the zone of tolerance of an organism to a particular condition, it can be remarkably difficult to establish an optimum. The physiology of the fish is influenced by a variety of factors, some of them exerting controlling effects upon metabolism, others exerting secondary or directing effects upon more specialized functions. An example of a controlling factor is temperature, which has its outstanding effect at the molecular level, governing rates of reaction in the fish. An example of a directing factor is sound, which may exert its effect by provoking a particular behavioural or hormonal response. Other important factors may act by restricting the energy which can be made available for regulation, or by placing an upper limit on all energy expenditure. Examples of such limiting factors are the metabolites, food, water and the respiratory gases. Limiting factors in general become operational at a particular level, this level marking a transition between a dependent and independent state.

All the various controlling, directing and limiting factors act together, often in an interactive way. Collectively, they establish the changing costs of maintenance and regulation by the animal under different environmental conditions, while also establishing the limits beyond which regulation is no longer possible. Close to the tolerable limits, the fish may be healthy and able to survive indefinitely, but the costs of regulation are high and there is little scope for the fish to show any other activity, or to withstand further environmental change. At such a point, the animal will react poorly to environmental stress or disease, and any small perturbation in the conditions of its existence will spell disaster. The key to keeping fish successfully in captivity is the realization that all the various environmental conditions must be controlled, and that an imbalance in any one condition will undoubtedly affect the capacity of the fish to withstand changes in another. If a fish is diseased, lacking particular amino acids, or at an extreme salinity, it will not be able to cope with too high a temperature or too much noise or light during the period when the imbalance is being rectified. The very act of confining an animal, restricting its sensory experiences, mobility and choice of food, limits its ability to regulate its internal state.

The habitat of any species is a complex of interlinked and interacting environmental factors. A research aquarium must often house a range of organisms from different habitats, and the aquarium environment is therefore inevitably a compromise, especially since it must also function as a working environment for the research scientist, whose needs must also be considered. In this essentially practical guide to fish-keeping, it is not our intention to document the great range of effects that the environment can have upon fish. A detailed review is given by Fry (1971). Instead, we shall consider in turn the most powerful factors which can affect fish and the means by which they can be controlled in the aquarium. It is the responsibility of the individual experimenter to determine the relative importance of these different factors and to reach a compromise appropriate to his or her particular circumstances.

B. Water Quality

Fish obtain their basic necessities from the water in which they live. The most characteristic feature of any aquarium system is therefore the quality of the water it contains. This water must be obtained from some source, pre-treated to make it suitable for the fish, delivered to the fish in sufficient quantities and maintained in good condition. Finally, it must be disposed of.

The water supplied to an aquarium is not pure, but contains dissolved and particulate materials, some necessary for the well-being of the fish, and others harmful. Such is the importance of water quality that Chapters 2, 3 and 4 of this book are devoted to the practical problems of obtaining and maintaining water in suitable condition. A topic of particular interest is the effect of release of the animal's own metabolic waste products into the water together with the breakdown of uneaten food materials. Methods for preventing the accumulation of such products and for restoring the quality of water which has been contaminated in that way are therefore considered in some detail, especially in Chapter 3. Contamination may occur not only at source or from the animals, but often takes place within the aquarium from the materials used in its construction. Chapter 6 considers the suitability of different materials for the aquarium.

The volume of water supplied to an aquarium may at first sight seem to restrict the number of fish that can be maintained within it. However, it is rarely the quantity of water *per se* which limits carrying capacity. The capacity is usually set by the consumption of dissolved oxygen and the accumulation of toxic metabolic products. There are relatively few studies which indicate that space or volume alone can limit growth and metabolism, though it is well established that secondary effects, like competition between individuals or the release of metabolic inhibitors can slow growth. Comfort (1956) does suggest that for guppies, the greatest growth is obtained in the greatest space, but studies which show that the absolute amount of space can influence growth quite independently of population density have been rare, however, despite the considerable importance of the subject. Many and varied secondary factors have usually proved to be responsible for any observed limitation. One of the most important factors is the presence in the water of ectocrines, or external metabolites, released by one organism and affecting the growth and well-being of others. Organic substances are produced by several species of tropical fish which exert inhibitory effects upon the growth of other individuals.

Extensive reviews of the toxicity of different chemical substances to aquatic organisms are given by McKee and Wolf (1963), Sprague and Drury (1969) and Koeman and Strik (1975). The effects of toxicants are often additive or synergistic, and the toxicity of any particular substance is often highly variable in natural waters, where factors like the hardness of the water and the pH often have great significance. Some of these aspects of water quality are considered in Chapters 4 and 6.

Perhaps the most pronounced and damaging changes to water quality originate with the aquarium inhabitants themselves. In particular, water quality is impaired by the end products of nitrogen metabolism. These include ammonia (either as the gas NH_3, or ammonium ion NH_4^+) urea, uric acid and other nitrogenous substances including proteins and amino acids. Ammonia, especially, is one of the most harmful substances to aquatic life, having a variety of detrimental effects, discussed in Kinne (1976). The conversion of the more toxic nitrogen compounds to less toxic nitrate is normally carried out in the aquarium with the aid of micro-organisms residing in water treatment units such as filters. In some aquaria, algae are also used in nitrogen recycling. The process of combating the effects of nitrogenous waste products is facilitated by low stock density, a high water turnover, aeration or oxygenation of the water, frequent cleaning, the removal of faeces and waste food and by the provision of special water treatment facilities.

Fish are not only affected directly by dissolved materials, but can detect very small concentrations of particular dissolved substances. The senses involved are those of smell, mediated by means of the paired olfactory organs on the snout; and taste, with sense organs scattered on the body and fins as well as in the mouth. In aquaria, and especially recirculating systems, the levels of dissolved metabolites and other chemicals can be very high and the ability of the fish to detect these same substances and others may be impaired by the high background levels.

C. Dissolved Salts

Fish in freshwater tend to take up water, with a dilution of their body salts and a loss of ions, while fish in sea water tend to lose water with concentration of their constituent salts. In both cases, the fish must maintain the composition of their blood to provide an osmotic pressure equivalent to about $10\%_{oo}$ (i.e. 10 parts per thousand) salinity.

Freshwater fish cope with body flooding by excreting a highly dilute urine, retaining salts and replacing from their food the small quantities of salts lost. In the sea, fish survive by drinking salt water, secreting the excess chloride ions via the gills and excreting isotonic urine.

The need for ion-osmoregulation is minimized by various structural and physiological adaptations in the acclimated fish, but some active adjustment is still necessary and costs energy. The metabolism of regulating fish in waters of different salinity has been examined by Rao (1968), Farmer and Beamish (1969) and others. Rao found that for rainbow trout, a species which can readily move from one salinity to another, the metabolic rate (measured as oxygen consumption) was least in an isosmotic dilution of sea water. The cost of ion-osmoregulation, at higher salinities or in freshwater, increased at a rate proportional to the overall metabolic rate. Thus, the costs of regulation appeared to be a function of respiratory exchange, confirming that the main interchange of water and dissolved salts takes place across the gills. In Rao's experiments, the fish could handle the additional costs of regulation, over and above those of physical activity. The ion-osmoregulatory load did not therefore limit activity. Under conditions of greatly increased oxygen demand, for example after heavy feeding, the costs of regulation may become limiting and may restrict the scope for activity.

Some fish are stenohaline; unable to tolerate changes in salinity. Examples are provided by many deep water and oceanic marine fish, and the strictly freshwater fish. Many euryhaline fish, on the other hand, can fully adapt to a range of salinities from freshwater to full sea water. Examples are the rainbow trout and flounder. Euryhaline fish with a damaged skin, whose osmoregulatory abilities are impaired, may have their osmotic problems alleviated if they are placed in an isosmotic solution. Stenohaline fish will rarely survive such treatment, however, because they are specifically adapted to only a narrow range of salinities.

Salinity within an aquarium is usually determined at the water source, though there may be a gradual increase in salinity from evaporation in still water or recirculating systems operated for long periods. The restoration of water lost by evaporation is discussed in Chapter 3. Marine aquaria which draw their water from coastal areas may show a reduced salinity, and it may therefore be necessary to restrict water abstraction to periods around high tide. Where oceanic or deep-sea species are to be kept, it may be necessary to increase the salinity of dilute or coastal water by the addition of sea-salt or synthetic salts. Sea water generally ranges between 32 and 37‰ salinity, though this may be much reduced in the vicinity of rivers, freshwater upwelling, or run-off from the land. Salinities of up to 40‰ are found in inland seas like the Great Salt Lake of Utah, or the Dead Sea.

The contamination of freshwater with high concentrations of dissolved salts may occur close to the sea coast, or in areas of very low rainfall. Also close to the coast, a layer of freshwater may sit upon a deeper layer of sea water, and may move up and down with the tide. The problems encountered in water with a very low concentration of salts, such as snow-melt water, are discussed in Chapter 4.

Salinity is normally defined as the total weight of solid material contained in one kilogram of sea water. Chloride accounts for about 55% of the salinity, and the chlorinity often provides the basis for determining salinity (see Appendix).

Chlorinity can be determined by titration with a silver nitrate solution in the presence of an indicator. However, salinity is most commonly determined by measuring the electrical conductivity of the water at a given temperature. A quick determination of salinity may also be made with a hydrometer (the specific gravity of sea water varies with salinity and temperature), or optically by means of a refractometer.

D. Dissolved Gases

The majority of aquatic organisms need oxygen and must obtain it from the surrounding water. The oxygenation or aeration of the water is therefore of fundamental importance in any aquarium, especially as the oxygen supply is one of the factors which may ultimately limit the capacity of a particular volume of water for carrying fish (Haskell, 1955).

The oxygen dissolved in water comes from two main sources: the atmosphere and green plants. The actual content is a function of temperature and salinity. Water of low salinity holds more gas in solution at saturation than water of high salinity. Cold water contains more gas at saturation than warm, so that if water is heated, oxygen and other gases will either escape into the atmosphere or the water will become supersaturated. The transfer of oxygen and other gases from the atmosphere to water and vice versa, is dependent upon the ambient pressure, high pressure driving more gas into solution. Thus, a reduction in atmospheric pressure can also result in previously saturated water becoming supersaturated. Oxygen diffuses only slowly through water, and the dissolved oxygen at depth is mainly derived from the circulation of water originally oxygenated at the surface. The oxygen level at depth therefore rarely exceeds that at the surface, though the carrying capacity of the water under pressure is higher.

Oxygen can also be derived from plants as a by-product of photosynthesis, which takes place only in the presence of light (in the dark, plants consume oxygen by respiration). On sunny days, in shallow water, so much oxygen is generated that the surface waters may supersaturate, releasing oxygen into the atmosphere.

Low oxygen levels can occur in deep water or water isolated from the atmosphere and the superficial photosynthetic layer, especially where the bacterial breakdown of dissolved organic material is taking place. Minimum oxygen layers therefore particularly occur below surface regions of high productivity, where thermal stratification inhibits mixing. A nocturnal depletion of oxygen can also take place near the surface, from the respiration of dense blooms of plankton.

Cold water, saturated with oxygen by contact with the atmosphere, rarely contains more than about 15 mg/l (ppm) of dissolved oxygen. At the other extreme, water containing less than 3 mg/l dissolved oxygen cannot be tolerated by many fish for long periods. Indeed for most fish, there is a critical oxygen level, below which the fish cannot survive indefinitely. As the level of environmental oxygen is progressively reduced from an initial high value, the animal first passes through a stage of respiratory independence, where oxygen uptake is unaffected by the environmental level, but at lower environmental levels, a stage of respiratory dependence ensues, where any further reduction in oxygen level results in a reduced oxygen uptake. This limitation in uptake severely restricts the scope for metabolic activity by the fish.

The level at which respiratory dependence occurs varies from species to species. Some fish can operate anaerobically to some degree, and can therefore withstand lower oxygen levels. Within a species, individual fish can be acclimated to low oxygen levels. The critical level is also greatly affected by the prevailing temperature. The coho salmon shows a reduction in its swimming ability at oxygen levels below about 10 mg/l at

20°C (Davis *et al.*, 1963), a value close to the saturation level. The goldfish shows impaired activity only below about 3 mg/l. Thus, whereas the former can only exhibit its full range of activity in well mixed and aerated water, the latter can show great versatility in its behaviour in quite poorly mixed, badly oxygenated environments. Some idea of the general level of resting oxygen uptake by fish is given by Brett and Groves (1979). These authors quote a mean of 89 ± 34 (SD) mg of O_2/kg/h, and an extreme range of 26 to 229 mg of O_2/kg/h for the standard metabolism of fish, fully acclimated to the test temperature. Standard metabolism, the minimum rate measured from resting fish, varies greatly with temperature, however. Brett and Groves (1979) have pointed out that a multiplier of 2.3 for a 10°C temperature change provides a near approximation for temperature effects close to the mid-point of a fish's normal environmental range. The size of a fish will also affect its standard metabolic rate, the oxygen consumption per unit weight decreasing with size.

Active 'game' fish may have a very high oxygen consumption even at rest, and like the coho salmon, may show a dependence of oxygen consumption and restriction of metabolic scope at quite high environmental oxygen levels. Certainly many workers have found these species difficult to maintain in captivity.

The greatest changes in oxygen demand by the fish are associated with changes in the pattern of locomotor activity. The active metabolic rate measured for very strongly swimming fish can exceed the standard or resting rate by a factor of 8 to 10 times, the highest rates approaching 1000 mg of O_2/kg/h for the best swimmers, whereas it only reaches about 300 mg of O_2/kg/h for a fish like the cod. The active metabolic rate appears to represent the highest rate of oxygen uptake possible for the fish through a limitation in the ability of the fish to extract more oxygen from the medium. The animal may make metabolic demands over and above those represented by the rate of oxygen uptake, particularly in contracting the great flank muscles for rapid escape swimming, but only by operating anaerobically and acquiring an oxygen debt which must later be paid off (Chapter 15). While the fish is paying off the debt, it may appear to be inactive but its oxygen consumption will be considerably higher than that for standard metabolism. It may also be suffering from acidosis resulting from the endogenous release of lactic acid, which may impede oxygen transport. Thus, newly caught or recently active fish may need special treatment to ensure they have enough oxygen. It is also important that fish in the aquarium should not be forced into excessive swimming or other activity, since this will greatly increase the oxygen demand. For game fish, especially, this high demand may force the fish into oxygen debt which cannot be paid off.

A particularly important factor affecting oxygen consumption by fish is the level of feeding. A resting fish, heavily fed, may have double the oxygen consumption of a starved fish, the increase gradually building up after feeding and falling back to the fasting level only after several days. In intensive fish culture, a key factor in determing the carrying capacity is therefore the relationship between oxygen consumption and the quantity of food supplied. Willoughby *et al.* (1972) give an average value for salmonids of 0.25 kg of oxygen being required to metabolize 1 kg of trout food at temperatures between 5 and 18°C. Under these intensive conditions, an oxygen level of above 5.0 m$_s$ O_2/l is advised, not only to supply the oxygen needs of the fish but also to counteract the effects of the other major limit to carrying capacity, ammonia accumulation (see Chapter 3). Downing and Merkens (1955) showed that the survival times of rainbow trout in the presence of high concentrations of un-ionized ammonia increased significantly with increasing oxygen concentration. As design limits for intensive salmon culture Westers and Pratt (1977) suggest a dissolved oxygen level of 90% saturation in the water supplied, and over 5.0 mg of O_2/l in the effluent. When considering the oxygen levels within an aquarium, it should be noted that the fish are not the only consumers of oxygen. Other organisms requiring O_2 are present both in suspension and on surfaces, while in a recirculating system, the nitrifying bacteria in the biological filter are oxygen consumers. These other organisms can sometimes consume as much oxygen as the fish (Chapter 3).

In some still water aquaria, sufficient oxygen is transferred to the water by passive diffusion from the atmosphere. The transfer is mainly a function of the surface area exposed to the atmosphere. Since diffusion is rather slow, the exchange can be promoted by circulating the water. In most aquarium systems, however, some form of active aeration is necessary to promote oxygen transfer, both by increasing the area of gas in contact with the water and by inducing movement and turbulence in the water itself. A thorough survey of various methods of aeration is given by Wheaton (1977). It should not be forgotten that one way of providing oxygen is by the cultivation of green plants and algae within the aquarium, although allowance must be made for the respiratory needs of the plants during darkness.

An excess of dissolved oxygen does not by itself appear to be harmful to fish except at very high partial pressures. However, the supersaturation of water with oxygen, air, or other dissolved gases can lead to a syndrome which has been termed 'gas bubble disease' (GBD). Symptoms of the disease in its most severe form are exopthalmia (or protruding eyes), an extended abdomen, gas bubbles in the inter-ray membranes of the fins and small skin blisters. Haemorrhaging may take place in the renal and other tissues, and gas bubbles may appear in the blood system. In mild cases, the only obvious external symptom may be a slight exopthalmia, though by the time the swelling is visible, the retina may already be damaged. Supersaturation of water with dissolved gases can occur where water is heated, where active photosynthesis is taking place, or where previously saturated water is exposed to a lower ambient pressure. In aquarium systems, it is common where the suction side of a pump is leaking, where pumping is intermittent and gas is entrained with the water, where water is aerated under pressure (for example at the bottom of a deep reservoir) and then fed to a shallow tank, or where water heats up in storage or in passing to the fish tanks. Air entrainment can also occur at source. Generally, supersaturation with oxygen is not the main problem since this gas is rapidly consumed by the fish; more often it is supersaturation with the remaining dissolved nitrogen that leads to gas bubble disease. A dissolved oxygen reading may indicate levels below saturation when a dangerous level of nitrogen supersaturation prevails. A saturometer, which gives a measure of total dissolved gases, can be useful in testing for this condition. Gas bubble disease has been reviewed by Harvey (1975), Wedermeyer *et al.* (1976), and Rucker (1972).

The accumulation of carbon dioxide produced by the aquarium inhabitants is not normally a problem in the aquarium provided that sufficient oxygen is present. It is only under rather special circumstances that carbon dioxide excess, rather than oxygen lack, becomes limiting. The commonest of these conditions occurs when fish are being transported (Fry and Norris, 1962). A discussion of acid–base imbalance, and the effects of high environmental carbon dioxide level upon oxygen uptake is provided by Spotte (1979).

The dissolved oxygen content of water may be measured in terms of mg of O_2/l (ppm) by the classical Winkler titration (Strickland and Parsons, 1968) but this method is rather tedious. A great variety of polarographic oxygen sensors are now available and are very convenient to use though they must be carefully and frequently calibrated. They may be calibrated against Winkler titration but a commoner technique is to place the electrode in water of known salinity, saturated with air at a given temperature and pressure. A table relating dissolved oxygen concentration to salinity and temperature is given in the appendix.

Oxygen electrodes essentially measure oxygen partial pressure rather than concentration. Thus, though air-saturated solutions of differing salinity at the same temperature and pressure may contain different concentrations of oxygen, they will give the same readings on an oxygen electrode. Conversely, if the temperature of a solution is changing rapidly with no gas exchange, the electrode will show a change in reading. Allowance must therefore be made for any change in salinity, temperature or pressure which takes place after calibration, if the oxygen content is to be expressed as mg O_2/l rather than as % saturation or mm Hg (see Appendix).

E. Light

Light is perhaps the most regularly periodic of the variables to which fish are exposed, and the one which usually conveys the most detailed information to the fish about its surroundings. Light is essentially directive in its effect, acting upon specific sense organs rather than upon metabolism, but it can trigger physiological responses, an example being the effect of photoperiod upon the endocrine organs.

The size and complexity of a fish's visual system is some guide to the importance of light in its natural habitat. The pike, *Esox lucius*, has well developed eyes and optic lobes and requires light for its predatory activities to be successful. On the other hand, many catfish living in turbid waters have much-reduced visual systems. Some of the cave-dwelling fish lose their eyes during development. The eyes of the eel are small and relatively unimportant during its freshwater phase, but as the fish prepares for and then embarks upon its long migration through the sea, the eyes enlarge and become more typical of those of deep-sea fish. Most shallow freshwater and coastal marine fish have eyes which can perform well by day or by night. Other fish, such as those from deep water, have eyes which are protected against high light levels and which operate efficiently only when light is scarce.

Visible light (that is, light to which the human eye is sensitive) is electromagnetic radiation at wavelengths of approximately 350 to 750 nm, extending from the ultraviolet to the infrared. This waveband includes only half the total energy received from the sun at the earth's surface, the total waveband extending from 290–3000 nm, and peaking at about 480 nm in the blue-green part of the spectrum. Sunlight is selectively and rapidly attenuated in water both by absorption and scattering, and the light spectrum is quite different at different depths. The first parts of the spectrum to be removed are the infrared and ultra-violet wavelengths. The spectral quality of underwater light varies according to the type and amount of dissolved and particulate matter in the water. Yellow dissolved organic material forms in most fresh and coastal waters, from the breakdown of plant materials, and selectively filters out blue light, allowing greatest penetration to green. The eyes of fish are often adapted to make best use of the light available in their particular habitat, and different species may have different spectral sensitivities. As a general rule, marine fish have their peak sensitivities shifted towards the blue (500–550 nm) in comparison with freshwater fish (540–620 nm).

Though the efficient use of available radiation may be critical in the natural environment, in the aquarium it is of much less significance. If the spectral quality of underwater light pertinent to a particular species must be reproduced, then green or blue filters may be used in conjunction with artificial light or daylight. The large non-inflammable acetate filters for theatre floodlights are suitable and are available in a wide range of colours, often with charts showing their detailed spectral characteristics. They can be used separately, or in combination.

The level of underwater light varies with many factors, including the altitude of the sun, the degree of cloud cover, water depth and clarity, and shadowing by plants. The light period varies diurnally and with season. It is a sensible rule of thumb that no fish should be subjected to light levels much higher than those encountered in the natural environment. The light level is especially important with animals of nocturnal habit, or those living in the deep sea, since normal laboratory light intensities may severely damage the visual system. With such animals, it is advisable to exercise care from the moment they are caught, bringing them to the surface in a shielded enclosure, and subsequently protecting them from high light levels. Fish subjected to too high a level may show pale colouration, loss of appetite, extreme nervousness and some of the symptoms of the stress syndrome described in Chapter 15. Such fish should be provided with shelter, or be continually maintained under dim lighting.

As long as feeding behaviour, general orientation and such behaviour patterns as schooling are maintained, there appears to be no disadvantage in keeping fish under a light regime that is dimmer than that of the natural environment. Where plants are not being kept, and there is doubt about the correct level of illumination, it is wise to err on the dark side.

Photosynthesis generally demands much higher energy levels than vision, and if plants are included in the aquarium, higher light levels are generally required. The photosynthetic efficiency shown by plants depends not only on the light intensity; particular photosynthetic pigments are involved and the wavelength of light is therefore important. For many higher plants at low light intensities, red light is more photosynthetically active than blue, but the difference is not great, and many plants can use a wide band of the spectrum of sunlight.

The photoperiod, and seasonal changes in the photoperiod, are important for many animals and plants. For fish from higher latitudes, maturation is accelerated in the spring spawning species by increasing day length, while autumn and winter spawners are affected by decreasing day length. Underwater, the variation in light level may cover 7–10 orders of magnitude over a 24 h period. Some visual systems adapt to the slow changes more rapidly than the human eye. Abrupt changes in the light level should generally be avoided in the aquarium since they may cause sensitive fish to panic, or may take place faster than the fish eye can adapt, so that the animals injure themselves by swimming into the tank walls. Fragile pelagic species, which do not normally contact any surfaces, are best continuously illuminated at a level where they can see the tank walls and any other obstructions.

Variations in day length may be obtained most easily by exposing the fish to daylight. If direct exposure to daylight is too bright, neutral density filters can reduce the level. Where the variation required is different to that of the natural prevailing cycle, artificial light is necessary, control being provided by switching in dimming circuits with a time clock. For most research aquaria, aritificial lighting generally offers greater flexibility and avoids the high levels of daylight which often lead to excessive growth of brown algae as well as affecting fish directly.

Under natural conditions, light shines down on fish from above, the precise angular distribution depending on the altitude and azimuth of the sun. Under cloudy conditions, in turbid water and with increasing depth, the angular distribution of light becomes more widespread. In some conditions of turbidity, or near a reflecting bottom, a high percentage of light is reflected upwards. In the aquarium, most light should come from above. If too much light comes from the side or beneath, the dorsal light reaction of the fish may be interfered with, and orientation disturbed. Light coloured or reflecting tank bottoms may also induce a state of extreme nervousness in captive fish.

Where artificial lighting is provided, fluorescent lamps have many advantages. They have a low heat output and long-life, though they may initially be more costly. Their diffuse cool light avoids local warming of the water. A wide range of spectral outputs are available, depending on the fluorescent coating of the tube. Warm white tubes have a high yellow/orange content, while other tubes closely replicate the spectrum of daylight, including the ultraviolet component. Some specialist tubes for plant growth have emphasized red and blue components, but can make plants appear pale to the human eye. The spectral quality of a particular tube can be altered, if required, with an acetate filter. The incandescent tungsten filament lamp has a yellow/red bias, making it suitable for plant growth and giving a natural appearance to the human eye. In addition, the lamps are relatively cheap to buy, the light is more readily directed and focussed, and more readily dimmed. When dimmed, the spectral composition shifts towards the red end of the spectrum but again the spectral output can be controlled with acetate filters. Diffuse light can be obtained from an array of many low-wattage incandescent lamps behind an opal plastic screen. High pressure quartz halogen lamps closely resemble daylight and are very efficient, but their initial cost is high. Sodium vapour lamps will provide good algal growth, though their spectral output in no way resembles daylight.

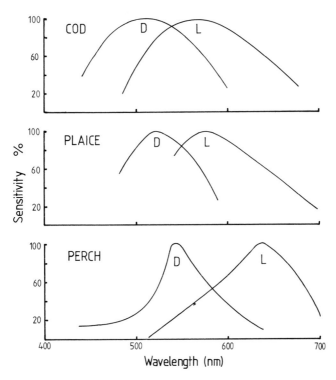

Fig. 1. Spectral sensitivity of three fish adapted to light (L) and dark (D) conditions, demonstrating the shift of sensitivity away from the blue end of the spectrum from deep marine (cod), to shallow marine (plaice), to freshwater (perch) habitats (from Protasov).

Commonly in the aquarium, lighting is required which is dim to the fish but which permits them to be observed and photographed. If the spectral sensitivity of the fish is known, then a lamp can be chosen with its energy peak well away from the sensitivity peak of the fish. A suitable arrangement for marine fish like the cod is to illuminate the tank with deep red light (with a spectrum above 650nm) and then to observe the fish with a red sensitive television camera (for example a simple silicon diode tube; low light level cameras, with an intensified tube, are generally green sensitive). In general, modern television equipment enables fish to be observed at much lower light levels than can be achieved with film cameras and allows observation in real time. If a silhouette of the fish is sufficient, then the light level can be further reduced by employing a reflective background. Infrared lighting, in combination with an infrared viewer (as used by the military for night observation) is effective only in very shallow water. The blue end of the spectrum offers even less scope for viewing fish. Blue lies nearer the peak sensitivity of most fish, and the short wavelengths are readily scattered, leading to poor resolution.

In measuring light levels in the aquarium, it is sensible to ensure that the spectral sensitivity of the light meter corresponds approximately to that of the animal of interest. Most commercially available meters are photometers, that is, they have a spectral response similar to the human eye under daylight conditions. The spectral range of many aquatic animals will be different and may vary with the overall light level. Since the spectral range of few aquatic animals is known, it may therefore be more satisfactory to measure light radiometrically, in terms of the energy in a specified wavelength interval. The most frequently measured quantity is irradiance, the energy falling on a surface per second from all directions, measured in watts/m^2. Alternatively, the quantity can be expressed in quanta/s/m^2 over a given wavelength interval. A photometer is normally calibrated in units of illuminance (the photometric equivalent of irradiance) and expressed in lumens/m^2 or lux. The measurement of illuminance or irradiance is normally done with the meter pointing upwards or towards the light source, and with a

Table I. Maximum illuminance in various underwater environments.

Habitat	Depth (m)	Illuminance (Lux)
Ocean type 1 (clear)	1	44 000
	10	22 000
	100	530
Coastal water type 1 (clear)	1	37 000
	10	5 900
Coastal water type 9 (turbid)	1	18 000
	10	50
River, clear	1	50 000
River, turbid	1	20 000

diffusing screen in front of the light–sensitive element. Values for the illuminance at different depths are given in Table I. It should be remembered that these values are appropriate only for organisms with the same spectral characteristics as the human eye.

F. Temperature

Temperature profoundly affects all biological systems. It alters the properties of most biological materials and determines the rate and type of biochemical reactions. Indeed, temperature is perhaps the most potent of all the environmental factors controlling and governing the metabolism of animals.

Water has a high thermal capacity compared to air; that is, it can absorb a large amount of heat energy for a small rise in temperature. It therefore provides a thermally stable environment. Changes in temperature of a large mass of water normally occur slowly in nature and the larger the mass, the slower the change. Small ponds, rock pools and shallow flats may, however, show dramatic fluctuations in temperature related to the time of day or the tidal cycle. In contrast, the surface waters of the oceans undergo daily temperature changes of only 0.2–0.3°C (Sverdrup *et al.*, 1942) and the deeper ocean waters are even more stable. Seasonal variations in water temperature are generally most marked at high latitudes and are nearly non-existent at the equator. Geographical variation in temperature in the oceans and long river systems will only affect migratory and wide-ranging species. However, spatial variations in temperature can be very marked at a thermocline and at the confluences of streams, rivers and ocean currents. The ability of fish to adjust to temperature change varies greatly from species to species.

Fish are thermal conformers, that is their temperature follows that of the surrounding water. There is evidence that some large, very active fish such as tuna and lamnid sharks are warm-bodied from metabolic heat production, but these are the exceptions. Fish are found in polar waters at temperatures down to $-2°C$ and in tropical swamps and hot springs where temperatures may rise to $40°C$, demonstrating the full evolutionary adaptability of the fish body (see Brett, 1970 for review). The tolerance range of individual species is of course much narrower. Some species (eurythermal types), have a wide range of temperature tolerance, while others are much more restricted in their range (stenothermal types).

Fry (1971) has drawn a distinction between the zone of tolerance of the organism (within which the lifespan of the organism is not directly affected by temperature change), and the zone of resistance (within which the animal will be killed in a determinate period of time). The boundary between the two is the incipient lethal temperature.

The thermal tolerances of fish vary greatly. Many cold water fish are still active at the freezing point of water. Indeed some marine fish can supercool (de Vries, 1971). Tropical species can have quite high lower lethal temperatures, for example around 12°C for the puffer *Spheroides maculatus*. The upper limit of some Antarctic species is about 5°C while some temperate and tropical species still thrive at temperatures above 30°C. Within the upper and lower limits of temperature tolerance for the species there is usually an optimum temperature zone for most efficient physiological functioning of the fish under prevailing environmental conditions. Different physiological activities have different thermal optima and a change of conditions may lead to a change in the preferred temperature. Brett (1971) has shown that the optimum temperature for growth in salmon becomes lower as food becomes scarcer.

If a fish's thermal environment lies outside the optimum temperature zone, the animal may still acclimate if given enough time. Temperature acclimation is accomplished not simply by changes in metabolic rate, but by metabolic reorganization involving different pathways and enzyme activities. The reorganization will proceed differently in different tissues, but the overall effect is to enable the fish to function more efficiently at the new temperature (Shaklee *et al.*, 1977). A further complication is that the degree and speed of acclimation shown by a fish will be affected by the temperature to which the fish was previously exposed. Thus, if similar fish from different temperature regimes are put together at a lower temperature, the fish from the lowest temperature will acclimate faster and have a lower limit of thermal tolerance. Individuals may also show ontogenetic variation in thermal tolerance, the youngest and oldest stages often being the least tolerant.

Temperature tolerance is often affected by other environmental factors including light, salinity and water chemistry, and also by endocrine activity and diet. For example, a change in the tolerance of fish may occur in anticipation of cold winter temperatures and be cued by photoperiod. Such anticipatory adjustment may be common in fish encountering widely varying seasonal temperatures and will be regulated by endocrine activity. Some tropical species may show only reactive adjustments. Exposure to sub-lethal concentrations of chemicals frequently results in a decrease of the upper limits of temperature tolerance. Temperature regulation in fish is largely behavioural, by avoidance of extremes and preference for the optimum, thereby minimizing any metabolic and physiological changes. Fish subjected to sudden temperature changes, however, show acute physiological responses, the effect upon metabolic rate being apparent as changes in cardiovascular activity and respiration. If the change is dramatic enough, the temperature of the animal will reach its critical thermal minimum or maximum and death will result.

In the aquarium, fish are largely denied the use of any behavioural regulation, and the aquarium design and management must compensate for this loss. Sudden changes of temperature in the aquarium should be avoided. Such thermal shocks are most likely to occur when fish are transferred from tank to tank or when they first arrive in the aquarium complex. A simple rule is to float transfer containers plus fish in their new tanks until the temperature has equilibrated, or alternatively to slowly mix the water in the container with that in the tank over half an hour or more. Increases in temperatures have the most distressing effect since respiration rate and excitability increase while the oxygen-carrying capacity of the water decreases. Such temperature increases in established tanks may result from refrigeration breakdown or thermostat malfunction. The damage caused by faulty thermostats in a heated system can be minimized by employing the minimum wattage heaters required for temperature control or by including a high temperature cut-out in the circuit. This could simply be a second thermostat in series with the first, but set to a slightly higher temperature so that it is on all the time during normal operations. Such a thermostat should, however, be serviced regularly to ensure it does not stick on.

The effects on fish of a reduction in temperature, as occurs during heater breakdown, may be less immediately apparent but equally damaging especially to those fish with a high optimum temperature and limited tolerance, for example coral reef fishes. Indeed, the characteristic difference between tropical and temperate fish lies in the lower and not the upper lethal temperature (Fry, 1967). The effects of chilling range from decreased respiration rate, sluggishness and loss of appetite to death when the critical thermal minimum is reached. Incipient effects of chilling, such as decreased resistance to infection, may become apparent sometime after the chilling has been remedied.

The aim of a temperature control system is to maintain the temperature of the aquarium water at or about the optimum for the species concerned. In addition, such changes as occur should be gradual and limited to the acclimation rate of the most sensitive species. It is generally true that acclimation to increased temperature occurs much more rapidly, often within 24h, than acclimation to lowered temperature, which may take several days or even weeks (Brett, 1970).

Where a great quantity of water is available at an appropriate temperature, there is no need for any elaborate temperature control.

Water is passed through the aquarium at sufficient flow rate to counter any heat transfer to or from the tank surroundings. Because no direct control is exercised over temperature, the obvious limitation is that the small fluctuations in water temperature that do occur must be acceptable to the tank inmates. Most fish farms and hatcheries operate in this way, a fast throughput of water being a normal part of the design in order to achieve high stock densities. Marine aquaria with continuous pumping from the sea may similarly operate at ambient temperatures. It is of course advantageous that supply pipes, distribution systems and even tanks themselves, be insulated if there is likely to be a high rate of heat transfer. Supply lines, in particular, may need to be buried. The big danger in such systems is that cool water may warm up sufficiently to become supersaturated with gases and give rise to gas bubble disease.

In many aquaria, some active temperature control is necessary, heat being removed or added to the tank water. The energy transfer may be arranged to occur in the tank itself, between the tank and the surrounding air (space heating or cooling) or, in the case of tanks linked to water circulation systems, at some point remote from the tank. Temperature control can be extremely expensive in aquaria with a fast turnover of water, and where a great deal of cooling or heating is necessary, it is usually applied to a separate closed circuit of smaller water volume.

Temperature is measured in degrees Celsius (°C). In small aquaria, without elaborate temperature control, temperature may be monitored with a conventional mercury in glass thermometer, but in larger systems, where temperature must continually be monitored or where the temperature is to be controlled, it is more common to employ electrical resistance thermometers either placed in the tanks or inserted into pockets in the pipeline.

G. Pressure

Fish live at widely different depths both in freshwater and in the sea and are therefore subjected to very different hydrostatic pressures. The effects of greatly increased pressure upon an animal acclimated or physiologically adapted to shallow depths can be profound. There can be immediate excitation of activity, the fish showing tremors and locomotor abnormalities. If the pressure is increased still further, this phase of neurological disturbance may be followed by a widespread contraction of the voluntary muscles (tetany), convulsions, paralysis and death. Rapid compression and decompression have deleterious effects on all but a few animals and even quite small pressure changes of a few atmospheres can have a severe effect upon fish containing a gas space like the swimbladder (see Chapter 7).

In the aquarium, organisms are rarely exposed to an increased hydrostatic pressure, but they must often live at a reduced pressure compared with their original habitat. In general, fish from as deep as 1200–1400 m (pressures of about 120–140 atmospheres) can survive with unimpaired vitality if they are brought to the surface carefully (Brauer, 1972). Creatures from greater depths may suffer more severe stress and show greatly altered behaviour.

Thus, if fish from depths of down to 1000 m or even greater are brought to the surface without mechanical damage or damage to the swimbladder, maintained at an appropriate temperature (3–5°C for many fish from the deep sea or deep lakes), salinity (deep-sea fish are stenohaline) and light level (deep-water species are accustomed to very low light levels), then they may be kept at atmospheric pressure without special difficulty. Many of the pelagic deep-sea fish undergo extensive vertical migrations and are not harmed at all by exposure to low hydrostatic pressures. This is not to say that such species are easy to keep. Deep-water fish are often very fragile and easily damaged, and the need to keep them at low temperatures and light levels may pose problems. Some deep-water organisms are accustomed to low oxygen levels and may be harmed by normal surface levels. The important thing is that there is no need for high pressures to be provided for these species. Fish from very great depths, however, show fundamental biochemical and other subcellular differences to their shallow-water counterparts and must therefore be maintained in high-pressure aquaria at hydrostatic pressures of between 100 and 1000 atmospheres. The very severe problems encountered in obtaining and maintaining fish at these high pressures are considered by papers in Brauer (1972). In general, high-pressure aquaria are suitable only for rather small organisms.

A particular problem which is encountered in the aquarium is that of fish being over-buoyant at normal hydrostatic pressures. Fish with swimbladders which are damaged during capture, and fish stressed by confinement or suffering from gas bubble disease, may over-produce gas. They bob about at the surface, becoming hyperactive, which results in more stress, setting up a vicious circle which is difficult to break. The symptoms can sometimes be alleviated by putting the fish in a larger deeper tank, or in some cases, by removing gas from the swimbladder with a syringe.

The sensitivity of fish to small pressure changes has recently been reviewed (Blaxter and Tytler, 1978). The saithe is sensitive to changes of the order of 0.5% of the adapted hydrostatic pressure. Many marine organisms respond in phase with tidal rhythms and may be entrained to tidal changes in hydrostatic pressure. Hydrostatic pressure is normally expressed in N/m^2, mm Hg, bars, or atmospheres (see appendix for conversion factors), and can be given either as absolute pressure or as gauge pressure (i.e. the pressure relative to atmospheric pressure). The atmosphere is often a very convenient unit, because hydrostatic pressure increases with water depth by very nearly 1 atm per 10 m. A great variety of pressure gauges and meters are available, and find their main aquarium application in indicating the performance of pumps.

H. Sound and Vibration

It is often forgotten that many fish are acutely sensitive to sound and other mechanical disturbances of the water. Though the hearing of most species is restricted to low frequencies (below 3 kHz for nearly all fish, and below 1 kHz for most), at these frequencies they can often detect very low level sounds, only just above the level of background noise in the natural environment. Moreover, they can distinguish between sounds of differing frequency, amplitude, and direction, and many species produce sounds, especially during courtship.

The aquarium is often a very noisy place, with underwater noise levels in aquarium tanks often very much higher than those in the sea or in freshwater. Much of the noise comes from the machinery, pumps and compressors associated with the aquarium, and characteristically contains strong single frequencies in its spectrum. Human footfalls, doors opening and closing, etc., can also be troublesome, and their strongly impulsive nature may evoke startle-responses from the aquarium inhabitants. Vibration is transmitted to the water mainly through the floor and tank supports, but also through the water pipes.

With particularly sensitive fish, or where the acoustical behaviour of fish is being studied, it may be necessary to reduce noise levels in the aquarium. Noise reduction is not a matter of eliminating airborne noise, however, since there is little direct coupling between sound in air and in water. Instead, it is necessary to reduce the transmission of vibrations, or structure-borne sound into the water. The main measures which must be taken are to remove any machinery well away from the aquarium tanks, preferably placing the pumps and compressors on anti-vibration mounts. In one aquarium system, this is achieved by having a separate floor for the plant room with the floors supporting the aquarium tanks floating on resilient material. Pipes joining the machinery to the tanks should be of large bore and should incorporate flexible couplings. The tanks themselves can be placed on a mat of resilient material, while the walkways should be covered with rubber or cork to reduce the impact of footfalls.

Underwater sound is measured by means of a hydrophone and sound level meter. The level is usually expressed in decibels relative to a reference pressure, which for water is normally taken as 1 μbar (1 dyne/cm^2) or 1 Pa (1 Pa = 1 N/m^2 = 10 μbars), which is quite different to the reference pressure normally used for sound in air (0.0002 dyne/cm^2). Ambient noise levels in the sea are described by Wenz (1964). There is little data available on noise conditions in freshwater lakes and rivers, though impairment of the hearing of a salmonid by high ambient noise levels is considered by Hawkins and Johnstone (1978).

II. AQUARIUM DESIGN

A. General

An aquarium is an enclosed volume of water containing a mixture of selected and unselected captive organisms. It is essentially unstable and to obtain stability must be carefully designed and managed.

As soon as water is placed in an aquarium tank, changes in water chemistry begin and these accelerate as the stocking density of the tank is increased. In an open, or flow-through aquarium system, the water is used only once and is then discarded. Though there may be some pre-treatment to adjust the sediment content, temperature or concentration of dissolved gases, the flow rate is usually sufficient to avoid contamination by the aquarium inhabitants. The tanks are generally arranged in parallel, rather than in series to minimize such effects. Thus, there is no need for elaborate water treatment. In a closed, or recirculating aquarium system, the water is continually recycled. Such systems are more independent of the environmental changes which affect open systems but the aquarium inhabitants tend to change the composition of the aquarium water. The nature of the various changes which occur in the aquarium water are detailed in Chapters 3 and 4. Unchecked, they would lead to a steady deterioration of water quality in terms of its ability to support animal life. When setting up any aquarium, large or small, the aim is to arrest this process of deterioration and thereafter exercise control over water quality.

Methods of control vary, of course, depending on such things as the size and complexity of the system and the sensitivity and stocking rate of the occupants. However, the main features are to ensure a supply of good quality water, and then to maintain its quality by the removal of accumulated metabolites (notably ammonia and carbon dioxide) and by maintenance of the correct levels of pH, temperature and dissolved gases.

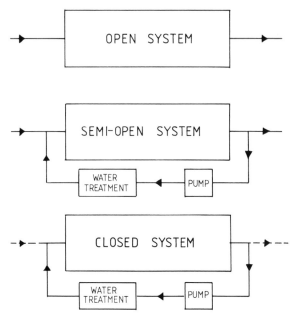

Fig. 2. Water circulation systems. In the open and semi-open systems, the water replacement is at a high rate and normally takes place continuously. In a closed system, the replacement rate is low and probably intermittent, most of the waste removal and detoxification being performed by filters.

The maintenance of water quality is accomplished using some combination of aeration, filtration and temperature control, often involving circulation of the water.

The complexity of aquaria can vary from the single static tank to the heavily stocked, multi-tank, flow-through and recirculating arrangements, common in farms and hatcheries. The small, single-tank system is considered in detail in Chapter 5. It is a common fallacy that such a tank can consist of a balanced system of animals, plants and bacteria where water quality control is effected by the living organisms themselves. It is certainly true that such a system may require a minimal input of essential metabolites and energy and only cursory management but the capacity of the still water aquarium for the self-correction of any imbalance is nevertheless very limited. A threat to stability usually arises when the respiratory demand on the system is increased. This might occur as a result of non-removal of dead organisms or uneaten food, the respiration of plants in darkness, the addition of extra animals, an elevated temperature or an outbreak of an otherwise non-lethal disease. Such effects can be especially severe where water is poorly mixed or becomes stratified. If the aquarium tank does not contain plants, and frequently even if it does, water quality may be improved by the application of a filter. Introducing a filter into a single tank turns it into a recirculating system since the filter can be considered as a separate entity with its own population of microrganisms and respiratory requirements.

B. Filtration

Filters have several roles. One is mechanical, involving the removal of inorganic and organic particles from the circulating water. Another is biological, the most important aspect of which is the conversion of toxic ammonia into much less toxic nitrate, by the bacterial populations of *Nitrosomonas* and *Nitrobacter* in the filter. A further function is the adjustment of pH. These processes are dealt with in detail in Chapter 3.

A clear understanding of filter function is essential in aquarium design. If mechanical and biological roles are to be combined in a single filter, as is frequently the case, the mechanical filtration should take place first, using the coarsest filter medium at the start to avoid premature clogging. In small filters, it should be possible to remove and clean the initial filter medium, be it nylon floss, filter pad or sponge, without affecting the biological filter medium which might be charcoal, gravel, lavalite, etc. Of course, all the media in the filter will contribute to the biological action if the flow rate is slow enough. The size of the functioning bacterial populations will be limited by the surface area of the filtering medium. Porous materials such as charcoal provide a very large total surface area in relation to their volume. Moving water to or from a filter requires either an airlift device or a water pump. Since a source of compressed air is often available, airlifts are the obvious choice where high flow rate and pressures are not required. They tend to be cheaper to run and have less to go wrong than do pumps. To work efficiently, they must be correctly adjusted and the aim is to produce a constant stream of water rather than the turbulent and erratic flow induced by too much air or too large a bubble size.

The water flow through the filter should be kept constant since the microbial population will have a certain oxygen demand which must be met. Cessation of flow will quickly result in anaerobic conditions and subsequent loss of the useful populations and impairment of the filtering function. If for any reason, such conditions have prevailed, the filter should be flushed through outside the tank, or cleaned completely, since highly toxic substances such as hydrogen sulphide may have accumulated. With an outside filter employing a siphon, the water should be pumped or airlifted from the filter to the tank with the siphon completing

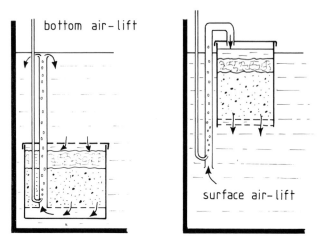

Fig. 3. Bottom and surface internal filters, operated by air-lift, as commonly used in small volume tanks. The filters are filled with nylon wool and charcoal, or some other porous material with a high surface area to volume ratio.

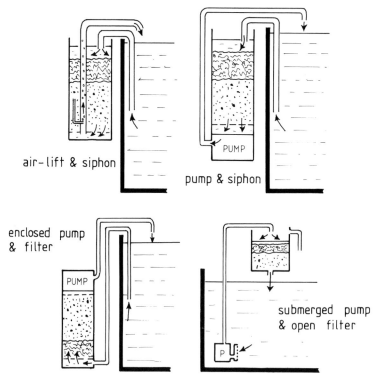

Fig. 4. Various types of external filters operated by air lift or pump.

the circuit from tank to filter. This avoids the aquarium being emptied by blocking or breaking of the siphon. Alternatively, the filter could be placed directly above the tank, thus avoiding the use of a siphon. This is common with large single tanks of a few hundred gallons. A container is sited above the tank with filtering material inside and a drain returns water to the tank. The top of such filters should be regularly cleaned since otherwise any overflow will return accumulated detritus to the tank.

Sub-gravel filtration systems are frequently employed in single tanks either alone or in conjunction with a high performance mechanical filtration unit such as a diatomite filter. Sub-gravel filters have a surface

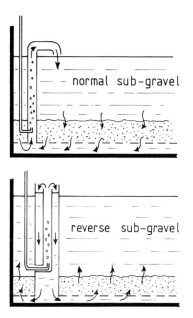

Fig. 5. Normal and reverse sub-gravel filters operated by air lift. An efficient alternative is to connect a modified reverse sub-gravel filter to the outlet of an enclosed pumped filter. This combines efficient mechanical filtration with a large-area biological filter free from detrital build-up.

area approaching that of the tank itself and are normally very efficient biologically. Uneven flow through the gravel can however lead to pockets of organic material building up. It must be remembered that these filters do not remove any particulate material from the tank but bind it into either the top or bottom layers of the gravel depending on the type of operation. Removal of excess detritus by other means therefore becomes more critical, along with partial water replacement. Where filters are not employed, and frequently even when they are, tanks containing fish are usually aerated.

C. Aeration

Introducing a stream of air bubbles into water not only ensures a local saturation with dissolved oxygen. The movement of the bubbles also sets up a circulation in the tank, breaking up any stratification caused by local temperature differences, and removing accumulated CO_2. The efficiency of gas transfer will depend largely on the total surface area of the bubbles. The smaller the bubbles, the larger the total surface area. The rule is that small bubbles provide good aeration and lift, while large bubbles induce turbulence.

A great variety of air diffusers are available ranging from wooden blocks to sintered glass, ceramics and perforated plastic. Diffusers are not, of course, the only aeration devices and alternatives such as venturi systems may be much more efficient (Scott, 1972). Aeration is also useful for removing gases from supersaturated water or for preventing supersaturation, for instance when water is being heated.

D. Water Circulation

When a number of tanks are to be set up, a common water treatment system is often employed, especially in the large aquarium. Such systems usually have a reservoir containing a greater volume of water than the tanks themselves, especially if a constant supply of new water is not available. The reservoir serves not only as a water store but as a buffer, averaging out the effects of temperature changes, or change of other conditions occurring in any one tank. There are many variations on the theme of common circulation but certain basic features must be adhered to if the system is to function efficiently. In individual tanks, inlets and outlets should be arranged so that the water volume is properly turned over or renewed. Water normally leaves the tanks via an overflow and so the simplest system directs the incoming water to the bottom of the tank. However, there are advantages in jetting or spraying the water in at the surface ensuring that the water is saturated with air, and preventing supersaturation. Then, it is possible to have a stand-pipe or extension tube system on the outlet either outside or inside the tank (Figs 6 & 7). The latter allows for adjustments to be made in water depth and promotes the removal of detritus by the outflowing water from the bottom of the tank.

All water leaving the aquarium tanks should be filtered before reentering the circulation system. The filters help to minimize the spread of any diseases but if ozone, ultraviolet light or other form of water sterilization is employed, this treatment should always be performed on cleaned, filtered water. All water returning to the reservoir in a filtered system should be cleaned. New water may be added to the reservoir if pre-filtered, but otherwise it should be bled in prior to the filter. Some large aquaria do not use filters at all, but rely on sedimentation in specially designed reservoirs, along with a large volume of water, to maintain water clarity and quality. Such filterless systems are usually sited close to a water source so that water is readily replaced. Their carrying capacity is lower than that of recirculating systems with filters, but since some planktonic organisms remain in the water, they can better support filter-feeding animals.

In all systems, a circulation pump will draw water from the reservoir and pump it either directly to tanks or to a header tank from where it will drain by gravity to the individual aquarium tanks. The tanks are

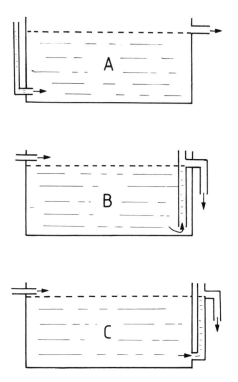

Fig. 6. Water flow arrangements in individual tanks. (A) Bottom inflow and simple overflow. (B) Top inflow and overflow incorporating internal extension pipe. (C) Top inflow and overflow incorporating external extension pipe.

generally arranged in parallel rather than in series, to minimize the effects of the aquarium inhabitants upon one another. An advantage of a gravity feed system is that it allows constant head of supply to the tanks up to the limits set by the length and size of the supply pipes. However, it does require either high level space in a building or a separate tower to contain the header tank (Fig. 9). Usually, the header tank is aerated to break up any water stratification and to ensure that the water is not lacking in dissolved oxygen, or alternatively, to prevent supersaturation.

The direct pumped system offers advantages in flexibility of layout and lack of building height requirement, but is more likely to suffer from fluctuating flow rate at inlets if take-off volumes as a whole are varying. The latter frequently occurs in the research aquarium. One solution is to vary pumping rate with demand but this requires sophisticated controls utilizing pressure-sensitive devices. Pumped circuits, do, however, have the advantages of permitting temperature control equipment to be slotted into circulation just before the aquarium tanks, since the pressure drop across a heat exchanger presents few problems.

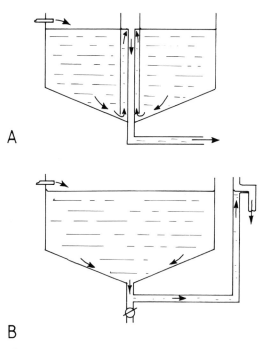

Fig. 7. Self-cleaning tanks with, (A) internal overflow and (B) external overflow. The overflow can be varied in height to permit different working depths. These tanks are most often employed when fish are to be kept at high stocking densities and high feeding rates.

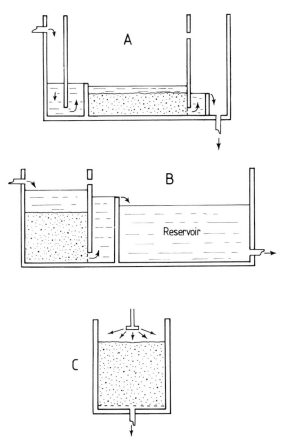

Fig. 8. Filters commonly used in large recirculation systems. (A) High-level flooded sand filter. (B) Low-level flooded sand filter, vulnerable to clogging because of limited head. (C) Trickling filter: this permits complete aeration of the filter bed allowing a higher effective flow rate to be maintained.

E. Temperature Control

Many experiments in aquaria call for some degree of temperature control, with either the heating or cooling of water; sometimes both. If the water volume to be heated or cooled is small, the temperature control can often be achieved by placing the tanks in a constant temperature room, though this solution may be rather uncomfortable for the experimenter. Where large volumes of water must have their temperature altered, the heating or cooling is best applied directly to the water.

Direct heating of tanks is usually accomplished by glass or silica-sheathed electrical heaters. These are preferable to metal heaters since the materials are less toxic but they are more fragile and care must be exercised to avoid accidental damage by the tank occupants or human error. One problem with such heaters is that they have a high surface temperature which may be dangerous for small animals which settle on them during an off period. A mesh shield may prevent this.

Cooling of water is carried out by means of a heat exchanger, where a cold refrigerant comes into thermal contact with the water over some form of heat conducting boundary. The simplest form of heat exchanger is a coil of metal or glass tubing, immersed in the water and containing the cooled refrigerant. Metal cooling coils often introduce corrosion problems, however, even if they are fabricated from stainless steel, and some modern systems employ PTFE and other plastics (see Chapter 6). A very successful type of heat exchanger is made from a block of graphite-containing material, bored with channels to carry the water and the refrigerant. The most common refrigerants are expanding gases like freon. However, more stable temperature control can often be achieved by the use of a liquid secondary refrigerant, operated at an intermediate temperature between the water to be cooled and the very cold gaseous refrigerant. An example is calcium chloride brine which has the advantage that it is much less toxic than a refrigerant gas should it ever leak into the water supply.

With a water supply pumped directly to the aquarium, a completely enclosed temperature control tank or tanks, incorporating heaters, heat exchangers, or both, can be inserted into the delivery line. Temperature control in a gravity-fed system is best carried out in a tank adjacent to the header tank. If this is not possible (the header tank may be at the top of a tower, where there is no room for a further tank), then a low level temperature control tank may be required, perhaps adjacent to the reservoir. A low level tank may require a secondary circuit, incorporating a pump, with its attendant risk of failure or breakdown.

The design of a versatile temperature control system, capable of heating and cooling, and maintaining the temperature constant within narrow limits is a matter for the specialist. Simple control systems characteristically overshoot on either side of a mean temperature, and may require some form of mixing tank or buffer, before the water passes to the fish.

F. Pumps and Pumping

When designing the aquarium circulation, it is important to employ the correct type and size of pump from the wide range available, and to site it correctly in the circuit. The materials suitable for pumps in the aquarium are covered in detail in Chapter 6. Toxic metals should be avoided especially in sea water recirculation systems where products of corrosion may build up to harmful levels. A wide range of materials is available to suit all service conditions.

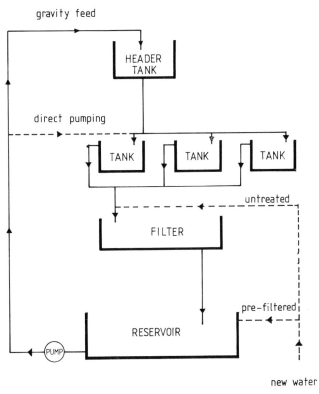

Fig. 9. Possible arrangement of gravity feed and direct pumping circulation systems.

The types of pumps used in aquaria fall into two basic categories, centrifugal or positive displacement.

In a centrifugal pump, a fast rotating impeller causes water in the pump chamber to move from the centre of the impeller to the outer edge of the chamber under the influence of centrifugal force. The water passes out at the tangentially arranged outlet port, entering the chamber in the middle opposite the impeller spindle. Features of this type of pump are its simplicity and lack of wear on the impeller under normal aquarium conditions. Also the water flow is continuous and the high speed allows direct coupling to AC or DC motors. Centrifugal pumps are essentially dynamic devices and generate a pressure head, the volume passed being dependent upon the pipework, valves, etc.

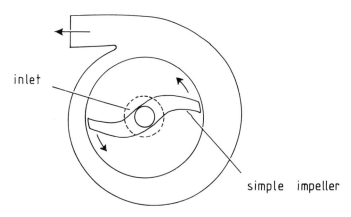

inlet

simple   impeller

Fig. 10.   A simple centrifugal pump.

If the discharge pressure is very high in a centrifugal pump, for instance in the extreme case of the outlet valve being closed, the pump will still rotate without immediate damage. If suction is very high, the impeller may cavitate; vapour bubbles form locally on the impeller and then refill with fluid. This reduces pump efficiency and can be damaging to the impeller. Another problem with many centrifugal pumps is that they cannot pump heavy particulate materials like sand, and may be severely damaged by such substances, especially if the body or impeller is constructed from plastic materials.

The impeller on a simple centrifugal pump cannot displace air and so it is not self-priming. It cannot operate until the pump chamber and suction pipes are filled with water. If the pump can be positioned below the level of the water it is pumping, then it is said to have flooded suction and this obviates the priming problems. Failing this, a foot valve may be fitted to the suction line so that once filled, it always remains full of water. Alternatively, a priming tank may be built into the line. Self-priming centrifugal pumps are available, the simplest of them having a vane impeller eccentrically mounted inside the casing. During the priming operation, this type of pump actively displaces the air along with the water, resembling in this respect the action of the second main category of pump which functions by positive displacement of the air/water in the pump chamber.

Positive displacement pumps operate by moving water through the

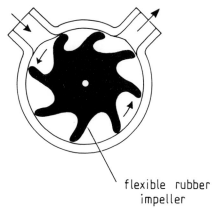

flexible rubber
impeller

Fig. 11. A self-priming pump with rotating flexible impeller.

pump in discrete parcels using a flexible close-fitting impeller, piston, eccentric cam, or a rotating, spirally shaped or screw-type rotor inside a spirally shaped housing or stator. In this last type of pump, the rotor is generally of stainless steel while the stator is moulded in rubber. This is

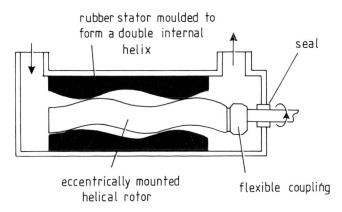

rubber stator moulded to
form a double internal
helix

seal

eccentrically mounted
helical rotor

flexible coupling

Fig. 12. A self-priming screw pump.

not an exhaustive list of the available types but they do have certain common characteristics. They deliver a certain volume of liquid against pressure and are intrinsically self-priming. The suction capability is usually good but, by the nature of their operation, they will not tolerate pumping against closed valves. The discharge may be more pulsatile than a centrifugal pump. Small organisms will survive better in passage through positive displacement pumps compared with centrifugal pumps.

This would be a consideration in the choice of pump if it were important to preserve the planktonic population of the pumped water. Many positive displacement pumps may also cope with heavy material like sand, and are therefore useful in aquarium systems where the water may become loaded with particulate material.

Both major types of pumps may be close coupled to the drive motor, that is the motor shaft passes straight into the pump chamber through a gland or seal. An alternative arrangement is to have a belt drive or clutch assembly to link motor and pump. The close coupled type occupies less space but the belt or clutch allows easier inspection and maintenance, keeps the motor remote from the pump and provides a degree of flexibility in the system, all more important in the larger pump sizes. Some small pumps have a magnetic coupling linking motor and impeller which not only prevents damage to the motor on overload, but also avoids the need for a gland or seal, since the shaft does not pass through the pump body. Glands or seals are the commonest cause of pumping problems, either permitting water to leak out or air to leak in. Regular maintenance and the provision of spare seals are the best precautions.

Operation in the aquarium environment makes it essential that pump motors are sealed and well maintained. All the pumps mentioned so far should be sited to avoid water splashes or floods, preferably on plinths above floor level. The exceptions of course are the submersible pumps. These normally centrifugal pumps have a totally enclosed and sealed motor and pump, often encased in resin or plastic. They are immersed in the water to be pumped and are cooled by it, and this addition of heat must be taken account of if temperature is a critical consideration in the aquarium. Submersible pumps have the great advantage of the absence of suction problems and are most frequently employed when setting up filters for individual tanks or for clearing sumps.

The performance of a pump will be given as a curve of pump output (in l/m, m³/h or gal/h) against total head (in metres or feet). The head represents the work the pump is required to perform. It includes the static delivery head, that is the difference in height between the pump and the highest point or water-level in the circuit, plus the friction losses from moving water through the pipework, valves and other fittings. Tables supplied by pipework manufacturers give the friction losses per length of pipe or per fitting, ready calculated in head figures to be added to the static head. Another factor to be considered is the static suction head, the difference in height between the pump and water intake. When setting up a pumping circuit, consideration of the various heads allows the correct pump and motor size to be chosen to give the required circulation rate. For a centrifugal pump, flow will only commence when the pressure head generated in the pump exceeds the total static head. Obviously the circuit should be designed to minimize the static head and especially to minimize the suction head. The maximum permissible suction head is limited by vapour pressure, by the presence of gases in the water and by the speed of the pump. Normal limits are 5 m for centrifugal pumps and 7 m for positive displacement pumps. In designing the suction line it is important to provide for smooth water flow by removing obstructions and sharp bends, and to eliminate all air leaks or air pockets. Any foot valve (to facilitate priming) should be large in size to reduce the friction loss to a minimum. Where the pump is below the level of the water to be pumped (i.e. with flooded suction) an inlet valve is necessary to close off water flow when the pump has to be removed from the circuit. Otherwise, inlet valves on the suction side should be avoided wherever possible because of their effect in reducing pump efficiency.

On the delivery side, a valve may be necessary to facilitate priming and to permit removal of the pump. Regulation of the flow by a delivery valve is not recommended for a centrifugal pump since it is wasteful of power. A delivery valve on a positive displacement pump should not be closed while the pump is operating or dangerously high pressures may develop. Non-return valves are often incorporated into delivery lines to avoid flow-back when the pump is off.

G. Pipes and Valves

The wide variety of materials available for constructing piping systems are discussed in detail in Chapter 6. The pipes most commonly used in aquaria now are unplasticized polyvinyl chloride (uPVC) and acrylonitrile butadiene styrene (ABS). The advantage these have over metal, glass or polythene is the combination of lack of corrosion or toxicity, ease of jointing and strength. The first choice for aquarium systems is ABS since it has much better impact resistance than uPVC especially at low temperatures. A characteristic common to all the modern thermoplastics is the very smooth bore which gives minimum resistance to flow and is much less susceptible to fouling by sessile organisms. Fouling can still occur of course and precautions should be taken to prevent this where long runs of inaccessible piping are involved, for instance in seawater intakes. Precautions may include prefiltering the water (Chapter 2), chemical treatment (chlorine will kill settled organisms and soften the byssal threads of attached mussels) and duplication of pipelines (allowing one line to be left static).

Another characteristic is the high coefficient of thermal expansion of thermoplastics compared with metals, approximately 10:1 for ABS and mild steel. However, because of the low thermal conductivity of plastic the contraction or expansion is often less than expected since it is the mean wall temperature which has to be considered. Nevertheless, the changes in length must be allowed for in piping layouts. Often changes of direction provide adequate flexibility as long as fixing brackets are not attached too close to the corner. If direction changes are not possible then expansion loops or purpose built expansion units may be incorporated. These problems are obviously more acute in industrial applications than in aquaria where temperature fluctuations are usually relatively small.

Thermoplastics may be jointed using solvent-welding, threaded fittings or bolted flanges. In solvent-welding, the cement chemically attacks the surfaces to be joined and the ensuing joint may be stronger than pipe or fitting alone. The process of jointing is described in detail in manufacturers' leaflets but basically consists of deburring and chamferring the pipe, then lightly abrading and cleaning both the pipe and fitting with special cleaning fluid. Finally, the solvent is applied to both pipe and fittings and the two pushed together (without twisting) and held for 10 s for smaller sizes such as 9 mm and up to 1 min for larger sizes of 200 mm or more. The drying time required will of course vary with the amount of solvent used, ambient conditions and the working pressure. With the low pressures in the aquarium, 1 h would normally be sufficient and minutes only may be needed where small bore or overflow system are being built. These types of joint are strong with few leakage problems but obviously cannot be taken apart.

Where meters, pumps or other fittings are to be included in the pipeline, it is normal practice to flange or use threaded fittings on either side so that they may be easily removed. The same applies to the larger valves although small valves are often solvent-welded in position if they do not have an integral threaded fitting.

Flange joints or couplings with flat gaskets or "O" rings on the mating surfaces are bulky and the nuts on them are prone to corrosion especially in the marine aquarium. Because the couplings or backing rings are also of metal, these joints may be heavy and require extra supporting brackets.

Screwed or threaded fittings are not as strong as the other joints and are normally only used on the smaller pipe sizes. Because of the thicker pipe required, they have smaller bore size than equivalent solvent-welded fittings and are most useful in making connections to tanks or setting up temporary systems which may be dismantled and re-used. When putting together threaded fittings, PTFE jointing tape or compound should always be applied to the male threads and the joints never over-tightened. Hand pressure plus a quarter turn with a strap wrench is all that is recommended. A wide range of sizes and type of fittings are made for both ABS and uPVC fittings. Although the size ranges for ABS and uPVC are identical they should not be mixed when solvent-welding. If this is unavoidable and is for low-pressure application, as for instance in overflows, then only PVC cement should be used.

The commonest types of valves used in aquaria are ball, diaphragm, gate, butterfly and needle. Ball valves allow full bore flow when open but precise control may be difficult to achieve, although once set they remain constant. Diaphragm valves make good on/off valves but again precise control is difficult especially for air, and there is a tendency for the set flow to change slightly, associated with the elasticity of the diaphragm. All valves, but diaphragm valves especially, should only be closed with minimum required force otherwise they may stick shut. Needle valves give good control but they are normally only available in the smaller sizes and they tend to have more resistance to flow when open than other types. Gate and butterfly valves are normally made in coated metal for the larger sizes and give good flow control. Non-return and foot valves, which may be of ball or flap type are employed in pipelines to avoid lines draining on cessation of pumping. They do add considerably to the head losses however, and if dirty water is being pumped, a screen should be incorporated to prevent them clogging or sticking open.

H. Tanks and Enclosures

The materials suitable for tank construction are detailed in Chapter 6 and the general principles of water circulation have already been dealt with. However, tank shape and construction can be of critical importance in the show or research aquarium especially where larger tanks are in use.

With show tanks in recent years, the tendency has been to get away from the box-shaped concrete tank. If the sides of a tank are sloped outwards at an angle of 45° from front to back, forming a trapezoidal shape, the side walls cannot be seen when viewing though the front glass. In a suitable wide tank, this creates the illusion of looking directly into the underwater world and is easier to decorate in a pleasing and natural manner. A similar effect can be obtained with a curved back and sides (Garnoud, 1977; Fraser-Brunner, 1960). The small triangular spaces left between adjacent tanks can be used for displaying sedentary animals such as coelenterates or crustaceans. Such tanks may be constructed in concrete or fibreglass.

In the research aquarium, rather different priorities take over, such as the experimental needs and the ease of cleaning, although of course the well-being of the inhabitants is still the prime concern. Except for very large tanks, the research aquarium does not normally contain built-in facilities since experimental needs constantly change. Glass, fibreglass, polythene, PVC and wood are all used although fibreglass is now by far the commonest because of its strength, non-toxicity and easy to clean surface. Square or rectangular tanks are easier to fit into a limited space but are less satisfactory for active animals which may damage themselves against the flat sides. Such animals often settle down more readily in circular tanks especially where a circulation of the water can be induced. Also, when made in fibreglass a rectangular tank is intrinsically less strong than a circular one and needs greater reinforcing per unit volume. Round tanks can be made large without internal bracing and can be constructed from sectional panels although these often have to be specially made. The circulation which can readily be induced in a round tank offers scope for the use of self-cleaning devices which are important when high stocking densities and feeding rates are combined.

Square or rectangular fibreglass panels are now commonly available and can be built up to form large fish-holding or reservoir tanks. Internal or external bracing is normally required. Annular tanks are useful in some research studies where fish are required to swim for long periods either against a current or in response to other stimuli. Such tanks may be elongated to form raceways or truly annular with a central island which can form an observation platform or chamber. The channel created avoids the problems of finite length associated with trough or flume tanks.

In all types of tanks, ponds and enclosures, the corners should be rounded where possible to facilitate cleaning. The tanks should generally contain a minimum of sand, gravel or other substrate, again to allow for easy cleaning, and should be as shallow as possible to prevent stratification of the water, and to allow for easy access. Where a natural substrate, like mud or sand, is placed in the tank, care should be taken that these materials do not get into the water circulation system. Water is best drawn off from the surface of such a tank by an overflow. Alternatively, a filter should be incorporated in the outflow. In a completely closed system, the tank could be placed on a separate circuit, with its own pumps and filters. It is rarely necessary for a tank to be deeper than 1.0 m, unless it is in a display aquarium, or required for some special purpose. Details of various types of ponds and tanks are given by Kinne (1976).

III. THE AQUARIUM AS A WORKING ENVIRONMENT

The people working in or visiting the aquarium have their own needs, which in some cases, will conflict with those of the aquarium inhabitants. Because these inhabitants are captive and because they are already in an artificial and potentially stressful environment, it is better that the humans adapt, rather than the animals. However, it is sometimes possible to prevent conflict, and to ameliorate the adverse effects on the people involved.

A. Space and Access

While it is tempting to fill the available space in an aquarium building with tanks, access must be provided for people to clean tanks, feed fish, view the animals and set up research apparatus. The most critical need, of course, is for essential cleaning and servicing of the tanks. The space required around a tank must depend on tank uses, shape and layout and the presence of outside fittings. Space must be left for any important moveable apparatus such as pumps and bins of water, and the area between tanks should be kept clear. This is easier when the tanks are arranged in rows paralleled, either above or below, by the essential services. Research workers are usually much more ready to build apparatus than to dismantle it and temporary concessions may end up as semi-permanent obstructions.

In exhibition aquaria, it is essential that lights, service pipes and items of equipment are hidden from the view of visitors. This may be achieved with small tanks by boxing them in with panelling. Access to the tanks is then gained from in front by hinged or sliding doors. While this is economical of floor space, the major disadvantage is that no work can be performed without obstructing the view. Larger show aquaria invariably have access from behind, usually in the form of a service corridor which may be as narrow as 60 cm at leg level. The height of show tanks is governed by the need for comfortable viewing, the centre of the tank usually being sited at around 1.5 m above floor level. The service corridor may require an elevated floor to ensure that the top edge of the tanks are not much more than 1 m above floor level. This gives easy access for servicing but may cut down drastically on available head height, and overhead hazards such as pipes and lights must be kept to a minimum.

In the working laboratory, the tanks are rarely of permanent construction, and are often being replaced or reconstructed for different experiments. Such a laboratory normally has the services on the walls or overhead, with taps and drains at frequent intervals. With a closed or recirculating system, it is a distinct advantage to have any drains which are returning water to the system mounted well above floor level. Though this arrangement means that the tanks must be mounted on plinths or tables to ensure free drainage, the raised drains prevent any spillages entering the recirculating water. The main drains, carrying water to waste, can then be placed at floor level with the floor pitched towards a drainage channel to facilitate cleaning and the removal of spilled water. The main drain should be large enough to cope with the high flow rates that occur when tanks are emptied.

B. Temperature

Where space heating or cooling is employed, then little can be done to make the people who must work in the aquarium more comfortable. Aquarium workers must dress appropriately and limit the time they are exposed to aquarium conditions. This can be achieved by automating where possible (self-cleaning tanks and automatic feeding systems) and by having separate work areas. Marine aquaria in temperate regions are often very cold to work in because of the need to keep the water at normal sea temperatures (generally within the range 5–15°C). To heat the rooms containing tanks with water at these temperatures is quite impractical and results in heavy condensation on the pipes and tanks. Separate dry working areas must be set aside. Should the cold water pipes pass through a dry area they must be insulated to prevent condensation.

C. Humidity

The humidity in an aquarium is normally high, making the environment feel damp and cold or alternatively unpleasantly hot. Heaters and/or fans may usefully be located at points of work. Electronic and electrical equipment may deteriorate rapidly in a damp environment and are best removed after use. Where they are permanently installed, they should be placed in cabinets which can be closed tightly. In some aquaria, small cubicles contain the electronic equipment and are fed by a separate air supply, with a slightly positive pressure to keep out the damp aquarium atmosphere. A duct connecting the cubicle to the exterior and containing an inflowing fan, is all that is needed.

Aquarium buildings are invariably damp and this factor must be borne in mind during their design and construction. Windows, walls, ceilings and pipes are especially subject to condensation. Windows should be double glazed, or removed altogether from the wet rooms. Walls and ceilings should be smooth and coated with a damp-proofing material and water pipes should be insulated in areas where they collect condensation.

D. Light and Sound

Few organisms in the aquarium require high levels of lighting, and those which do can generally be specially catered for. Most organisms require dim or subdued lighting and this is best supplied artificially. Thus, windows should be kept to a minimum in the aquarium building (as we have already said, they are often also a troublesome site for condensation to occur). Only the plant rooms, and various dry working spaces should constantly be brightly lit. In other parts of the aquarium, it is necessary to provide bright lighting only for periodic use: for example, for cleaning, servicing and repair of the water system, but this should be switched off for normal aquarium working.

The light level required for the human occupants of the aquarium building varies according to the tasks they are performing. If they have merely to negotiate areas kept at low light level, then dim red lights near floor level are advantageous. For more complex tasks, the minimum necessary level and spread of light may be obtained using dimmable spotlamps. The best policy, of course, is to separate work areas from the fish and thereby remove the conflict. Individual tanks of fish can be effectively isolated using curtains of black polythene sheeting or separate rooms can be provided for particular experiments. When planning the aquarium and designating experimental areas, remember that opening and closing doors can allow in unwanted light and curtains or double doors may be needed if this is critical.

Opening and closing doors can, of course, also generate noise and vibration which is readily transmitted through the structure of the building. Such sudden noises can be very disturbing to fish and may render some types of experimental work almost impossible. Sensitive animals or experiments should be sited as far away as possible from such noise sources, and the noise should be minimized as detailed earlier. Where especially critical work is being performed, special rooms may be required.

E. Electrical Safety

The close proximity of electrical current sources and water in the aquarium presents a constant hazard. The problem is especially severe in the sea water aquarium, both because sea water is a better conductor, and because it promotes corrosion of electrical apparatus, power sockets and switchgear. It is often impractical to instal waterproofed power sockets, which may require every electrical item to be fitted with a special plug. However, some form of conventional socket which can be closed off by a waterproofed seal when not in use is a useful safety measure. In general, wall-mounted power points should be placed as high as is practical, well above the level where water can be splashed. Electrical fittings, which often include copper, should not be placed directly above tanks, where the products of corrosion may fall into the water. It is also a useful safety measure for the power circuits to incorporate an earth leakage circuit breaker which switches off the power when any current is shorted to earth. Such devices provide an early indication of potentially dangerous electrical faults in any apparatus used in the aquarium and can also protect the user of a faulty device from electrocution. Small portable earth leakage breakers are available for use with individual items of equipment.

A further potential source of trouble in a working aquarium environment, where often few power sockets are provided, arises with the use of long extension cables. Any plugs or sockets along the cable should not be placed in a position where they may come into contact with water. In addition, the cables should not be left tightly wound on a drum if large currents are being drawn because heat is generated which may melt or burn the cable insulation.

It is especially important to warn all aquarium users of the inherent dangers in using electrical equipment in a wet environment or with wet hands or clothes. Electrical safety notices should be prominently displayed in every working aquarium.

F. Ancillary Facilities

An aquarium for experimental studies does not simply consist of a set of rooms containing tanks but must include other facilities. In this account, we have stressed the need to keep dry areas separate from wet. The dry areas where the staff keep most of their scientific equipment, their stocks of chemicals and other consumables, are the spaces to which they retire when the atmosphere of the wet areas becomes unpleasant. Facilities which should be available in the dry areas include wash hand basins, a plentiful supply of paper towels, dry, well ventilated cupboards, extensive storage space, deep-freeze cabinets, conventional refrigerators, waste-disposal units and workshop facilities. Wet rooms, where the aquarium tanks are sited, need a hose connection to a freshwater supply and good drainage facilities as discussed earlier. The aquarium building itself should have wide doorways, should include few changes in level (to facilitate the transport of heavy objects to and from the aquarium rooms), and should have an entrance, perhaps equipped with a hoist, to which trucks can be brought.

Most aquarium buildings do not stay the same size but progressively grow larger. They should therefore be designed so that they can easily be extended, and the machinery upgraded.

IV. REFERENCES

Blaxter, J. H. S. and Tytler, P. (1978). Physiology and function of the swimbladder. *In* "Advances in Comparative Physiology and Biochemistry" (O. Lowenstein, ed.), Vol. 7, 311–367. Academic Press, London.

Brauer, R. W. (1972). "Barobiology and the Experimental Biology of the Deep Sea", p. 428. North Carolina Sea Grant Program, Chapel Hill, NC.

Brett, J. R. (1970). Temperature. *In* "Marine Ecology" (O. Kinne, ed.), Vol. 1, 515–560. Wiley, New York.

Brett, J. R. (1971). Energetic responses of salmon to temperature. A study of some thermal relations in the physiology and freshwater ecology of sock eye salmon (*Oncorhynchus nerka*). *American Zoologist* **11**, 99–113.

Brett, J. R. and Groves, T. D. D. (1979). Physiological Energetics. *In* "Fish Physiology" (W. S. Hoar, D. J. Randall and J. R. Brett, eds), Vol. VIII, 279–352. Academic Press, New York and London.

Comfort, A. (1956). "The Biology of Senescence". Routledge and Kegan Paul, London.

Davies, G. E., Foster, J., Warren, C. E. and Doudoroff, P. (1963). The influence of oxygen concentration on the swimming performance of juvenile Pacific salmon at various temperatures. *Trans American Fisheries Society* **92**, 111–124.

de Vries, A. L. (1971). Freezing resistance in fishes. *In* "Fish Physiology" (W. S. Hoar and D. J. Randall, eds), Vol. VI, 157–190. Academic Press, New York and London.

Downing, K. M. and Merkens, J. C. (1955). The influence of dissolved oxygen concentration on the toxicity of un-ionized ammonia to rainbow trout (*Salmo gairdnerii*, Richardson). *Annals of Applied Biology* **43**, 243–246.

Farmer, G. J. and Beamish, F. W. H. (1969). Oxygen consumption of *Tilapia nilotica* in relation to swimming speed and salinity. *Journal of the Fisheries Research Board of Canada* **26**, 2807–2821.

Fraser-Brunner, A. (1960). Towards the perfect public aquarium. *In* "Ier Congrès International D'Aquariologie Monaco 1960" *Bulletin de l'Institut Ocanographique de Monaco 1963* **IC**, 1–14.

Fry, F. E. J. (1967). Responses of vertebrate poikilotherms to temperature. *In* "Thermobiology" (A. H. Rose, ed.), 79–135. Academic Press, New York and London.

Fry, F. E. J. (1971). The effect of environmental factors on the physiology of fish. *In* "Fish Physiology" (W. S. Hoar and D. J. Randall, eds), Vol. VI, 1–98. Academic Press, New York and London.

Garnaud, J. (1977). Construction de l'aquarium public. *Bulletin de l'Institut Ocanographique* **72**, No 1433.

Harvey, H. H. (1975). Gas disease in fishes: a review. *In* "Chemistry and Physics of Aqueous Gas Solutions" The Electrochemical Society Inc., Princeton.

Haskell, D. C. (1955). Weight of fish per cubic foot of water in hatchery troughs and ponds. *Progressive Fish Culturalist* **17**, 117–118.

Hawkins, A. D. and Johnstone, A. D. F. (1978). The hearing of the Atlantic salmon, *Salmo salar*. *Journal of Fish Biology* **13**, 655–673.

Kinne, O. (ed.), (1976). "Marine Ecology" 557. John Wiley and Sons, London.

Koeman, J. H. and Strik, J. J. T. W. A. (eds), (1975). "Sublethal Effects of Toxic Chemicals on Aquatic Animals" Elsevier Scientific, Amsterdam.

McKee, J. E. and Wolf, H. W. (1963). "Water Quality Criteria—2nd edn", Publ 3A Res. Agency California State Water Quality Control Board, Sacramento, California.

Rao, G. M. M. (1968). Oxygen consumption of rainbow trout (*Salmo gairdneri*) in relation to activity and salinity. *Canadian Journal of Zoology* **46**, 781–786.

Rucker, R. R. (1972). Gas Bubble Disease of Salmonids: A critical review. Technical Paper 58 of the Bureau of Sport Fisheries and Wildlife, United States Department of the Interior, Fish and Wildlife Service, Washington DC.

Scott, K. R. (1972). Comparison of the efficiency of various aeration devices for oxygenation of water in aquaria. *Journal of the Fisheries Research Board of Canada* **29**, 1641–1643.

Shaklee, J. B., Christiansen, J. A., Sidell, B. D., Prosser, C. L. and Whitt, G. S. (1977). Molecular aspects of temperature acclimation in fish: contributions of changes in enzyme activities and isozyme patterns to metabolic reorganisation in the green sunfish. *Journal of Experimental Zoology* **201**, 1–20.

Spotte, S. (1979). "Seawater Aquariums". John Wiley, New York.

Sprague, J. B. and Drury, D. E. (1969). Avoidance reactions of salmonid fish to representative pollutants. *In* "Advances in water pollution", *Research Proceedings Fourth International Conference* held in Prague, 1969, Vol. I, 179–189 Pergamon Press, Oxford.

Strickland, J. D. H. and Parsons, T. R. (1968). "A Practical Handbook of Sea Water Analysis". Bulletin of the Fish. Research Board of Canada No. 167, 3rd Edition, 311. Fish Research Board of Canada, Ottawa.

Sverdrup, H. U., Johnson, M. W., and Fleming, R. H. (1942). "The Oceans" Prentice-Hall Inc., Englewood Cliffs, NJ.

Wedermeyer, G. A., Meyer, F. P. and Smith, L. (1976). Environmental stress and fish diseases. *In* "Diseases of Fishes Book 5" (S. F. Snieszko and H. R. Axelrod, eds), T. F. H. Publications Inc., Nepture, New Jersey.

Wenz, G. M. (1964). Curious noises and the sonic environment in the ocean. *In* "Marine Bioacoustics" (W. H. Tavolga, ed.), 101–120. Pergamon Press, Oxford.

Westers, H. and Pratt, K. M. (1977). Rational design of hatcheries for intensive salmonid culture based on metabolic characteristics. *Progressive Fish Culturalist* **39**, 157–165.

Wheaton, F. W. (1977). "Aquacultural Engineering" 708. John Wiley & Sons. New York.

Willoughby, H., Larsen, H. N. and Bowen, J. T. (1972). The pollutional effects of fish hatcheries. *American Fishes and US Trout News*, **17**, 6–20.

Chapter 2

Sea Water Abstraction

G. Cansdale

SWS Filtration Limited, Morpeth, England

I. INTRODUCTION

In any marine biology laboratory, sea water of a quality that allows direct feed into working systems should be freely available. The economical and ample provision of such water should have priority in the location and design of any new project.

II. SOURCES OF SEA WATER

A. Open Intake in Shallow Water

This method is perhaps the commonest way of providing a continuous or semi-continuous supply, but it has three disadvantages:

(1) The grille which protects the intake becomes obstructed by sea wrack, especially after storms, and may become fouled with algal growth. The mesh is a compromise decided by local sea conditions; fine mesh excludes more suspended particles but is more quickly blocked. Routine clearing is needed either by a diver or by hoisting the intake out of water.

(2) The ingestion of silt usually makes sedimentation and/or screening necessary, for no grille can exclude fine particles. Both treatments are expensive in plant and labour, especially if the water is to be filtered to exclude very fine particles.

(3) Pipe-line fouling by mussels, sea squirts and other organisms is almost inevitable. These enter in larval form and colonize the walls, where they grow rapidly by feeding on nutrient particles in the raw, oxygenated water. Constant flow at above 2 m/s prevents colonization of straight runs, but turbulence allows settlement on bends, valves etc. and once the organisms have settled they can withstand higher velocities. All methods of control are expensive. In the industrial plant, the periodic use of chlorine at up to 60 mg/l has been routine, but this is unsuitable for aquarium and laboratory intakes and is becoming unacceptable generally for environmental reasons, especially on coral coasts. Other methods of control are:

(a) Designing the pipeline so that it can be dismantled for cleaning by rodding, or building-in facilities for insertion of a pig, a cleansing projectile which is pumped through the line. Inevitably, the supply is periodically interrupted.

(b) Providing two complete systems in parallel which are used alternately. In the dormant system, any organisms exhaust the available oxygen and die, but annual treatment with hydrochloric acid (commercial grade, diluted with twice the volume of water) may be needed to remove calcareous remains.

(c) Filling all unused sections with freshwater for several days twice a month.

(d) By omitting a foot valve, allowing the pipeline to drain between periods of pumping. A self-priming pump is necessary and the entrainment of air with the water may result in a supply which is supersaturated with dissolved gases (see Chapter 3).

Where no alternative method appears possible, the site must be chosen after careful consideration, particularly of the following factors:

(a) The intake must be anchored securely, if need be to a pile or rockface. There are advantages in placing the intake at the foot of a protective outer tube, through which it can be withdrawn for cleaning.

(b) A study of the available coastline may show sites with minimum silt disturbance and little loose wrack.

(c) An intake near the sea bed will ingest more silt, but one in midwater is more liable to physical damage.

(d) Surface freshwater, sewage and other pollutants must be avoided.

(e) The submerged pipe must be dimensioned to have no noticeable friction head at maximum flow (see Chapter 1).

B. Open Intake in Deep Water

Water of high quality containing few fouling organisms can sometimes be drawn from below the thermocline fairly close inshore. The Bergen Aquarium is well serviced in this way (Rollefson, 1962). Other deep inlets may also be suitable, but deep water conditions in both summer and winter must be carefully monitored to avoid taking up water low in oxygen or loaded with decaying material. The following factors are important:

(1) A long run of pipeline with the necessary diameter may be expensive. For instance, a flow of 22 m³/h requires a pipe of diameter 100 mm for a 200 m suction line; for 500 m this must be 125 mm.

(2) Water from below the thermocline will normally be much colder than water drawn close inshore. Only actual pumping will show how much the water temperature is raised by passage through shallow inshore water and beach. Any subsequent warming will result in supersaturation with gases.

(3) The water may be very low in oxygen but this is simply corrected.

C. Pumping from Aquifers of Salt Water

A few marine projects are situated over porous strata in direct communication with the open sea which can be tapped directly by a well at low cost. This is most frequently true of coral formations but moraines, sandstone and even coarse limestone can occasionally serve as marine aquifers. The geology is usually unfavourable but the possibility should always be considered. This water is sometimes warmer than surface water and very low in oxygen. The water quality and especially the salinity, should be tested from a test well before scaling up, for there is always a danger of the water picking up unwanted metallic salts in transit, or of tapping fresh water-bearing strata (Clark and Eisler, 1964).

D. Batch Supply by Tanker

The distance from a suitable or accessible sea source or a combination of adverse factors may make a piped supply impossible and batch-filling by tanker may be necessary. The tank must be protected from corrosion (Chapter 6). The main cost of this transport is in tanker charge and labour so that mileage is relatively unimportant. The water can be drawn directly from the sea or from a sub-sand source (see below, p. 51): even pumping at only 6 m^3/h, the largest tanker will be filled in about 3 h over high tide, with minimum suction head and run. When not in use, the suction hose can be capped off and buried, but the site must be chosen carefully to avoid damage by vandals.

E. Synthetic Sea Water

Sea water can be made up from various salts (Chapter 3). This involves sinking an intake into the beach and withdrawing water from the substrate. (See next section.)

F. Pre-filtered Water, Drawn Sub-sand

Many of the problems listed above are solved by sub-sand working. Sub-sand abstraction also has the following advantages:

(1) Particulate material, including fouling organisms, detritus and a high percentage of bacteria and yeasts is removed. In established systems, the filtration is very effective (Table I). Water can often be used that is too dirty for an open intake, and design is simplified and costs reduced because fouling of the pipeline is not a problem.

(2) As the sub-sand system develops, it is made aerobic by the passage of oxygenated water from the surface; buried organic matter decays rapidly and there is no further production of hydrogen sulphide or methane. In addition, ammonia is oxidized to nitrite and then to nitrate; BOD and iron are reduced by up to 90%.

Table I. The efficiency with which naturally occurring particles of different sizes are removed by sub-sand filtration. Water drawn from a shallow sand and shingle shore near Aberdeen, Scotland by means of screen wells.

Average particle size µm diameter	No. of particles per ml		Filtration efficiency %
	Inlet	Outlet	
2.2	11416	10674	6.5
2.8	7990	1448	81.9
3.6	5737	808	85.9
4.5	4185	269	93.6
5.7	3174	111	96.5
7.1	2492	81	96.7
9.0	1756	43	97.5
11.3	1146	13	98.9
14.2	654	5	99.2
17.9	314	2	99.3
22.6	152	1	99.3
28.5	84	<1	(100)
35.9	37	<1	(100)
45.2	16	<1	(100)
57.0	7	0	100

(3) There is some evidence that heavy metals are held.

(4) The system is unaffected by surface pollutants such as oil which are now a constant hazard on most coasts. Installed systems have been able to continue in full operation during local oil spillages.

(5) The whole system, including the rising main, can be completely buried, thus avoiding overheating in hot weather and exposure to vandalism.

Perhaps the main disadvantage of sub-sand abstraction is that the water is deficient in suspended food for filter feeders.

III. SUB-SAND ABSTRACTION

A. Principles

A sub-sand intake converts the surrounding area into an induced-gravity slow sand filter, for the pump creates a negative pressure at the slotted grid intake. At the same time, it creates a well system with a permanent head of water, or if placed above low water, it gives a supply twice daily around high water. Since the pump can only apply a negative head of under one atmosphere, the system is not a pressure filter. Although there is still not full agreement about certain theoretical aspects of sand filtration, it is clear that the process has two interdependent stages. Suspended particles, multi-cellular organisms, cluster bacteria, etc. are held on the fine felted mat that forms on the bottom surface, called *Schmutzdecke* and usually less than 10 mm, rarely to 25 mm deep. In the sea, this is subject to continual tidal and wave movement and is self-cleansing, helped by benthic organisms.

Below this, an aerobic, biologically active zone is created. A range of multi-cellular organisms are active in removing material. Other organisms, mainly bacteria, process ammonia, reduce BOD and convert iron into the insoluble ferric form. This zone does not simply filter out the bacteria and noxious chemicals; these are processed into harmless soluble materials. An exception is iron, which is precipitated in ferric form within the bed or, by delayed action, in the actual pipeline. The depth of this layer varies with the terrain and the rate of flow, for it has been shown that populations of bacteriophages per column increase with flow.

B. Application of Sub-sand Working

Some early examples consisted of elaborate structures sunk in the sea bed some 500 metres or more off-shore. Examples are given by Joice and Davenport (1964), Hettler *et al.* (1971; 1974) and Kinne (1976). Some of these systems need frequent back-washing, with monthly alternation of the delivery lines to miminize fouling. Other units have been severely undercut by strong currents. The system described below does not need repeated backflushing and completely excludes fouling organisms. Certain types of shore are wholly unsuitable; these are deep soft mud, steep cliffs and exposed rocky shores. Areas with strong coastal currents must also be avoided.

The following factors affect the choice of site and details of the system:

(1) Nature of terrain
Sites with a range of particle size distributions can be utilized but the system demands a permeable bed of a minimum depth 1 m. Ideally, the sand should be a mixture of particles ranging in size from *c.* 0.5 to 5.0 mm, but the presence of at least 25% of larger material can be tolerated. The mineral nature of the medium is not important provided that it does not release harmful substances. Following a careful study of bed texture and depth with pumping trials, a complex of abstraction points is designed to provide the required flow.

(2) Tidal amplitude
This can vary from under 1 m to over 10 m. The smaller the range the better, for the maximum suction lift is usually from low water spring tide level. A very large amplitude may demand the use of submersible pumps. The lower the intake on the shore the better, to ensure a continuous supply of water.

(3) Tidal recession
The shorter the distance between low- and high-water mark the better, to reduce both length of run and pipe diameter. However, if the sand in the intertidal zone is deep, it is sometimes possible to pump continuously from this, using it as both a filter and a reservoir which is recharged twice daily.

(4) Distance and height of pump chamber
On any site, this is the only factor that may be controlled. The nearer to the abstraction point the better, to minimize the suction run. On some sites, the pump chamber can be sunk, thus reducing suction lift.

(5) The presence of pollution
It is normally safe to use a site not less than one kilometre from a sewage outlet, provided that the current does not consistently bring pollution directly over the site. If there is doubt, a temporary source should be established and developed for two weeks before monitoring all relevant parameters.

(6) Salinity
On some sandy beaches, especially at the head of bays, freshwater springs up-well even below low tide level and these areas must be avoided. Fresh water aquifers may occur under impermeable strata a metre or two deep.

(7) Vulnerability to damage
Burying pipes deeply is the only practical way of reducing this danger.

(8) Coastal stability
The construction of harbour works, breakwaters and other coastal defences may cause severe beach erosion or sand deposition. Some shores are inherently unstable.

C. Appliances

An essential component of the efficient sub-sand system is an intake with a pattern of tapered slots. This allows development of the source (see page 58) before bridging by coarse sand grains forms a screened entrance, while the reverse taper prevents blocking of the slots. A range of slot sizes is used on screen wells, mostly from 1.5 to 2.5 mm on the narrow side. The slot diameter has no direct bearing on the removal of fine suspended particles; it is related solely to the sand to be retained and in theory bridging is effected by grains one third of the slot size. This slotted intake can be applied in two ways:

(1) As a false ceiling in an open-bottomed GRP box or unit (Fig. 1).

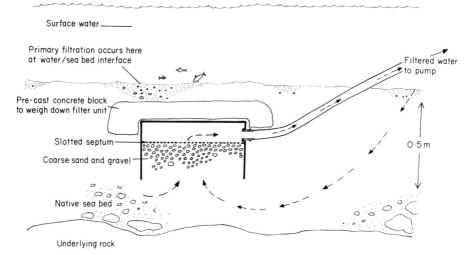

Fig. 1. Sub-sand abstraction unit, consisting of a GRP box with a slotted septum, designed for areas where the sand is shallow. The armoured hose can be buried for protection.

The standard slot diameter is 2.5 mm. This unit is used underwater and, in particular, where the sand is shallow. It is also used where the site is such that a hole must be excavated and filled with suitable medium. Dimensions of 60 × 30 cm with a depth of 30 cm give a unit of a size and weight that can be handled by one person in sites where mechanical aids are not always available. In a favourable medium, and fully developed, the potential initial flow is 22 m³/h drawn through a zone up to 10 m in diameter. To scale up it is technically sounder to use several units at about 10 m centres with 50 mm diameter take-offs than fewer larger ones, which would require 100 mm take-offs and would be very difficult to handle. Installed in the sea bed at a convenient point below spring low tide away from strong currents, so that at least 15 cm and preferably 30 cm sand covers it when stabilized, such a unit is free of scouring, while the continuous suction holds it firm in the bed. To keep the unit stable, a paving slab can be placed on top.

(2) Around a cylindrical screen well, either inserted below low tide mark or in the inter-tidal zone. Large diameter screens are used in deep wells on land but for sea work, the usual diameter is 50 or 75 mm, with an intake length of 30 or 60 cm. This is inserted vertically and can only be used successfully when the sand is at least 1.5 m deep and contains at least 50% grains above 1 mm. It can be driven in, but is more usually inserted by connecting a jet probe to the outlet of a portable pump and sliding the screen well down alongside it. With experience, the jet probe provides useful site data; changes of texture are palpable, while the upwelling water brings successive sand samples. The optimum depth for abstraction can then be confirmed by pumping.

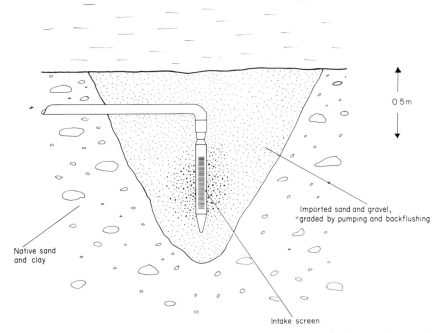

0·5m

Imported sand and gravel, graded by pumping and backflushing

Native sand and clay

Intake screen

Fig. 2. Screen well, for sub-sand extraction where the sand is deep. In this case, imported sand is used. The well is jetted in by back-pumping water, and the surrounding substrate then graded by alternative pumping and backflushing.

In the inter-tidal zone, the intake should be up to 3 m deep, allowing more water to be drawn between the tides, for the foreshore acts as both filter and a reservoir that is charged twice daily. An important advantage of inter-tidal wells is that the suction run is reduced and also, because of the capillary action of the sand, the maximum suction head. Yield varies with site factors but the potential flow is lower than in the sea, where $22 \ m^3/h$ should be possible from a 50 mm screen 60 cm long. Where the sand depth allows screen wells to be used, they are much easier to install and maintain than units. The principle of working at 10 m centres applies equally to screen wells, giving the formula stated below for made beds i.e. *c*. $3 \ m^2$ surface for $1 \ m^3/h$ flow.

Fig. 3. A plastic bag for sea water transport. The bag holds approximately 3000 litres of water, and can be filled with a gasoline driven pump carried on the truck. The bag is secured to the bed of the truck with ropes.

D. Difficult Sites

(1) Compacted foreshore with shallow sand
Such sites are often gently shelving with wide inter-tidal zones. A trench of 1.5 m depth and suitable area can often be excavated, the unit or screen well installed and the hole filled with sand. It is essential to fill the hole thoroughly and not allow a hollow to form in which organic matter collects on the falling tides.

(2) Rocky foreshores with little or no sand
If the formation allows, blasting can prepare a series of craters of suitable

volume which can be filled with sand. The shape is unimportant. Blasting may be possible below low tide mark, with greatly increased potential. The size of excavation for either type of site will be decided by the topography of the shore, the position of the hole relative to low water, the volume of water required and whether pumping is to be continuous.

A surface area of *c*. 3 m² is desirable for a flow rate of 1 m³/h; i.e. for a flow of 20 m³/h, a pit of some 4 × 15 m surface area is needed. However, a higher pumping rate may be possible without loss of quality, and can be found by experience. The trench is filled first with *c*. 30 cm gravel/stones to stop the unit bedding down and also give free lateral access for water, thus utilizing all the surface area. Coarse sand is then added, and the unit put in position when a depth of *c*. 10 cm has been tipped in. Because of its position, the pit will be full of water before sand is added and this avoids the delay in development caused by air trapped within the sand.

Above low tide, continuous pumping may be made possible by placing the trench as near low tide mark as possible, with a small sea water channel to give water access at all times from the tide. If the site does not allow this, the trench can be so constructed that it holds enough water to last until the tide returns. The dimensions recommended above give only up to 1 h reserve, but on some shores there is continuous run-off which will be caught by a trench parallel to the tide line, adding markedly to capacity. Further, the increase in suction head toward low tide may severely reduce the flow rate and extend the period of pumping. If the system is to supply an open circuit, a third variation may be possible on some terrains. The pipe bearing the aquarium effluent can run parallel with the rising main and be allowed to flow on to the shore well above the trench. This will then mix with other water at low tide and be filtered thoroughly while allowing continuous pumping.

These variations are clearly of limited capacity and difficult to install, and it may be preferable to work higher up the beach and pump into storage for up to 6 h over each high tide. Although continuous pumping is ideal, a fully developed system remains aerobic even if pumped at intervals of several days in cool climates. Such a system will be much cheaper, with lower head, shorter suction line and perhaps, a pipeline of smaller bore.

(3) Fine sand
Uniform sand of under 0.5 mm is unsuitable on its own; it is not permeable enough, while particles are too small to start bridging the slots and sand will pass indefinitely. If a much finer slot size is used, the flow is very limited and blocking tends to be more frequent. It is sounder to introduce coarse sand (*c*. 1 mm to 5 mm) into the excavated hole before

the unit is placed in position and then to pile coarse sand around it. The unit itself should be pre-filled with coarse sand or pea gravel (2 mm to 5 mm), held in by a piece of wood which is pulled out after the unit has been put in position. Much of the surplus fine material is evacuated during development and the coarse medium, in effect, forms a larger perimeter and thus gives easier access for the water. Assuming the diameter of the introduced material to be 1.2 m, the perimeter is nearly 400 cm compared to 16 cm for a 50 mm jet well.

(4) Shingle foreshores
There is such variation that the only general solution is for a sand bed to be prepared for the unit, but it must be emphasized that a surface examination is never sufficient. Fist-sized stones may cover suitable sand, while a fine stratum may be underlain by or covered by an ideal sand mixture. Some sites must be treated almost as (1) above; elsewhere the shingle may be fine and mixed well enough to allow the unit to be installed in a small sand-filled hole, while loads of sand are tipped around it and allowed to work in.

E. Development of the System

It must again be stressed that the slots of the plate or well screen affect filtration only indirectly but are essential for successful development and working of the sub-sand system. Failing to understand this principle, some workers have used 0.25 mm slots, drawing little more than 100 l/h per point. Development serves two purposes:

(1) By hydraulically classifying the medium in and around the unit or screen well and evacuating the fine material, it increases flow until the intake has no intrinsic friction head loss.

(2) By drawing oxygenated water continuously through the bed it makes it aerobic and thus allows the biological filter layer to form.

The process will therefore be described in detail; it applies equally to screen wells and units but for simplicity the latter will be named. As soon as the unit is in position, the suction line is connected to a portable self-priming petrol-driven pump of 2 to 4 hp. This specification is important, for the speed must be controlled in the early stages. As soon as the pump primes, the speed is reduced until it runs steadily. At first, for a period varying from one minute to many minutes, silt and fine sand are pumped, sometimes almost as sludge, but the water progressively clears and when it appears clean the pump is stopped and at once restarted. This release of vacuum allows the bridged sand grains to rearrange themselves, so that a further dirty stream emerges, again followed by clean water. As this process continues, the flow steadily improves and the flush of dirty water becomes less marked. At the same time, the motor speed is gradually increased. Each sequence expands the perimeter of bed which is being exploited. After a period which may vary from a few minutes to several hours (the latter for difficult sites containing much fine silt) the motor is at full power and stopping and restarting no longer have any effect. For sites developing very slowly, two variations are possible:

(a) Instead of just stopping the pump, the suction line is loosened, allowing the water to run back and purge the unit briefly.

(b) The suction and delivery lines are interchanged and the water is pumped back to the unit for some two or three minutes while a man stands on the unit to stop it lifting, remaining there until normal pumping starts again. (In river sites, this is remarkably effective in speeding progress.)

With several units, each must be individually developed before connecting to the sea main. The system should then be matured by pumping continuously, or at least for 6–8 h daily, for a period that can only be decided by monitoring. On ideal clean sites, it can perhaps be used freely after 24 h; on poor sites with polluted inshore water and bed, pumping for up to two weeks may be needed. On many sites, very small numbers of discrete grains of sand may come through long after development. These are from the lower bed and are clean and sterile; they drop out immediately a baffle chamber or storage vessel is reached.

F. Pumps and Plumbing

Only pumps guaranteed for marine work must be used; these include stainless steel, marine bronze and plastic materials (Chapter 6). Marine bronze can be used safely only where water quality is not important. Though there may be no copper accumulation, there is always a risk of it. However, such pumps may cost only one third of stainless steel models of similar capacity.

The need for self-priming limits the choice but several series of pumps are available, the precise characteristic needed being determined by maximum flow, total suction and delivery heads. A shore-based pump is likely to be better maintained, but on some sites, only submersible pumps can be used. The latter are usually very efficient and any extra capital cost may be recovered in power economy within 2 years. In several submersible models, the standard slotted grille can be replaced by a housing connecting directly to the take-off from one or more units. This pump need not be completely submerged at all times, but can be conveniently mounted on a pile so that it is exposed at low spring tides for easy maintenance. A disadvantage of such pumps is that an armoured power cable must traverse the beach, but it is possible for this to enter the pipeline at the delivery end and emerge through a special gland at the pump collar, thus affording it complete protection.

Pipelines are calculated to reduce friction head loss to a minimum on the delivery side of the pump and to have a low suction head. Capacity of a line rises much more steeply than cost; e.g. the cost of a 100 mm diameter line is roughly twice that of a 50 mm diameter one but for the same head loss, the flow is about 6 times greater. Failure to apply this principle causes permanent waste of energy for pumping and possible pump damage by cavitation. Bends and valves add disproportionately to friction head loss so that the pipe-work should be as simple as possible, especially around the pump. Provision for back-washing should be made; this may also be useful for filling the suction line when restarting the pump. Facilities for pumping to waste are essential.

G. System Maintenance

From experience, a properly developed sub-sand system requires negligible maintenance other than periodic pumping back. In particular, surface blocking has seldom been recorded though there is a decline in flow rate with time. The following points, however, should be noted:

(1) In the case of a submersible pump system with a large volume of water in the pipeline, if the pump is switched off, this water must not be allowed to run rapidly back to the unit, for it may flush it out of its bed. A valve must be used to allow the water to run back slowly even though the unit is held in position by a concrete slab.

(2) Reduction of flow rate is normally caused by an accumulation of fine material around the unit or screen well and this is aggravated by erratic pumping. It is quickly cleared by pumping back for approximately 5 min at gradually increasing volume. A study of flow pattern, taking account of variation caused by tidal movement, will indicate if such action is needed and a routine can be worked out. The interval between action is likely to be weeks rather than days.

(3) The jet probe is a very effective tool for cleaning the bed, either just the surface or to any depth required.

(4) In some beds, including those with high organic content before development, iron is leached in soluble form and then oxidized and this becomes deposited on the pipeline walls in the form of iron-rich bacteria. While pumping of aerated water continues, most material remains attached to the wall but when the flow has stopped, it becomes detached and is washed out when pumping restarts. This phenomenon is usually only temporary.

(5) Overpumping must be avoided. It is better to develop a unit or screen well to maximum capacity and then to pump at not above 80% of the maximum.

H. General Points

Any scheme demanding a continuous supply should be duplicated up to and including the pumps to allow for pump maintenance; it is usually enough to provide two systems each with 75% of maximum demand. Absence of fouling makes a duplicate delivery line unnecessary. With a complex of approximately 10 units, a similar principle applies, but less over-provision is needed: e.g. three systems of 4 units or screen wells each would allow one system to be taken out for a day's maintenance while some 80% of the maximum demand is provided.

Access to clean water tends to increase demand. It is much more economical to allow for this at first, when a further 50% capacity might add only about 10% to total costs. Added subsequently, it would cost nearly as much as the original scheme. It is therefore essential to make accurate projections of need.

Installation normally requires actually working in the sea. In warm climates, the timing will be dictated by tide and local weather, for calm water and daylight are needed. In northern latitudes, the short daylight hours, rough weather and cold water limit work to the summer months. There must be careful planning, with study of the tide tables, especially when the amplitude varies widely. These systems are equally valuable for abstracting clean water from rivers and lakes and, in fact, find their main application there.

IV. REFERENCES

Clark, J. R. and Eiser, R. (1964). Sea water from ground sources. *In* "Sea Water Systems for Experimental Aquariums" A collection of papers (J. R. Clark and R. L. Clark, eds) *Research Report of US Fish Wildlife Service* **63**, 173–184.

Hettler, W. F. Jr (1974). A filter and chiller for an open seawater system. *Progressive Fish Culturalist* **36**, 234–238.

Hettler, W. F. Jr, Lichtenheld, R. W. and Gardy, H. R. (1971). Open seawater system with controlled temperature and salinity. *Progressive Fish Culturalist* **33**, 3–11.

Joice, D. K. and Davenport, D. (1964). Sea water system of the marine laboratory of the University of California, Santa Barbara. *In* "Sea Water Systems for Experimental Aquariums" A collection of papers (J. R. Clark and R. L. Clark, eds) *Research Report of US Fish Wildlife Service* **63**, 143–146.

Kinne, O. (ed.) (1976). "Marine Ecology Vol. III Cultivation Part I". 681 J. Wiley and Sons, London.

Rollefsen, G. (1962). The Aquarium in Bergen. In "1er Congrès International d'aquariologie" Monaco 1960. *Bulletin Institut ocèanographique Monaco* Vol. 1B 167–172.

Chapter 3

Sea Water Treatment

J. F. Wickins and M. M. Helm

Fisheries Experiment Station, Conwy, North Wales

I. INTRODUCTION

A. General Aspects

The principal objective of anyone who wishes to keep marine organisms is to provide an environment capable of supporting the natural behaviour, growth and development of the cultured species. Furthermore, the animals held should be able to realize their reproductive potential and provide vigorous, viable offspring. These criteria are of equal importance both to the amateur aquarist and to the research worker. Unfortunately, from the moment that water is drawn from the sea, changes occur in its physico-chemical and biological characteristics. The rate of change is accelerated as soon as the organisms to be cultured are introduced. Many of the changes are subtle, difficult to monitor and in many cases, incompletely understood. The objective is therefore to reduce the rate of deterioration of sea-water quality and by good management, to control the more important parameters within acceptable limits. This necessarily involves continuous, or at least frequent analyses of physico-chemical and biological factors of known importance and the application of suitable corrective measures.

Developments in the fields of aquarium technology and water quality control continue, but much still depends on the experience and skill of the individual — colloquially known as the "wet thumb". Our objective in this chapter is to provide the reader with current information on a wide range of water treatment equipment and to describe analytical techniques of proven value in water quality control. Wherever possible, we have drawn from our own experience at the Fisheries Experiment Station, Conwy. This is largely in the field of bivalve and crustacean rearing in various types of culture systems. No attempt has been made to fully review literature on the subject as this has been amply covered by Kinne (1976). Further references have been included together with selected literature which will enable the reader to pursue the topic.

B. Properties of Sea Water

Table I shows the composition of natural sea water both for coastal and offshore waters and the Conwy laboratory supply. References to analytical techniques used are shown in Table XV. Also in Table I is a list of references which provide detailed information on the properties of sea water. Variations within wide limits of some of the quoted factors are associated with seasonal biological activity and climatic conditions; variations in other factors are less readily explained. An example is in the concentrations of magnesium and calcium at Conwy (Elderfield, 1971). The ratios of these cations in relation to the concentration of sodium indicate that variations cannot be explained by dilution of sea water by land drainage.

Sea water from different sites, or taken from the same source at different times of year, may vary in its ability to support the growth and development of marine invertebrate larvae (Wilson, 1951; Wilson and Armstrong, 1958; Millar and Scott, 1968; Helm, 1971). Ways of improving water which is sub-standard are mentioned later, but the precise causes of the problem remain to be identified. A fundamental knowledge of the ways in which organisms react to changes in their environment is essential to further developments in aquarium science. Such knowledge would stimulate research into improved methods of sea water treatment and water quality control.

C. Basic Aquarium Systems

Marine culture systems are conveniently divided into three types: still water, through-flow and recirculation systems. These have already been described in Chapter 1. The rest of this chapter is divided into two main

Table I. Values for a range of sea water parameters. Data from the Conwy laboratory sea water supply are provided for comparison.

Parameter	Sea water	Conwy laboratory
Salinity	30–34‰	26.4–30.0‰ (1977)
pH	8.1–8.3[a]	7.75–8.33 (1977)
Inorganic carbon	28 mg C/l[a]	15.7–26.3 mg C/l (1977)
Carbonate alkalinity	2.34 meg/l[a]	1.8–2.4 meg/l (1972)
Particulate inorganic material (ash)	—	2.4–26.8 mg/l (1977) *
Particulate organic material	0.1–1.0 mg C/l[b]	5.6–66.8 mg/l (1977) †
"Dissolved" organic carbon	1–5 to a max. of 20 mg C/l[b]	0.9–19.4 mg/l (1977) ‡
		0.5–18.0 mg C/l (1977) †
Na	10.561 g/kg[a]	7.5–10.4 g/l[e]
Mg	1.272 g/kg[a]	0.67–1.24 g/l[e]
Ca	0.400 g/kg[a]	0.31–0.42 g/l[e]
K	0.380 g/kg[a]	0.27–0.44 g/l[e]
Cl	18.980 g/kg[a]	13.8–18.7 g/l[e]
SO$_4$	2.639 g/kg[a]	1.9–2.6 g/l[e]
B	0.0046 g/kg[a]	0.004–0.005 g/l[e]
NH$_3$	0.1–2.0 to a max. of 10 µg at.N/l[c]	0.02–0.04 mg N/l[f]
NO$_2$	0.01–4.0 µg at.N/l[c]	0.01–0.04 mg N/l[f]
NO$_3$	0.01–40.0 µg at.N/l[c]	0.1–0.2 mg N/l[f]
PO$_4$	1–60 µg/l[d]	0.03–0.04 mg P/l[f]
Zn	8–14 µg/l[d]	0.5–470 µg/l[e]
Bacteria	10– >100/ml[d]	9–9900/ml (1977)

* Material filtered on to Whatman GF/C papers and ashed.
† Difference between oven dried and ash weight of the above.
‡ Dry weight of all particulate material retained on 0.22 µm membrane.

[a] Sverdrup et al. (1942)
[b] Head (1976)
[c] Kinne (1976)
[d] Harvey (1945)
[e] Elderfield (1971)
[f] Wickins (1976b)

themes. First, we deal with the treatment of sea water for through-flow systems and the more sophisticated preparatory treatment for still and recirculation systems. We then consider the maintenance of water quality in recirculation systems.

II. SEA WATER TREATMENT

Sea water treatment is the stage of water quality control between extraction from the sea and its use in an aquarium system. The purpose of treatment is to render the sea water suitable for the culture of the required species. The extent of treatment is dependent upon the tolerance of the culture subjects to prevailing sea water quality (quality being defined as the ability of the sea water to support the species cultured).

A. Sea Water Abstraction and Storage

(1) Choice of abstraction site and method of abstraction
Ideally, water should be drawn from a source where natural populations of the desired culture subjects flourish, but this is not always possible. Many establishments draw their water supply from adjacent estuaries or coastal waters. In some cases, off-shore water is shipped and transported overland in tankers to inland establishments and to coastal sites where it may be more satisfactory for certain applications than the local supply. Chapter 2 discusses the choice of a suitable site and the more common methods of abstraction. Sub-sand abstraction would appear to be the most attractive technique for most applications.

(2) Sea water storage
When water of the required quality cannot be continuously obtained, it must be stored. The water supply may benefit from a period of storage which allows solid material to settle out. At Conwy, the laboratory's water supply is drawn from the adjacent estuary. Outdoor concrete storage tanks (450 m³), which are topped up by about 30% of their volume at each high tide, help to buffer variations in salinity.

Storage may also be necessary as a back-up water supply in the event of a drastic, long-lasting deterioration in sea water quality. At Conwy, an annual bloom of the colonial alga *Phaeocystis pouchetti* renders water unsuitable for culturing unicellular algae or for rearing bivalve larvae during the period mid-May to July. A 450 m³ uncovered outdoor concrete storage tank is filled with water of proven suitability during spring tides at the beginning of May. Once blooming of *Phaeocystis* begins, the laboratory sea water supply is drawn from the storage tank. With careful management, this supply will last for 6–8 weeks. Some deterioration in quality becomes detectable towards the end of this period but at this time, it is often still better than water from the estuary. The design of storage tanks is considered in Chapter 1, and materials suitable for their construction in Chapter 6.

B. Improving Water Quality

(1) Removal of large particles
The extent to which particulate material needs to be reduced depends on a number of factors. These include the method used in abstraction from the sea, the prevailing nature and quantity of such matter, the subsequent steps of treatment employed, the type of culture system used and a knowledge of the tolerance or requirement of the culture subject to such matter. The reduction of the particulate content is usually the first stage in sea water treatment (Fig. 1). An exception, discussed later, is where foam separation is applied. Generally the latter technique precedes fine filtration. The following is a guide to commonly used filtration methods.

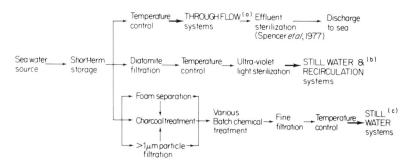

Fig. 1.   Various stages of sea water treatment at Conwy for holding and rearing marine animals: (a) for holding bivalve breeding stocks; (b) for rearing bivalve and crustacean larvae and juveniles; (c) experimental treatment units being tested for the modification of sea water quality for bivalve embryos and larvae.

(a) Sub-sand abstraction.   A properly installed and maintained sub-sand filtration unit as described in Chapter 2 can be a highly cost-effective method for sea water clarification. With such a facility, the further filtration of larger particulate material is unnecessary. Another advantage where long pipelines from the extraction point are unavoidable is the very considerable reduction in the risk of pipe

occlusion through the growth of fouling organisms. The major biological disadvantage is that phytoplankton, other micro-organisms and organic detritus which together constitute the food source of filter feeding animals are excluded. For those working with filter feeders, particularly if held in through-flow systems, the problems of cultivating suitable foods are introduced. The water extracted should be directly suitable for any of the procedures for sub-micron filtration, chemical pre-treatment or sea water sterilization detailed later. If, however, any pre-filtered sea water is allowed to stand in storage tanks for an appreciable amount of time, filterable material will develop by the normal processes of particle formation in the sea (Riley, 1970) and from air-borne contamination. The development of particles will be enhanced if the storage tanks are subject to wind action or are aerated.

(b) Sedimentation.   Where sub-sand abstraction is either impractical or undesirable, many coastal sited establishments pump directly from the sea into storage tanks. Depending upon the periodicity of pumping, tank size and configuration and the rate of water usage, these tanks can fulfil the role of settling tanks. Negatively buoyant material will settle according to the difference in specific gravity between the particles and sea water. Buoyant materials, including the foam which is produced from organic material during pumping, will rise to the surface initially and may need to be removed by skimming. After peaks of phytoplankton blooms in spring at Conwy, crusts of floating decomposing organic matter are periodically removed with manual skimmers, otherwise they can sink and generate anaerobic conditions at the bottom. The rate of particle settlement is enhanced in shallow tanks, but wind-induced turbulence can impede settlement and further contribute to the particulate content of the water. Settlement tanks especially designed for this purpose are used in freshwater treatment plants, and at the mussel station at Texel, Holland. Some are circular; others are long V-shaped channels.

A relatively recent innovation developed primarily for waste water treatment and the chemical industry is the tilted plate or tube separator, sometimes referred to as a particle interceptor. Because they operate at a rapid flow rate, they are suitable for filtering water at source. Essentially, water is pumped upwards through parallel tubes or plates arranged to ensure a laminar flow. Close packing of the elements permits the minimum of distance for particles to settle out on to the surfaces. The angle of tilt is adjusted to ensure that the particle aggregates slide against the direction of flow into a sediment trap. These devices will not, however, work efficiently with finely divided solids which are reluctant to move off the inclined surfaces. In this case, a stable floc formed by chemical treatment improves efficiency. Tilted plate separators are being operated by the National Marine Fisheries Service in a closed-system shrimp culture project at Galveston, Texas (Mock *et al.*, in preparation). Parker and Simco (1973) also describe the use of a tilted tube unit in the culture of fresh water fish in closed systems.

(c) Mechanical filters

(i) Meshes and wadding filters, in their simplest form, comprise either a mesh screen or a wad of glass or synthetic wool held in a suitable container. They are widely used to remove large particles from recycled water. With proper maintenance, they provide a cheap method of partial water clarification. Mesh screens, usually manufactured of mono-filament nylon or other synthetic materials, are essentially two dimensional filters, and have a limited life between cleaning operations. In-depth "wool" filter media (e.g. Perlon, Nylon or Terylene) are more efficient in removing particles, particularly when partially clogged, and are longer lasting. Clarification efficiency is dependent upon the depth of medium used, its packing and the length of time it has been in operation. Neither meshes nor wadding are of value in clarifying large volumes of incoming water. Wadding can be effective when used as a crude filter for low turnover, open flow systems where more sophisticated methods may be very costly. We use nylon mesh filter bags of 45 μm or 61 μm aperture to remove filter-feeding organisms, but not their food, from the incoming water supply to recirculation systems for rearing juvenile bivalves. These systems have a complete water change two or three times each week. Crude filters are rarely built in to pipelines because they need frequent cleaning or replacement.

(ii) Sand and diatomite filters are commonly used for water clarification, both being particularly useful because they can be used on-line with other water quality control equipment such as charcoal filters, foam separators, ultraviolet light treatment or sub-micron filters (Fig. 1). They can cope with small or large batches of water or can be used in continuous operation. As well as the filtration of water at source, they are often used to control the particulate content in recirculation systems either by intermittent or continuous operation. Among their advantages are the use of chemically inert, insoluble filter media, the lack of moving parts and their all-plastic construction.

Sand filters are classified either as slow or rapid. Slow filters are unpressurized and water dispersed over the surface of a bed of clean graded sand and gravel percolates through the media to a discharge pipe. The filters are either constructed as discrete units or they can be built into aquarium tanks to provide *in situ* sub-gravel filtration. Examples of both applications are illustrated in Spotte (1970) and Kinne (1976). A schematic diagram of a typical unit is shown in Fig. 2. Layers of coarse

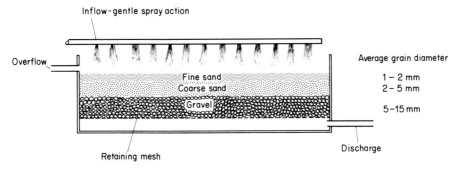

Fig. 2. Schematic representation of a slow sand filter.

sand and gravel act as a support for a thinner layer of fine sand and ensure an even water flow. It is important that the different layers be well delineated and evenly packed. Uneven particle distribution and packing reduces both the capacity of the filter and its efficiency and can draw suspended material into the bottom layers of the media. The capacity of the filter is increased more by providing a greater surface area of bed than by increasing its depth because it is the upper layer of fine sand which is the site of filtration. Here, suspended particles which bridge adjacent media granules are trapped.

As the layer of fine sand gradually becomes blocked, the efficiency of particle removal improves. Eventually, with continuous use, the rate of water flow drops below acceptable limits and there is a danger that the dissolved oxygen content within the filter bed will fall below that necessary to support the developed biomass of aerobic micro-organisms. These are of considerable importance in degrading organic material trapped within the filter bed. When clogged, the top layer of fine sand is gently stirred and the turbid over-layer of water siphoned off. Kinne (1976) recommends that the top layer should be replaced once or twice each year with fresh graded sand. Backflushing should be avoided as this leads to uneven particle distribution and packing.

Slow filters are most commonly used in recirculation systems because of their biological action. They are too slow to be of value in filtering water at source. The water flowing through a rapid sand filter is usually propelled by pressure, the filter media being encased within a robust housing. Being operated in this way, rapid filters provide a much greater throughput of water per unit area of filter bed than slow sand filters and can, therefore, be used at source. They act primarily as mechanical filters as there is insufficient time for microbiological activity to modify water quality. This limits their use in recirculation systems solely to particle removal. The filter medium, usually sand, is uniform in particle size. One reason for this is that maintenance of such a unit involves backflushing which would disrupt the integrity of graded layers. Anthracite or a similar material, may serve as a coarse aid to filtration above the sand bed. An advantage of anthracite is that it permits greater depth penetration of suspended material within the sand bed and thus increases the duration of a filter run. Having a lower specific gravity than sand, anthracite will settle back as a discrete layer above the sand after back-flushing.

In passage through the filter bed, particles are removed by a straining effect, dependent on the size of medium granules and their packing, the attachment of suspended material to medium granules and settlement of solids in interstices sheltered from the main flow. Efficiency of filtration improves with time of operation until progressive clogging results in a rapid pressure drop between the inlet and outlet. At this point, the unit needs backflushing to restore its efficiency. Pressure gauges are usually fitted to the ports to give warning of impending loss of efficiency. Manufacturers quote efficiency on the basis of 90–95% particle removal down to a specific particle diameter. The minimum particle size retained is related to the grade of medium used. A fine, uniform medium with an effective size of 0.3 mm will theoretically remove 95% of particles to 6 μm diameter, while a coarser medium of 0.45 mm is efficient in retaining 15 μm particles. Achieved efficiency is dependent on prevailing site conditions (manufacturer's data).

Diatomite filtration involves the propulsion of water, usually under pressure rather than vacuum, through filter septa which have a layer of diatomite deposited upon their inflow surfaces. Diatomite is the siliceous skeletal remains of fossil diatoms. Filter septa may be of a porous ceramic or plastic material in the form of plates, candles or paper filter mats. When deposited from recycled water onto the filter septa, the layer of diatomite provides a strong but highly permeable coating (the pre-coat) with an intricate matrix which entraps suspended solids from sea water. As with sand filtration, the efficiency of particle removal is dependent on the grade of filter medium, the flow rate and the period of time that the filter has been in operation. The majority of commercially available diatomite filters have vertical septa to facilitate backflushing when the medium is blocked with particles. Others with horizontally arranged filter papers as septa require the strip-down of the unit for cleaning.

At Conwy, diatomite filters have been used for many years in the batch filtration of water for rearing bivalve and crustacean larvae and early juveniles. For the majority of applications, the grade of diatomite used has been '545 Celite' (Johns-Manville Celite Division). This is a coarse grade with an average particle size of 30 μm and yet the intricate structure of the medium enables effective filtration of particles to 2.5–5.0 μm diameter. Finer grades are available which improve the efficiency of filtration and retain smaller particles but reduce the length of a filter cycle. Data from a typical run with a filter of vertical ceramic candles (filter area 1 m²) coated with '545 Celite' are shown in Fig. 3.

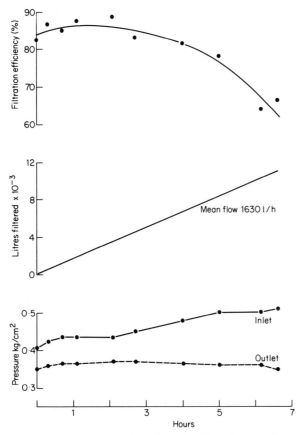

Fig. 3. Data of a typical run with a diatomite filter. See text for explanation.

Previously untreated sea water containing 61 500 particles within the size range of 2.5–5.0 μm diameter per ml was filtered. Filtration efficiency was determined as the percentage removal of particles within that size range using a Coulter Counter. Note the gradually increasing inlet pressure as the diatomite layer blocks and the resulting drop in filtration efficiency which results from the layer breaking up. In this run, the unit should have been backflushed after 5 h of operation.

The efficiency with which particles within various size ranges are removed by diatomite filters using grade '545 Celite' is shown in Table II. These values were obtained early in the filter cycles and would alter towards greater efficiency as the runs proceeded. The reduction in efficiency of filtration of the larger size raɪ.ʒe of particles is probably an artefact where smaller particles have aggregated after passing the filter medium.

Table II. The efficiency with which naturally occurring particles of different sizes are removed by diatomite filtration using grade '545 Celite' as the filter aid.

	Particle size μm diameter	No. of particles/ml Inlet	Outlet	Filtration efficiency %
	1.5– 2.5	337 720	228 120	32.4
	2.5– 5.0	35 140	13 625	61.2
Run 1	5.0–10.0	5 869	1 758	70.0
	10.0–20.0	484	161	66.7
	1.5– 2.5	229 120	173 810	24.1
	2.5– 5.0	27 640	7 190	74.0
Run 2	5.0–10.0	6 343	798	87.4
	10.0–20.0	467	124	73.4

Figure 4 shows the number of particles within the range of 2.5–5.0 μm per ml in the laboratory sea water supply during 1977 and the efficiency with which they were retained by a diatomite filter. Samples for efficiency determinations by means of a Coulter Counter were taken approximately 1 h after the start of filtration of a batch of sea water. Average efficiency over the year was 77.5%. The relationship between particle count and filtration efficiency was not significant. This demonstrates that the nature of particulate material is an important factor in filtration. Further evidence suggests that certain phytoplankton species with cell sizes which should ensure efficient entrapment are sufficiently plastic to enable passage through the filter medium.

Information on rapid sand or diatomite filters is most readily available from manufacturers or suppliers of swimming pool or aquarium equipment. Filters of these types should either be used with gravity head feed or

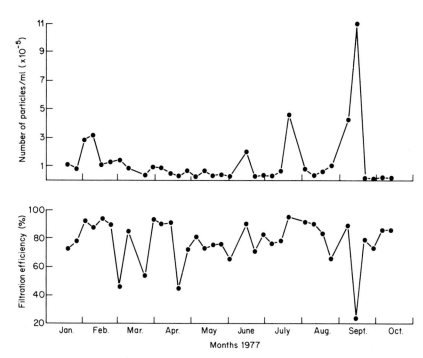

Fig. 4. The number of particles per ml within the size range 2.5–5.0 μm diameter in the Conwy laboratory sea water supply and the efficiency with which they were removed by diatomite filtration during 1977.

centrifugal pumps. Positive displacement water pumps can result in a pressure differential building up between the inlet and outlet ports which disrupts the filter medium and could damage equipment.

(iii) <u>Cartridge filters</u> are much smaller units and are suitable for in line filtration to small aquaria. They are frequently used as pre-filters for subsequent sub-micron particle filtration although they can also be used independently. A range of types is commonly available with retention ratings ranging from 1 μm to 10 μm particle diameter. The cartridges are usually mounted, either singly or in clusters, in a suitable housing. For sea water applications, plastic housings are preferred. The filter elements which may be of ceramic, pleated paper, resin-bound fibres or pleated or woven synthetic plastic material are generally, but not always, replaceable and must be disposed of when blocked. Cartridge life can in some cases be extended by careful backflushing. Ceramic candles can be reused repeatedly by backflushing followed by soaking in a hydrogen peroxide solution overnight.

(2) Reduction of sub-micron particles and dissolved substances

(a) Sub-micron filtration. For small aquaria, sub-micron filtration is generally achieved by cartridges manufactured of a thin-pleated plastic membrane perforated with pores of uniform size. The membrane is arranged around a rigid plastic core and is retained by an outer plastic mesh. Usually about 80% of the volume of a membrane filter is void space, providing high flow rates in relation to pore size. Filter membranes are fibre-free to preclude the risk of contaminating the filtrate. Sub-micron filters have two principal uses in aquaria. They are frequently used with cartridges of 0.2 μm pore size to filter the air supply to sealed vessels used in the culture of bacteria, yeasts, unicellular algae, etc. minimizing air-borne contamination. They are also used to remove or reduce the number of water-borne micro-organisms in the incoming water supply. The choice of porosity of filter is of great importance. While manufacturer's data show that 0.45 μm membranes will retain coliform bacteria, there are bacteria in sea water which are not completely retained even by 0.2 μm filters.

The use of suitable pre-filters, e.g. diatomite or cartridges, is strongly recommended to extend the life of these membranes as they are expensive items. Sterility of the filters is an important consideration. A recent development is in autoclavable membrane cartridges which, alternatively, can be steam-sterilized *in situ*. These are of particular value in the filtration of sea water media for the culture of micro-organisms. The manufacturers of non-autoclavable filters recommend chemical sterilization either with ethylene oxide gas, sulphur dioxide or solutions containing free chlorine.

The importance of suspended particulate material which cannot be removed by diatomite or sand filtration is shown in Fig. 5. Data are from

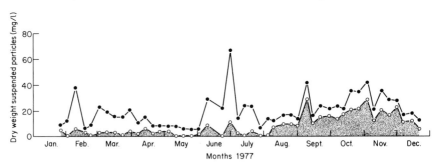

Fig. 5.   The dry weight of particulate material in the Conwy laboratory sea water supply in 1977 and the quantity which passed a Whatman GF/C filter paper but was retained on a 0.22 μm membrane (shaded area).

the Conwy laboratory sea water supply in 1977 and show the quantity of suspended material passing through a Whatman glass-fibre GF/C filter paper but retained on a 0.22 μm membrane in relation to the total dry weight of all suspended particles. The former is the predominant fraction from late summer through to early winter. There is no evidence that this fraction is particularly harmful; it is not closely correlated with the quantity of organic carbon. However, it can severely limit the useful life of a membrane cartridge.

(b) Activated charcoal is a highly adsorptive, porous material which is used to control the quantity of micro-particulate and dissolved organic material in aquaria (Spotte, 1970; Kinne, 1976). It acts by chemically attracting organic molecules to adsorptive surfaces. The most commonly used form is granular coconut charcoal, 1 kg of which may have a total surface area in excess of $10\ 000\ m^2$ (Kinne, 1976). Activated charcoal will also function as a mechanical filter in much the same way as a slow sand filter. However, it is important to pre-filter the sea water to prevent premature loss of adsorption efficiency through the coating of granules with particulate matter. Replaceable glass or synthetic wool wadding pre-filters are often used in recirculation systems for this purpose.

Activated charcoal filters are generally used in recirculation systems. They remove organic metabolites and leachings from uneaten food and dead animals and therefore aid the control of micro-organisms. Charcoal will also remove soluble organic compounds which form slicks at the water–air interface and interfere with the free exchange of gases. Both Kinne (1976) and Spotte (1970) describe the design and operation of charcoal filters for a range of sizes and types of aquarium systems, but little information is available on the effective life of the filters or their efficiency in removing organic substances. Filter life and efficiency are dependent upon the prevailing load and nature of adsorbable organic compounds which, from our experience, can show considerable variation from day to day. The medium needs changing when the carbon content of the water is not reduced in transit through the filter. Regeneration of the charcoal is difficult and costly.

Activated charcoal treatment can also serve in the batch or continuous treatment of extracted sea water subjected to prior coarse particle filtration (Fig. 1). Current work at this laboratory is investigating the use of charcoal treatment as a means of improving prevailing sea water quality for the early developmental stages of Pacific oyster (*Crassostrea gigas*) larvae. Small filter units of the type illustrated in Fig. 6 are used, each having a 100 ml packed bed volume of distilled water washed, granular, activated coconut charcoal. The surface area of the bed is

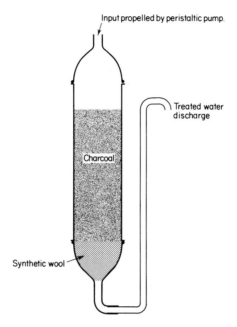

Fig. 6.   Diagram of model 100 ml bed volume granular coconut charcoal column used at Conwy. See text for explanation.

approximately 5 cm². Water samples of 2 litre volume are pumped through the units at different flow rates and are tested for their ability to support the normal development of embryos to completely shelled bivalve larvae. Data of one such trial are shown in Table III. They show the success of the treatment in removing naturally occurring organic substances and the mechanical filtration effect of the charcoal. There is an improvement in the ability of water to support normal embryonic development at the higher flow rate but too slow a flow rate through the filter bed is a hazard. In this latter case, the restoration of water quality by the addition of EDTA and sodium metasilicate following charcoal treatment suggests that natural chelating substances are removed by the treatment.

(c) Foam separation.   This treatment is sometimes referred to as dispersed air flotation, air stripping or protein skimming. Small air bubbles are introduced into a column containing water which is to be treated. As the bubbles rise, a skin of surface-active micro-particulate and dissolved organic substances forms at the air–water interface. When the bubbles reach the surface and burst, the skins are left behind, material

Table III. The effect of charcoal filtration at different flow rates on the quantities of organic carbon and particulate material in sea water treated as a medium for the development of Pacific oyster larvae.

Flow rate ml/min	Organic carbon mg C/l	Dry weight of particulate material (GF/C) mg/l	% Development of embryos (95% Confidence limits)
245	5.5	2.63	60.0–65.1
110	3.7	2.40	48.6–52.1
27.5	1.7	2.27	0[b]
Pre-treated sample	10.5–12.6[a]	4.01	49.4–53.3

[a] Sample lost: values are for 3 days before and 3 days after the experiment.
[b] % development 54.0–58.3 for water treated with 1 mg/l Na$_2$EDTA and 20 mg/l Na$_2$SiO$_3$.5H$_2$O after charcoal filtration.

accumulating in the froth being carried continuously away through a discharge outlet situated above the water level. Some skins sink, as do other small particles, forming nuclei for the further aggregation of organic material. Both Spotte (1970) and Kinne (1976) provide useful diagrams of foam separation equipment. While foam separation is usually used to improve water quality in recirculation systems (Short and Olson, 1970; Zillioux and Lackie, 1970), we have used it to treat sea water for the early developmental stages of oyster larvae.

The configuration of a small experimental foam separator used at Conwy, a modification of the design of Wallace and Wilson (1969) to permit treatment of a continuous flow of sea water, is shown in Fig. 7. Sea water is introduced two-thirds of the way up a 50 cm height, 7 cm diameter column at a flow of 180 ml/min. The water is treated by injecting a flow of compressed air at a rate of 1 l/min (inlet pressure 0.25 kg/cm^2) through a 1 cm diameter, grade 3 sintered glass disc (20–30 µm nominal pore size) at the base of the column. The height of the foamed water output tube is adjusted to permit an output of 160 ml of foamed water per minute; the remaining 20 ml/min being run-off through the foam discharge tube. Average retention time within the 1600 ml column is about 9 min.

Table IV shows the proportion of Pacific oyster embryos which develop to normally shaped straight-hinged veliger larvae in untreated and foamed sea water. These results, collected during and immediately after natural blooms of phytoplankton in the Conwy estuary show the beneficial effect of foam separation. Water quality is rarely impaired by

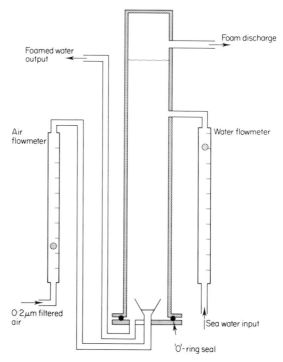

Fig. 7.   Diagram of a model foam separator based on the design of Wallace and Wilson (1969) used at Conwy for the treatment of a continuous flow of sea water. See text for explanation.

Table IV. The percentage of Pacific oyster embryos which developed to straight-hinged veliger larvae in sea water before and after foam separation and in a synthetic medium.

Date	Development %		
	Before foaming	After foaming	Control synthetic medium[a]
13.6.77	10.2	13.5	—
15.6.77	61.8	46.3	59.8
20.6.77	6.0	60.3	57.3
28.6.77	4.6	22.7	80.5
1.8.77	51.3	50.0	64.3
6.9.77	2.5	35.3	71.2
20.9.77	43.3	64.8	55.3

[a] Zaroogian *et al.* (1969).

this treatment. The efficiency of foam separation is dependent upon the size of air bubbles and the contact time between the water and air. The dispersion of a given volume of air as small bubbles provides a greater surface area for the attraction of surface-active substances than the same volume dispersed as large bubbles. Thus an open-ended pipeline is less efficient than an air–stone or a sintered screen with a nominal porosity of 20 μm. Contact time is improved by constructing taller or wider columns. These criteria are more important when considering a single pass unit rather than one installed in a recirculation system where water is continually recycled through the separator.

A foam separator may lead to an increase in the quantity of filterable particulate material in the treated water. Zillioux and Lackie (1970) showed a loss in particles as the result of foam separation but only counted particles ranging from 5 μm to 100 μm diameter. Our data show a similar trend for larger particulate material, i.e. that proportion which is filterable using Whatman GF/C filter papers. Table V gives the oven-dried weights of particulate material per litre of sea water foamed before and after treatment, and in the foam produced. Also shown is the weight of organic matter determined by ashing samples at 500°C for 24 h in a muffle furnace. The procedures were as described in Strickland and Parsons (1968). In this experiment, the results of which are representative of a number of trials made following a standard method, weights of particulate material passing a GF/C but retained by the finer GF/F grade papers are given. This fraction almost invariably shows a marked increase as the result of foam separation. Foam separators are best placed in front of fine filters. Since particulate materials act as nuclei for the further removal of dissolved organic substances (Batoosingh *et al.*, 1969), the separators may even precede coarse filtration in a treatment plant.

Table V. The dry weight and (in parentheses) the organic weight of particulate material retained on Whatman GF/C and GF/F filter papers per litre of sea water foamed.

| Filter | Particulate material mg/l of water foamed | | |
	Before treatment	After treatment	In foam discharged
GF/C	2.02 (1.32)	1.26 (0.95)	2.25 (1.38)
GF/F	3.56 (2.86)	7.30 (3.26)	2.79 (1.50)
Total	5.58 (4.18)	8.56 (4.21)	5.04 (1.88)

Foam separation can also be an efficient method of oxygenating water or for driving off excess dissolved gases such as oxygen or carbon dixoide. With a mixture of ozone and air, the treatment will oxidize organic substances, potentially toxic metabolites, e.g. nitrites and ammonia, and will also control the growth of micro-organisms. This topic is reviewed by Kinne (1976).

(d) Ion exchange resins.   Information on the application of ion exchange resins to marine culture is limited. However, there is increasing interest in the use of resins to remove potentially toxic metals from sea water in marine pollution studies. Davey *et al.* (1970) showed that the purified sodium form of Chelex–100 (Bio-Rad Laboratories) can selectively remove contaminant trace metals which are often present in natural and artificial sea waters. Levels are reduced to allow growth of marine phytoplankton and the development of the early stages of some marine invertebrates. The major cation/anion composition and natural chelation capacity of the sea water remain unaltered. Although this resin is expensive it can be repeatedly regenerated which may make it an attractive proposition to researchers requiring small volumes of metal-free sea water. Treatment with the resin should follow clarification of the water, preferably by sub-micron filtration.

(e) Alternative treatments.   In dealing with larger volumes of sea water, where batch treatment presents no problems, alternative methods of physico-chemical treatment can be used at low cost. Little is known of the precise mode of action of the treatments, but all are capable of reducing or removing growth and development-retarding substances from filtered sea water. The effectiveness of the treatments varies according to changes in water quality, but rarely is quality impaired. Lewis *et al.* (1972) found that the calanoid copepod, *Euchaeta japonica*, showed improved survival in copper-contaminated sea water when the water was treated with a range of particulate and water-soluble agents. Among successful treatments were clay minerals, diatoms, ascorbic acid, sewage effluents and aqueous extracts of humic acids and various soils. Substances such as clay minerals adsorb metals, organic substances and organo-metallic compounds (Chester, 1956; Siegel, 1966) while certain phytopankton species concentrate metals, e.g. Morris (1971).

Recent unpublished work at Conwy has compared the development of Pacific oyster embryos and the growth of larvae in filtered, non-chemically treated sea water and in filtered water—treated with a variety of additives. These included disodium EDTA, sodium metasilicate, aluminium oxide and Fuller's earth either as single treatments or in various combinations. Experiments showed that the greatest improvements in water quality were obtained when the agents were added to an aerated vessel containing a batch of filtered water 16–24 h before the batch was required. Data in Table VI show the effectiveness of treatments. Greatest improvements were obtained during and following phytoplankton blooms and following periods of stormy wet weather. Various actions of the chemicals are suggested, including complexing of trace metals by chelators and the adsorption of metals, organic substances and organo-metallic complexes. Willey (1977) has shown the coprecipitation of insoluble metal silicate compounds in metal-enriched sea water in the presence of sodium metasilicate. Sodium metasilicate and Fuller's earth may also act as flocculents, removing sub-micron particulate material from suspension. All the methods are cheap, although their effectiveness in improving water for the culture of less delicate organisms has yet to be demonstrated. With Fuller's earth, further filtration or settlement must follow the treatment but this is not the case with other materials.

Table VI. The percentage of Pacific oyster embryos developing to normally shaped veliger larvae in Whatman GF/C filtered sea water treated with various agents.

Trial	No agents	1 mg/l EDTA and 20 mg/l sodium metasilicate	1 mg/l EDTA and 150 mg/l Fuller's earth	Control synthetic medium[a]
1	24.2	49.8	54.2	49.3
2	43.0	84.3	92.7	—
3	49.0	80.0	87.3	78.8
4	35.0	66.2	74.2	79.7
5	50.0	80.7	82.8	81.5
6	8.3	13.3	13.2	—
7	15.0	63.3	64.2	57.3

Trial	No agents	EDTA and sodium metasilicate	Aluminium oxide 20 mg/l		Control synthetic medium[a]
			Alone	With EDTA and sodium metasilicate	
8	29.2	47.5	33.2	46.7	48.2
9	2.5	62.2	62.7	65.5	71.2
10	43.3	63.8	55.8	68.3	55.3
11	0	0.8	0	40.8	25.0

[a] Zaroogian *et al.* (1969).

(3) Sea water sterilization

Sea water sterilization is usually the last step in treatment. At this stage, it may be desirable to control the number of potentially harmful micro-organisms entering an aquarium system. At present thinking is against the use of antibiotics and other anti-microbial agents in culture systems, except in special circumstances. Micro-organisms are most commonly controlled by filtration or ultraviolet light treatment of sea water intended for the aquarium. We believe that control of the organisms which inevitably bloom within still or closed systems is rarely necessary. Good husbandry generally minimizes detrimental effects. Should control be essential then sterilizing filtration, ultraviolet light treatment or antimicrobial chemical treatment can be implemented.

(a) Filtration.   Filtration of sea water through sterile 0.2 µm membrane cartridges has none of the potentially detrimental effects associated with the other methods. It should be noted that absolute retention of bacteria will not necessarily be achieved.

(b) Ultraviolet light.   Within the wavelength range 240–280 nm (peak effect at 254 nm) ultraviolet light disinfects sea water rather than sterilizes it (Kinne, 1976). It reduces the reproductive capacity of bacteria and is therefore bacteriostatic rather than bactericidal (Wood, 1961). It has similar effects upon fungi. Depending on the amount of ultraviolet energy emitted, organic matter in sea water may be oxidized (Armstrong *et al.*, 1966). The efficiency of ultraviolet light treatment is dependent upon the amount of particulate material and natural yellow substance in sea water. To improve efficiency, it is advisable to reduce particulate content by prior filtration or if the water is markedly coloured, to employ charcoal treatment.

Wood (1961) and Shelbourne (1964) describe suitable ultraviolet light apparatus and quote optimum flow rates for the maximum bacteriostatic effect. A range of commercially manufactured equipment is also available. At Conwy, ultraviolet treatment is used routinely on sea water prior to its use in still or recirculation systems for bivalve and crustacean-rearing. The equipment emits 16 mW s/cm^2 within the bacteriostatic wavelengths. At a flow of 600 l/h of diatomite-filtered sea water, an average reduction of colony-forming units of 85.4% was obtained during 1977 (95% confidence limits 78.8%–92.1%). Analysis showed no relationship between the number of particles remaining after diatomite filtration and the efficacy of treatment. Efficiency was below 60% on a number of occasions between mid-May and the end of June, coincident with the use of a stored sea water supply during the decline of the spring phytoplankton bloom. Oxoid nutrient agar medium was used in plating bacteria. The range of colony-forming units in the Conwy laboratory supply during 1977 is shown in Table I. Further data suggest that colony-forming units which develop on Oxoid TCBS medium, which has a high specificity for *Vibrio* species, are 100% deactivated at the ultraviolet light dosage and water flow rate quoted.

(c) Ozone treatment. Ozonation, if used with caution, can be a powerful means of improving sea water quality. Dissociating rapidly in sea water to provide a highly active oxygen atom, ozone will both disinfect and sterilize sea water, oxidize organic material and oxidize potentially toxic nitrite to nitrate. On the other hand, ozone is highly toxic to both man and to many of the species cultured, is corrosive to aquarium equipment and will destroy natural chelating materials, e.g. humic acids. Evidence suggests that some essential trace elements, e.g. manganese, may be removed from solution by ozonation (Rosenthal, 1974). The potential hazard of stable, toxic ozonides being formed under certain conditions has also been suggested (Kinne, 1976).

Recent papers by Honn and Chavin (1976) and Honn *et al.* (1976) describe the design and application of an ozone generator for use in both through flow and recirculation systems. The benefits of dosing ozone at a rate of 0.132 mg/h/l of sea water in a 2270 litres recirculation system with biological filtration are discussed. Nurse sharks, *Ginglymostoma cirratum*, were the experimental animals and provision was made to spatially separate the reservoir into which ozone was introduced from the aquarium tanks and the biological filter. Bacterial numbers were kept within acceptable limits and ammonia and nitrites were oxidized. Sander (1967) combined foam separation with ozonation at an ozone dose of 0.05 mg/h/l of water foamed. He recommended that prior to recycling treated water from the separator to the aquarium, it should be filtered through carbon to absorb residual ozone. Rosenthal *et al.* (1978a) suggest that low biodegradable organics are degraded by ozone treatment into compounds which are more readily digested by bacteria in biological filtration. Their experiments were made in brackish water fish culture recirculation systems (S = 8‰) and applicability of the findings to fully saline conditions is unknown. Fauvel (1962) discusses ozone as a sterilizing agent for the continuous treatment of a flow of sea water in the cleansing of shellfish. An ozonizer capable of introducing a maximum of 0.6 mg ozone/l of water rapidly eliminated *E. coli* from the purification tanks.

In calculating an effective dosage of ozone, allowance should be made for factors which contribute to ozone consumption, e.g. chemical oxygen demand, turbidity, salinity, dissolved substances and microbial and planktonic densities. Guidance on this subject is provided by equipment manufacturers. Ozonation of the water in through-flow systems where filter feeding animals are cultured should be viewed with caution.

(d) Chlorine.   As a sterilizing agent in sea water, chlorine has largely been superseded by ozonation which is a more effective treatment (Kinne, 1976). Chlorine has many of the disadvantages of ozone in that it is toxic both to man and to marine organisms, corrosive, and may form toxic stable complexes with organic compounds. Chlorine as sodium hypochlorite (bleaching powder or as a concentrated solution) is used at Conwy and elsewhere to treat water for shellfish cleansing or to sterilize effluent from culture systems prior to discharge in the sea (Spencer *et al.*, 1977).

C. Synthetic Sea Water

Synthetic sea water is frequently used in the aquarium either as a substitute for natural sea water or as a comparative culture medium. Either commercially prepared salt mixes are used or individual researchers prepare media from published recipes. With commercial preparations, problems have occurred when manufacturers have altered formulations without notice (Kinne, 1976). All artificial preparations have a common disadvantage. Their constituent salts are contaminated with inorganic and organic impurities. Although the ratios of the more abundant elements can be controlled by careful preparation, this is not the case with trace components which may differ considerably, both in quantity and quality from natural sea water. Thus, while many preparations are successful as support media for a range of marine animals and plants, none are sufficiently precise to imitate the subtle complexity of the natural medium.

Kinne (1976) and Ukeles (1976) provide details on the formulation and preparation of a number of the better known non-commercial recipes as media for marine animals and plants respectively. Some recent references to commercial and published formulations for the holding and culture of marine animals are given in Table VII. At Conwy, a number of formulations have proven to be of value in the culture of oyster larvae and juveniles. Lyman and Fleming synthetic sea water will support the development of *Ostrea edulis* larvae through metamorphosis, providing yields of viable juveniles equivalent to those obtained with natural sea water. Various commercial preparations are also satisfactory for rearing oyster larvae including "Instant Ocean", "Tropic Marin" and "Büsum

Meersalz". Zaroogian synthetic sea water is an excellent medium for developing Pacific oyster larvae (see Table IV) but not if EDTA and sodium metasilicate are omitted in preparation. Synthetic formulations will not support all marine animals. Some organisms, e.g. echinoderms, require the addition of natural sea water to the artificial medium (Kinne, 1976).

Table VII. Some recent applications of synthetic sea waters in the holding or cultivation of marine animals.

Artificial sea water	Purpose	Reference
Published formulations:		
Lyman and Fleming *In* Sverdrup *et al.* (1942)	Culture of oyster larvae, *Ostrea edulis*	Helm *et al.* (1973)
Courtright *et al.*	Bioassays with mussel embryos, *Mytilus edulis*	Courtright *et al.* (1971)
Zaroogian *et al.*	Embryonic development of oysters, *Crassostrea virginica*	Zaroogian *et al.* (1969)
Tusov and Davis	Culture of colonial hydroid, *Bougainvillia* sp.	Tusov and Davis *In* Kinne (1976).
Commercial formulations:		
Instant Ocean	Nurse sharks, *Ginglymostoma cirratum* in recirculation systems	Honn and Chavin (1976)
Instant Ocean	Culture of lobster juveniles	Gallagher and Brown (1976)
Instant Ocean	Culture of prawn larvae, *Macrobrachium rosenbergii*	Maddox and Manzi (1976)
Instant Ocean and Utility Seven Seas Marine Mix	Culture of crab larvae, *Rhithropanopeus harrisii*	Sulkin and Minasian (1973)
Simplified recipes:		
	For storing lobsters and the depuration of oysters and clams	Wood and Ayres (1977)

III. WATER QUALITY IN RECIRCULATION SYSTEMS

Recirculation systems are a prerequisite for the laboratory study of living marine organisms where good quality sea water is not readily obtainable or where particular conditions need to be maintained. The word "closed", often applied to such systems, is misleading since new water, either salt or fresh (see below), must be added periodically to keep the aquarium inhabitants alive and healthy. The proportion of water changed and the frequency of changing varies from a continuous "bleed in" of new water to systems that contain artificial sea water which is renewed only infrequently. It is advisable to start with sea water that has been pre-treated by filtration and perhaps sterilization and afterwards to maintain water quality by continuous monitoring and treatment. Four treatments are usually performed:

    (A) Control of temperature and light;

    (B) Replacement of physical losses of water;

    (C) Stabilization of chemical changes, by replacement of depleted substances (1) and by detoxification and dilution of substances which accumulate (2);

    (D) Control of particulate and dissolved organic matter.

A. Temperature and Light

Temperature control near ambient temperatures is most conveniently achieved through thermostatically controlled heaters or coolers acting directly upon the water. In temperate climates, if temperatures of more than 5–7°C above or below ambient are required, both aquaria and treatment plant are best placed in controlled-temperature rooms to reduce supersaturation of the atmosphere and condensation. Condensation is both corrosive to equipment and dangerous in conjunction with electricity. Rapid overheating or overcooling when equipment fails is minimized if the temperature of the surrounding air maintains the temperature of the water. Where cooled or heated water passes through laboratories, or areas where staff work, the pipes must be insulated. Where tanks are lit, illumination must be restricted to the appropriate aquaria to prevent the growth of algae in other locations where they might block filters and pipes. In some recirculation systems, the growth of algae is encouraged as part of the water treatment facility (see Fig. 15), and of course many organisms require light if they are to thrive.

B. Water Loss

Small losses of water from leaks, splashing or sampling, do not alter water quality, except in systems with a small total volume where new water must be added to maintain a constant biological load on the treatment plant. On the other hand, evaporation losses affect water quality by increasing salinity, nitrate and the concentrations of most other dissolved substances. Losses are ideally made good with distilled water or aged softened tap water. The quantity of freshwater may be calculated from

$$Va = Vi \left(1 - \frac{Si}{Sn}\right)$$

where $Va \equiv$ volume to be added; $Vi \equiv$ the initial volume of sea water in the system; $Si \equiv$ the initial (preferred) salinity; $Sn \equiv$ the salinity after evaporation.

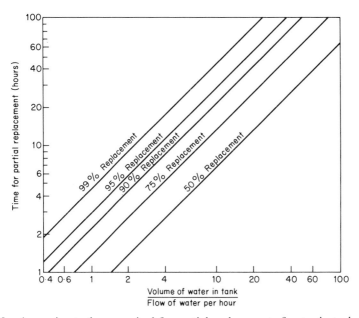

Fig. 8. Approximate times required for partial replacement of water in tanks, under constant flow conditions. Example: for a tank containing 30 litres; with a flow of 10 l/h, there would be 50% replacement of water in the tank in about 2 h; 75% in about 4 h; 90% in 7 h, and 95% replacement in 9 h. Another time period could replace hours, but the same time must be used on each axis, and the same unit of capacity must be used for volume and flow. Based on information supplied by Alfred Hensner (Sprague, 1969).

C. Stabilization of Chemical Changes

During recirculation some compounds (such as dissolved oxygen), some anions (bicarbonates, carbonates) and some cations (magnesium, calcium) become depleted. Others, such as ammonia, nitrite, nitrate, phosphate, carbon dioxide and dissolved organic compounds accumulate. While the former can be replaced or their depletion prevented with moderate ease, the latter (particularly ammonia and dissolved organic compounds) are more difficult to control.

(1) Substances which are depleted and their restoration

(a) Oxygen. Within a recirculation system oxygen demand has broadly three major components:

  (i) the organisms being studied;
  (ii) other heterotrophs, in suspension and attached to surfaces;
  (iii) nitrifying bacteria.

Together, these make up the Biological Oxygen Demand of the system (B.O.D.). The term Chemical Oxygen Demand (C.O.D.) refers to the oxygen consumed by chemical compounds, both oxidizable and biodegradable. In artificial sea water systems, measurements of C.O.D. are likely to be misleading since some freshly prepared solutions of commercial sea salts have a C.O.D. value two to three times higher than that of natural sea water. In fresh water, and low salinity, brackish water systems, refactory organic substances contributing to the C.O.D. may be degraded by ozonation into compounds more easily oxidized by bacteria living in conventional biological filters (Rosenthal *et al.*, 1978a).

Usually, the oxygen requirements of the organisms being studied in research aquaria are readily met with moderate aeration and water flow rates because relatively few animals are being kept in a large water volume. A useful review of the minimal oxygen requirements of a variety of species has been made by Davis (1975). In heavily stocked commercial systems, however, much oxygen is consumed not only by the cultured animals but also by other heterotrophs and nitrifying organisms throughout the system. In a compact recirculation system, Scott and Gillespie (1972) found that the oxygen consumed by the biological filter was nearly equal to that consumed by their fish. The oxygen demands of a biological filter in a recirculation system are greatest in submerged filters and in percolating filters with small void spaces where both dissolved and particulate organic matter are oxidized by heterotrophs. Speece (1973) reported that about 40% of oxygen removed during passage through a freshwater biological filter was due to nitrification of trout wastes, the remainder presumably due to heterotroph respiration. Oxygen consumed during nitrification and biodegradation in relation to the carrying capacity of a filter are further discussed later.

(b) Replenishment of oxygen. The solubility of oxygen in sea water is some 20% less than in fresh water for a given temperature, and varies with pressure and salinity. At a pressure of 760 mm of mercury, the saturated concentration of oxygen (mg/l) in water of salinity S‰ and temperature T°C is given by the simplified equation of Truesdale and Gameson (1957):

$$\text{mg oxygen/l} = \frac{475 - (2.83 - 0.011 \text{ T}) \text{ S}}{33.5 + \text{T}}$$

Supersaturation of sea water with a gas is to be avoided because it causes "gas bubble disease" as bubbles form in or on the tissues of cultured organisms. Supersaturation with air can occur where water is warmed on passing from a reservoir tank to the culture aquaria, or when a pump develops a leak on the suction side and cavitates. Supersaturation with oxygen may occur when photosynthetic algae are growing in a system or when chemicals are used to provide oxygen. Supersaturation with nitrogen may be introduced by a significant amount of denitrification in anaerobic areas. Any gas introduced under pressure into the culture aquarium will result in supersaturation. Equilibrium between the water and atmosphere is obtained by aeration at atmospheric pressure by sprays, cascades, splashing and wave-making, or at slightly elevated pressures with plain nozzles, air dispersers and venturis.

Scott (1972) compared the efficiency of five combinations of venturis, sprays and air dispersers (air stones) and showed that a venturi discharging through a nozzle near the tank bottom was twice as effective as air diffusers and sprays directed at the surface. Further improvements in efficiency are obtained if the gas bubbles are made smaller in diameter (1 mm or less) by pressurization in a U tube (Speece, 1969), by the shearing action of a rapidly moving stream of liquid or when contact time between water and bubble is increased. The latter two methods decrease the risk of accidental supersaturation compared with the former and avoid the need for degassing towers (see Speece, 1969). Kils (1977) found that increases in salinity and temperature increased the effectiveness of a venturi and of a rotation aerator in which turbulence pulled bubbles into sea water.

Aeration can physically injure delicate organisms or prevent small predatory forms from catching their food. When such animals are to be held in recirculation systems, aeration is best restricted to the water treatment facility, and gaseous exchange is achieved by an adequate flow of water through the aquaria (see Serfling *et al.*, 1974). In calculations of the flow rates necessary to provide cultures with sufficient oxygen (or to remove metabolites), it is necessary to compute the displacement time of the water in the tank. This is most readily done by reference to Fig. 8 (Sprague, 1969).

Aeration failure due to breakdown in power supplies at commercial installations is usually minimized by auxiliary power generators but with small research aquaria, aeration failure can kill fish or render whole experiments useless. A small apparatus that has proven useful in such circumstances is shown in Fig. 9. It supplies air pressurized by a laboratory vacuum filter pump attached to a cold water supply.

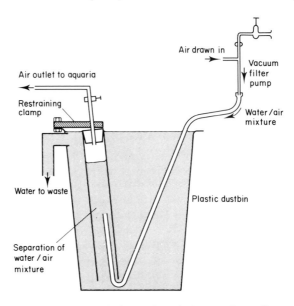

Fig. 9.   An emergency compressed air supply unit that can be easily constructed from basic laboratory equipment.

In heavily stocked systems, it may be necessary to inject pure oxygen directly into the water. This is most useful as a therapeutic measure to revive failing organisms after aeration or flow failure. Direct oxygenation as a continuous process has recently been applied in the through-flow culture of marine fish at high density and at least one commercial freshwater trout farm in the UK has direct oxygen injection into a through-flow system. The addition of chemicals (hydrogen peroxide, urea, potassium permanganate, sodium perborate and calcium peroxide) serves mainly as a therapeutic measure in critically polluted water and as a prophylactic during transport of fish larvae over long distances. As a general rule, however, we feel their use is best avoided.

Air lift pumps are frequently employed to move water in small recirculation systems and are particularly useful because they also assist gaseous exchange, Spotte (1970) and Castro *et al.* (1975). In addition to providing oxygen to oxygen-depleted cultures, aeration removes excess carbon dioxide, thus tending to increase and stabilize pH.

(c) Loss of buffering capacity (inorganic carbon).   Buffering in sea water is from the classic reaction:

$$2HCO_3^{1-}, \text{ total} \rightleftharpoons H_2CO_3 + CO_3^{2-}, \text{ total.}$$

Boric acid (H_3BO_3) plays a relatively minor role. The equilibrium depends upon pH, and at pH 8.1–8.2 about 89% of the carbon is in the form of bicarbonate, 10% as carbonate and 1% as carbon dioxide. When nitrification occurs in recirculated sea water, the H^+ ions produced (0.14 mg H^+ per mg $NH_4 - N$ oxidized to nitrate) lower the pH and unbalance the carbonate–carbon dioxide equilibria:

$$H^+ + CO_3^{2-} \rightarrow H^+ + HCO_3^{1-} \rightarrow H_2CO_3 \rightarrow H_2O + CO_2 \uparrow.$$

In addition, a small amount of inorganic carbon (0.09 mg C/mg $NH_4 - N$ oxidized to nitrate) is assimilated by the bacteria during nitrification. Unless the recirculated water has adequate buffering capacity, there is at first a gradual and then a rapid drop in pH as inorganic carbon is lost (as carbon dioxide) to the atmosphere during normal aeration. Loss of carbon dioxide in relation to foam treatment is discussed later. The change occurs at about pH 7.7 where buffer capacity is minimal (Fig. 10).

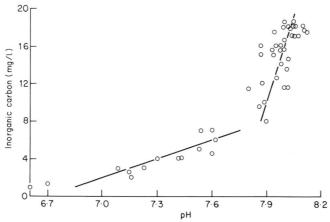

Fig. 10.   The change in the relationship between pH and inorganic carbon (carbonates, bicarbonates and carbonic acid) in sea water above pH 7.7.

Ammonia removal in the first 60 cm of a through-flow model filter was reduced from over 50% at about pH 7.9 to nearly 20% at about pH 5.9, Forster (1974). Complete inhibition occurred at pH 5.5. In contrast, reduced pH favours the oxidation of nitrite to nitrate by marine nitrifiers.

The rate of loss of inorganic carbon varies with the rate of nitrification. In model recirculation systems of about 40 l capacity, dosed with ammonium chloride at 40, 80 and 320 mg NH_4–N/day, where the only external carbon source was atmospheric carbon dioxide, carbon was lost at rates of 0.6, 1.5 and 2.3 mg C/day respectively (Fig. 11). In similar

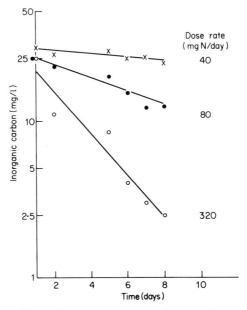

Fig. 11. The rate of loss of inorganic carbon (carbonate, bicarbonate, carbonic acid) from a model sea water recirculation system (40 litres) dosed with 40, 80 and 320 mg NH_4–N/day.

experiments also made with plastic filter media, nitrification was inhibited at pH 6.8 when carbon levels fell below 3 mg inorganic carbon/litre. The occurrence of 20% ammonia removal at pH 5.9 in Forster's (loc. cit.) system may have been because more substantial buffering from the water created a more favourable environment for ammonia oxidizing bacteria. The rate of loss of alkalinity (V) from marine recirculation systems increased as the weight of food fed/day (F) increased (Hirayama, 1970):

$$V = (0.92 \ F + 2.52) \ 10^{-3}$$

In his systems, the sources of inorganic carbon were carbon dioxide from the air, respiration of the cultured fish and microheterotrophs feeding on uneaten food, and presumably from carbonates in the food (shrimp). The rate of acidification or carbon loss therefore depends on the amount of nitrification, on the amount of carbon dioxide produced by the animals and micro-organisms in the system and on the buffering capacity of the system.

(d) Maintenance of buffering capacity. In research aquaria, the most convenient and trouble-free method to counteract acidification is to recirculate the water through magnesium-bearing calcium carbonate such as crushed bivalve shells or dolomite limestone. These materials provide a large surface area and act as a substrate for nitrifying bacteria. When the filter material is suitably graded, it may also act as an efficient mechanical filter in which biodegradation of organic materials also takes place. Biological filters constructed in this way serve four major functions, nitrification, mechanical filtration, biodegradation and buffering. Buffering occurs when calcium carbonate dissolves in the presence of carbon dioxide:

$$CaCO_3 + CO_2 + H_2O \rightleftharpoons Ca^{2+} + 2HCO_3^{1-}.$$

This occurs more readily below pH 7.7 as the proportion of H_2CO_3 (CO_2) increases. The dissolution is enhanced by excess carbon dioxide and magnesium and is prevented when dissolved organic compounds coat the carbonate particles. Phosphate, which accumulates in recirculation systems, may precipitate out as an acid-insoluble apatite on the filter matrix (Siddall, 1974). Although washing in acid will remove some of the organic material it has little effect on dolomite exposed to 0.83 M Na_2PO_4 for 24 h. Dry tumbling for 10 min to abraid the surfaces increased the buffering capacity by 53% as the acid insoluble coating was removed. Loss of buffering contribution from the filter is most readily overcome by periodically renewing a proportion of the shell or dolomite and by more frequent changes of water. This can be inconvenient, however, if this removes a significant proportion of the system's nitrifiers, and time has to be allowed for new populations to develop. A filter can thus only be relied upon to maintain pH for a time that is related to the load placed upon it. Little information has been published on the rates of loss of buffer contribution under different conditions of load.

In heavily stocked commercial systems, other methods of maintaining buffering capacity and hence pH control are necessary. The methods outlined below are independent of the nature of the filter substrate and can be applied either to new filters to help maintain their contribution to buffering capacity or to old filters to replace their contribution to buffering capacity entirely. Solutions of sodium hydroxide (< 40 g/l in fresh water) and sodium carbonate and bicarbonate ($Na_2CO_3 10H_2O$, 71.5 g/l or Na_2CO_3, 26.5 g/l and $Na HCO_3$, 21.0 g/l have been administered with success for a number of years at Conwy in systems (1000–10 500 l capacity) using either mixtures of silica gravel and dolomite limestone chips or inert plastic rings as a filter matrix. The quantities added daily to control pH in these tropical marine systems ($28°C$ and $30‰$) which were stocked with up to 2.6 kg of prawns ranged from 0.1 to 4.6 g of carbon (sodium carbonate or bicarbonate) and 0.8 to 16.9 g of sodium hydroxide. There was no clear relationship between the quantity of chemicals added and the animal load because each system also contained large and fluctuating numbers of microheterotrophs which were judged to have contributed substantially to ammonia production and hence nitrification. While sodium carbonate and bicarbonate contribute to the buffering capacity directly, sodium hydroxide works indirectly by neutralizing excess H^+ ions and increasing pH so that more carbon dioxide from respiration and the atmosphere is converted to bicarbonate.

(e) Calcium and magnesium. Both calcium and magnesium exist in moderately large amounts in natural sea water (Table I) but in marine recirculation systems they may be lost by precipitation with phosphate and through uptake by cultured organisms, particularly Crustacea and molluscs. For example, 50 000 oyster spat (6 mg live weight) grown in 1000 l of sea water removed 9% of the available calcium in one week. Calcium and magnesium losses are unlikely to be equal and can result in a change in the Mg/Ca atom ratio (Table VIII). In this particular example, part of the change may have been due to variations in magnesium content of the laboratory sea water supply.

Large variations of the magnesium/salinity ratio from 0.0231 to 0.0409 compared with 0.0370 and 0.0369 in offshore water, were found by Elderfield (1971). The calcium/salinity ratio was less variable and ranged from 0.0107 to 0.0140 compared with 0.0118 in offshore water. Replacement by the addition of lime (calcium oxide) or magnesia (magnesium oxide) or calcium and magnesium carbonates (as coral and shell) has proved satisfactory, although the levels of calcium and magnesium that result from such treatments are likely to be substantially different from those in natural sea water. Levels of $640–790 \pm 150$ mg Ca^{2+} /l (calcium/salinity ratio 0.0224 to 0.0287) were found by Beard and Forster (1973) in a recirculation system containing a biological filter of

Table VIII. An example of the variation in calcium and magnesium levels in a marine recirculation system during the culture of the banana prawn (*Penaeus merguiensis*). Temperature and salinity were 28°C and 30‰ and 30% of the system volume was replaced with filtered sea water each week.

Concentration (mg/l)	Laboratory sea water	Months 1	2	3	4
Calcium	350	300	395	370	240
Magnesium	1140	930	1190	1030	680
Ratio Mg/Ca	3.26	3.10	3.01	2.78	2.83

gravel topped with crushed oyster shell. The mean pH of the system over 16 weeks of culture was pH 6.8; salinity was 28‰.

(2) Substances which accumulate and their treatment

(a) Ammonia and nitrite. Ammonia is the major nitrogenous product of many aquatic organisms although some amino acids, volatile amines and urea may also be excreted. Ammonia is present in water in two forms, an un-ionized portion (NH_3) which is highly toxic and an ionized portion (NH_4^+) which is relatively non-toxic. The proportion of each depends primarily upon hydrogen ion concentration (pH) but also on temperature, salinity and pressure (Whitfield, 1974). There is approximately ten times more un-ionized ammonia nitrogen in sea water at pH 8 than at pH 7. Knowledge of the rate at which ammonia is produced by the species to be cultured is useful in the design of treatment plants and some examples are given by Kinne (1976). As a general guide, a standard rate of nitrogen excretion is often assumed: 0.5 g N/kg wet weight animal/day. Our experience has been to allow 1 g/kg/day, especially when rapidly growing juveniles are being cultured (Wickins, 1976b).

Ammonia is also likely to be produced by heterotrophs living elsewhere in the system, primarily in the filter matrix, substrate and water. Ammonia production during biodegradation may be represented by Richards (1965) equation for the decomposition of plankton:

$$(CH_2O)_{106} \ (NH_3)_{16} \ H_3PO_4 + 106 \ O_2 \rightarrow$$
$$106 \ CO_2 + 16 \ NH_3 + H_3PO_4 + 106 \ H_2O.$$

The removal of ammonia from both fresh and sea water may be achieved by biological nitrification, air stripping, break-point chlorination, ion exchange, micro and macro algae. The most popular method for marine aquaria and closed-system aquaculture is biological nitrification which has been the subject of a recent review by Sharma and Ahlert (1977). McCarty and Haug (1971) summarized the overall reactions of nitrification and assimilation:

$$55\ NH_4^+ + 5CO_2 + 76O_2 \xrightarrow{\text{Nitrosomonas}} C_5H_7O_2N + 5\ NO_2^-$$
$$+ 52\ H_2O + 109H^+ \qquad \textbf{(1)}$$
$$400\ NO_2^- + 5\ CO_2 + NH_4^+ + 195\ O_2 + 2H_2O \xrightarrow{\text{Nitrobacter}} C_5H_7O_2N$$
$$+ 400\ NO_3 + H^+ \quad \textbf{(2)}$$

Gundersen and Mountain (1973) calculated the oxygen consumed during the oxidation of ammonia to nitrate by nitrifying bacteria in the sea to be 21% of that consumed during the complete decomposition of plankton to nitrate. Estimates of the ratio of oxygen consumed to nitrogen oxidized range from 4.25 to 4.57. The lower values take into account the oxygen released during the fixation of carbon dioxide (Painter, 1970). In aquarium systems, nitrification may be accomplished in several ways, by percolating and submerged filters, rotating biodiscs, activated sludge and bio-sedimentation. Little is known of the long-term operation of the latter two methods in sea water. The safest and probably the most versatile is the percolating filter, where water trickles downwards over the filter matrix. Submerged filters, which may be up-flow or down-flow, are more prone to the development of anaerobic conditions when circulation fails or when dead spaces occur due to blockage with sloughed bacterial film or detritus. This risk is of course reduced if the matrix has a large void space and does not also serve as a mechanical filter.

Nitrification was inhibited in marine submerged filters when oxygen levels fell to about 0.6 to 0.7 mg O_2/l (Forster, 1974). These values were in good agreement with those given for fresh water nitrifiers. The chemical changes that occur when unfiltered sea water spiked with ammonia is recirculated through new, unseeded gravel filters, were illustrated by Forster (1974). Figure 12 shows similar changes when the load on an established filter was increased, for example from 2 to 40 mg N/day. As ammonium chloride was added (40 mg $NH_4 - N$/day) there was an initial rise in the ammonia nitrogen followed by a decrease as the ammonia was oxidized to nitrite by developing populations of *Nitrosomonas* bacteria. A similar delayed peak for nitrite followed as it was further oxidized to nitrate by *Nitrobacter* and *Nitrocystis*. Nitrate increased as a result of the activity of the latter. After 17 days, the water was completely changed and the daily dose of ammonium chloride

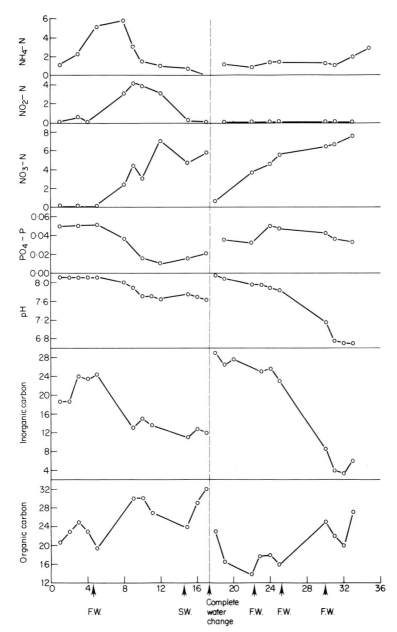

Fig. 12. Fluctuation in the levels of nitrogen, phosphorus, carbon and pH in recirculated sea water (27°C; 30‰ salinity) following an increase in load from 2 to 40 mg $NH_4 - N$/day on an established nitrifying filter incorporating a plastic matrix. Additions of fresh or salt water are shown by arrows.

continued. Ammonia and nitrite levels remained constant as nitrate increased. Ammonia rose when nitrification ceased after about 32 days when levels of inorganic carbon fell to 3 mg/l and pH to pH 6.8. Phosphate tended to decrease (there were no animals present) and organic carbon fluctuated with the fresh water that was added to compensate for evaporation.

Factors that influence the rates of oxidation of ammonia in marine biological filters are similar to those extensively studied in freshwater systems, although most of the freshwater studies were made in through-flow systems at relatively high ammonia and organic loadings. One important factor is hydraulic load. The effect of hydraulic load on through-flow marine percolating filters of 6–12 mm gravel dosed with 1 mg $(NH_4)_2 SO_4 - N/l/day$ was studied by Forster (1974) who found that the weight of ammonia nitrogen removed in the first 60 cm of gravel was 50.1, 111.2 and 217.8 g N/m^3 gravel/day at hydraulic loads of 20, 82 and 246 m^3 water/m^3 gravel/day.

If the specific surface area of the gravel was 350 m^2/m^3, then the corresponding rates of ammonia removal would be 0.14, 0.32 and 0.62 g N/m^2/day. Filters with plastic media in model recirculation systems typically oxidized 0.3 g N/m^2/day at hydraulic loads of about 280 m^2/m^3/day. These figures provide a guide to the rates of nitrification

Table IX. The specific surface area m^2/m^3 of media used in biological filters. Data on graded material kindly supplied by Water Research Centre, Stevenage, UK.

Nominal maximum size (mm)	Graded material		Approximate % voids
	Granite	Crushed gravel	
13	350[a]	300[a]	< 38[a]
25	185–237	169–208	40–50
37	129–149	120–140	45–50
50	94–111	86–101	40–50
63	73– 85	67– 77	45–60
Plastic media[b]	164		93

[a] by extrapolation
[b] plastic media are available in a variety of shapes and sizes. They have a high proportion of voids for a given specific surface area compared with conventional media. One example is "Filterpak" YTH 1130 with a specific surface area of 164 m^2/m^3 from Mass Transfer Ltd, Kendal, UK.

that can be expected from conventional marine systems with relatively low rates of organic load. The specific surface areas of those materials are given in Table IX. The published information on the time taken for population of nitrifying bacteria to become established in marine recirculation systems is limited. Saeki (1963) reported that 82 days were required before levels of nitrite nitrogen had fallen to <0.1 mg N/l in the sea water in the Veno (Japan) Aquarium system.

In a system described by Rolf (1972), establishment took about 60 days at 10°C. Siddall (1974) determined that filters could be more rapidly "conditioned" by adding ammonium chloride and ammonium sulphate in the absence of organic material. Conditioning of new filters with solutions of ammonium chloride, sodium nitrite and mixtures of both was tested in model recirculation systems (40 litre capacity) under different conditions of pH and temperature. The results are shown in Table X. For comparison, data from larger systems, some stocked with animals, or given an "organic feed" are included. In each case, unfiltered sea water was relied upon to supply the initial nitrifying bacteria though some were probably present on the gravel, animals and their food. Nitrification was established, on average, after 34 days, range 24 to 41 days. Animals that were cultured in the systems during the establishment phase did not usually survive or grow well and, in the case of individually held juvenile lobsters (*Homarus gammarus*), mortality continued for some time after nitrification was established.

As might be expected, new filters may be "seeded" with nitrifiers by the transfer of a proportion of the media from an established filter. In fresh water, establishment took 10.7 days in a seeded system compared with 22.2 days in an unseeded system (Carmignani and Bennett, 1977). Examples of the levels and ranges of concentrations of ammonia nitrogen and nitrite nitrogen that were found in established marine systems (1000 to 3000 litres) are given in Table XI. Wide fluctuations in nitrite levels often occurred in the systems and may have resulted from the changes in load placed on the filter as the animals grew and their food ration increased. Such fluctuations would not be expected in larger or less heavily stocked research aquaria (Rosenthal *et al.*, 1978) and can, at least in brackish water systems, be reduced by careful ozonation (Rosenthal *et al.*, 1978a).

(b) Nitrate and phosphate. In recirculation systems, nitrate levels increase as a result of nitrification although some nitrate may enter with new sea water. Examples of the levels obtained in experimental marine systems are shown in Table XI. Also shown are values for phosphate. Phosphate arises from the excretion and decomposition of animals and, by leaching,

Table X. The establishment of nitrification in marine biological filters determined from the time taken for concentrations of nitrite nitrogen to fall to 0.1 mg N/1 or below.

Single initial dose (mg N/l) in model recirculation systems of 40 litre capacity	Filter medium	pH	Temperature (°C)	Organic carbon (mg C/l)	Time to establishment of nitrification (days)
NH_4 Cl 50	Gravel	7.0	26	14.0	29
NH_4 Cl 50 Na NO_2 50	Gravel	7.3	26	11.0	41
Na NO_2 50	Plastic	6.8	28	14.8	Not established after 38 days
Na NO_2 50	Gravel	7.9	34	16.0	Not established after 38 days
Na NO_2 50	Gravel	8.2	34	16.0	Not established after 38 days
Na NO_2 50 Acidified with HCl	Gravel	7.8	34	15.8	38
Na NO_2 50	Plastic	8.2	28	14.7	20% $NO_2 - N$ oxidized in 38 days
Na NO_2 50 Acidified with HCl	Plastic	6.6	28	14.4	20% $NO_2 - N$ oxidized in 34 days
Na NO_2 50	Gravel	8.1	26	11.0	34
Repeated doses or live animals in recirculation systems of 500 to 2000 litre capacity NH_4Cl 0.5 to 2 mg N/l/day	Plastic	8.2	20	3.9	37
NH_4Cl 1 mg N/l/day plus live lobsters	Plastic	8.2	24	9.4	35
Live prawns $(NH_4)_2SO_4$ 1 to 4 mg N/one or two days plus 50 g mussel/day	Plastic	8.1	26	14.8	37
Forster (1974)	Gravel	—	28	—	24–35
Mean					34.4
Range					24–41

from their food stuffs. Figure 13 shows the relationship between the increasing levels of nitrate and phosphate in six of our recirculation systems. In the absence of animals, tests in model systems (40 litres) dosed

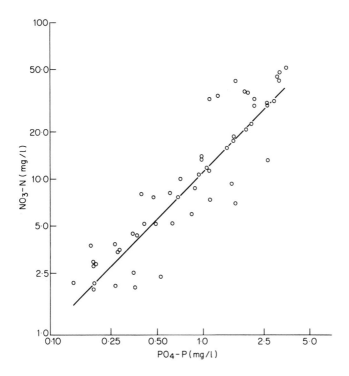

Fig. 13. The increase of nitrate nitrogen and inorganic phosphate phosphorus in marine recirculation systems stocked with 400–1500 g of tropical prawns at 28°C for periods of 60–120 days. The calculated regression line is drawn. The data were compiled from six separate systems.

with 40–320 mg NH_4–N/day showed that inorganic phosphate decreased with increase of nitrate (Fig. 14—see also Fig. 12). In sea water, concentrations of phosphate rarely exceed about 6 mg P/litre since precipitation occurs with calcium from the water or any calcareous material present (shells, limestone). As a result, calcium and magnesium may be lost from the system (Table VIII). Nitrate and phosphate are relatively non-toxic to marine organisms and, although some denitrification may occur, levels are commonly controlled by dilution or periodic replacement of a proportion of the culture water.

The culture of algae in marine systems ("algal filters") may prevent the build-up of nitrate by assimilation of ammonia or nitrate nitrogen and may control levels of phosphate (Siddall, 1974). Cultures may be run continuously or for discrete periods. One advantage of algal filters that are continuously illuminated is that the acidification common with nitrifying filters is not so marked, since algae that are assimilating nitrate

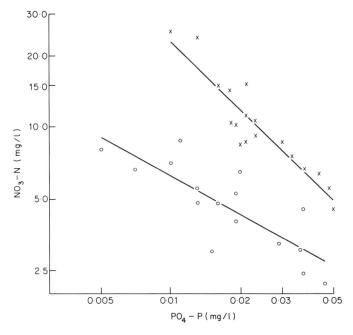

Fig. 14. The decrease in inorganic phosphate phosphorus with increase in nitrate nitrogen in two model marine recirculation systems dosed with 40–320 mg NH_4–N/day for periods of 4–8 days (28°C; 30‰ salinity). The calculated regression lines are drawn.

produce OH^- ions and remove carbon dioxide during photosynthesis. When ammonia nitrogen is assimilated, however, H^+ ions are produced and may cause some acidification (Brewer and Goldman, 1976). Under natural light-dark regimes, tumbling cultures of *Ulva* (initially 6 kg wet weight) maintained in a 4500 litre prawn culture system produced large diurnal fluctuations in pH, sometimes as much as 0.6 units, from pH 7.4 in the early morning to pH 8.0 in the afternoon despite vigorous aeration. In preliminary trials with the prawn *Penaeus merguiensis*, the algae failed to cope with the increase in ammonia production as the prawns grew and levels rose to 22 mg NH_4–N/l (equivalent to 0.2–0.3 mg un-ionized NH_3–N/l at pH 7.55).

Table XI. The mean levels and ranges of concentrations of nitrogen and phosphorus in marine recirculation systems used for nursery maintenance of fish and crustacea (constant load) and for grow-out trials (increasing load). Load was calculated from the weight of animals held divided by the total volume of water used (including the initial charge) throughout the culture period (g/l).

Type of system (number of trials in parentheses)	Systems holding 290–400 g of juvenile lobsters for periods of 44–186 days		System holding 1–30 kg of turbot for periods of 175 days	System holding[a] 0.4–7 kg of tropical fish for 314 days	Systems holding 400–2600 g of juvenile and adult prawns for periods of 90–352 days	
	Nursery (2)	Grow-out (3)	Grow-out (1)	Grow-out (1)	Nursery (9)	Grow-out (3)
Temperature (°C)	20	20	24	23–27	28	28
Load	0.057	0.054	0.093	0.5–0.6 estimated	0.063	0.124
pH	8.09	8.07	7.79	7.7–8.0	7.95	7.59
$NH_4 - N$ (mg/l)						
mean	0.04	0.05	4.80	0.04	0.20	0.27
range	0.01–0.21	0.01–0.18	2.9–8.4	0.01–0.12	0.03–0.81	0.04–0.61
$NO_2 - N$ (mg/l)						
mean	0.03	0.04	0.03	0.04	0.08	0.34
range	0.01–0.60	0.01–0.36	0.01–0.11	0.01–0.12	0.01–0.51	0.05–3.52
$NO_3 - N$ (mg/l)						
mean	—	—	—	—	16	55
range	—	—	—	45–102	0.02–111	11–95
$PO_4 - P$ (mg/l)						
mean	—	—	—	—	1.47	3.71
range	—	—	—	—	0.08–5.48	1.45–8.19

[a] From Rosenthal et al. (1978b) Date recalculated in terms of nitrogen content.

J. F. Wickins and M. M Helm

Table XII. Some examples of particulate and organic matter in warm water marine recirculation systems (28°C) holding 44–2400 g of juvenile and adult prawns for periods of 28–196 days. Load is calculated from the weight of animals held divided by the total volume of water used (including the initial charge) throughout the culture period.

	Grow-out systems				
System number	13	14	6	5	Beard and Forster, 1973
Load (g/l)	0.012	0.096	0.104	0.166	0.102
Total wet weight of food given (kg)	1.4	54.3	40.8	44.4	over 73.8
Weight of particles >1 μm (mg/l)					
mean	2.25	5.12	6.29	10.55	8.59
range	1.5–4.3	1.6–11.3	1.4–19.2	1.5–35.5	5.3–12.6
% Organic matter					
mean	59.25	58.92	60.53	62.70	—
range	32.7–86.1	19.2–87.0	10.0–92.6	31.6–86.3	—
Total organic carbon (mg/l) mean	6.37	8.98	9.43	14.6	—
range	3.7–8.5	4.0–13.5	1.7–16.2	7.5–25.0	—
Weight of sub-micron particles (mg/l) mean	3.33	8.25	8.56	38.90[a]	—
range	0.1–6.7	0.1–34.1	0.9–50.4	0.0(1)–104.4	—
Bacteria/ml × 10³ mean	—	1674	1251	—	7527

[a] Analysis did not cover entire period.

There are a number of problems with algal filters:

(i) continuous illumination is expensive and when sunlight is used as a supplement temperature problems may result (see Shelbourne, Riley and Thacker, 1963);

(ii) the efficiency and speed of nitrogenous waste removal by algae is thought to be less than that of nitrifying filters (Kinne, 1976);

(iii) algal cultures are more difficult to maintain than nitrifying filters, being vulnerable to smothering and competition by epiphytic and epizootic growths;

(iv) a change of physical, chemical or nutritional status in the sea water may precipitate reproduction or fragmentation of the alga causing it to lodge in inaccessible parts of the system. Despite these difficulties, there is no reason why algal filters cannot be used in lightly stocked systems in conjunction with separate nitrifying and mechanical filters as shown in Fig. 15a. In the arrangement shown, detritus from the aquaria is collected by coarse filtration on synthetic wool, settlement in the sump and fine filtration in the mechanical filter and may be removed daily. Some dissolved nitrogen, phosphorus and organic compounds are removed in the algal and percolating nitrifying filters. The latter filter also acts as a degassing tower to prevent supersaturation with oxygen from the algae. Sloughed bacterial film or algal fragments are also collected by the synthetic wool filter. An important feature of this treatment system is that the flow to each facility can be independently adjusted. High nitrate levels may also be removed by anaerobic bacterial denitrification but this process requires the careful balance of an organic carbon source (usually methanol) with the influent concentration of nitrate and oxygen. A successful brackish water system (Otte and Rosenthal, 1978) incorporating a bacterial denitrification and an ozonation unit is shown in Fig. 15b.

(c) Carbon dioxide. Free carbon dioxide in sea water increases with decrease in pH from about 0.8 mg/l at pH 8 to 9.0 mg/l at pH 7. Its solubility depends upon salinity and temperature. Droop (1969) formulated the equilibrium relation between partial pressure of carbon dioxide in the air, concentration of bicarbonate and carbonate and the pH of sea water:

$$\log [HCO_3^-] - \log P_{CO_2} = pH - 7.6$$
$$\log [CO_3^{2-}] - \log P_{CO_2} = 2\ pH - 16.6$$
$$\text{where } \log P_{CO_2} = 3.5 \text{ for normal air.}$$

Excess carbon dioxide is not normally a problem as it is readily removed by aeration. The effects on pH of vigorous aeration (foaming) and normal aeration are compared in Fig. 16. Fig. 16a compares the decrease in pH in systems where buffering was inadequate because the water was not changed throughout the trial. In Fig. 16b, lower pH in the unfoamed system was accompanied by high levels of total inorganic carbon indicating that carbon dioxide, released by H^+ ions from nitrification or during respiration, or both, was partly responsible for pH depression. Its removal (or the prevention of its formation) by foaming maintained the higher pH values.

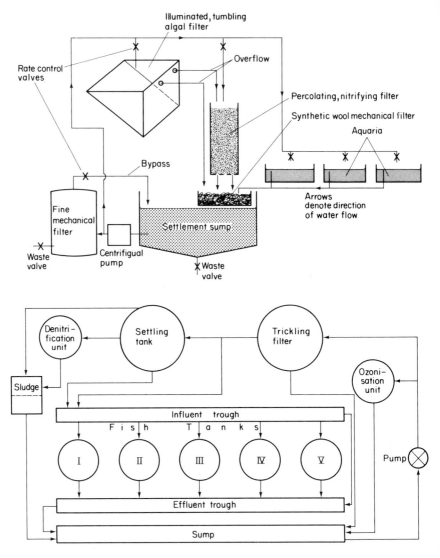

Fig. 15. Examples of water treatment systems incorporating algal and mechanical filters (above, original) and denitrification, ozonation and settlement units (below, Otte and Rosenthal, 1978) in addition to percolating, nitrifying filters. In both systems the flow to each treatment unit can be separately controlled.

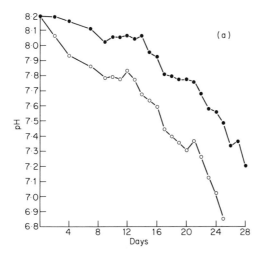

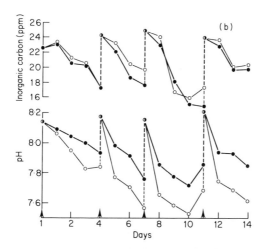

Fig. 16. (a) The rate of decrease in pH in foamed (solid circles) and unfoamed (open circles) recirculation systems in which the water was not changed. (b) The rate of change in pH and inorganic carbon levels in foamed (solid circles) and unfoamed (open circles) recirculation systems. Water changes are denoted by arrows.

D. Control of Particulate and Dissolved Organic Matter

(1) Carrying capacity

A number of parameters are widely used for the measurement of organic material in recirculated sea water and are based on the oxygen consumed during their degradation. They include redox potential, B.O.D., C.O.D. and O.C.F. (Oxygen Consumed during Filtration). The ratio of oxygen used to carbon oxidized is 2.67 (Richards, 1965). Calculations to determine the carrying capacity of a biological filter are often based on the O.C.F. (Hirayama, 1974). The results obtained from one culture regime, however, are not always applicable to another since qualitative and quantitative differences in filterable substances and B.O.D. occur between species and between diets. The O.C.F. method is satisfactory when it is used for a particular species fed with a particular diet, for example, in commercial fish culture or with low to moderately stocked research systems. Predictions based on O.C.F. measurements agree with the criteria described by Goldizen (1970) for *Octopus bimaculatus* which were applied to systems ranging from 80 to 30×10^4 l capacity in which animals as diverse as the sponge *Microciona prolifera* and the dolphin *Tursiops* have been held. Goldizen's criteria for 1 kg of a delicate species (*Octopus bimaculatus*) or 5 kg of the sea urchin *Stronglocentrotus purpuratus* or 7 kg of the lobster *Homarus americanus* were:

(a) 500 l water/kg animal;
(b) 0.1 m³ filter bed of 2 to 5 mm particles of magnesium bearing calcium carbonate;
(c) hydraulic load of 80 l/m² of filter bed surface/min;
(d) replacement of 25% of culture water/month.

Certain precautions concerning the interpretation of calculations of carrying capacity were suggested by Kinne (1976). The effective carrying capacity of a system will decrease:

(i)   per unit of animal weight if smaller rather than larger animals are cultured;
(ii) with increasing metabolic activity of the animals;
(iii) with increasing pollution by uneaten food;
(iv) as the culture period increases;
(v)   if animals are to breed.

Siddall (1974) suggested that a factor which would take into account the nitrifer : heterotroph ratio in the system was necessary in calculations of carrying capacity.

We have found it convenient to divide the organic material into two fractions: micro-organisms and particles larger than 1 μm, and sub-micron material. The latter includes bacteria, some colloids and particles, and dissolved organic compounds.

(2) Particulate matter larger than 1 μm
Particulate matter in marine recirculation systems arises predominantly from uneaten food, faecal material, dead organisms, exuviae, sloughed film from biological filters and aggregates caused by agitation (aeration, pumping, foaming). In some marine systems at Conwy, examples of the concentrations of particles retained on a *c.* 1 μm filter (Whatman GF/C) and the proportion of organic material they contain are shown in Table XII. Levels were high and ranged from 2.25 to 10.55, mean 6.58 mg/l, of which about 60% was organic material. The removal of particulates or suspended solids is probably one of the most important objectives for display aquaria. In intensive commercial aquaculture, their removal can be a major cost item, increasing the requirement for new water and labour. In research aquaria, changes in particulate loads can perturb the whole system. Recirculation systems for the maintenance of filter feeders may be considered a special case and lightly stocked systems sometimes rely solely on settlement. In more heavily stocked systems where food (e.g. algal cells) is added, a proportion will be lost to the mechanical filtration system.

Mechanical water treatment to remove particulate organic material may be achieved by sedimentation, centrifugation and mechanical filtration. Each has advantages and disadvantages. Settling tanks are perhaps most suitable for pretreatment where water flow is slow and where the treatment plant may be sited outside so that laboratory space is not lost. In commercial recirculation systems operated at controlled temperatures compact sedimentation devices (e.g. tilt plate filters) may be of more value since they can be sited within the culture building with little loss of production space. It might be expected that nitrifying and heterotrophic bacteria would colonize the multiple surfaces, thereby reducing sedimentation efficiency but increasing biological filtration activity. It would be of value to know if an effective balance between these functions could be achieved in marine systems. Centrifugation is expensive and most marine operators tend to avoid devices with moving parts because of the risks of corrosion and subsequent maintenance costs.

The development of microbial populations in mechanical filters, particularly in rapid sand filters and sand, gravel and stone filters, is highly desirable in many circumstances. In addition to the mechanical filtering action of the media itself, detritus and living matter accumulate in the finest layers of sand or gravel and trap even smaller particles. A desirable balance is achieved when the rates of deposition and biodegradation of the particles are equal. The problems arise when the efficiency of filtration decreases or oxygen consumed during filtration rises and cleaning becomes necessary. Cleaning invariably disturbs the ecological balance within the filter and results in a change in water purification capacity, at least temporarily. Heating due to biodegradation may also take place in such filters.

In a heavily stocked marine recirculation system (800 litre capacity) using a 75 litre filter of 1–2 cm gravel, we have noted that the temperature of the filter bed rose sufficiently high to heat the water an average of 2°C above normal running temperature (28°C), and on some days up to 5°C higher. Under such load conditions, where 1–2 kg of prawn are grown in 800–2000 litre capacity systems and fed with 40–80 kg of wet food over 16–38 weeks, we endeavour to separate mechanical from biological filtration. Ammonia and dissolved organic compounds are degraded biologically in percolating filters packed with plastic media with a large proportion of void spaces (93%). Particulate matter is removed by separate mechanical filters in which the establishment of nitrifiers is prevented by daily washing.

Mechanical filters with disposable or washable media (synthetic wool, diatomaceous earth, cartridges) are ideal for intermittent use at peak load times, after feeding, or for continuous use under low load conditions. Continuous use of these filters in high load commercial systems requires a relatively high level of daily maintenance and energy input but in return, a reliable high standard of water quality can be achieved. By separating mechanical and biological filtration, the populations of beneficial micro-organisms are not disturbed when the mechanical filters clog or are back flushed. Competition between nitrifying bacteria and an over-abundance of heterotrophs for available oxygen is thereby reduced.

(3) Sub-micron particles and dissolved organic compounds
The sub-micron particles retained by 0.22 μm membrane filters ranged in our experiments from 3 to 39 mg/l with a maximum of 0.01–104 mg/l in one experiment (Table XII). The reasons for the wide variation were not clear and there was no correlation between the weight of sub-micron particles and the number of bacteria present. Measurements of total organic carbon made on unfiltered samples from our experiments with tropical prawns showed an increase with increasing animal load in the system from 5 to 13 mg C/l at loads of 0.01–0.26 g prawn/l of water used (Fig. 17). Dissolved organic compounds include free amino acids, carbohydrates, lipids and humic substances, and some may be necessary for life support. Organic processes in estuarine conditions have been reviewed by Head (1976). Dissolved organic compounds are thought to be

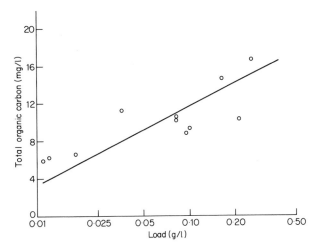

Fig. 17. The increase in total organic carbon with increasing load in nine marine recirculation systems. Load was calculated from the weight of animals held divided by the total volume of water used (including the initial charge) throughout the culture period. The calculated regression line is drawn.

responsible, at least in part, for the supersaturation of surface sea water with calcium carbonate. In recirculation systems, the gross accumulation of dissolved organics and subsequent effect on B.O.D. and hence carrying capacity of the system is of most concern to the aquarist. Dissolved organic compounds arise by leaching from food, exudation from and decomposition of damaged and dead organisms respectively; when eggs are spawned and hatch; and from secretions and excretions of living organisms (including moulting in Crustacea).

Dissolved organic compounds may be controlled by dilution and by biological filters, including filters made with a high percentage of voids. They are degraded and assimilated mainly by bacteria, but also by other small heterotrophs. The same process probably occurs in the majority of activated carbon filters in all but the most lightly loaded marine recirculation systems, unless efficient pre-filters are used. The ability of carbon filters to adsorb dissolved organic compounds is not disputed, but the cost and difficulty of ensuring that they are functioning correctly mitigate against their commercial use. Foam separation, an effective way of removing excess dissolved organic compounds from sea water (Kinne, 1976), can also contribute to the formation of particulate matter. This is not a problem unless the particles are carried into the culture system, for example by an excessive water flow through the separator. Ozone can be used in foam separators (Rosenthal *et al.*, 1978 a, b) but little data is available to the authors on the use of this combination in marine recirculation systems. "Yellow substances", aqueous extracts of decaying plants or melanoids of animal origin from fish foods, accumulate in some systems, particularly those using activated sludge for biological filtration, and may be removed by ozonization (Otte, Hilge and Rosenthal, 1977). Under some circumstances, however, "yellow substances" may ameliorate the effects of toxic concentrations of copper (Lewis *et al.*, 1972). The relative effectiveness and costs of biological filters, activated carbon and foam separators to remove dissolved organic material from marine systems has not, to our knowledge, been compared.

In Fig. 18, fluctuations in the sub-micron fraction in foamed and unfoamed oyster spat culture systems are shown. Higher levels of organic carbon (measured by combustion) occurred in the foamed system and

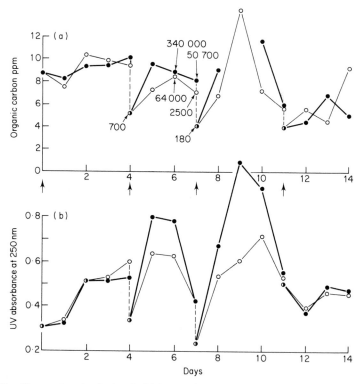

Fig. 18. Fluctuations in the level of (a) organic carbon (measured by combustion) and (b) u/v absorbance at 250 mm of filtered (submicron) samples from foamed (solid circles) and unfoamed (open circles) oyster spat culture systems. Figures in parentheses are numbers of bacteria/ml. Water changes are denoted by arrows.

may have been associated with bacteria which were 5 to 20 times more numerous. The foamed system also showed increased ultraviolet light absorption at 250 nm indicating an increased level of dissolved organic carbon. In contrast foamed prawn culture systems showed much lower numbers of bacteria than unfoamed systems (Table XIII) and little difference in ultraviolet light absorption and levels of organic carbon.

Table XIII. The effect of foaming on the numbers of bacteria found in warm water marine recirculation systems (28°C).

Replicate	Foamed		Not foamed	
	a	b	a	b
Experiment 1 Day	Number of bacteria/ml × 10^3			
44	8	7	980	1700
51	13	11	54	360
Experiment 2 Day				
2	145	256	1325	1175
9	55	2	270	110
16	36	60	65	200
23	45	67	338	1000
30	42	34	340	400

These results are open to two interpretations; one is that foaming removes bacteria but under some circumstances can create a more favourable environment for their growth while the other is that foaming may also create an unfavourable environment, which inhibits bacterial growth. Very high numbers of bacteria were found, 2.35 to 7527×10^3/ml (Tables XII and XIII), and were probably related to the elevated levels of organic material and high temperatures (28°C) of our prawn cultures. More acceptable levels (10–250/ml) were recorded by Bayne and Thompson (1970) for their studies on mussels where a gravel filter (2.5 m^3) which was large in relation to the total system volume (3500 litres) was followed by ultraviolet irradiation. The development of bacterial films on the water surface in non-agitated reservoir tanks may also be controlled by ultraviolet irradiation.

It is evident that although a proportion of dissolved organic compounds are readily degraded by conventional biological filters, there are several compounds that are not. In pilot scale commercial trials, in which water is used very intensively, these refractory substances may contribute significantly to the C.O.D. and possibly also have toxic effects. There is a pressing need for the chemical nature of these compounds to be determined and their effects in culture systems evaluated if recirculation systems are to be applied in commercial aquaculture. Much of the technology of municipal waste water treatment has been applied directly to pilot aquaculture systems. This is despite the fact that (a) lower organic loads (BOD) are desirable in aquaculture compared with municipal plant effluents and (b) so little is known about the nature of organic substances in fish farm effluents. It is therefore, likely that direct application of municipal waste water technology may not produce an economically viable mode of water treatment.

E. Animal Husbandry and Water Quality

One advantage of recirculation systems is that diseases are not being continually introduced by the incoming water. However, if disease is introduced, it may spread rapidly. To prevent the introduction of disease, water may be pre-treated. Some foods, particularly compounded feedstuffs, may be cleaned or sterilized, and to some extent, animals may be quarantined before entering the system. Effluent may be treated before discharge to minimize the risk of infection of existing quarantined or local stock (see appendix).

It is generally accepted that many of the animals kept in aquaria experience stress at some time or another (Chapter 15). Such stress can be induced by inadequate diet, water quality or living space, and may be revealed by reduced growth and survival, increased fighting and cannibalism, reluctance to breed and greater susceptibility to pollutants and disease organisms. Stressed animals may also release growth-inhibiting substances and other potent dissolved organic compounds. Wounds can give rise to accumulations of pathogenic organisms, and in recirculated water, latent pathogens can become virulent and spread quickly throughout the entire system. The control of pests and pathogens by water-borne therapeutic agents (chemical and antibiotic) in freshwater recirculation systems is thought to be possible (Levine and Meade, 1977), but little is known of their effects in marine biological filters (Collins, Gratzek, Dawe and Nemetz, 1976). Sometimes, infestation is only eradicated by completely dismantling and cleaning the whole system. Particular attention should be paid to the biological filter media which can become a reservoir of infection.

In addition to stress from malnutrition, the husbandry of feeding plays a vital part in the control of sea-water quality in recirculation systems. Regular removal of faeces and uneaten food (manually or by water currents in self-cleaning tanks) is necessary to prevent the occurrence of localized anerobic conditions where toxic and highly diffusable hydrogen sulphide is rapidly formed. Perhaps more important is feeding in a controlled way that is in sympathy with the natural feeding behaviour of the animals.

Some penaeid prawns, for example, consume a large proportion of detrital material of low nutritional value by continuous browsing. Such animals may be unable to efficiently utilize foods given at infrequent intervals. Oyster spat filter optimally at a particular concentration of algal food cells above which little growth advantage is obtained and the culture system is likely to become unnecessarily burdened. Compounded feeds are widely used in marine aquaria and must be suitably bound to minimize loss of ingredients by leaching and fragmentation. Tests with a number of binding agents (e.g. guar gum, casein, polyvinyl alcohol) showed that even with the best binders, 20–30% of the dry weight of prawn diets was lost to the water after 16 h of gentle but continuous agitation (Forster, 1972).

F. The Measurement of Water Quality

The tolerance of cultured species to the changes that occur in recirculated sea water are determined by conventional acute and chronic toxicity tests (see Chapter 6). In acute tests, animals are exposed for 48 or 96 h and survivors placed in clean water for a further 5 days to check for "overkill". Other, more rapid methods, use the residual oxygen concentrations after death by asphyxiation in the presence of the toxin to measure acute toxicity. In chronic tests, physiological and behavioural parameters are measured, e.g. food consumption, growth, activity, disease resistance, and can give a good practical guide to "safe" levels. Safe levels are best expressed in terms of the concentration that affects only 1% of the population (EC_1) in a specified time, and can be calculated from the EC_{50} by conventional log-probit analysis. Bioassay methods for acute and chronic toxicity tests and their interpretation have been reviewed by Sprague (1969; 1970; 1971). Some examples of recommended acceptable levels given by various authors are shown in Table XIV. For precise ecological studies, many of these levels may be considered to be at the very limits of acceptability, but in high density and commercial cultures, they may often be exceeded (see Table XI). A review of the water quality requirements of fish and shellfish cultured intensively has been prepared (Wickins, 1980).

Table XIV. Some examples of acceptable levels of various parameters for captive marine organisms.

Parameter	Desirable level greater than:	Studies made with:	Author
Oxygen	85% saturation	Kuruma prawn *Penaeus japonicus*	Liao, 1969
Alkalinity	1.0 mEq/l	Black sea bream *Mylio macrophalus*	Hirayama, 1970
pH	pH 7.5	Black sea bream *Mylio macrophalus*	Hirayama, 1970
Alkalinity	1.4 mEq/l	Pearl oyster *Pinctada fucata*	Kuwatani and Hishii, 1969
pH	pH 7.78	Pearl oyster *Pinctada fucata*	Kuwatani and Hishii, 1969
Calcium	100 mEq/l ($\sim$ 200 mg/l)	Greentail prawn *Metapenaeus bennettae*	Dall, 1965
Calcium	7.5 mmol ($\sim$ 300 mg/l)	Shore crab *Carcinus maenas*	Greenaway, 1976

	Desirable level equal to or less than (mg N/l)		
Un-ionized ammonia	0.001	For ecological experiments	Kinne, 1976
Un-ionized ammonia	0.04	Dover sole *Solea solea*	Alderson, in Hampson, 1976
Un-ionized ammonia	0.09	Turbot *Scophthalmus maximus*	Alderson, in Hampson, 1976
Un-ionized ammonia	0.09–0.11	Six species of prawn *Penaceus*	Wickins, 1976
Un-ionized ammonia	0.14	American lobster *Homarus americanus*	Delistraty, 1977
Nitrite	0.1	For research aquaria	King and Spotte, 1974; in Kinne, 1976
Nitrite	1.4	Prawn larvae *Macrobrachium rosenbergii*	Armstrong *et al.*, 1976
Nitrate	20	For research aquaria	King and Spotte, 1974; in Kinne, 1976

Table XV. Some suggested methods for the analysis of water quality, parameters in recirculated sea water.

Parameter	Method	Single sample volume (ml)
Temperature	Mercury thermometer; thermograph	*in situ*
Salinity	Goldberg T/C optical refractometer model 10419, American Optical Corporation	0.1
Oxygen	Dissolved oxygen probe model 54, Yellow Springs Instrument Co	500
pH	Research pH meter, model PHM 64, Radiometer calibrated to Hansson's sea water activity scale with Tris buffers (Hannson, 1973; Almgren *et al.* (1975))	100
Carbon (inorganic)	Rapid combustion, Beckman total carbon analyser model 915	50 µl
Calcium Magnesium	Atomic absorption spectrometry	100
Ammonia (total)	Modified Solorzano, 1969 (Hampson, 1975)	50
(un-ionized)	Calculated from total ammonia, pH, temperature, salinity, from Whitfield, 1974 (Hampson, 1977)	—
Nitrite	Bendschreider and Robinson, 1952	50
Nitrate	Wood *et al.* (1967)	50
Phosphate (inorganic)	Modified Strickland and Parsons, 1968	50
Particulates	Vacuum filtration (12–15 mmHg) through Whatman GF/C (1 µm) and Millipore 0.22 µm filters. Residue washing with 0.9% ammonium formate (Strickland and Parsons, 1968)	500 and 100 respectively
Carbon (organic)	Rapid combustion, Beckman total carbon analyser model 915	50 µl
Bacteria	Nutrient agar or ZoBell pour plating. Oxoid TCBS medium pour plates as rapid method for *Vibrio* sp.	1 ml with appropriate dilution

(1) Methods of analysis

Details of many of the methods used for the determination of water quality in sea water are described by Strickland and Parsons (1968) and Carlberg (1972). In Table XV, the methods which we believe to be most convenient for use in recirculated (polluted) sea water are given. Practical aspects of three of the methods are presented below.

(a) pH. In the opinion of Almgren *et al.* (1975), it is almost meaningless to measure the pH of sea water in the traditional way with electrodes standardized in low ionic strength phosphate or borate buffers. Such "pH" values are not a measure of H^+ ion concentration or the activity of H^+ on any activity scale (Hansson, 1973). pH measurements made in this way are elevated by about 0.05 to 0.16 pH units at 35‰ according to the type of electrode (and the filling) by comparison with measurements made with electrodes standardized in buffers with an ionic strength similar to that of sea water. An example of the latter is the "Tris"/artificial sea water buffer (Tris is 2 amino—2 hydroxymethyl propane 1, 3 diol) used by Hansson (1973).

To prepare the "Tris" buffer, two solutions are prepared in distilled water and can be stored indefinitely:

	Solution A g/l^{-1}	Solution B g/l
NaCl	18.65	24.08
KCl	0.76	0.75
Na$_2$SO$_4$	4.07	3.98
MgCl$_2$ 6H$_2$O	11.23	10.98
CaCl$_2$	1.14	1.11
HCl	10.01 ml	—

10 m mol of "Tris" base are added to 50 ml of solution A and made up to 1000 ml with solution B. The salinity of this buffer is 35‰ but can be adjusted by altering the concentrations of the first five ingredients in proportion. The pH of the buffer depends on temperature and salinity according to the equation:

$$pH = \frac{4.5 \times S‰ + 2559.7}{273.15 + T°C} - 0.5523 - 0.01391 \times S‰$$

The salinity of the prepared buffer should not differ more than 10% from that of the sea water sample. For example, a 35‰ buffer is effective for samples ranging between 31.5 and 38.5‰ (Almgren *et al.*, 1975).

(b) Ammonia. Total ammonia nitrogen in marine recirculation systems is commonly determined by the indo-phenol blue reaction (see Solor-

zano, 1969). Recent modifications to the method were made by Dal Pont *et al.*, 1974 and Liddicoat *et al.*, 1975, and were combined in the procedure described by Hampson, 1975. Although the reaction is specific for ammonia, it is suppressed by nitrite and amines, particularly when the concentration of these exceeds that of the ammonia on a nitrogen atom basis. Hampson (1975) showed how measurements could be corrected by the use of internal calibration standards. The proportion of un-ionized ammonia nitrogen was calculated using the model of Whitfield (1974) and a convenient computer program for its determination in fresh, brackish and sea water from measurements of total ammonia nitrogen, hydrogen ion activity (Hansson's sea water pH scale), salinity, temperature and pressure has been described by Hampson (1977). Table XVI gives values of total ammonia nitrogen that correspond to 0.1 mg un-ionized ammonia nitrogen/litre at selected values of temperature, pH and salinity. It gives a quick guide to what might be called the "maximum acceptable levels" for general aquarium systems.

Table XVI. The concentration of total ammonia nitrogen (mg/l) that corresponds to a calculated level of 0.1 mg/l un-ionized ammonia nitrogen in water at a constant pressure of 1 atmosphere at different values of salinity, temperature and pH.

Salinity (‰)	0			15			25		
Temperature (°C)	10	20	28	10	20	28	10	20	28
pH									
7.4	21.4	10.2	5.7	23.7	11.3	6.2	25.3	12.0	6.7
7.7	10.8	5.2	2.9	11.9	5.7	3.2	12.7	6.1	3.4
8.0	5.5	2.6	1.5	6.0	2.9	1.6	6.4	3.1	1.7
8.3	2.8	1.4	0.8	3.1	1.5	0.9	3.3	1.6	0.9

Salinity (‰)	30			35		
Temperature (°C)	10	20	28	10	20	28
pH						
7.4	26.2	12.5	6.9	21.1	12.9	7.1
7.7	13.2	6.3	3.5	13.6	6.5	3.6
8.0	6.6	3.2	1.8	6.9	3.3	1.9
8.3	3.4	1.6	0.9	3.5	1.7	1.0

(c) Phosphate. The method given by Strickland and Parsons (1968) was found to be extremely sensitive and necessitated considerable dilution of our samples which contained up to 5–8 mg PO_4-P/l. By doubling the concentration of each reagent, linear spectroscopic absorption was obtained up to 1.0 mg PO_4-P/l at 8850A and enabled routine measurements to be made on the majority of samples without excessive dilution. Straightforward addition of the reagents enabled estimation of reactive inorganic phosphate. After irradiation with ultraviolet light, any organic phosphates present (such as ADP, ATP) were broken down to the inorganic form allowing determination of the total (inorganic and organic) phosphates present. Further hydrolysis with hydrochloric acid enabled polyphosphates in solution to be determined.

IV. ACKNOWLEDGMENTS

We are grateful to Mr C. W. Baker of the Radiobiological Laboratory, Hamilton Dock, Lowestoft, for calcium and magnesium determinations; D. Harrington of the Water Research Centre, Stevenage, for data on filter material; Dr F. J. Whitley of I.C.I., Brixham, for information on analytical methods; Dr J. R. W. Norfolk, Marine Resources Research Unit, Portsmouth, and our colleagues, especially Mrs S. D. Utting, R. W. Sedgwick and B. E. Spencer, and J. L. Coburn, who allowed us to use some of their unpublished data.

V. REFERENCES

Almgren, T., Dryssen, D. and Strandberg, M. (1975). Determination of pH on the moles per kg sea water scale (M_w). *Deep Sea Research* **22**, 635–646.

Armstrong, D. A., Stephenson, M. J. and Knight, A. W. (1976). Acute toxicity of nitrite to larvae of the giant Malaysian prawn, *Macrobrachium rosenbergii*. *Aquaculture* **9**, 39–46.

Armstrong, F. A., Williams, J. P. M. and Strickland, J. D. H. (1966). Photo-oxidation of organic matter in sea water by ultraviolet radiation: analytical and other implications. *Nature, London* **211**, 481–483.

Batoosingh, E., Riley, G. A. and Keshwar, B. (1969). An analysis of experimental methods for producing particulate organic matter in sea water by bubbling. *Deep Sea Research*, **16**, 213–219.

Bayne, B. L. and Thompson, R. J. (1970). Some physiological consequences of keeping *Mytilus edulis* in the laboratory. *Helgoländer wiss. meersunters* **20**, 526–552.

Beard, T. W. and Forster, J. R. M. (1973). A growth experiment with *Penaeus monodon* Fab. in a closed system. I.C.E.S., Shellfish and Benthos Committee, C.M. K. 39 (mimeo), 6 pp.

Bendschreider, K. and Robinson, R. J. (1952). A new spectrophotometric method for the determination of nitrite in sea water. *Journal of Marine Research* **11**, 87–96.

Brewer, P. G. and Goldman, J. C. (1976). Alkalinity changes generated by photoplankton growth. *Limnology and Oceanography* **21**, 108–117.

Bryan, G. W. (1976). Heavy metal contamination in the sea. *In* "Marine Pollution", (R. Johnston, ed.) 185–302. Academic Press, London and New York.

Carlberg, S. R. (1972). New Baltic manual with methods for sampling and analysis of physical, chemical and biological parameters. Internat. Council Explor. Sea Coop. Research Report, A, **29**.

Carmignani, G. M. and Bennett, J. P. (1977). Rapid start up of a biological filter in a closed aquaculture system. *Aquaculture* **11**, 85–88.

Castro, W. E., Zielinski, P. B. and Sandifer, P. A. (1975). Performance characteristics of air lift pumps of short length and small diameter. Proceedings 6th Annual Workshop Wld. Mariculture Soc., Seattle, Washington, 27–31 January 451–461.

Chester, R. (1965). Adsorption of zinc and cobalt on illite in sea water. *Nature, London* **206**, 884–886.

Collins, M. T., Gratzek, J. B., Dawe, D. L. and Nemetz, T. G. (1976). Effects of antibacterial agents on nitrification in an aquatic recirculating system. *Journal Fisheries Research Board Canada* **33**, 215–218.

Courtright, R. C., Breese, W. P. and Krueger, H. (1971). Formulation of a synthetic sea water for bioassays with *Mytilus edulis* embryos. *Water Research* **5**, 877–888.

Davey, E. W., Gentile, J. H., Erickson, S. J. and Betzer, P. (1970). Removal of trace metals from marine culture media. *Limnology and Oceanography* **15**, 486–488.

Delistraty, D. A., Carlberg, J. M., Van Olst, J. C. and Ford, R. F. (1977). Ammonia toxicity in cultured larvae of the American lobster (*Homarus americanus*). I.C.E.S., Fisheries Improvement Committee. C. M. 1977, E. 63.

Elderfield, H. (1971). Some geochemical aspects concerning oyster rearing at Conwy, North Wales. Research Report, Applied Geochemistry Research Group, Department of Geology, Imperial College, London.

Fauval, Y. (1962). Utilisation de l'ozone comme agent stérilisateur de l'eau de mer pour l'épuration des coquillages. *Comité international de l'Exploration scientifique Mer de la Méditerranée Rapp. et P.V.* **17**, 701–706.

Forster, J. R. M. (1972). Some methods of binding prawn diets and their effect on growth and assimilation. *Journal du Conseil permanent international Exploration de la Mer* **34**, 200–216.

Forster, J. R. M. (1974). Studies on nitrification in marine biological filters. *Aquaculture* **4**, 387–397.

Gallagher, M. L. and Brown, W. D. (1976). Comparison of artificial and natural sea water as culture media for juvenile lobsters. *Aquaculture* **9**, 87–90.

Goldizen, V. C. (1970). Management of closed-system marine aquariums. *Helgoländer wiss. Meersesunters.* **20**, 637–641.

Greenaway, P. (1976). The regulation of haemolymph calcium concentration of the crab *Carcinus maenas* (L.). *Journal of Experimental Biology* **64**, 149–157.

Gunderson, K. and Mountain, C. W. (1973). Oxygen utilization and pH change in the ocean resulting from biological nitrate formation. *Deep Sea Research* **20**, 1083–1091.

Hampson, B. L. (1975). The analysis of ammonia in polluted sea water. I.C.E.S. Hydrography Committee, C. M. *c.* 16, 8 pp. (mimeo).

Hampson, B. L. (1976). Ammonia concentration in relation to ammonia toxicity during a rainbow trout rearing experiment in a closed freshwater-sea water system. *Aquaculture* **9**, 61–70.

Hampson, B. L. (1977). Relationship between total ammonia and free ammonia in terrestrial and ocean waters. *Journal du Conseil permanent international Exploration de la Mer* **37**, 117–122.

Hansson, I. (1973). A new set of pH scales and standard buffers for sea water. *Deep Sea Research* **20**, 479–491.

Harvey, H. W. (1945). "Recent Advances in the Chemistry and Biology of Sea Water", p. 164. University Press, Cambridge.

Head, P. C. (1976). Organic processes in estuaries. pp. 53–91. *In* "Estuarine Chemistry" (J. D. Burton and P. S. Liss, eds), Academic Press, London and New York.

Helm, M. M. (1971). The effect of sea water quality on the laboratory culture of *Ostrea edulis* L. larvae. *I.C.E.S., Shellfish and Benthos Committee* C. M. 1971, Doc. K:28 (mimeo).

Helm, M. M., Holland, D. L. and Stephenson, R. R. (1973). The effect of supplementary algal feeding of a hatchery breeding stock of *Ostrea edulis* L. on larval vigour. *Journal of Marine biological Association of the UK* **53**, 673–684.

Hirayama, K. (1970). Studies on water control by filtration through sand bed in a marine aquarium with closed circulating system. VI. Acidification of aquarium water. *Bulletin of the Japanese Society for Scientific Fisheries*, **36**, 26–34.

Hirayama, K. (1974). Water control by filtration in closed culture systems. *Aquaculture* **4**, 369–385.

Hirsbrunner, W. R. and Wangersky, P. J. (1976). Composition of the inorganic fraction of the particulate organic matter in sea water. *Marine Chemistry* **4**, 43–49.

Honn, K. V. and Chavin, W. (1976). Utility of ozone treatment in the maintenance of water quality in a closed marine system. *Marine Biology*, **34**, 201–209.

Honn, K. V., Glezman, G. M. and Chavin, W. (1976). A high capacity ozone generator for use in aquaculture and water processing. *Marine Biology*, **34**, 211–216.

Kils, U. (1977). The salinity effect on aeration in mariculture. *Meeresforsch.* **25**, 201–206.

Kinne, O. (1976). Cultivation of marine organisms: water quality management and technology. *In* "Marine Ecology 3 (1)" (O. Kinne, ed.), pp. 19–300. Wiley, London.

Kuwatani, Y. and Nishii, T. (1969). Effects of pH of culture water on the growth of the Japanese pearl oyster. *Bulletin of the Japanese Society for Scientific Fisheries* **35**, 342–350.

Levine, G. and Meade, T. L. (1977). The effects of disease treatment on nitrification in closed system aquaculture. Proceedings 7th Annual Workshop. Wld. Mariculture Society, San Diego, California, U.S.A., 25–29 January 483–492.

Lewis, A. G., Whitfield, P. H. and Ramnarine, A. (1972). Some particulate and soluble agents affecting the relationship between metal toxicity and organism survival in the calanoid copepod, *Euchaeta japonica*. *Marine Biology* **17**, 215–221.

Liao, I. L. (1969). Study on the feeding of Kuruma prawn. Reprinted from *China Fisheries Monthly*, **197**, pp. 17–18. *In* "Tungkang Marine Laboratory, Collected Reprints, Vol. 1, 1969–1971", pp. 17–24.

Maddox, M. B. and Manzi, J. J. (1976). The effects of algal supplements on static system culture of *Macrobrachium rosenbergii* (de Man) larvae. Proceedings 7th Annual Workshop. Wld. Mariculture Society, 1976, San Diego, California, U.S.A., 25–29 January 677–698.

McCarty, P. L. and Haug, R. T. (1971). Nitrogen removal from waste waters by biological nitrification and de-nitrification. *In* "Microbial Aspects of Pollution" (G. Sykes and F. A. Skinner, eds), pp. 215–232. Academic Press, London and New York.

Millar, R. H. and Scott, J. M. (1968). An effect of water quality on the growth of cultured larvae of the *Ostrea edulis* L. *Journal du Conseil permanent international Exploration de la Mer* **32**, 123–130.

Mock, C. R., Ross, L. R. and Salser, B. R. (in preparation). Design and preliminary evaluation of a closed system for shrimp culture.

Morris, A. W. (1971). Trace metal variations in sea water of the Menai Straits caused by a bloom of *Phaeocystis*. *Nature, London* **233**, 427–428.

Otte, G. and Rosenthal, H. (1978). Water quality during a one-year operation of a closed intensive fish culture system. *I.C.E.S. Mariculture Committee*, C.M. 1978, F.7. (mimeo).

Otte, G., Hilge, V. and Rosenthal, H. (1977). Effect of ozone on yellow substances accumulated in a recycling system for fish culture. *I.C.E.S. Fisheries Improvement Committee*, C.M. 1977, E.27. (mimeo).

Painter, H. A. (1970). A review of literature on inorganic nitrogen metabolism in micro-organisms. *Water Research* **4**, 493–450.

Parker, N. C. and Simco, B. A. (1973). Evaluation of recirculating systems for the culture of channel catfish. Proceedings 27th Annual Conference Southeastern Association of Game and Fish Commissioners, 474–487.

Pasveer, A. (1966). Consideration on the efficiency of the aeration process. *Air and Water Pollution* **10**, 477–493.

Prince, J. S. (1974). Nutrient assimilation and growth of some seaweeds in mixtures of sea water and secondary sewage treatment effluents. *Aquaculture* **4**, 69–79.

Richards, F. A. (1965). Chemical observations in some anoxic sulfide-bearing basins and fjords. *In* "Advances in Water Pollution Research". Proceedings of the 2nd International Conference, Tokyo, 1964, **3** (E. A. Pearson, ed), 215–232. Pergamon, Oxford.

Riley, G. A. (1970). Particulate organic matter in sea water. *Advances in Marine Biology* **8**, 1–118.

Roff, J. (1972). The nitrogen cycle in nature and culture. *Sea Scope* **2**, 1, 7–8.

Rosenthal, H. (1974). Selected bibliography on ozone, its biological effects and technical applications. *Fisheries Research Board of Canada, Technol. Report* 456.

Rosenthal, H., Krüner, G. and Otte, G. (1978a). Effects of ozone treatment on recirculating water in a closed fish culture system. *I.C.E.S. Mariculture Committee* C.M. 1978, F.9 (mimeo).

Rosenthal, H., Westernhagen, H. V. and Otte, G. (1978b). Maitaining water quality in laboratory scale sea water recycling systems. *I.C.E.S. Mariculture Committee.* C.M. 1978, F.10 (mimeo).

Sanders, E. (1967). Skimmers in the marine aquarium. *Pet Fish Monthly*, May, 48–51.

Scott, K. R. (1972). Comparison of the efficiency of various aeration devices for oxygenation of water in aquaria. *Journal of the Fisheries Research Board Canada* **29**, 1641–1643.

Scott, K. R. and Gillespie, D. C. (1972). A compact recirculation unit for the rearing and maintenance of fish. *Journal Fisheries Research Board Canada* **29**, 1071–1074.

Serfling, S. A., Van Olst, J. C. and Ford, R. F. (1974). A recirculating culture system for larvae of the American lobster, *Homarus americanus. Aquaculture* **3**, 303–309.

Shelbourne, J. E. (1964). The artificial propagation of marine fish. *Advances in Marine Biology* **2**, 1–83.

Shelbourne, J. E., Riley, J. D. and Thacker, G. T. (1963). Marine fish culture in Britain. 1. Plaice-rearing in closed circulation at Lowestoft 1957–60. *Journal du Conseil permanent international de l'Exploration de la Mer* **28**, 50–69.

Shigueno, K. (1975). Shrimp culture in Japan. Ass. for int. Tech. Promotion, Tokyo, Japan.

Short, Z. and Olson, P. R. (1970). Oyster shells and foam formation used to improve quality of water recirculated in a fish hatchery incubator. *Progressive Fish Culturalist* **32**, 180–183

Siddall, S. E. (1974). Studies of closed marine culture systems. *Progressive Fish Culturalist* **36**, 8–15.

Siegel, A. (1966). Equilibrium binding studies of zinc-glycine complexes to ion-exchange resins and clays. *Geochimica cosmochim.* Acta **30**, 757–768.

Simpson, H. J. and Broecker, W. S. (1973). A new method for determining the total carbonate ion concentration in saline waters. *Limnology and Oceanography* **18**, 426–440.

Sharma, B. and Ahlert, R. C. (1977). Nitrification and nitrogen removal. *Water Research* **11**, 897–925.

Solorzano, L. (1969). Determination of ammonia in natural waters by the phenolhypochlorite method. *Limnology and Oceanography* **14**, 799–801.

Speece, R. E. (1973). Trout metabolism characteristics and the rational design of nitrification facilities for water re-use in hatcheries. *Trans. American Fisheries Society* **102**, 323–334.

Spencer, B. E., Helm, M. M. and Dare, P. J. (1977). Recommended quarantine measures for marine molluscs. *Tech. Rep. MAFF Direct. Fish. Res. Lowestoft*, (32).

Spotte, S. H. (1970). Fish and invertebrate culture: water management in closed systems. Wiley-Interscience, New York.

Sprague, J. B. (1969). Measurement of pollutant toxicity to fish. I. Bioassay methods for acute toxicity. *Water Research* **3**, 793–821.

Sprague, J. B. (1970). Measurement of pollutant toxicity to fish. II. Utilizing and applying bioassay results. *Water Research* **4**, 3–32.

Sprague, J. B. (1971). Measurement of pollutant toxicity to fish. III. Sublethal effects and "safe" concentrations. *Water Research* **5**, 245–266.

Strickland, J. D. H. and Parsons, T. R. (1968). A practical handbook of sea water analysis. *Bulletin of Fisheries Research Board of Canada* **167**, 1–311.

Sulkin, S. D. and Minasian, L. L. (1973). Synthetic sea water as a medium for raising crab larvae. *Helgoländer wiss. Meeresunters.* **25**, 126.

Sverdrup, H. U., Johnson, M. W. and Fleming, R. H. (1942). The Oceans: their Physics, Chemistry and General Biology. Prentice-Hall, New York.

Truesdale, G. A. and Gameson, A. L. H. (1957). The solubility of oxygen in saline water. *Journal Conseil permanent international de l'Exploration de la Mer* **22**, 163–166.

Ukeles, R. (1976). Cultivation of plants 367–466. *In* "Marine Ecology" **3** (1), 367–466 (O. Kinne, ed.), Wiley, London.

Wallace, G. T. and Wilson, D. F. (1969). Foam separation as a tool in chemical oceanography. Naval Research Laboratory, Washington D.C., NRL–6958.

Whitfield, M. (1974). The hydrolysis of ammonium ions in sea water—a theoretical study. *Journal of the Marine Biological Association of the UK* **54**, 565–580.

Wickins, J. F. (1976a). Prawn Biology and Culture, pp. 435–507. *In* "Oceanography and Marine Biology: An annual review" **14** (H. Barnes, ed.), Aberdeen University Press.

Wickins, J. F. (1976b). The tolerance of warm-water prawns to recirculated water. *Aquaculture* **9**, 19–37.

Wickins, J. F. (1980). Water quality requirements for intensive animal aquaculture: A review. E.I.F.A.C. Symposium on new developments in the utilization of heated effluents and of recirculation systems for intensive aquaculture. Stavanger. Doc. R2.

Willey, J. D. (1977). Coprecipitation of zinc with silica in sea water and in distilled water. *Mar. Chem.* **5**, 267–290.

Wilson, D. P. (1951). A biological difference between natural sea waters. *Journal of the Marine Biological Association of the UK* **30**, 1–19.

Wilson, D. P. and Armstrong, F. A. J. (1958). Biological differences between sea waters: experiments in 1954 and 1955. *Journal of the Marine Biological Association of the UK* **37**, 331–348.

Wood, E. D., Armstrong, F. A. J. and Richards, F. A. (1967). Determination of nitrate in sea water by cadmium −copper reduction to nitrite. *Journal of the Marine Biological Association of the UK* **47**, 23–31.

Wood, P. C. (1961). The principles of water sterilization by ultraviolet light and their application in the purification of oysters. *Fishery Investigations London (Ser. 2)* **23** (6).

Wood, P. C. and Ayres, P. A. (1977). Artificial sea water for shellfish tanks. *Lab. Leafl., MAFF Direct. Fish. Res., Lowestoft*, (39).

Zaroogian, G. E., Pesch, G. and Morrison, G. (1969). Formulation of an artificial sea water media suitable for oyster larvae development. *American Zoologist* **9** (Abstract No. 549), 1144.

Zillioux, E. J. and Lackie, N. F. (1970). Advances in the continuous culture of planktonic copepods. *Helgoländer wiss. Meeresunters.* **20**, 325–332.

Chapter 4

Freshwater Quality

R. Lloyd

Fisheries Laboratory, Burnham on Crouch, England

I. INTRODUCTION

It is a common experience among those who are setting up freshwater aquaria to find that the organisms which they wish to keep become unhealthy and die. The initial assumption is made that a potable water supply, with perhaps some additional aeration, is a satisfactory medium in which to keep fish or other aquatic organisms. However, sooner or later, it is realized that a water supply which is wholesome for humans to drink is not necessarily of a satisfactory quality to provide a healthy environment for aquatic life.

In this chapter, the basic requirements of a satisfactory freshwater supply to support aquatic organisms are outlined, together with sources of contaminants which can render that supply unsatisfactory. Such sources may be in the primary water supply: rivers, lakes or underground water, or may be derived from water treatment works, from the pipework in the water supply system, from the design of the aquatic systems, or from the excretion of organisms in them. There is more information on the effects of such contaminants on freshwater fish than on other aquatic organisms although it is likely that conditions satisfactory for species of fish known to be sensitive to harmful substances will be also suitable for most other animals. Limiting values for contaminants will be given, where possible, together with methods for overcoming particular problems.

II. SOURCES OF WATER

Water may be drawn from three main sources: rivers, lakes (including reservoirs) and from underground sources. This section deals with the characteristics of such waters insofar as they affect aquatic life.

Natural River Water

(1) Dissolved salts and acids
The chemical composition of a river water can fluctuate both in the short- and long-term. These fluctuations may be induced by geological or geographical factors, rainfall and runoff, or by the river biota. Factors such as pH, dissolved oxygen and carbon dioxide can show daily variations, particularly if there is an abundance of aquatic plants present.

Among the geological factors, water hardness, sodium chloride and pH are the most important. Most freshwater fish and invertebrates can live within a wide range of calcium concentrations from 1 mg/l upwards, and sodium chloride within a range of a few mg/l upwards to about 9 g/l. However, at the lower end of these ranges, fish may have difficulty in maintaining homeostasis since sodium chloride has to be absorbed from the water to replace that lost by diffusion and excretion. It is well known that fish have difficulty in surviving in constantly renewed distilled water. Although they may be able to live in water with a low calcium, sodium and chloride content, they may be more susceptible to other adverse factors under these conditions. For example, recent Scandinavian work has shown that the toxicity of low pH to fish increases as the concentration of these ions decrease; one measured effect is that the blood osmotic pressure cannot be maintained (Leivestad and Muniz, 1976). Snow-melt water may have an especially low ionic content. In general, the hardness of the water should be greater than 10 mg/l as $CaCO_3$, and the sodium chloride content should be greater than 5 mg NaCl/l. Although natural waters may contain lower values and still support a good fish population, there is always the danger that the artificial conditions of the aquarium may result in stress which is accentuated in water of low ionic content. If the water supply is of a low ionic content, it may be sufficient to add (in a semi-controlled way) sufficient calcium and sodium chloride to raise the concentrations to those of a moderately hard water.

Some natural waters draining granite regions may be acid, especially if they also drain through peat bogs where the production of humic acids can reduce the pH to 4.0 or even lower when the bogs are flushed by heavy rain following prolonged drought. In the latter case, the acidification may be of too short a duration to harm aquatic life. However, in general, the pH of the water (after aeration to bring the carbon dioxide concentrations into equilibrium with air) should not be below 6.0 and not above 8.5, although some aquatic species can live within the range 5.0–9.0. If the pH of the water supply is outside this range, the necessary adjustments can be made by adding hydrochloric acid or sodium hydroxide. The water should then be aerated vigorously to bring the carbon dioxide concentration into equilibrium with air.

(2) Temperature
Since the usual temperature of a natural river water is below the ambient air value, it is probable that during passage through water pipes and storage systems, the supply to the aquaria will rise by several degrees C, especially during the daytime. In some cases, the temperature of the aquarium water may rise to levels close to or exceeding the upper end of the natural range for the aquatic organisms to be kept, and this can cause increased susceptibility to disease or even mortalities. As a general rule, the temperature should be at least 5°C below the lethal level, as measured

by exposing the organisms to a steadily increasing temperature of 1 °C per hour, and recording the temperature at which mortalities occur.

As water becomes warmer, so the solubility of dissolved gases becomes less. If the excess gas remains in solution, the total dissolved gas pressure is greater than the saturation value, a condition known as supersaturation. This problem is described later in greater detail. Small volumes of water can be readily cooled and there are many types of equipment available for this purpose. But the cooling of large quantities of water is expensive and should be avoided if possible, either by locating the aquarium system elsewhere or providing an alternative source of colder water.

(3) Effect of aquatic life on water quality
Most lowland rivers contain an abundance of aquatic plants. Respiration and photosynthesis during the summer months can cause considerable daily fluctuations in the dissolved oxygen concentration of the water. It is not unusual for dissolved oxygen concentrations to rise to 140% of the air saturation value (ASV) during the day and to fall to 50% ASV during the night. Daytime photosynthetic activity can remove free carbon dioxide from the water and under some conditions (such as in moderately hard water), the pH may rise to above 10.0. There are records of fish mortalities in such situations. Vigorous aeration is usually sufficient to restore the dissolved oxygen and pH of the water to normal values.

B. Lake or Reservoir Waters

(1) Dissolved salts and acids
The problems which may be encountered with lake and reservoir sources are similar to those for river waters in respect of sodium, calcium, chloride and pH, except that fluctuations in concentrations are usually much less pronounced.

(2) Dissolved gases
The concentration of dissolved oxygen and carbon dioxide in the surface waters can fluctuate in the same way as in rivers as a result of plant respiration and photosynthesis. However, where a lake is thermally stratified, it is usual to find that the dissolved oxygen concentration of the deeper water is less than the air saturation value, depending on the rate of oxidation of organic matter in the sediments. Where water is drawn from such levels, vigorous aeration is all that is required to make the water satisfactory for fish.

Even if the hypolimnion has an acceptable dissolved oxygen content, the water may nevertheless contain an unsuspected hazard, that of supersaturation with dissolved nitrogen gas. Such supersaturation may be widespread (not confined to lakes and reservoirs) and can arise from a number of causes. The mechanism whereby deep waters in lakes and reservoirs become supersaturated is uncertain. It is obvious that at increasing depths, the water under pressure can hold more nitrogen than that at the surface, but whether the nitrogen accumulates there by diffusion from the surface or from denitrification of organic matter in the sediments, or a combination of both, is not known.

When water saturated with a mixture of oxygen and nitrogen (the oxygen concentration being usually less than the ASV) at the pressure present at the abstraction point is brought to aquaria at the surface where it is at atmospheric pressure, the gas can come out of solution as bubbles. The formation of the bubbles depends on the presence of particles or surfaces. Often the bubbles collect on the walls of aquaria and if this happens, supersaturation with dissolved gases should be suspected. The principle is similar to that of soda water from a siphon or pressurized bottle.

When aquatic animals are exposed to water supersaturated with nitrogen, the internal fluids tend towards equilibrium with the gas pressure present in the ambient water. Internal bubbles can then form and block the circulation systems, forming a condition similar to "bends" in deep sea divers. In fish, these bubbles can be seen in the fins between the fin rays, although mortalities are probably caused by blockages to vital arteries. In less extreme, sub-lethal cases, there is some circumstantial evidence that small bubbles can accumulate in the dorsal fin of fish, causing degeneration of the distal tissues and giving the appearance of a fin–selective fin rot. In cases where the dorsal fins (and occasionally the caudal fins as well) are eroded away, yet the paired fins are unaffected, supersaturation of the water with nitrogen should be suspected. Other locations where gas may collect include beneath the cornea, and the loose connective tissues around the eye, causing exopthalmia or "pop-eye".

Until recently, the measurement of the dissolved nitrogen content of the water has been difficult, with errors arising from the sampling methods and the gasometric analytical techniques used. However, dissolved gas pressure can now be measured *in situ* by a manometric technique and a simple analyser has been described recently by D'Aoust *et al.* (1976). Simultaneous measurement of the dissolved oxygen concentration by conventional electrode techniques will enable the nitrogen supersaturation to be calculated. It must be stressed that it is supersaturation with respect to atmospheric pressure which is important, not supersaturation with respect to the ASV. For example, fish are not affected by water through which oxygen has been bubbled to give concentrations considerably in excess of the ASV, and where the total pressure of dissolved gases is at the normal atmospheric pressure.

There is no limiting dissolved nitrogen pressure above which fish are harmed; what firm evidence there is (US EPA, 1972; Fickeisen and Schneider, 1976) indicates that pressures above 110% of atmospheric pressure may harm fish. Both these references contain excellent descriptions of "gas bubble disease". Where nitrogen supersaturation is suspected, or the conditions are such that it may occur, the gas tension in the water can be equilibrated to atmospheric pressure by vigorous aeration which "strips" the surplus dissolved gas from solution. A cheaper and perhaps more reliable method is to trickle the incoming water down a tower packed with a high surface area filter medium as used for the biological treatment of sewage. Such a method has been used successfully for many years at the Water Research Centre, Stevenage, England. At St Johns, Newfoundland, a similar passive "degasser" has proved effective with seawater; the system consists of a square section column containing a series of baffles perforated by 3 mm-diameter holes.

(3)   Pollutants in surface waters

Some rivers, and to a lesser extent lakes, can be subjected to sporadic or continuous pollution from domestic, industrial or agricultural sources. Such waters should not be abstracted for aquaria use without treatment. A biological survey of the watercourse upstream of the abstraction point may give some indication of water quality, even though this cannot usually indicate the chemical contaminants responsible for an abnormal flora or fauna. Where poor water quality is suspected, samples of water have to be analysed for the suspected contaminants.

It is impossible in this chapter to list the limiting concentrations of all the pollutants likely to occur in freshwaters; such information for specific chemicals can be found in the specialist literature. For those pollutants which occur most frequently in water, literature reviews such as Alabaster and Lloyd (1980) and Train (1979) provide estimates of the maximum concentrations which can be tolerated by fish for long periods under different environmental conditions. Other source books contain data on the toxicity of a large number of chemicals, usually obtained from short-term toxicity tests on fish and other aquatic organisms. Such data have to be interpreted with care; if the concentration of a chemical exceeds that known to be acutely toxic to a sensitive aquatic animal, then it is most likely (but not certain) that the water will be unsatisfactory. However, only if the aqueous concentration is at least 4 orders of magnitude less than the acute toxic concentration, can it be said with any certainty that the water is safe. Higher concentrations may be safe, but further toxicity data would be required to prove that this was so.

However, some protection to aquaria supplied directly from a river or lake which is liable to pollution, can be obtained by keeping fish in the water near the abstraction point. Such monitoring techniques generally depend on the automatic detection of changes in the behaviour of fish swimming in a chamber through which a constant flow of water is passed. The response may be a reduction in swimming ability, changes in behaviour pattern, or alteration in heart rate or opercular rhythm. The latter physiological responses may be more sensitive to sub-lethal changes in water quality than changes in the swimming ability, but they may produce a greater number of false alarms. A brief outline of these techniques, together with a short bibliography is given by EIFAC (1975).

C. Underground Water Supplies

Water from a borehole with a composition similar to natural surface water, is often more suitable than surface water because the ionic composition remains fairly constant and pollutants are unlikely to be present unless the borehole or well is shallow. However, even with deep boreholes, particular problems can occur.

(1) Dissolved gases
Water supplies from borehole sources can be supersaturated with dissolved gases, but whether this excess pressure is present at source or arises from the pumping operation and subsequent supply is not always easy to determine. A water pump which draws in some air as well as water can readily supersaturate the water with dissolved gas. For all underground water, supersaturation with dissolved gas should be looked for, and if present, remedial action should be taken as described earlier. Submersible pumps are less prone to cause supersaturation than conventional pumps with a long suction line.

Borehole waters taken from chalk strata frequently contain high concentrations of dissolved carbon dioxide, often in the range 20–40 mg CO_2/l, giving pH values for the hard water of between 7.2 to 7.6; the air saturation value is about 1.5 mg CO_2/l with a corresponding pH of about 8.1–8.3. It is known that fish can adapt to concentrations of free CO_2 of up to at least 20 mg/l, but this concentration may have adverse long-term effects. Recent investigations have shown that farmed rainbow trout reared in borehole water containing elevated concentrations of free CO_2 (about 20 mg/l) developed kidney stones (G. Smart, personal communication).

Cascading water over artificial filter media, as described in Section

II.B.(2) may remove sufficient free carbon dioxide to prevent this disease occurring, but additional aeration to strip the surplus gas may also be necessary. Alternatively, sufficient lime can be added to react with the carbon dioxide, although this can be inconvenient.

(2) Dissolved iron
Some acidic underground waters (as well as acid-polluted surface waters) may contain dissolved iron if the pH is below 5.0. If these waters are made more alkaline, as recommended earlier, the salts will precipitate out, possibly as the hydroxide. There is increasing evidence that freshly precipitated iron can be lethal to fish at concentrations above 0.4 mg Fe/l, although after a short period, the precipitate may become less toxic. The evidence has been reviewed by Alabaster and Lloyd (1980). Treatment of such waters may require a pre-treatment tank in which the incoming water is made alkaline and the precipitated iron allowed to settle out.

D. Water Treated for Human Consumption

In most cases, the water supply to a laboratory or other building, has been processed through a water treatment works to render it fit for human consumption. Some of the problems encountered with such supplies may be similar to those with direct abstraction of natural waters. For example, dissolved toxic substances may be present at concentrations which are within those set for public health, but which may nevertheless be harmful to aquatic organisms. Some of the processes involved in water treatment and their possible effects on fish and other freshwater aquatic organisms are described below.

(1) Chemicals used in water treatment
One of the main problems in reservoir storage is the growth of algae which not only block sand filters but can also impart a taint to the water. Treatment can be by means of algicides, the most common being copper sulphate which is added to give a concentration of about 1–2 mg Cu/l (Tuwiner, 1976). In moderately hard water, most of the copper will be precipitated as the unsoluble carbonate, or absorbed on to organic matter, thus making it relatively harmless (McIntosh, 1975). Nevertheless, although there is unlikely to be a serious copper contamination from this source, the possibility should not be overlooked.

Within the treatment works, water may be treated with floculating agents to trap and settle out suspended matter. Also, the water may be artificially softened by the addition of soda-lime to precipitate some of the calcium present and then treated with floculating agents followed by acid to restore the pH to close to neutral. None of these processes are likely to lead to a deterioration of the water quality insofar as aquatic organisms are concerned, but they may cause additional fluctuations in the ionic composition of the water.

(2) Chemicals used in water sterilization
Most public water supplies are sterilized by the addition of chlorine, which also removes taints and odours from the water. Natural waters contain small amounts of soluble organic matter which react with the added chlorine, and a slight excess has to be present to kill pathogenic bacteria. Normally, the amount of chlorine remaining in the water by the time it has passed through the distribution system is less than 0.5 mg Cl_2/l, but even concentrations as low as this can be harmful to fish. Moreover, occasions can arise, either with a fluctuating concentration of organic material in the water, or a malfunctioning of the chlorination plant, which can result in a much higher concentration occurring for a short time. It is likely that excess free chlorine is one of the commonest causes of an unsatisfactory water supply for aquatic animals, and for this reason a full description will be given of its toxic properties.

When chlorine or chlorinating compounds are added to water, the following reactions occur:

$$Cl_2 + H_2O \rightleftharpoons HCl + HOCl$$
$$HOCl \rightleftharpoons H^+ + OCl^-$$

Of the compounds formed, hypochlorous acid (HOCl) is probably the toxic agent and little free chlorine (Cl_2) is likely to be present. If the water contains ammonia (which is commonly present even in slightly polluted rivers), the addition of chlorine leads to an initial formation of chloramines. Addition of further chlorine converts these compounds to chloride ions and nitrogen. However, if residual chloramines are present, they can dissociate to form an equilibrium with a small concentration of hypochlorous acid and thus be toxic to aquatic life.

The proportion of hypochlorous acid present in water containing free chlorine decreases with a rise in pH value. For example, at a pH of 5.0 and 25°C, almost all the chlorine is present as HOCl, whereas at pH 7.0 about 70% is present as HOCl, at pH 8.0 about 26% and at pH 9.0, 3%. For this reason, the toxicity of chlorine is very much reduced at pH values above 8.5. A reduction in temperature also slightly reduces the proportion of hypochlorous acid present.

The literature on the toxicity of chlorine to European freshwater fish and some aquatic invertebrates has been reviewed recently by Alabaster and Lloyd (1980). Salmonid fish appear to be most sensitive to chlorine and for long-term exposure, it is recommended that HOCl concentrations should not exceed 0.004 mg/l. Other species of fish and invertebrates are less sensitive, although the fecundity of *Gammarus pseudolimnaeus* was reduced by long-term exposure to 0.004 mg HOCl/l. Much higher concentrations of chlorine (up to 0.1 mg HOCl/l) can be withstood by both fish and invertebrates for short periods without causing apparent permanent damage, although 1 mg/l can be rapidly fatal. The concentrations in water which contain 0 004 mg HOCl/l are given in Table I.

Apart from effects on the survival of aquatic organisms, chlorine can combine with phenolic compounds in water to form chlorophenols, some of which can produce tainting of fish flesh at concentrations as low as 0.001 mg/l. Where there is a possibility that chlorine may be present at concentrations greater than those given in Table I, the problem can best be overcome, or forestalled, by the installation of an activated carbon filter on the incoming supply. Specialist advice should be sought on the size and capacity of the filter and the frequency of renewal of the activated charcoal in relation to the amount of chlorine and organic matter in the water. Recently, the efficiency of activated carbon filters in removing chlorine from water has been questioned (Seegert and Brooks, 1978) and it is possible that ultraviolet (UV) light could be superior in some instances. Ultraviolet light would also have the additional benefit of sterilizing the water supply.

Table I. Concentrations of free chlorine in water which correspond to 0.004 mg HOCl/l.

Temperature °C	pH			
	6	7	8	9
5	0.004	0.005	0.011	0.075
25	0.004	0.005	0.016	0.121

In those circumstances where only small volumes of water are required at infrequent intervals, a less expensive remedy might be to add sufficient sodium thiosulphate to the water to react with the chlorine present. The organic matter in the aquarium itself will also react with a small quantity of chlorine and so reduce the possible hazard. In some cases, sodium bisulphite or sodium dioxide are added to potable water in order to remove excess chlorination after sterilization; both these compounds are highly toxic to fish and before a potable water supply is used for supplying aquaria, the possible presence of these compounds should be investigated.

In a few water treatment plants, ozone is used as a water sterilant. Although it is more expensive than chlorination; it has some additional advantages. Ozone has a relatively short life in water and after about $\frac{1}{2}$ h, organisms coming into contact with it will not be harmed (Ogden, 1970).

III. WATER SUPPLY SYSTEMS

A. Materials used in the Supply System

After abstraction and treatment, water passes to the point where it is used. Considerable changes can occur in the water quality during such passage. Some of the changes can occur from contact with various materials used in the construction of the pipelines, in storage facilities and in the aquaria themselves; these are described in detail in Chapter 6. Freshwater supplies are most likely to be affected by metal pipes, galvanized iron, copper and lead, but asbestos-cement and cement-lined iron pipes have also caused problems in soft water (Sprague, 1964). Whenever possible, water should not be allowed to come into contact with such surfaces, and non-toxic plastic pipes should be substituted. It must be stressed that aquatic organisms may be much more sensitive to dissolved heavy metals than man, so that water safe for human consumption may not be suitable for aquatic life. Also, at concentrations close to lethal levels, the toxicities of chemicals to fish are usually additive, so that lethal mixtures can be produced although the individual chemicals may be below lethal concentrations.

B. Control of Biological Growth in Pipes

Because most water supplies contain nutrients in solution, the water mains can become coated on the inside with saprophytic growths and some species of invertebrates. The problem can be severe in mains which supply untreated water abstracted from rivers which carry a high organic load. The growth of zebra mussels and sponges can considerably reduce the effective internal diameter of the pipeline (Clark, 1952). Control of microbiological and invertebrate communities is usually achieved by chlorination. In at least one area of the UK, problems have occurred with colonies of chironomid midge larvae in mains supplying treated water; partial control is achieved by addition of natural or synthetic pyrethrums to the water as it enters the supply mains, every spring and autumn. The concentration of insecticide used is lethal to sensitive species of fish as well as to the midge larvae, and aquarists in the area are warned when treatment is about to begin.

Enquiries should be made of the water supply company about the use of biocides to control such infestations in the mains, and appropriate action taken. Chlorine and pyrethrum may both be removed by activated carbon filters.

C. Increase in Temperature

A considerable increase in temperature may occur during the cold season between the point of abstraction and the aquarium. Much of this temperature increase may occur within the building housing the aquarium, especially if it is heated. Such temperature increases are not necessarily unacceptable unless the limit for cold water species is exceeded but problems may occur if the water becomes supersaturated with dissolved gas especially if the rise is greater than $10°C$. Problems of supersaturation and their remedies have been described earlier.

D. Dissolved Oxygen

It is unlikely that the dissolved oxygen content of a treated water supply will be reduced significantly while passing through the mains; any deficiency would probably be derived from low dissolved oxygen concentrations at the source. However, raw water supplies abstracted from organically polluted waters can, in extreme cases, become anaerobic, with the formation of hydrogen sulphide. Such sources should not be used for aquarium supply unless continuous vigorous aeration can be guaranteed.

E. Artificial Water Supply

In those areas where the only convenient sources of water are unsuitable for aquarium use because of the presence of harmful chemicals or unacceptable fluctuations in ionic composition, it may be necessary to use an artificial water supply. This is achieved simply by de-ionizing the water and adding measured quantities of salts to restore a near-natural ionic composition. Commercial de-ionizing plants are readily available and not too expensive to operate. It should be remembered that if sodium carbonate is used to regenerate the anionic exchange resin, the de-ionized water will contain a high concentration of free carbon dioxide which will have to be reduced by aeration to below 20 mg/l before delivery to the aquarium. At some stage, the water should be passed through an activated carbon filter if harmful concentrations of free chlorine or organic substances are likely to be present.

If large quantities of water are required, some saving in cost can be achieved by first passing the water through a calcium/sodium exchange resin, followed by filtration through a reverse osmosis unit which can remove up to 90% of the dissolved salts. Prior water softening is essential since calcium can block the membrane pores. The water can then be deionized by ionic exchange resins which, because of the reduced ionic content of the feed water, need less frequent regeneration. Salts can then be added automatically to obtain the required ionic composition in the water. A system based on this principle has been recently described by Slooff, Rab and Spierenburg (1978).

Several recipes for reconstituted water have been published; one is given below (ASTM, 1962):

(1) Stock Solution 1: Dissolve 71.0 g $MgSO_4.7H_2O$, 6.5 g K_2SO_4, and 0.2 g $MnSO_4.4H_2O$ in water and dilute to 1 litre.

(2) Stock Solution 2: Dissolve 18.6 g $CaCl_2.H_2O$ in water and dilute to 1 litre.

(3) Stock Solution 3: Dissolve 25.0 g $NaHCO_3$, 3.0 g NH_4NO_3, and 1.1 g $K_2HPO_4.3H_2O$ in water and dilute to 1 litre.

(4) Stock Solution 4: Dissolve 32.2 g CaO in water and dilute to 1 litre. Bubble CO_2 gas through this mixture to make a $CaCO_3$ slurry.

(5) Stock Solution 5: Dissolve 62.6 g $Na_2SiO_3.9H_2O$ in water and dilute to 1 litre.

(6) Stock Solution 6: Dissolve 1.2 g $FeCl_3.6H_2O$ in water and dilute to 1 litre.

For each litre of standard reference water to be prepared, add 1 ml each of solutions 1, 2 and 3. Disperse pure CO_2 gas into this solution by means of a gas diffuser for 15 min. The pH of the solution at this point should be about 4.3. Add 1 ml of solution 4 to each litre of standard reference water and introduce CO_2 gas until the solution becomes clear. The pH at this point should be about 5.1. Then diffuse compressed air through the solution for 25 min to raise the pH to about 7.9. Add 1 ml each of solutions 5 and 6 to each litre of water and aerate for 60 min. The final pH of 7.9 remains constant within 0.1 pH units.

IV. CHANGES IN WATER QUALITY WITHIN THE AQUARIUM

Water quality changes within the aquarium system can arise from two major sources: materials and techniques used in the aquarium design and construction, and from the aquatic organisms themselves. Problems which can be encountered from the first source are described fully in Chapter 6.

Aquatic organisms can have a major effect on the quality of the water. Production of faeces is an obvious source of pollution and should not be allowed to build up in the aquarium; proper aquarium design and maintenance can reduce this concentration of organic matter which may consume oxygen and also form a substrate for potentially pathogenic bacteria and fungi. The consumption of oxygen by the organism and concomitant production of carbon dioxide can be balanced by the provision of aeration. The two remaining potential problems arise from the excretion of nitrogenous wastes. Ammonia is the common form in which nitrogen is excreted by freshwater organisms as a metabolic end-product. Normally, the ammonia is oxidized to nitrite and then to nitrate which is relatively non-toxic; ammonia and nitrite toxicity will be considered separately.

A. Aeration

Where the dissolved oxygen in the incoming water, or the rate of surface aeration is insufficient to meet the oxygen requirements of the aquatic organisms present, extra oxygen has to be supplied.

For small aquarium units, there is a range of miniature air compressors designed for ornamental systems and these are suitable providing they are robust and reliable for extended use. Compressed air cylinders can be useful in areas where there is no power, but otherwise they can be expensive. For larger, more extensive aquarium systems, an industrial air compressor should be used in conjunction with a high pressure reservoir tank. The commonest form of air diffuser is a porous block of stone which breaks the air flow up into fine bubbles. These are cheap and effective, but in very hard waters, they can become blocked due to deposition of calcium carbonate in the pores, and have to be replaced at intervals. All joints between the air compressor and the diffuser stones should be firmly secured; the air pressure in the tube leading to the aeration stone should not exceed 10 lb/in^2 and ideally should be within the range 3–5 lb/in^2.

Air compressors provide few problems. Care must be taken to absorb any oil which may reach the air supply lines and efficient oil filters should be fitted. Care must also be taken to site the air intake where the air is not liable to contamination. For example, a series of unexplained mortalities of fish at weekends during wintertime was thought to be caused by the siting of the air inlets in a coke-fired central heating boiler house; the coke fires were "damped down" at the weekend and the atmosphere became contaminated with fumes, including carbon monoxide. The air intakes were resited and fish no longer died.

Most air compressors are driven by electric motors and failures should be infrequent. Furthermore, many large buildings have standby generators which operate in the event of a failure in the electricity supply. However, because aquaria with a high biomass and low incoming water flow can become rapidly anaerobic when the aeration system fails, a useful safeguard is to have a cylinder of compressed air connected into the air supply line. This system requires that the cylinder head reducing valve is of a design which does not allow the outlet gas pressure to rise above the value set. Thus, if the main air supply line pressure is set at 5 lb/in^2, the outlet gas pressure of the cylinder is set at 3 lb/in^2. A non-return air valve is incorporated into the air supply line upstream of the cylinder input. If the air pressure in the supply line falls to below 3 lb/in^2, the air in the cylinder is released and aeration to the aquarium is maintained. A similar system can be used with multiple banks of compressed gas cylinders; the cylinder-head reducing valves are set at, for example, 15, 12, 9 and 6 lb/in^2 respectively, with a final pressure-reducing valve in the air supply line to maintain the final delivery pressure at 5 lb/in^2. With such a system, the gas cylinders exhaust in sequence, the ones with the highest set outlet pressure emptying first, followed by the second highest. Empty cylinders can then be replaced with minimum wastage of gas.

Although most aquatic animals can survive without harm in water containing less than the ASV of dissolved oxygen, it is very difficult to balance the incoming supply of oxygen (either in the water flow or from air diffusers) against the respiratory demand to provide a sub-saturation oxygen equilibrium. The margin for error is usually so small that it is safer to provide excess aeration and so maintain the dissolved oxygen concentration close to the ASV. It is sometimes necessary to aerate the incoming water before introducing it into the tank, either to maintain the water at the ASV of dissolved oxygen, or by aeration with a mixture of air and nitrogen, to maintain a sub-saturation concentration. A common method of achieving such dissolved oxygen control is to pass the water down a column up which gas is bubbled from an aerator at the base. Gas exchange is thus achieved on a counter current principle. However, if the aeration column is long (>3 m) the water may become saturated with dissolved gas at a pressure higher than that in the aquarium and supersaturation may then occur, especially if the water in the aquarium is subsequently heated without further aeration. Packing the column with a high surface-area medium and allowing the water to trickle over it is one solution; the depth of water at the bottom of the column should not exceed the depth of the aquarium.

B. Ammonia

Ammonia production by aquatic animals is usually a problem only in aquaria containing a high density of organisms and where the water flow is insufficient to remove the waste products at a sufficient rate.

The toxicity of ammonia to aquatic organisms is complicated because it dissociates in water to form an equilibrium between ionized ammonia (NH_4^+) which is thought to have a low toxicity, and non-ionized ammonia (NH_3) which is the toxic form. The proportion of the toxic non-ionized ammonia in an ammonia solution increases as the pH of the water becomes more alkaline and also increases with a rise in temperature. Therefore, ammonia is more toxic in warm alkaline water than in cold acid water. From the considerable volume of experimental data on the toxicity of ammonia to freshwater fish, it would seem that there is little difference between the sensitivity of different species to this pollutant, and it is generally accepted that the maximum safe concentration of non-ionized ammonia is 0.025 mg NH_3/l (Alabaster and Lloyd, 1980). Concentrations of total ammonia which contain this amount of non-ionized ammonia, for a range of temperature and pH, are given in Table II.

Table II. Concentrations of total ammonia ($NH_3 + NH_4^+$) which contain 0.025 mg NH_3/l, for a range of temperatures and pH.

Temperature	pH			
	7.0	7.5	8.0	8.5
5	19.6	6.3	2.0	0.65
10	13.4	4.3	1.4	0.45
15	9.1	2.9	0.93	0.31
20	6.3	2.0	0.65	0.22
25	4.4	1.4	0.47	0.17
30	3.1	1.0	0.33	0.12

Fish, and possibly other aquatic organisms, become more sensitive to non-ionized ammonia as the dissolved oxygen concentration of the water is reduced below the ASV, but if such a reduction is accompanied by a rise in carbon dioxide concentrations (and this usually occurs), the concomitant reduction in pH causes the ammonia to become less toxic.

The reverse occurs if the aquarium contains green plants; active photosynthesis increases the dissolved oxygen content of the water, but the carbon dioxide concentration is reduced and the pH rises, thus making the ammonia more toxic. A further complication is that fish, and possibly other aquatic organisms, can become acclimatized to sub-lethal concentrations of non-ionized ammonia. For example, fish reared under conditions of intensive culture can withstand up to four times the ammonia concentration shown in Table II. It is possible that non-ionized ammonia may be more toxic to fish in cold water ($<8°C$) but there is little information on this point. In general, freshwater invertebrates are more resistant than fish to non-ionized ammonia, although *Daphnia magna* is only slightly more resistant than rainbow trout.

A build-up of ammonia concentrations can be avoided by maintaining sufficient water flow through the aquaria, but where this is not possible, or where a recirculation system is used to conserve warmed water, a biological filter may be needed to facilitate nitrification. Nitrifying bacteria live on surfaces, so a filter with a large surface area is required. One of the problems with downward-flow filters containing sand is that faeces and other waste matter can block the surface, thus impeding water flow. Recent research has shown that upward-flow sand filters, in which the sand grains are maintained in semi-suspension, are highly efficient for oxidizing ammonia (Short, 1975) since there is no channelling of water through the filter bed, and the surface area of each sand grain is utilized. A filter of this design has the additional advantage that it is less liable to become blocked by solid wastes.

C. Nitrite

Compared with ammonia, the potential harmfulness of nitrite has received little attention. However, recent studies on fish kept in intensive culture systems with recirculated water have shown that harmful concentrations of nitrite can be formed. For salmonid species, concentrations above 0.1 mg NO_2/l as N can be harmful, but other fish species may be more resistant. Nitrite causes the formation of methaemoglobin in the blood and consequent loss of respiratory efficiency although another as yet unknown, toxic action may be the cause of death (Crawford and Allen, 1977).

It appears that when a nitrifying flora is being built up on a biological filter, the *Nitrosomonas* bacteria become established first, so that ammonia is oxidized to nitrite, whereas the *Nitrobacter* bacteria which oxidize nitrite to nitrate become established more slowly. Therefore, in a new biological filter, conditions may occur during the first few weeks where the nitrite concentration can be high. Presumably, this would also occur in any enclosed aquarium system in which a natural nitrifying flora was being built up. One possible solution to this problem may be to maintain a lower animal population density in the aquarium while the nitrifying flora was becoming established, thereby reducing the rate of ammonia production.

V. SUMMARY

The lessons to be drawn from this chapter are clear. In setting up a freshwater aquarium, the water supply should be traced to its source, and information obtained on its physical and chemical quality, together with possible causes of variation in quality. Every intermediate stage between source and final supply to the aquarium and within the aquarium itself, should be examined for potential contributions of pollutants or other adverse water quality characteristics. A similar examination should be given to any air supply. Almost certainly, some problems will be encountered which have not been described in this chapter, but it is hoped that the description of the various potential sources of trouble will help find the cause.

VI. REFERENCES

Alabaster, J. S. and F. S. H. Abram (1965). Estimating the toxicity of pesticides to fish. *Pest Articles and News Summaries (C)* **11**, 91–97.

Alabaster, J. S. and R. Lloyd (eds), (1980). "Water Quality Criteria for Freshwater Fish", Butterworths, London.

ASTM (1962). "Standard method of test for evaluating acute toxicity of industrial waste water to freshwater fishes. Manual on Industrial Water and Industrial Waste". ASTM Publication D1345–59, 2nd ed. 500–508.

Clarke, K. B. (1952). The infestation of waterworks by *Dreissensia polymorpha*, a freshwater mussel. *Journal of the Institute of Water Engineers* **6**, 370–378.

Crawford, R. W. and G. H. Allen (1977). Seawater inhibition of nitrite toxicity to chinook salmon. *Trans. American Fisheries Society* **106**, 105–109.

D'Aoust, B. G., White, R. and H. Seibold (1976). An electronic monitor for total dissolved gas pressure. In "Gas Bubble Disease" (D. H. Ficheisen and M. J. Schneider, eds), Technical Information Center; Office of Public Affairs, Energy Research and Development Administration, USA, CONF–741033, pp. 106–110.

EIFAC (1975). Report on fish toxicity testing procedures. EIFAC Tech. Pap. **24**, FAO, Rome.

Fickeisen, D. H. and M. J. Schneider (1976). "Gas Bubble Disease". Technical Information Center, Office of Public Affairs, Energy Research and Development Administration, USA, CONF-741033.

Leivestad, H. and Muniz, I. P. (1976). Fish kill at low pH in a Norwegian river. *Nature, London* **259**, 391–392.

McIntosh, A. W. (1975). Fate of copper in ponds. *Pesticides Monitoring Journal* **8**, 225–231.

Ogden, M. (1970). Ozonation today. *Industrial Water Engineering* **June 1970**, 36–42.

Seegert, G. L. and A. S. Brooks (1978). Dechlorination of water for fish culture: Comparison of the activated carbon, sulphite reduction, and photo chemical methods. *Journal of the Fisheries Research Board of Canada* **35**, 88–92.

Short, C. S. (1975). Removal of ammonia from river water. Water Research Centre UK Technical Report 3.

Sloof, W., Rab, E. and T. P. Spierenburg (1978). Continuous standard water delivery system for bioassays with aquatic organisms. *Progressive Fish Culturalist* **40**, 112–114.

Sprague, J. B. (1964). Highly alkaline water caused by asbestos-cement pipeline. *Progressive Fish Culturalist* **26**, 111–114.

Train, R. E. (1979). Quality criteria for water. Castle House Publications Ltd.

Tuwiner, S. B. (1976). Copper sulphate helps control microorganisms in reservoirs. *Water and Sewage Works* **123**, 68–70.

US EPA (1972). Water Quality Criteria 1972. NAS/NAE, Washington DC. EPA. R3.73.033.50.

Chapter 5

Small Aquaria

D. Ford

Animal Studies Centre, Melton Mowbray, England

I. INTRODUCTION

Much research is performed with small species of fish kept in self-contained aquarium tanks in general laboratories. Many different fish are suitable and available, some of them reared for generations in tanks or under laboratory conditions. Such fish can often be kept at high densities without expensive equipment and are to the fish biologist, what the common rat is to the mammalian biologist. This chapter describes the small-scale aquarium, whether a single temporary tank on the laboratory bench, or a complete aquarium laboratory with tanks containing many different species.

II. SITING THE TANKS

Though the small aquarium may range from a single tank, established for a particular experiment, to the much larger installation, the problems of siting are essentially the same. The tanks should be placed on a firm and substantial base, in a position where the fish will not be stimulated by extraneous noises or other physical disturbances. They should be away from doors or equipment such as vacuum pumps or typewriters, which may vibrate the bench or floor. Ideally, the fish should be maintained under a controlled regime of lighting and temperature, which is best obtained by keeping them in a room set aside for the purpose. Where fish must be kept in an ordinary room, it is best to place the tank on a separate plinth or stand away from the window, preferably in a corner. Extraneous stimuli can be reduced by enclosing the corner of the room with a plywood screen.

If the laboratory is a complete fish house, serving no other function, the tanks can be mounted on stands around the periphery with a central island filled with the normal laboratory benches, drawers, cupboards and services. Any office facilities or electronic equipment are best kept separate, or partitioned-off from the part of the room containing the fish. Commonly, the fish are kept for a specific purpose, for example to monitor water quality for a factory, and in this case it is often sensible to remove the fish from the main building and place them in a shed or annex where they will not be disturbed. Basic services which should be included in the unit are a clean water supply, drainage, an electricity supply and bench and cupboard space.

III. EQUIPPING THE AQUARIUM

Each item of aquarium equipment is available in many forms, and choice must depend on purpose and budget.

A. The Tank

The traditional aquarium that has existed for many years has a rectangular iron frame with glass sides embedded in putty. This design is heavy even when empty, readily corrodes and tends to leak if moved or if the water level is changed. The putty dries out with age resulting in minor leaks that are difficult to seal without emptying the tank. However, many of these older tanks are available second-hand. If the laboratory is on a tight budget, banks of these tanks may be installed at low cost. Local newspapers often advertize complete aquaria at very low prices when some houseowner wishes to dispose of an ageing set-up.

The leaking problem can be overcome by sealing the internal corners with a silicone sealer. Any bare metal must be primed with a non-toxic paint and given several coats of a good quality polyurethane paint. Such metal framed tanks are not really suitable for sea water but may be pressed into service if the painting and silicone sealing is meticulously carried out. There must be no physical contact between sea water and any bare metal or putty. High quality stainless steel frames are excellent for all types of aquaria. However, if putty is used, the inside corners must be silicone-sealed for sea water usage.

Some modern tanks have metal frames sealed with a nylon or polyurethane coating prior to glazing. These tanks are suitable for all uses, but again if putty is used, the inside corners must be silicone sealed for sea water. Nylon coatings on frames and stands generally outlast polyurethane, the latter tending to crack after a year or so. With the introduction of aquaria made from glass sheet, bonded with silicone sealer, decorative frames made from lightweight alloy, aluminium or plastic have been marketed. All are suitable for laboratory use, but the usual precautions are necessary to ensure that sea water does not directly contact metallic frames.

All-plastic tanks have been popular in recent years because they are non-toxic, light and require no maintenance. The rising cost of plastics, however, has made these tanks expensive and some manufacturers have changed back to glass. Small plastic tanks (2–60 litres) manufactured from a single mould, are useful for handling fry and for quarantine and treatment purposes. A problem with plastic tanks is that the surface can be easily scratched making the sides opaque, so abrasive cleaning materials must be avoided.

Other non-glass aquaria can be virtually any container that is stable and non-toxic. In emergencies, a wooden or strong cardboard box can be lined with a large polythene bag. Polystyrene boxes, plastic baby-baths, even plastic dustbins can be used. Partly glazed aquaria can be made from asbestos, concrete or wood. Marine ply sheets can be pinned and screwed into large aquaria at much lower cost than the all-glass aquaria. These wooden tanks need a liberal coating of glass-fibre reinforced resin internally, to render them water-tight and non-toxic, especially for sea water. Such tanks should have a cutaway section at the front for glazing with a suitable thickness of glass. In all cases, the glazing can be done with silicone sealer.

The ideal tank is probably the all-glass silicone-sealed unit. This is simply a glass box and can range in size from 10 to 2000 litres. Small tanks of up to 100 litres can be made from glass of 4 mm thickness, but 6 mm glass is preferable. The front, back and base can be 6 mm thick with the side 4 mm. For tanks of more than 100 litres capacity, 6 mm glass should be used throughout, while for tanks of more than 200 litres, 10 mm glass is necessary. Large aquaria of 1000 litres need 20 mm glass which must usually be specifically ordered. Small tanks can be made from clear glass sheet, but for larger tanks with thicker glass, polished or floated plate glass is better for distortion-free viewing. In older tanks, the base may be slate and the rear may be the cheaper pebble or reinforced glass, mounted in a steel frame. These materials are not suitable for silicone-sealing since the strength of the join is achieved by using very clean, polished, flush-fitting joints. The reverse face of a pebble glass may sometimes be smooth enough to serve, however.

Silicone sealer can be obtained in small tubes or cartridges, the latter requiring a specially designed caulking gun. Glass should be bought in a cut and polished state and the edges cleaned with acetone or a degreasing agent prior to sealing. Some manufacturers of silicone sealer supply details of tank construction with their products. The hobby press often publishes articles on all-glass tank manufacture. An internal bead of silicone sealer adds to the strength of joints, but the silicone rubber is easily cut by sharp objects and tank cleaners such as razor blades or metal scrapers should not be used. The sealer sets in one hour but full strength is not achieved for 48 h. During the setting stage, the sealer produces acetic acid and any residue must be flushed away with water. Silicone sealer will not work with plastic sheet since it will not form a water-tight seal. Specially shaped tanks can be made from Perspex, Lucite, Darvic or similar materials. Perspex needs a solvent adhesive but the thermosetting plastics may be welded.

The size of the tanks should be carefully considered prior to installation. If only one technician is available, the largest tank he can comfortably handle is $80 \times 35 \times 30$ cm $(30 \times 15 \times 12$ in). On the other hand, the larger the tank, the easier is the maintenance. Uniformity of size will make measurements easier since aquarium posology (dosage levels) can be standardized. Another advantage is that all the accessories are interchangeable. If second-hand tanks are used, they will probably be based on Imperial linear units in the UK or USA. European and contemporary tanks are measured in metric units (aquaria sizes are usually quoted in centimetres) which gives a greater variety of tanks sizes. Traditional sizes are listed in Table I.

Table I. Traditional aquarium sizes. The water volumes are for furnished tanks in the presence of gravel, rocks, plants, etc.

| | Imperial | | Metric | |
| | U.K. | U.S.A. | | |
Inches	Gallons	Gallons	cm	Litres
$7 \times 5 \times 5$	$\frac{1}{2}$	$\frac{1}{2}$	$30 \times 20 \times 20$	10
$12 \times 6 \times 10$	$1\frac{1}{2}$	$1\frac{1}{4}$	$60 \times 35 \times 37$	60
$18 \times 10 \times 10$	6	5	$80 \times 35 \times 41$	90
$20 \times 10 \times 12$	9	$7\frac{1}{2}$	$100 \times 40 \times 41$	120
$24 \times 12 \times 12$	12	10	$100 \times 42 \times 50$	150
$30 \times 15 \times 12$	16	13	$135 \times 42 \times 53$	200
$36 \times 15 \times 12$	20	17	$140 \times 42 \times 53$	220
$48 \times 15 \times 12$	43	36	$150 \times 42 \times 53$	250

A full aquarium is very heavy and adequate support is essential, not only the aquarium stand, but also the floor beneath it must be strong. The water pressure within the tank is a function of height, and a tank one metre or more deep needs a supporting frame, which adds to the overall weight. The average hobbyist's aquarium of $24 \times 12 \times 12$ in (about $60 \times 30 \times 30$ cm) with accessories and full of water weighs almost 90 kg (200 lb). The traditional angle-iron stand is adequate for vertical banks of 1, 2 or 3 tanks and is available from most domestic aquarium suppliers. Custom-built stands can be made from strong timber or Dexion-style fittings. To compensate for inequalities in such stands, especially with all-glass tanks, a buffer of expanded polystyrene is necessary. Kitchen ceiling tiles are ideal. With sea water aquaria, iron or galvanized stands will corrode (see Chapter 6). Painting or coating with epoxy resin is rarely satisfactory. Plastic coating is expensive and may crack in time. Nylon coating is effective if correctly applied by the hot-dip process. The most suitable cheaper alternative is to use timber frames that can be replaced when the wood rots.

All tanks must be emptied before being moved. Even a little water can slop about within a tank and build up a twisting torque that can crack the glass or cause a leak.

Every tank must have a top cover otherwise dust can get in, the fish may leap out and heavy evaporation losses will be suffered. A simple sheet of glass or plastic is sufficient. The glass may be 3 or 4 mm (window glass) but rigid plastic of this thickness will sag with age and some support is necessary, one method being to drill and screw the centre line to a suitable length of timber. The cover may rest on the top of the aquarium, but a better system is to arrange flush fitting within the tank. This ensures condensation returns to the tank rather than running down the outside. With framed tanks, stainless steel or plastic clips designed to hold coverglasses within the tank can be bought from most pet shops. With all-glass tanks, supporting strips of glass or vitrolite can be silicone-sealed into place inside the tanks. These can support plastic runners for cupboard doors. The coverglass can then be cut into overlapping halves that slide within the runners to give easy access for feeding and maintenance. Manufactured covers are available for most standard sized tanks and these will accept overhead lights and are close fitting.

The bottom of the tank should always be covered so that the fish can orientate properly. Hobbyists cover the base with a gravel of split pea size (5 mm), usually spread over a plastic undergravel, air-lift operated, filter. For reasons detailed later, undergravel filters are best avoided. Without such filtration, a smaller sized gravel may be employed; this is better for plant roots and individual stones are less likely to block the mouths of sucking feeders such as goldfish. A type called bird's-eye gravel (about 2 mm) is ideal. Sand is a possible medium but can be too fine and compaction may occur. Compact sand can give rise to anaerobic conditions and may therefore pose pollution problems.

B. Heaters, Thermostats and Thermometers

The average laboratory temperature is too low for most tropical freshwater and marine specimens, so additional heating is necessary. The standard glass-sheathed equipment produced for the hobby trade is ideal. It is possible to have a master thermostat controlling a series of heaters in a bank of tanks. However, it is preferable for each tank to have its own heater and thermostat since this will minimize losses in the event of failure. The simplest form is a combined heater and thermostat wired for direct mains supply. Separate thermostats can be purchased and of these the outside fitting variety is more accessible for adjustment. Wattages for heating tanks are not critical but Table II is a guide.

Table II. Heater wattages for tanks of different size.

Metric (cm)	Imperial (in)	Wattage required
45 × 25 × 25	18 × 10 × 10	25 to 50
60 × 30 × 30	24 × 12 × 12	75
90 × 40 × 45	36 × 15 × 18	100 or 2 × 60
120 × 40 × 45	48 × 15 × 18	150 or 2 × 100
180 × 45 × 60	72 × 18 × 24	2 × 150 or 3 × 100

A combined heater/thermostat should be sited according to the manufacturer's instructions, usually vertically in a rear corner. If an aerator is placed near the instrument, the water flow helps dissipate the heat. A separate heater may be placed horizontally on the gravel; this position aids convection. Extra long heaters are available which have a low heat content per unit area. This allows the heater to be buried beneath the gravel without the danger of the glass cracking. The advantage is only an aesthetic one, however. For a similar reason, there are undergravel flexible heaters and under-tank heating blocks available, but the standard heating element in a glass tube is recommended for ease of use and maintenance. (To meet electrical regulations in many countries, these heaters are now double insulated, usually by an internal or external metallic sheath or external PTFE sheath.)

Duplicate or multiple heaters have the advantage of spreading the heating effect throughout a large tank. The heaters should be wired in parallel, with electrical connections outside the tanks, well-insulated against condensation or accidental spillage of water. Ceramic or plastic block connectors, sealed with a smear of silicone sealer and wrapped in PVC insulating tape are recommended. It should be stressed, however, that electrical insulation is extremely important in a fish house and the advice of a qualified electrician should be sought. This is particularly important with marine tanks where salt crusts develop with age; these creep away from the tank on any surface and work into the electrical connections giving rapid corrosion and electrical short-circuits. For the lighting circuit of a marine tank, the author runs a cable through polythene tubing sealed with silicone sealer at the connection to a fluorescent tube and at a point at least a metre away from the tank.

Some fish-breeding establishments avoid the high cost of direct electrical heating of the water by heating the space surrounding the tanks to a temperature of 25°C. The heating may be by steam pipes, the tanks being placed directly above the pipes to give good heat transfer. Other techniques include space heating with paraffin heaters or electric fan heaters. Such methods may have low running costs but a high ambient temperature is unpleasant for staff to work in.

Each tank needs a thermometer to monitor the water temperature. The cheap hobbyist thermometer is notoriously inaccurate and a mercury-in-glass chemical thermometer is preferable. Some aggressive species of fish may break such thermometers and the temperature in this case can be monitored with a liquid-crystal digital thermometer. The latter will adhere to the outside of the glass and though the reading may be a degree or so low, the error is consistent. The temperature of the water involved in water changes or fish transfers should always be checked with a thermometer because rapid temperature changes will severely stress the fish.

C. Aeration

Continuous aeration is very good husbandry since it mixes the water, supplies oxygen for the fish, and removes carbon dioxide. It is only unnecessary where stocking levels are very low; on the other hand, it should not be relied upon to support high stocking levels because of the danger in even temporary failure. Many cheap airpumps are available in the hobby trade, though they are often noisy, are of limited power and may frequently fail. If only one or two tanks are required, such small vibratory diaphragm pumps are acceptable, but a spare pump and several replacement diaphragms should be stocked. The pump should be mounted above the tank level or the air-line fitted with a non-return valve to prevent back-siphoning when the pump is stopped or fails. A loop in the air-line 8 cm (3 in) vertically above the tank's water level will also prevent back-siphoning by absorbing the oscillations when the air-flow stops. With banks of aquaria, one or more large air-pumps or preferably a compressor can be used. To give a uniform rate of airflow, the pump should operate a pressure line in a closed circuit system with individual airlines to each tank.

D. Filtration

The undergravel filter used by the hobbyist is best avoided because it retains waste materials within the tank and the water flow through the gravel adversely affects aquatic plants. Gross material can be removed by operating one or more corner or box filters containing polyester filterwool. Glasswool must not be used because irritant glass splinters can be released into the tank; cottonwool is also to be avoided because this will quickly rot and pollute the water. Several models of box filter are available; all are operated by air lifts. To clarify the water, a diatomaceous-earth filter can be used.

These filters consist of a motorized pump that draws water through a glass jar containing a nylon mesh bag. Diatomaceous-earth powder is added to the jar and the water flow coats the nylon bag with the powder. The water then has to pass through the powder which within an hour or two will "polish" the water to a high clarity. One filter can routinely treat 20 or 30 tanks weekly. A fresh change of diatomaceous-earth is usually required for each tank.

Marine fish require their water to be biologically filtered and on a small scale, this filtration is normally done by means of undergravel filters. A better system is to use an external power filter. The power filter is more efficient than an undergravel one, gives a better water flow within the tank, and can easily be cleaned without disturbing the fish. Any filter medium with a large surface area is suitable, including silica sand, coral sand, gravel, glass beads and various resins. The author favours carbon and polyester wool. The carbon is not included for its adsorptive properties (which are quickly saturated), but for its large surface area. Since biological filtration relies on surface-active nitrifying bacteria the filter medium with the highest surface area will be the most effective. The carbon granules should be packed loosely in a mesh nylon bag, and to prevent them becoming clogged with solids, the bag should be sandwiched between polyester wool which removes gross material and gives a final mechanical filtration before the water flows back into the tank. Table III is a guide to pump sizes that have been shown in practice to keep saltwater nitrite levels near zero.

Table III. Powerfilter sizes for saltwater tanks.

Tank Size	Flow Rates	Examples of filters
Up to 50 l	Over 100 l/h	Eheim No. 2016 Martin No. 300
Up to 200 l	Over 150 l/h	Eheim No. 2018 Martin No. 400 Nuova Turbo Filter
Up to 500 l	Over 300 l/h	Eheim No. 2026 Interpet No. 200
About 1000 l	1000 l/h	Eheim No. 2030 or No. 2034

E. Decoration

Most fish seem to prefer a tank decorated to resemble their natural environment. Even generations of tank-bred fish need some cover, and a bare tank may stress them. Any rocks, pebbles or ornaments placed in the tank must be non-toxic and sterilized with boiling water. Rocks must be lime-free to avoid increasing the water hardness, and should not have sharp edges. Granite, river-washed boulders or rounded lumps of glass are ideal. Aggressive species like many Cichlidae need caves built from rocks to give territories and safe retreats. Many coral-fish need pieces of coral to weave through (these are usually bleached white when sterilized). Sensitive fish such as the Discus need dense plants (real or plastic) to hide in, while burrowing fish like certain wrasses (Labridae) need coral sand of at least 3 cm depth. Even a tank used to house a fish temporarily should have a gravel base and a plastic plant.

To give a better view of the fish, the back glass may be made opaque. An effective method is to cover the outside rear glass with a liberal coating of a white emulsion paint (best applied with the tank lying face down, prior to installation).

F. Lighting

Most fish prefer dim lighting conditions. The bright lighting of the aquarist's display tank is not necessary unless plants are present. Many fish are diurnal in habit, requiring a regular light/dark cycle. For many species, maturation is triggered by changes in the day length. Table IV is a guide to the Wattage for an 8 h period of lighting where plants are present.

Table IV. Light intensity for planted aquaria.

Length of Tank	Wattage of filament bulb	Wattage of fluorescent tube
Up to 50 cm (approximately 18 in.)	40	8
60 cm (approximately 24 in.)	2 × 40	15
75 cm (approximately 30 in.)	2 × 60	20
90 cm (approximately 36 in.)	3 × 40	2 × 20
120 cm (approximately 48 in.)	3 × 60	2 × 30

Larger tanks than those listed in Table IV can be lit by dichroic spotlights mounted over the tanks. The only cover required is then a top-glass. A 2 m long tank can be lit by two 150 W cold running spotlights. Ordinary tungsten filament bulbs are cheaper to buy than fluorescent tubes and heavy starter units are avoided, but the usual sideways mounting of these bulbs in a standard cover gives a short life due to sagging filaments. Lifting the cover while the lamps are lit often breaks the filament. The bulbs also heat the surface of the water to unacceptably high levels for many fish, such as coldwater species or the Anabantidae. The heat can also create condensation problems, but this and the surface heating, can be overcome by placing a glass sheet between the lamps and water, mounted either in the cover or the tank top. The bayonet or screw fitting of the bulb can be protected from condensation by a few inches of tubing cut from a bicycle inner-tube.

Fluorescent tubes have the advantage of being cool and are cheaper to run. The starter unit is best housed on a wall behind the tank rather than on or in the cover. This is is because its heavy weight creates a danger of the whole lid falling into the water if dislodged. Spring clips will hold the tubes in the lids but these must be of stainless steel or nylon-coated steel. Electrical connections can be smeared with silicone sealer.

Domestic wiring is sufficient for all normal aquaria and hence a wide range of readily available accessories can be used. Each tank may be lit from a universal ring main or all the tanks may be lit from a single circuit with a masterswitch that can be controlled by a timer. With the latter, overide switches should be fitted to allow individual tanks to be switched off. The lighting of individual tanks can, of course, be controlled by a separate timer if required.

G. Electricity Supply

A ring main of sufficient amperage should be available to operate the banks of aquaria. The average tank described earlier has a rating of 0.5 amp, but to allow for surges, a rating of 1 amp should be used in calculations. The wiring from the ring main should be via a suitable socket outlet for each unit of 1, 2 or 3 tanks. This will allow one tank, or unit, to be electrically isolated before any handling. A lead of 3 amp, 3 core, domestic cable can be taken from the socket and plug to a junction box near the tanks. The hobby trade sell junction boxes under the name "cable-tidy". This junction box in turn feeds the thermostat, heater, lights, pump and power filter as required. External parts can be earthed, including the frame of the tank and the stand, if these are made from metal. The water itself should preferably not have an earth connection because of the danger of corrosion of the metal and subsequent pollution.

Where it is necessary to earth the water (perhaps to eliminate mains hum from any electronic monitoring equipment in the tank), then highly toxic metals such as copper and brass must be avoided. Steel may be used in freshwater though any rusting is unsightly. An ideal earth for all aquaria is a carbon rod (e.g. taken from a dry cell). Electrical safety regulations of most countries will soon require all electrical accessories to be double insulated. An ideal arrangement for a tropical fresh water tank is shown in Fig. 1.

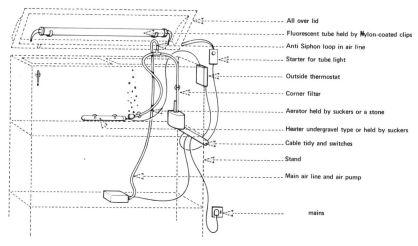

All over lid

Fluorescent tube held by Nylon-coated clips

Anti Siphon loop in air line

Starter for tube light

Outside thermostat

Corner filter

Aerator held by suckers or a stone

Heater undergravel type or held by suckers

Cable tidy and switches

Stand

Main air line and air pump

mains

Fig. 1. The well-appointed tropical fish tank.

IV. SETTING UP THE TANK

A. Installation

Wash the tank with water and a disinfectant that does not contain detergent (e.g. sodium hypochlorite or potassium permanganate solutions). Strong soap or detergents are highly toxic to fish and should not be used in case traces are left in the aquarium. Place the tank in position and add any gravel or sand. This must previously be thoroughly washed to prevent fine material clouding the water. The best method is to half fill a bucket with the gravel or sand, push a hosepipe to the bottom and flush with running water until the overflow is clear.

Add the ornaments, accessories, cables and tubing. Plastic suckers are available to aid mounting, but the suction tends to fail with time, so an acrylic resin or silicone sealer can be used to fix the suckers permanently in position. Fill with water using a dish to spread the water flow and prevent it disturbing the substrate. If a plastic garden hose is used, it must be flushed to waste for a short while to prevent any of the toxic plasticizer contained within the coils entering the tank.

B. Water

Water quality must be tested and adjusted to optimal values for the chosen species of fish. Tapwater is for drinking, not for keeping fish. It is sterile, chlorinated, sometimes fluoridated and often very hard and alkaline. Most tropical species require soft, slightly acid, biologically active water. Chlorine may be removed from tapwater by adding a few drops of 1% sodium or potassium thiosulphate solution or by leaving the water to mature for a day or two, especially with strong aeration. Hardness can be reduced by adding de-ionized or preferably distilled water.

The pH can be lowered by adding sodium dihydrogen orthophosphate (NaH_2PO_4) and acidic water can be neutralized with sodium bicarbonate $(NaHCO_3)$. An ideal water source is rainwater, provided that industrial air-pollution is not present. The collecting area must also be non-toxic and the water stored in the dark and kept covered to prevent infestation. Pond and river waters may introduce parasites and disease.

Some fish require hard, alkaline waters (e.g. some Cichlidae) and crushed cockleshell, dolomite or marble chips may be added to the substrate to help maintain these conditions. Other fish need some sodium chloride (e.g. many *Poecilia sp.*). Seasalt, rocksalt or even A.R. sodium chloride can be used, but not table salt because iodine (as an iodide) and/or flow agents such as magnesium carbonate have often been added.

Once the ideal chemical balance has been achieved, it must be monitored and maintained, particularly during routine water changes. Sudden changes in the chemical equilibrium will stress the fish. The water can be biologically matured by seeding with water from an established tank or pond or rainwater tub, providing disease or parasites are not present. Proprietary water conditioners are available for new aquarium water. These contain buffers and chelating agents and may reduce any inflammation of the fish's gills resulting from dissolved substances such as metallic ions.

Fish should be introduced over several days, or even weeks. The tank is then well understocked during the critical period of maturation. The fish's excreta (ammonia, urea and faecal matter) will encourage bacteria to develop, which in turn "softens" the water and makes it more suitable for the fish. Eventually a balance is set up between fish and water that can be maintained by frequent but partial water changes. Twenty per cent weekly has proved to be the optimum in the author's laboratory. Since each aquarium is practically a closed system, this partial water change is important to dilute the steady build-up of dissolved solids.

Various alternative sources of sea water are described in Chapter 2, but remember that synthetic sea water has to mature. This process is easily monitored by testing the nitrite (NO_2^-) concentration. Colorimetric equipment is available from laboratory suppliers, and kits are available from pet shops.

The ammonia and consequent nitrite are converted to the much less toxic nitrate (NO_3^-) ion by denitrifying bacteria that develop in the filter system, so to establish the bacterial colony, nitrogenous material must be made available. This can be by the addition of a material such as shrimp flesh, left to decay in the water, or by adding a marine fish that can tolerate the nitrite crisis e.g. the lionfish *Pterois volitans* (but note that this species is venomous). A cheap freshwater fish that will tolerate both saltwater and nitrite is the black molly (*Poecilia sphenops* var.).

C. Stocking Levels

The limiting factor to stocking level in the small aquarium tank is the oxygen content of the water. This is often dependent on gaseous solution (and exchange with carbon dioxide) at the air–water interface. Hence, the stocking levels are dependent on the surface area, not the volume, of the aquarium. The size of the fish is also important.

To calculate maximum stocking levels in freshwater aquaria, measure the water surface area in square centimetres. Measure the fish's length excluding the tail and group into small (up to 3 cm), medium (3 to 5 cm) and large (5 to 10 cm). Divide the surface area by 70 to give the maximum number of small fish, by 120 to give the maximum number of medium fish and by 140 to give the maximum number of large fish. Very large fish need swimming room as well as adequate oxygen levels, so allow at least 20 litres of water per fish. Table V shows the average number of fish that can be housed in five sizes of typical aquaria.

Marine fish must be stocked at about half the freshwater fish level, because of the lower solubility of oxygen in sea water. At $20°C$, saturated sea water contains about 20% less oxygen than saturated freshwater. Table V refers to adult fish. If fry or young fish are installed, the initial density may be higher but the fish must be culled, or some fish moved, as they grow. If a permanent fish population is required, allowance must be made for growth. The species to be kept will of course depend on the research work, but a general rule is to house at least a trio of a given species. To prevent stress by bullying, the preferred ratio is usually one male to two females.

Table V. Stocking levels.

Surface area (cm²)	Tropical fish	5–8 cm goldfish
700	10 (small)	3
1800	15 (medium)	5
2800	24 (medium)	7
4600	40 (medium)	12
8400	70 (medium)	20

D. Plants

Real plants can prove beneficial in the aquaria since when illuminated, they oxygenate the water and help remove nitrates from solution. In marine aquaria, few higher plants can be cultivated (the author has had some success with *Caulerpa sp.*). However, the common algae can be encouraged to grow with bright lighting. The disadvantage of real plants is that unless conditions are ideal, they rot and pollute the tank. When conditions are good, growth can be vigorous necessitating constant attention e.g. pruning and thinning.

If plants are required, a suitable rooting medium is necessary. This can be provided by small plastic pots filled with peat and Innes potting compound topped with gravel, each container housing individual or groups of plants. To grow directly from the gravel or sand base, a layer of peat 2 or 3 cm thick should be laid before the gravel or sand is placed in the tank as a top covering. The best peat is the commercial variety available for gardening but it must be free of added fertilizers. Pre-soak the peat for several days and squeeze dry before layering. This removes much of the humic acid and colour which otherwise would alter the pH and stain the aquarium water.

The requirements of the chosen plants need to be studied just as much as the needs of the fish. Some plants require soft water and others hard, some need bright and others dim conditions. For photosynthesis, the lighting must be of sufficient brightness per unit area, hence the same intensity of lighting is necessary whether the aquarium contains one or one hundred plants. If only a few plants are present, small algae will proliferate and these may spread on to the plants, stunting growth or even killing them. Therefore, if plants are required, plant a sufficient number. There should be at least one plant per litre.

E. Adding the Fish

Fish imported from the tropics arrive in plastic bags blown up with oxygen. The bags are packed in shredded paper or polystyrene to maintain the high water temperature. These packs must be opened in dim light to reduce panic and stress. The plastic bag should be cut open, not burst and left floating in the receiving tank for the temperature to equilibrate. The bag must be opened because gas diffusion through the plastic from the water is poor. Slow, partial water changes are not recommended. Excreted ammonium ions (NH_4^+) can be converted to toxic ammonia (NH_3) during this procedure. Direct transfer is better.

Fish bought from a local dealer must be chosen carefully. The fish should be active and alert, with erect fins and no superficial blemishes. Other fish in the dealer's tank must be free of any obvious disease or parasite. New marine fish particularly must be fully quarantined before placing in a tank with established fish since all are wild stock, imported with endemic diseases and parasites. The new animals should remain in the quarantine tank for at least several days.

V. MAINTAINING THE AQUARIUM

A. Foods and Feeding

If the trials do not involve nutritional studies, the best basic diet for the small aquarium fish is a commercial flake food. The advantage of flake is that it will at first float for top feeders, sink slowly for middle feeders and lay discretely on the bottom for bottom feeders. Carnivorous fish have a higher requirement for protein and vitamins per body weight than omnivorous mammals and the usual mammalian foods (e.g. kitchen scraps) are nutritionally deficient. The ideal diet would be a live one such as Daphnia, Tubifex, etc. but such a diet is sometimes difficult to provide and can lead to the introduction of diseases or parasites. Sterile prepared foods are preferable. Most flake foods are made from the dried meals of fish, meat, cereals, etc. Because processing to a meal tends to heat damage amino acids, the total protein content of these foods is high to bring the limiting essential amino acids up to the levels required by the fish. A better balanced diet is achieved with lower levels of a higher quality protein source, as in flakes made directly from wet mixes of whole fish and meats.

Fry need feeding frequently to maintain a full stomach. This is easily checked with a hand magnifying glass. Carnivorous fish need one good

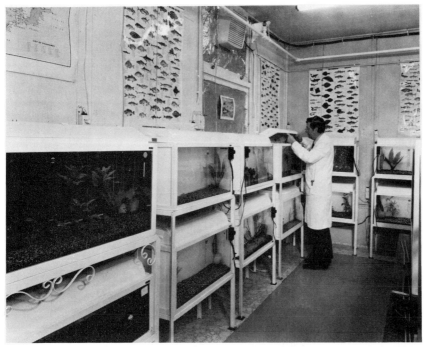

Fig. 2. The Aquarian Laboratory, where nutritional trials are performed for Aquarian products. The aquaria are housed on the periphery of a laboratory of 80 m². Some 30 tanks, each 80 × 35 × 30 cm are used in banks of two, each tank being a self-contained unit. The air supply is via a polythene tube, silicone sealed into a hose hung from the ceiling.

meal daily. Omnivorous fish can be fed twice daily and herbivorous fish several times. Individual needs of the actual species must be considered, of course. Feeding can be weekdays only (except small fry) and weekend working by laboratory staff is usually unnecessary.

B. Routine Cleaning

Routine partial changes of the water are most important. The changes are necessary to dilute the build-up of soluble materials. The ideal is to replace 20% of the tank volume weekly. Too great a dilution will change the water chemistry and thereby stress the fish. The aquarium should not be left until it is very dirty and then cleaned by emptying, scrubbing out and refilling with fresh water. A well-established tank kept clean by routine, partial water changes has gin-clear water and a sweet odour. Solid excreta or mulm, is removed during the water changes by "hoovering" the gravel with a siphon tube. This siphon is a few metres of polythene tubing of 8 or 10 mm internal diameter. Smaller tubing tends to block, while larger tubing tends to remove the gravel. Algal growth or mulm settling on the internal face of the glass is removed with a soapless scouring pad as required.

The cleaning can be done by hand; the hands should be washed after the job and not before because of the danger of introducing soap into the water. The outside of the tank should be wiped down with a damp cloth or paper tissue. Floor areas get wet and so a mop and pail is useful. A bucket of water with added disinfectant should be conveniently placed to receive used fish nets. Sufficient of these nets in a range of sizes should be available so that immediately after use in any one tank, they can be immersed in the disinfectant. This prevents cross-infection of diseases or parasites. The nets can be washed and dried routinely as required. In this case, most commercial brands of disinfectant may be used, but all traces must be rinsed away before re-use in the aquarium. The nets must be made from synthetic fibre to withstand this treatment. The mesh should also be very fine. The barbels, spines and gill covers of many species catch in large open meshes, causing wounds when the fish are disentangled.

Evaporation losses should be replaced by distilled water in freshwater aquaria. Tapwater is adequate for salt-water aquaria. In laboratories with banks of aquaria, the volume of distilled water required can be quite large, and having a distillation unit is an advantage. Steam-distillation is the preferred method and automatic models for chemical laboratories are available. A 4-litre still can cope with 30 or 40×100 l tanks.

VI. AQUARIUM PROBLEMS

A. Algal Growth

The most common problem for the inexperienced aquarist is excessive algal growth. There are many species of algae that can flourish in the aquarium and the problem can be green water, sometimes as thick as pea soup, filamentous growth that chokes plants, or a blanket forming over the gravel and rocks. There are green, brown and red varieties. Three factors contribute to this problem and each must be examined and corrected:

(a) *Lighting:* excess lighting will encourage algal growth, particularly daylight or direct sunlight. Photosynthesis is dependent upon illumination per unit area, and if plants are included, the same level of lighting is necessary for many or a few plants (see section IV D, Plants). If only a few plants are present, the remaining area can be utilized by algae.

(b)   *Balance:* the water must be in biological balance by the ageing process and continuous dilution described under "Routine Cleaning". A sudden growth of algae in an established tank is a sure indication of imbalance due to excess nitrogenous material in solution.

(c)   *Overfeeding:* the most common reason for an excess of soluble material is overfeeding. Freshly hatched fry can eat almost their own body weight daily in natural foods such as *Artemia salina*, but only 3 or 4% of body weight in dried foodstuffs. An adult fish's requirements falls to about 1.5% of body weight since growth almost ceases and only a maintenance diet is required. Furthermore, some fish have the ability to ingest continuously, but only absorb their nutritional requirements, simply excreting the surplus. With such fish, to feed to satiation is to pollute the aquarium with excess food. Growing fish should be fed for 2 or 3 min at each feeding and any excess siphoned or netted away. Adult fish can be fed similarly but the frequency reduced to once or twice daily according to species. A 20-g pack of Aquarian flake food should last 100 adult community tropical fish about one month.

B. Diseases and Parasites

Parasites and diseases are the second major problem in small aquaria. The confines of the tank favour explosive growth of the more common parasites, such as white spot (*Ichthyopthiriasis*), various fungi (*Dermatomycosis*) and in saltwater, *Oodinium* (*Oodiniasis*). These parasites are present in any body of water but healthy fish can resist them. Poor husbandry, stress or damage from fighting or handling, leads to unhealthy fish that may then be troubled by parasites. Treatment for various parasites and diseases is described in chapter 10. Once an outbreak has been contained, the underlying fault in husbandry should be sought and corrected.

VII. MARINE SPECIES

Many of the marine fish kept in aquaria are more sensitive to their aquatic environment than the majority of freshwater species. In the marine aquarium, the pH, nitrite and specific gravity levels in the marine aquarium should be monitored routinely and swiftly corrected if necessary.

Most marine species require a pH of about 8.2, but biological filtration systems tend to produce acidic by-products which slowly reduce the pH. Alkaline materials can be added to the tank such as crushed shells, dolomite granules, marble chips or sodium carbonate. Nitrite levels should be zero a few days into the maturing period, after an initial crisis level. A value over 0.1 mg/l should be taken as an indication of some problem in the system. This could be blocked or dirty filter beds, a dead fish or invertebrate, overcrowding or inadequate water-changing. It is advisable to keep a supply of made-up synthetic sea water for partial water changes when a high nitrite reading is obtained. The water may be kept at normal or double strength (to reduce bulk storage) and should be housed in a plastic dustbin with a lid. Black or grey plastic is better, since coloured plastics may contain toxic dyestuffs. Some aeration keeps the water moving and prevents precipitation, especially if double strength solution is stored.

VIII. SUITABLE FISH FOR THE RESEARCH LABORATORY

The species of fish to be housed in the laboratory will depend on the purpose of the research. The following are examples of fish that are commonly the subject of scientific study.

A. Toxicity Screening and Water Quality Research

The International Organisation for Standardisation has issued a document (ISO, 1976) detailing proposals for screening chemicals and commercial products for their acute toxicity to freshwater fish. The test species recommended is the zebra fish, *Brachydanio rerio*. An extensive review of the biology of this fish has been given by Laale (1977).

Other species commonly employed for assessing the effects of pollutants are as follows:

threadfin shad (*Dorosoma petenense*)
brook trout (*Salvelinus fontinalis*)
rainbow trout (*Salmo gairdneri*)
northern pike (*Esox lucius*)
emerald shiner (*Notropis atherinoides*)
fathead minnow (*Pimephales promelas*)
white sucker (*Catostomus commersoni*)
channel catfish (*Ictalurus punctatus*)
white bass (*Roccus chrysops*)
blue gill (*Lepomis chrysops*)
largemouth bass (*Micropterus salmonides*)
yellow perch (*Perca flavescens*)

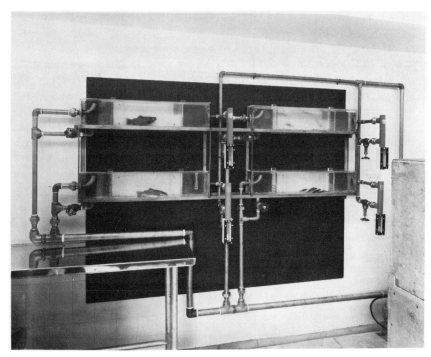

Fig. 3. A unit for monitoring water quality. Water piped to a food processing factory passes through a settlement tank. Water is drawn directly from this settlement tank to four aquarium containing rainbow trout. Each aquarium holds 20 litres of water and is fed at a flow rate of 10 l/min. The fish are viewed continuously on a TV monitor by factory security personnel.

B. General Biological Studies

The equivalent of the laboratory rat for much behavioural and physiological research is the goldfish, *Carassius auratus*. The aquarium requirements of this fish are described by Hervey and Hems (1968). The rainbow trout, *Salmo gairdneri*, is also a common laboratory species, though it requires cool, well oxygenated water. Based on sales figures, the ten most popular and readily available freshwater fishes are given below. They are compatible species, and can be mixed in a community tank. They are also the easiest fish to keep in the aquarium:

 angel fish (*Pterophyllum scalare*)
 guppy (*Poecilia reticulata*)
 swordtail (*Xiphophorus helleri*)
 black molly (*Poecilia sphenops* var.)
 neon tetra (*Paracheirodon innesi*)

zebra fish (*Brachydanio rerio*)
platy (*Xiphorus maculatus*)
white cloud mountain minnow (*Tanichthys albonubes*)
dwarf gourami (*Colisa Ialia*)
catfish (*Corydoras* sp.)
All these fish are described in any good aquarist's book on tropical fish.
See, for example, McInerny and Gerard (1966) and Hoedeman (1974).

IX. REFERENCES

Hervey, G. F. and Hems, J. (1968). "The goldfish", Faber and Faber, London.
Hoedeman, J. J. (1974). "Naturalists Guide to Freshwater Aquarium Fish", Elsevier, Amsterdam.
ISO (1976). Document No. 150/TC 147/SC5/WG3. 11 Nov. 1976., BS1, Park Street, London.
Laale, H. W. (1977). The biology and use of zebrafish, *Brachydanio rerio*, in fisheries research. *Journal of Fish Biology* **10**, 121–173.

Chapter 6

Materials for the Aquarium

A. D. Hawkins[1] and R. Lloyd[2]

Marine Laboratory, Aberdeen[1] and Fisheries Laboratory, Burnham on Crouch,[2] UK

I. INTRODUCTION

A wide range of natural and synthetic materials with very varied physical properties is now available for general engineering work. However, for aquaria, especially of the marine variety, the choice of materials is often very restricted and fraught with difficulty. Sea water destroys or corrodes a great many of the substances that are placed in contact with it. This chapter outlines the properties of materials for aquarium use, identifying the problems of constructing and maintaining a freshwater or marine aquarium system which is free of toxic and corrodible substances.

II. METALS

Metals tend to corrode when wet or immersed in water, some more rapidly than others. The corrosion is particularly bad in soft or acid water and sea water. In the aquarium, the breakdown of metal components leads to difficulties with maintenance and servicing, and may result in mechanical failure and a loss or restriction of water supply with serious consequences. In addition, many of the products of metal corrosion are highly toxic to fish and their presence in small quantities is difficult to monitor, so that they form the most elusive of the potential contaminants. As a general rule, especially for closed-circuit marine aquaria, metals should not be allowed to come into contact with the water. If this avoidance is not possible, the metals must be carefully selected and subsequently subjected to regular checking. Major pieces of aquarium equipment, such as pumps and heat exchangers, should not be installed without a preliminary search for corrodible metallic parts, and should not be ordered without a guarantee from the manufacturer that the item is suitable for the aquarium. The best assurance that an item is acceptable is that it has been successfully used in another aquarium for several years.

A. Metal Corrosion and its Causes

The likelihood of a particular metal corroding in a weak solution of an electrolyte like sea water is given by its corrosion potential, measured against a reference electrode. Metals can be arranged in a galvanic series, from the most electronegative to the most electropositive; the latter being much more resistant to corrosion than the former. The corrosion potentials of a series of metals are given in Fig. 1.

An important group of metals, including aluminium, the stainless steels and titanium cover themselves with a protective oxide film. Such metals in the so-called "passive" state are much more resistant than their composition would suggest and they therefore take a higher place in the galvanic series. However the "passivity" can be lost, particularly in the presence of chlorides and this loss is followed by a fall of potential and

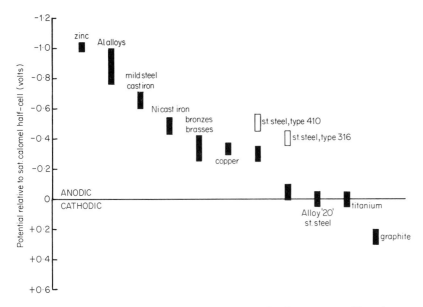

Fig. 1.   The corrosion potentials of various metals in flowing seawater. Note that some alloys may show a more active potential under certain conditions, indicated by an open box.

accentuated corrosion, the latter often being strongly localized. Corrosion can often be most severe when metals are touching one another and in contact with a solution. Such galvanic corrosion, where a current flows between one metal and the other, has two effects: an increased corrosion of one material, and a decreased corrosion of the other. If the two metals have similar corrosion potentials, then the change in corrosion properties is slight and they can be considered compatible. However, any contact between highly dissimilar metals will result in a greatly accelerated corrosion of the more active one which acts as the anode of a cell, with the more noble metal as a cathode. Very concentrated corrosion occurs where the area of the anode is small compared to the cathode. Titanium is a valuable material in a corrosive environment since it is almost always passive, yet it does not have too adverse an effect upon adjacent metals. On the other hand, most of the resistant and noble metals are efficient cathodes which promote the corrosion of adjacent less noble metals. Graphite, though not a metal, is electrically conductive and a good cathode which can stimulate the corrosion of any metal connected to it.

For some marine applications, galvanic corrosion is deliberately sought by placing a sacrificial anode of a cheap material like zinc, aluminium or steel in contact with the more noble metal which is to be protected. Examples are the galvanization of mild steel by a layer of zinc or the protection of stainless steel with an adjacent anode of mild steel. Such protective measures are out of place in the aquarium, particularly with zinc where the soluble corrosion products are highly toxic. Indeed, galvanic couples should normally be avoided, and even certain types of stainless steel should not be mixed (for example the stainless steels known as types 410 and 416 are not compatible with the 300 series). If dissimilar metals must be used, they are best separated by non-conducting materials, with the key component in the more noble material, and the larger area formed from the less noble. Tables of galvanically compatible metals in sea water are given by Tuthill and Schillmoller (1967). Plating an active metal like mild steel or brass with a more noble metal like nickel or chromium is not always successful in sea water though the plating metal is resistant to corrosion. Any scratch or break in the plating sets up a corrosion cell where the noble metal acts as a cathode to the less noble anode. The underlying metal therefore corrodes severely where it is exposed, the corrosion spreading under the layer of plating. Plating, therefore, should be restricted to objects which are not likely to be abraded or eroded.

Copper and its alloys, while not forming films as protective as those on the truly passive metals, do form relatively adherent protective layers of oxides and other compounds and this film has the additional feature of being toxic, which prevents the settlement of fouling organisms. Many types of bronze, aluminium–bronze and nickel–copper are used in marine engineering, but because of their potential toxicity, they are generally rejected for the aquarium. Though the toxic surface film is very tenacious, the consequences when such materials do contaminate the water are too severe to be risked.

Most low alloy steels show some resistance to extreme rusting by virtue of the adherent rust film which forms on them, largely as a result of the small quantities of copper and nickel they contain. Other special steel alloys have been formulated which can more easily be rendered passive and which develop more resistant protective films. These steels (Table V), which contain large quantities of nickel, chromium and molybdenum are especially suitable for the aquarium, though their noble position means that they should not be mixed with low alloy or mild steel. With some alloys, one component may be preferentially attacked. Iron is selectively removed from cast iron, the more noble carbon remaining as a graphite network which retains the appearance of the original, but is greatly weakened. However, the newer highly-alloyed nickel cast irons are extremely unlikely to suffer from this defect. Intergranular corrosion

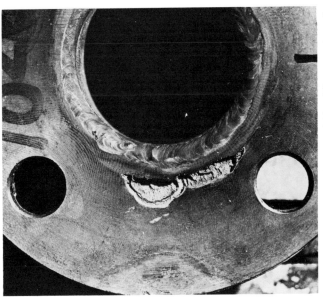

Figs 2a and 2b. The corrosion of stainless steel in the marine aquarium. (Left) Severe crevice corrosion of a type 316 stainless steel flange forming part of a heat exchanger in a closed circuit aquarium. (Right) Pitting of a type 316 stainless steel temperature probe on the shaft and on the thread.

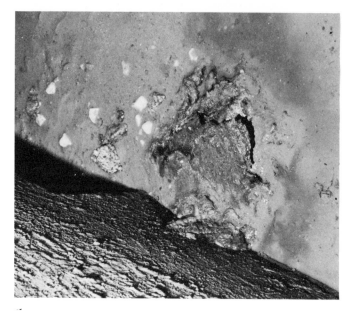

Figs 3a and 3b. Spalling of concrete as a result of rusting of the steel reinforcement.

Figs 4a qnd 4b.   Corrosion of mild steel nuts and bolts in a sea water aquarium.   The only solution is replacement with type 316 stainless steel fittings, though even these are not entirely immune from attack. Note the potentially dangerous corrosion of the electrical socket above the water pipes (right).

Figs 5a and 5b. Moulded tanks of GRP (glass reinforced plastic or "fibre-glass") are satisfactory for many purposes in the aquarium, and are available in a great variety of sizes and types. The circular tank shown is sectional, the parts being held together by stainless steel bolts, sealed with mastic. Up to three tiers can be added.

of some stainless steels may occur at welded joints and can be prevented by welding only with low carbon or "stabilized" grades of these alloys.

The many factors which can effect the rate of corrosion of a metal are discussed by La Que (1975). Increased temperature accelerates the corrosion of all materials, and oxygen normally promotes the rusting of mild steel and the corrosion of other metals. Many of the common stainless steels are particularly susceptible to local corrosion where the oxygen content of the water is depleted, for example at flange joints, under washers or in crevices. At such a crevice, a local concentration cell is formed in which the metal surface inside the crevice becomes anodic to the adjacent passive areas of metal and may suffer severe localized corrosion. Corrosion products are released from the crevice as an acidic stream and may create new local concentration cells, spreading the corrosion to adjacent areas. The common stainless steels can also show severe pitting beneath fouling organisms, and in the presence of micro-organisms which are often present in aquaria at sites where detritus collects. The stainless steels with high molybdenum content are more resistant to local pitting and crevice attack (for example BS and AISI type 316, BS and AISI 317, and 20 Cr–25 Ni–4.5 Mo–1.5 Cu–Fe). High water velocities or turbulence can also promote corrosion, especially of copper, copper alloys and mild steel. With many stainless steels, however, a high water velocity results in a more stable surface film. In addition, fewer fouling organisms settle and local concentration cells are dispersed, so that the metal is less vulnerable to pitting.

B. The Toxicity of Metals

Fish, and many other aquatic organisms are very susceptible to poisoning by metals (see Bryan, 1977 for a general review). In the marine aquarium, contamination is usually a result of corrosion in and around the aquarium itself, but where a marine or freshwater aquarium takes water from a river or coastal area subjected to industrial pollution, then the contaminants may enter with the water supply. Domestic freshwater supplies may be delivered by way of copper, zinc-coated or even lead pipes, and the problems arising from their use will be described later in the chapter. Zinc and copper compounds may also be used to treat certain infections in fish, and thereby accumulate in an aquarium system.

The likelihood of a particular metal harming fish depends on the solubility and form of its corrosion products. The physical chemistry of an individual metal in aquarium water is much more complicated than in distilled water since the medium already contains a mixture of inorganic and organic materials, both soluble and insoluble, together with a range of micro-organisms. Metals not only go into simple ionic solution but form inorganic and organic complexes with other materials. Particulate compounds of the metal may be bound or adhere to suspended material or be taken up by the micro-organisms. The load of metallic material carried by aquarium water may therefore be very much higher than that supposed from simple solubility considerations. Table I lists typical quantities of particular metals to be found in clean filtered river and sea water. Natural levels may be much higher than the quoted figures, especially if particulate material is included. The quantities will also vary with temperature, salinity, pH, water hardness etc.

Table I. Natural levels of dissolved metals in the sea and in freshwater (µg/l or ppb) (after Johnston, 1977).

Metal	Concentration in freshwater	Concentration in sea water
Ag	0.3	0.3
Al	400.0	3.0
As	2.0	3.0
Cd	0.5	0.03
Co	0.2	0.5
Cr	1.0	0.05
Cu	7.0	2.0
Fe	670.0	10.0
Hg	0.07	0.03
Mn	7.0	2.0
Mo	1.0	10.0
Ni	0.3	2.0
Pb	3.0	0.03
Sb	1.0	0.3
Se	0.2	4.0
Sn	0.04	3.0
V	0.9	2.0
Zn	20.0	10.0
Ti	3.0	1.0

Higher levels of these trace elements will not necessarily be harmful to fish or other aquatic organisms, and because of the wide range of sensitivities of aquatic organisms to toxic substances and the marked effect which other chemical parameters of the water have on the toxicity of particular chemicals, it is impossible to give a table of maximum concentrations of these elements which are harmless to aquatic life. For example, various organisms are affected differently by particular metals and their response depends on the form of the metal. Though in general it is the soluble salts that are most toxic, some aquarium inhabitants, especially filter feeders, may remove even insoluble particulate material and accumulate it. The sensitivity of individual organisms will also vary with age, sex and physiological state. In addition, various metals may have additive, synergistic and even antagonistic effects upon one another, although the usual joint action is additive. In freshwater, the water hardness significantly affects toxicity, the heavy metals being more toxic in soft waters. Therefore, it is not possible to specify "safe" levels for a given metal, which will apply in all circumstances. One figure which is commonly given as a measure of toxicity is the LC_{50}, the concentration that kills half a test population in a specified time. A series of LC_{50} values for different metals and for several marine and freshwater organisms is given in Table II.

In the research aquarium, it is rarely the lethal concentration of a metal that is important. A gradual change in the behaviour or physiology of test subjects may be as damaging to an experiment as their sudden death. To minimize such effects, it is wise to resist the introduction of any metals. The heavy metals, silver, mercury, copper, cadmium, nickel, lead and zinc are the most toxic and since the levels of all these metals in natural fresh and sea water is normally very low, they can be increased by quite minor local contamination. Any increase in their aquarium level must be considered potentially damaging to the occupants, though paradoxically, copper, nickel and zinc must be present in trace quantities for the well-being of the animals. Methods of determining the levels of various metals in freshwater are given by (Anon., 1972) and analytical methods for sea water by Riley (1977).

Materials which produce insoluble corrosion resistant surface films, like the alloys of copper and nickel, do not normally release significant quantities of toxic products into the water. It is important to remember, however, that at very high water velocities (above 1–2 m/s), the toxic protective film is eroded. Mild steel and cast iron rust in the aquarium but the products of corrosion are largely insoluble and relatively harmless to most aquatic organisms. Thus, rusting can sometimes be tolerated where corrosion of non-ferrous materials cannot. The only effect of rusting may be a heavy staining of adjacent materials like concrete and weakening of the ferrous structure.

C. Metals in Freshwater Supply Pipes

Freshwater aquaria are often supplied with water prepared for human

Table II. The relative toxicities of metals to aquatic organisms (after Bryan, 1977; and Anon., 1971). Concentrations expressed as ppm (mg/l).

Metal	Freshwater Fish Lepomis macrochirus (96h LC_{50})	Marine Fish Fundulus heteroclitus (96h LC_{50})	Marine Crustacean Crangon (48h LC_{50})	Marine Crustacean Balanus balanoides (96h LC_{50})	Marine Bivalve Crassostrea virginica (48h LC_{50})	Marine Bivalve Cardium edule (embryo) (48h LC_{50})	Estuarine Polychaete Nereis diversicolor (192h LC_{50})
Ag	–	0.04	–	0.2	0.009	–	0.5
Cd	1.94	–	3–10	–	3.8	100–300	100
Cr^{6+}	110	55	100	–	10.3	1	10
Cu	0.74	3.2	24	0.24	0.128	–	0.27
Fe^{3+}	–	–	56	–	–	190	–
Hg	–	0.23	5.7	0.5	0.006	9	–
Ni	5.18–39.6	–	–	–	1.19	>500	130
Pb	23.8–442.0	188	–	–	2.46	>500	>5
Zn	1.7–12.2	66	110	8	0.34	257	30

consumption and transported through metal pipes. Because of corrosion of the metals, dissolved zinc, copper and lead are potential hazards, especially since the limits set for many metals in potable water are higher than those known to be harmful to aquatic organisms.

(1) Galvanized iron pipes: zinc
It is unlikely that harmful concentrations of zinc will occur in a public water supply, unless the source is contaminated by mine workings or spoil heaps, or by atmospheric fall-out from ore smelters. The major source of zinc contamination is likely to be from galvanized iron pipes, tanks, fittings, and bronze fittings. In some areas, bronze fittings undergo rapid dezincification, leading to higher concentrations in the water. Zinc plating is more likely to be dissolved by acid soft waters. For example with a batch of rainbow trout transported in a galvanized iron tank containing soft water, sufficient zinc dissolved within 18 h to be lethal to the fish, despite the tank being coated with a non-toxic paint.

The toxicity of zinc to aquatic organisms increases as the water becomes softer. For example, the 48-h LC_{50} for rainbow trout is 0.5 mg Zn/l in soft water (12 mg/l $CaCO_3$) compared with 4.8 mg Zn/l in hard water (504 mg/l as $CaCO_3$). The protective action of calcium may be internal since rainbow trout kept in hard water retain their resistance to zinc for at least 5 days after transfer to contaminated water. The literature on zinc toxicity has been reviewed by EIFAC (1973). Non-salmonids (the minnow, *Phoxinus phoxinus* is an exception) are generally more resistant to zinc poisoning than are trout. The maximum safe concentrations of zinc are given in Table III. Higher concentrations than those shown can be withstood for short periods, and fish can acclimate, in that fish reared in sub-lethal concentrations (from public water supplies) can be more resistant to otherwise toxic concentrations.

Table III. Maximum safe concentrations of zinc for freshwater fish (EIFAC, 1973).

Water hardness (mg/l as Ca CO_3)	Concentration, mg Zn/l	
	Salmonids	Non-salmonids
10	0.03	0.30
50	0.20	0.70
100	0.30	1.0
500	0.50	2.0

Although galvanized and bronze materials may not give rise to zinc contamination in hard water areas, the risk is always present, and non-toxic plastics or stainless steel are more satisfactory.

(2) Copper pipes and fittings

Most natural waters contain traces of copper. The levels are generally too low to affect aquatic organisms except in areas where mining and smelting activities take place. The addition of copper sulphate to reservoirs for algal control (Chapter 4) can also raise the level in the water supply. However, the main source of copper contamination in aquaria is from copper pipes and brass or bronze fittings, especially when these are new. The permitted level of copper in drinking water is much higher than the maximum safe concentration for fish. Because copper can form non-toxic complexes with organic matter, the setting of precise limits for copper toxicity presents considerable problems. The recent literature is critically reviewed by EIFAC (1976).

The major factors affecting toxicity of copper are the hardness and organic matter (especially humic acids). Copper is 16 times more toxic to rainbow trout in soft water (12 mg/l as $CaCO_3$) than hard water (320 mg/l as $CaCO_3$) over a 7-day exposure period. The mechanics of the protective action of calcium is poorly understood. Little is also known of the complex-forming capacities of copper and organic matter though it is well established that the toxicity of copper in soft water containing humic acids is much less than would be predicted from the total copper content. In hard waters, the copper may be precipitated in a colloidal form which may further reduce its toxicity.

Table IV. Maximum safe concentrations of copper for rainbow trout in freshwater (EIFAC, 1976).

Water hardness (mg/l as $CaCO_3$)	Concentration, mg Cu/l
10	0.005
50	0.02
100	0.04
300	0.11

Table IV presents some limiting values for copper to rainbow trout; it is assumed that all the copper present is in a toxic form. Some fish, like the rudd, carp and perch may be more sensitive, while pike and eels seem to be more resistant. A hard water supply can be passed through copper pipes without any harm to fish. However, intermittent flow through the pipes could lead to problems. There is no satisfactory alternative to non-toxic plastic or stainless steel pipes and fittings. Copper and zinc may be found together in water supplies. At concentrations within an order of magnitude of those shown as lethal to fish their toxicities are additive. That is, half a lethal concentration of zinc plus half a lethal concentration of copper equals a lethal solution.

(3) Lead pipes
An early material for water supply pipes was lead, though it is now known to be harmful to man and its use has been discontinued. In some areas, particularly those with soft water, lead is being replaced by copper or galvanized iron. Where lead piping is still in use, the concentration in potable water can exceed 0.01 mg Pb/l. Until recently, lead was thought to be relatively non-toxic to fish especially in hard water where it is less soluble. However, recent research with brook trout has shown that fish can be harmed by exposure to lead concentrations in excess of 0.08 mg Pb/l in water with a hardness of 44 mg/l as $CaCO_3$ and a pH range of 6.8–7.6 (Holcombe, Benoit, Leonard and McKim, 1976). There is also evidence that fish absorb lead more rapidly at lower pH values, so it is likely that even lower concentrations are harmful in softer, more acid waters.

D. The Choice of Metals for the Aquarium

When metals must be used in the aquarium, the most commonly available material is type 316 stainless steel (AISI type 316; BS 316S16, formerly known as type EN 58J). This molybdenum-containing alloy is more resistant to pitting and crevice corrosion than lower alloy steels and can easily be worked, welded and polished. For welding, a low carbon grade (AISI type 316L; BS 316S12) is preferred. Type 316 steel is not entirely immune from attack and is not a high-strength steel. Kirk (1972) has discussed the selection of high-strength steels for such purposes as high pressure tanks. He points out that high tensile stresses can cause cracks in stainless steels immersed in a corrosive liquid like sea water. A more attractive choice for many high stress applications is known as 18% nickel maraging steel, though this material is only slightly more resistant to corrosion than mild steel. Newer high-strength corrosion-resistant alloys have been developed and are probably more suitable: for example Inconel 625, Hastelloy C-276, A-L6X, a variety of titanium alloys and in some cases titanium itself.

E. The Coating of Metals

Naturally corrosion-resistant materials need no additional protection. Protective coatings can be applied to corrodible metals, though few of them can be regarded as permanent. For many commercial applications, inhibitive synthetic coatings are employed, the inhibitor minimizing the effects of any break and restricting corrosion of the bare metal surface. Inhibitors are included as pigments in a priming coat or in the coating itself, zinc chromate and lead chromate being common. Both these materials, and the highly successful metallic zinc primers are best avoided in the aquarium because of their high toxicity.

Where a synthetic coating is necessary, the preparation of the surface is a most important step in its application. A clean surface, roughened by sandblasting or abrasion, is desirable for good adhesion of the first coat. A great variety of coatings are now available, the epoxy types appearing to give the best protection in the aquarium if the manufacturer's application procedure is strictly followed. Very severe corrosion may take place if only a small area of an active metal forming part of a galvanic couple is exposed to sea water. The corrosion may spread beneath the coating and not be noticed; in such circumstances the coating is disadvantageous. Some metal components and instruments for the aquarium are provided with thick factory-applied coatings of materials like epoxy resins, polytetrafluoroethylene (PTFE) or polypropylene. These have proved satisfactory only where there is no likelihood of mechanical damage or abrasion. Some coating materials may initially release toxic compounds and should be thoroughly soaked before use.

III. CONCRETE

Concrete is commonly used in the aquarium for the construction of reservoirs, fish tanks, raceways, filter beds, etc. Though primarily a material with a strong resistance to compression, its lack of tensile strength can be overcome by embedding steel wire or bar inside. Up to 4% of steel by volume can be added, the metal generally being placed near the outer skins of members to more effectively withstand the loads applied. Reinforcing steel may also be used to increase the shear resistance of a concrete structure, while for some applications, concrete may be stressed with high tensile steel wire prior to loading.

Concrete is highly alkaline for some time after its construction because of free lime produced by the hydration reaction of cement. Small quantities of chromates and other materials may also leach out for a period. Asbestos-cement, or cement-lined iron pipe can cause freshwater supplies to become highly alkaline for extended periods. If the water is hard, and especially if it contains excess carbon dioxide, the additional alkali will have little effect. This is also the case with sea water, with its natural buffering capacity. However, if very soft freshwater with little buffering capacity is passed through the pipes, the pH can be considerably raised. One example of such an effect has been described by Sprague (1964) where a water supply changed from pH 6.6–6.9 (total hardness 10–14 mg/l as $CaCO_3$) to pH 9.5 (15–19 mg/l as $CaCO_3$). The pH was restored to 7.3 by vigorous aeration, and at high flow rates, by bubbling CO_2 through the water followed by aeration. There was no lessening of the amount of alkali leading from the pipe over a period of $2\frac{1}{2}$ years.

Thus concrete structures in the aquarium should be thoroughly washed before fish are admitted. After several coats of sodium silicate solution (water–glass) which acts as a sealant, the concrete should be soaked with water for a period of several weeks with periodic renewal of the water. The small quantities of alkaline materials which may subsequently continue to leach from the concrete can be prevented by coating or lining the concrete structures with a resin paint. If the coat is well applied and continuous, marine fish can be placed in the aquaria after several days of washing the lining.

Concrete is a very durable material with a long life even in sea water. Sea water-resistant concrete is normally made with a cement that contains less tricalcium aluminate and more tetracalcium aluminoferrite than ordinary Portland cement to inhibit sulphate attack (sulphate-resisting Portland cement, to BS 4027:1972). Browne (1974) suggests that where the structure is likely to be subjected to severe freezing during construction, the strength can be maintained by entraining air during mixing to allow for water expansion. The water/cement ratio should not exceed 1:2 by weight to ensure low permeability, while the cement content should not be less than 350 kg/m^3, providing adequate binder to block aggregate voids. To minimize the penetration of oxygen and salts to the reinforcement, a layer of at least 50–75 mm of thoroughly compacted concrete must lie between the steel and the medium, forming a watertight layer. Where possible, the concrete forming a water tank should be poured in a single operation to avoid sutures. Quick-setting high alumina cements should not be used in the aquarium because prolonged exposure in a wet environment may result in their crumbling.

When concrete breaks down in the aquarium, it is usually because the reinforcing steel is attacked by sea water or acid water. The steel is normally passivated by the high alkalinity of the concrete. A break in the concrete cover or any increase in permeability which allows both sea water and oxygen to contact the steel will destroy the passivation, setting up a corrosion cell between the exposed steel and the deeper passivated steel and causing the metal to rust. As the steel rusts, the overlying concrete becomes stained and then eventually splits away or spalls, as a result of the increase in volume of the corrosion products (Figs 3a and 3b).

To repair spalled concrete, the porous concrete is broken away and the corroded steel and remaining concrete thoroughly washed with freshwater. The steel can then be sealed with an epoxy or polyester resin and finally the hole refilled with well compacted mortar or concrete. An area of poor concrete can be protected with a synthetic resin coat, and with some modern resins, such a coat can even be applied to wet or submerged concrete. It is probably good sea water aquarium practice to coat new tanks and raceways with resin both on the inside and on the outside where water will be splashed. Resin paints are normally supplied with a separate hardener and possibly a separate pigmented filler. The components must be mixed precisely according to the manufacturers' instructions and special care must be taken to ensure that the temperature is high enough for proper curing. Epoxy resin mortars have recently been developed and can be used not only for repairs but to screed concrete tanks with a minimum of surface preparation.

IV. OTHER MATERIALS

A wide range of chemically inert materials are now available for the aquarium. They include thermoplastics, thermosetting resins, synthetic rubbers and ceramics with a wide variety of mechanical characteristics. Many of them replace older natural materials like wood, rubber, bitumen, stone and glass. Some of the synthetic polymers, or plastics, lack strength or show properties that are time, load, or temperature-dependent, and materials like glass fibre or textiles are therefore incorporated to increase the strength and versatility.

Many polymers, and especially polyvinylchloride (PVC), deteriorate in sunlight. The breakdown can be inhibited by incorporating carbon black, or by painting the material to screen off ultraviolet light. The great majority of plastics and resins are non-toxic to aquatic organisms. However, many additives are mixed in with polymers to act as antioxidants, colourants, catalysts, plasticizers, flame-retardants, fillers and stabilizers. These chemicals may include lead salts, phenols, aromatic amines, aromatic hydrocarbons and isocyanates. The additives are often surrounded by polymers and cannot always leach out.

Nevertheless, plastics and resins should not be accepted uncritically for the aquarium, and new items should always be well washed before use, even if made from the more common polymers. New or unfamiliar synthetic materials should preferably be tested for toxicity if their use cannot be supported by the testimony of other aquarists. Recycled plastics should especially be avoided, because additives readily leach out of them. They are commonly sold more cheaply than new plastics: for example, as recycled polyethylene bags. Materials graded as suitable for use with foodstuffs are most acceptable. Carmignani and Bennett (1976) have shown that toxic dioctyl phthalate leaches from many plastics commonly used in aquarium systems, and recommend a 10-day soaking period for all such materials.

Wood was formerly common in the aquarium and though it has now largely been superseded by more modern synthetic materials, it is still a useful material for the construction of tanks and tank supports. Well-seasoned and dried heartwood is the most durable, and the heavier timbers like teak and afrormosia are the most resistant to decay. Mahogany, oak and western red cedar are also suitable. Any plywoods must be of the marine variety, where the glues and veneers are water-resistant. Many wood preservatives are toxic, and only untreated wood should be used.

V. MATERIALS FOR PARTICULAR APPLICATIONS

A. Pumps

The cheaper domestic and industrial water pumps have a cast iron body with bronze or cast iron impeller and bronze or steel shaft. The impellers may need frequent replacement in sea water, and pumps containing bronze should be avoided in the closed-circuit marine aquarium or in acid water areas because of the possible accumulation of toxic copper compounds. Pumps with more resistant copper alloy bodies and nickel-copper impellers are common on naval vessels and may be used in some open-circuit aquaria if water quality is not too important. Pumps with nickel-cast iron bodies, type 316 stainless steel impellers and type 316 or nickel-copper shafts are more satisfactory and give good aquarium service with sea water for long periods. Where pumps containing metal parts are used only intermittently for pumping sea water, it is good practice to flush them out with freshwater immediately after use, and before re-use.

The most suitable pumps for closed-circuit aquaria, or where water quality is important, are made from inert synthetic materials, with any metallic parts insulated from the liquid being pumped (these parts may include the drive shaft, bearings, and bearing sleeve). Such pumps are specifically sold for use with chemicals, foodstuffs or corrosive liquids. The weakest component in most of them is the seal or gland where the drive shaft enters the pump. This part should be frequently checked for leaks and for subsequent corrosion of the metal parts outside the pump body. For small scale aquaria, magnetically driven pumps avoid all contact between the drive motor and the sealed inert pump.

B. Pipework and Valves

Formerly, cast iron, lined steel, stainless steel and even copper and lead pipes were fitted in aquarium systems. Some freshwater mains may still contain ferrous materials, copper and lead, or contain pipes made from asbestos cement or concrete. In general, however, most aquarium systems have pipework made from inert synthetic materials like high density polyethylene and PVC. Metals are now only found in heavy duty valves and fittings which may be made with nickel cast iron bodies and stainless steel trim, but these too have now largely been superseded by alternatives made from synthetic materials.

Flexible hoses for the aquarium are often made of PVC and other plastics, sometimes reinforced with textiles like nylon. The hoses may contain traces of softening agents or plasticizers which are toxic and which must therefore be washed out before use. High density polyethylene pipes are strong and slightly flexible, and are commonly used in delivery pipelines. Most rigid pipework and associated fittings are of high impact PVC or unplasticized PVC (uPVC) and this material is satisfactory for most applications though it may contain very small quantities of lead. Acrylonitrile butadiene styrene (ABS) pipes and fittings are often preferred because this material is completely non-toxic and is less brittle at low temperatures. The range of fittings available is often more restricted, however. The rigid plastics are light and easy to handle, though they need independent support especially where valves or weighty components are fitted. They are all much more prone to thermal expansion than metals, so that clips and supports must be loose fitting to allow for movement. Laid below ground there may be no need to consider thermal movement but above ground expansion joints or loops in the pipes may be necessary.

Solvent-welded joints are usual with plastic pipework, though specific solvents are used for uPVC and ABS. A common fault in solvent jointing is an excess of solvent. Joints with threaded fittings are also possible though the fittings are not always available in ABS. The joints are usually sealed with PTFE tape. Threading the tube may reduce the working pressure that the pipe can contain. Flange joints sealed with neoprene or some other synthetic rubber are common where pipework must periodically be dismantled to service machinery or to clean off fouling organisms. Mild steel nuts and bolts are satisfactory at the flanges but in a salt-laden marine aquarium they quickly rust. Since the rust does not come into contact with the water inside the pipes, it is relatively harmless, though the nuts themselves may seize. Type 316 stainless steel is a good substitute, and where high strength is not required, nuts and bolts of a synthetic material can be used. Coated nuts and bolts are only successful if frequently checked, while galvanized ones are potential sources of contamination even if they are overcoated with a layer of PTFE or some other plastic.

C. Aquarium Tanks

In the past, aquarium tanks were commonly made from glass and angle-iron, wood, asbestos or even steel, and were often coated with bituminous paints. Tanks are now available in a much wider variety of materials including the virtually unbreakable polyethylene or polypropylene (the latter being harder, more rigid, and with a higher melting point), the more brittle polystyrene and uPVC, and the transparent acrylic materials (Perspex, Lucite). Larger tanks are moulded from glass-fibre reinforced polyester resin (GRP or "fibre-glass") in a wide range of sizes and shapes, often incorporating wooden or steel beams and ties to give additional strength. GRP tanks are also available in sectional form, as panels, rings or part-rings, which can be bolted together with type 316 stainless steel fittings. The joints can be sealed with a synthetic non-toxic strip. It is not always prohibitively expensive to have a GRP tank custom-built to a particular size or shape. Large tanks for sharks have been tailor-made from resin/fibre coated plywood. Both faces of this material are coated with a mixture of cellulose fibres and a phenol-formaldehyde resin which meets a US military specification for chemical tank construction. At completion, any exposed wood is covered with polyester resin. The internal surface of a tank should be smooth, for two reasons: it makes cleaning easier and prevents damage to the more delicate fish. Fish kept in rough concrete tanks may have damaged ventral and caudal fins from constant rubbing against the rough surface.

Many large tanks or raceways are made from concrete, but large containers can also be made, relatively cheaply, by lining a suitably excavated hole or depression with plastic sheeting. The sheeting must be backed by sand or clay to provide a firm and smooth support for the sheeting, whch is easily torn or broken by sharp stones. Plastics reinforced with nylon and other textile fibres are stronger and less likely to rupture, and such sheets can be slung from tubular steel frames to provide inexpensive tanks. If such tanks are exposed to bright sunlight, additional layers of black sheeting may be necessary to slow down the deterioration from ultraviolet light.

From the point of view of good husbandry, it is often better to build tanks from transparent materials or to build windows into the side. The first signs of disease or aberrant behaviour are often more readily noticed if fish are viewed from the side. Glass windows can readily be fitted to tanks made of the more rigid materials like concrete. They may even be fitted to GRP tanks provided that the area surrounding the glass is strengthened against bending and if the face against which the glass must lie is flat and smooth. The flat smooth surface can be obtained by coating the surface with epoxy or polyester resin and flattening it with a sheet of glass previously smeared with a release agent. Ordinary putty should not be used to seal an aquarium window in place because it may contain lead as a hardening agent. Special non-toxic aquarium putties are available. Silicone rubber sealants are also sold for the aquarium though acetic acid may leach out of these for a period and the newly glazed tank may need a good wash before fish are allowed in. Silicone sealants for household use may contain fungicides and should be avoided.

D. Support for Aquarium Tanks

Portable aquarium tanks generally need some form of support to raise them from the floor, either for the convenience of the user, or to allow satisfactory drainage. In some cases, it is necessary to arrange many tanks on shelves, one above the other. Wood is a good material for support. It may rot with time and need replacing, but it is non-toxic (if untreated) and has some "give" to it. Wooden legs can be built into GRP tanks, protected from rot by covering with GRP.

Stainless steel shelving has been used in aquaria but it is expensive and is not immune to corrosion. Coated or painted mild steel is rarely satisfactory since the covering is easily broken and rusting ensues. Permanent benches and stands can be made from sea water-resistant concrete, which may be coated with resin paint for additional protection.

E. Heat Exchangers

Most polymer materials do not conduct heat well. Particular difficulty has therefore been experienced in selecting heat exchangers for the aquarium. Glass is satisfactory only for relatively small installations and nickel, stainless steel and titanium have usually been chosen as alternatives. However, nickel and even type 316 stainless steel heat exchangers have failed with sea water through crevice corrosion or failure at welded tube ends, and titanium has proven the only reliable metal. Recently, the development of graphite-impregnated resins, with a higher thermal conductivity than many metals, has allowed heat exchangers to be constructed from this relatively inert material. The heat exchangers are normally made up of plates or blocks of the material drilled axially and radially to create flow channels for the coolant and the water. Joints are sealed with PTFE. The resin has little tensile strength and the whole structure is therefore held under compression within a mild steel shell (which does not come into contact with the water being cooled). Heat exchangers constructed from bundles of fine bore PTFE tubing are also available.

F. Heaters

Heating water can sometimes pose an even greater problem than cooling. For the small electric aquarium, glass heaters are in general use, while for larger installations, several fused-silica heaters can be placed in an open tank. Stainless steel sheathed heaters have generally been found unsatisfactory in the marine aquarium, and in some cases have had to be replaced by titanium ones. Rather than applying heat directly, water may also be heated by passing it through a heat exchanger, perhaps linked to a domestic heating system. The control of water temperature is considered in Chapter 1.

G. Aquarium Instrumentation

Thermometers, pressure gauges, flow meters, water level recorders and a variety of other instruments are commonly found in the aquarium, and many of these items contain metallic parts. Type 316 stainless steel, the newer corrosion-resistant steel alloys and titanium are the preferred materials. These metals are also suitable as passive electrodes for detecting the presence of electrical signals in water (e.g. the electrocardiogram of freshwater fish) though metal electrodes cannot be used to examine the detailed characteristics of DC electrical signals.

Care must also be taken in selecting metals as active electrodes to which a voltage is applied (for example to measure the resistance of the medium in some water-level monitoring systems). Stainless steel and even

Table V. Metals for use in seawater.

Metal or alloy	Aquarium use	Corrosion characteristics in seawater	Designation	Composition
Cast iron	pump and valve bodies, pipework	good corrosion resistance of unalloyed steel but iron leaches out leaving only the graphite		Fe, C, traces of other metals
Mild or carbon steel, low alloy steel	should be avoided unless coated	poor corrosion resistance, corrosion products are non-toxic but stain		Fe, C, traces of other metals
Austenitic nickel cast iron	pump and valve bodies	good corrosion resistance, compatible with stainless steels type 304 and 316		Fe, Ni, Cr, percentage depending upon type (Ni 13–36%)
Stainless steel type 304	pump impellers, valve trim	suffers deep pitting and crevice corrosion, compatible with stainless steel type 316	BS 304S15 (EN 58E) AISI 304	Fe, Cr 18, Ni 10, C, 0.06%
Stainless steel type 316	thermometer pockets, heat exchangers, probes, pump impellers, valve trim	the preferred steel for the aquarium, easily worked but subject to some pitting and crevice corrosion only low carbon grade suitable for welding	BS 313S16 (EN 58J) AISI 316 BS 316S12 AISI 316L	Fe, Cr 18, Ni 10, No 3 C 0.07% C 0.03%
Stainless steel alloy 20	As above	more resistant to pitting and crevice corrosion than type 316		Cr 20, Ni 29, Mo 2, Cu + Nb 3%
Stainless steel alloy 25–20	As above	resistant to pitting and crevice corrosion	2RK65 904L	Cr 20, Ni 25, Mo 4.5, Cu 1.5
Nickel–molybdenum–chromium alloys	As above	virtually inert in seawater	Hastelloy C Inconel 625	typically Ni 59, Mo 1, Cr 16, Fe 5, W 4% Ni 61, Mo 9, Fe 4, Cb 4
Titanium	As above	virtually inert in seawater		Ti
Nickel–copper alloys and marine bronzes	pumps and valves for many marine applications	highly resistant to both corrosion and fouling, but potentially toxic, not compatible with some stainless steels		

titanium electrodes will corrode when large electrical currents are being passed through them, while the polarization which occurs with direct current will necessitate even higher voltages to overcome the surface barriers that have formed. Carbon electrodes are perhaps the best choice for applying a voltage to water without creating toxicity problems. Some of the more modern instruments are either completely inert, or contain a minimum of metal. Thus, electromagnetic flowmeters with very small titanium, platinum or resistant alloy electrodes replace older varieties with moving metal parts and level measuring devices employing active stainless steel electrodes can now be replaced by capacitance-measuring devices with coated probes.

H. Electrical Cables

Plastic sheathed electrical cables may occasionally need to be immersed in water. The cables may carry substantial currents to machinery like pumps, or conduct very small signals from instruments, and may sometimes be armoured. Immersed cables sheathed in plasticised PVC have failed in several marine applications where the cable has been attacked by organisms or has become permeated by water. Polythene is more resistant to both forms of attack, but is easily abraded. Polyurethane and synthetic rubber are satisfactory. Underwater connectors are available in a wide range of synthetic materials.

VI. TESTING AQUARIUM MATERIALS

There is an extensive literature on toxicity testing and bioassay procedures. Recent reviews on testing methods are provided by Anon., 1971.

In general, for the *in situ* aquarium testing of materials, only a simple procedure is necessary. The following comments are given for guidance:

(1) The test animals should be selected from those aquarium inhabitants which are believed to be most susceptible to contaminants. However, there is some advantage in selecting organisms like the rainbow trout, *Salmo gairdneri*; fathead minnow, *Pimephales promelas*; brown shrimp, *Crangon vulgaris*, and *Daphnia*, for which extensive toxicity data are already available.

(2) The animals should previously have been quarantined and be acclimated to the general test conditions and to the chosen assay water (usually typical aquarium water). Ideally, a control group of fish should be maintained in parallel with those being tested.

(3) The test can be performed in a closed tank with or without the renewal of water, or in flowing water. However, it should be noted that in a closed body of water, there may be an adaptation to the toxicant. In general, chemicals are toxic at lower concentrations under continuous flow conditions. Toxicants may only leach from some materials for a short period and to test such materials satisfactorily, some water renewal is necessary.

(4) As well as recording and removing dead fish, any signs of distress, rapid gill ventilation, loss of equilibrium, disease or unusual behaviour should also be noted.

VII. REFERENCES

Anon. (1971). *Water Quality Data Book 3*. US Environmental Protection Agency Washington DC.

Anon. (1972). "The analysis of raw, potable and waste waters", p. 316. HMSO, London.

Browne, R. D. (1974). The performance of concrete structures in the marine environment. *In* "Corrosion in the Marine Environment". Institute of Marine Engineers, London.

Bryan, G. W. (1977). Heavy metal contamination in the sea. *In* "Marine Pollution" (R. Johnston, ed.), Academic Press, London and New York.

Carmignani, G. M. and Bennet, J. P. (1976). Leaching of plastics used in closed aquaculture systems. *Aquaculture* **7**, 89–91.

EIFAC, F.A.O. (1973). Water quality criteria for European freshwater fish. Report on dissolved oxygen and inland fisheries. *Tech. Rep.* **19**.

EIFAC, F.A.O. (1976). Water quality criteria for European freshwater fish. Report on copper and freshwater fish. *Tech. Rep.* **27**.

Holcombe, G. W., Benoit, D. A., Leonard, E. N. and McKim, J. M. (1976). Long-term effects of lead exposure on three generations of brook trout. *Journal of the Fisheries Research Board of Canada* **33,** 1731–1741.

Johnston, R. (1976). "Marine Pollution", Academic Press, London and New York.

Kirk, W. W. (1972). Corrosion of high strength materials in seawater. *In* "Barobiology and the Experimental Biology of the Deep Sea" (R. W. Brauer ed.), p. 428. University of North Carolina Press, Chapel Hill, N.C.

La Que, F. L. (1975). "Marine Corrosion", p. 332. J. Wiley & Sons, New York.

Riley, J. P. (1975). Analytical chemistry of sea water. *In* "Chemical Oceanography, Vol. 3" (J. P. Riley and G. Skirrow, eds), p. 564. Academic Press, London and New York.

Sprague, J. B. (1964). Highly alkaline water caused by asbestos-cement pipeline. *The Progressive Fish Culturalist* **26**, 111–114.

Tuthill, A. H. and Schillmoller, C. M. (1973). "A Guide to the Selection of Marine Materials", p. 24. Inco Europe Ltd, London.

Chapter 7

Fish Capture and Transport

D. J. Solomon[1] and A. D. Hawkins[2]

Fisheries Laboratory, Lowestoft,[1] and Marine Laboratory, Aberdeen,[2] UK

I. FISH CAPTURE

A. Introduction

For most research on live fish, it is important that the experimental animals are healthy. The greatest damage to health is usually sustained during capture. Quite apart from direct physical injury, such as scale loss, the stress of capture and handling affects the ease with which fish are transported, and may subsequently render them vulnerable to a variety of ailments (see Chapter 10).

B. Damage During Capture

Fish are often damaged by abrasion during netting or handling. The integument may be particularly susceptible to damage, especially the delicate mucoid and epidermal layers that overlie the scale and normally provide waterproofing and disease protection. In freshwater fish, the damage can lead to the absorption of water and a loss of body salts by leaching or enhanced excretion, while with marine fish, it may lead to loss of body water. Such fluid balance problems can sometimes be temporarily alleviated by placing the fish in an isotonic external medium. Superficial wounds can also be infected with pathogens, later affecting the health and survival of the fish. Further stress results from the exhaustion of the fish during capture (Chapter 15). With some fishing methods, there is a period of sustained swimming or struggling which places the fish in a vulnerable physiological state.

Particular difficulties are encountered in obtaining fish from deep waters. The decompression experienced by fish as they are brought to the surface may damage them. Those fish lacking a gas phase may be little affected by the change in static pressure but others, especially those with a gas-filled swimbladder, can be severely injured. The main damage is from expansion of the swimbladder. Thus, in coming from a depth of 10 m to the surface, the volume of the gas inside this organ may double. In some fish, notably the carps, herrings and salmonids, the swimbladder communicates with the exterior, and excess gas may be voided. In others, the swimbladder is closed and unable to sustain the expansion of the contained gas. The organ may split or burst, releasing gas to the exterior or into the abdominal cavity. Alternatively, the organ may expand, everting the stomach or forcing the intestine from the cloacum. As a result, there may be severe abdominal bleeding and damage to the surrounding organs.

Fish damaged by decompression can survive, but their capture is almost always traumatic and at the very least a period for recovery must be allowed. For some experimental work, even the carps, salmonids and herrings may need to replace the gas voided during capture. Decompression effects can be minimized by taking fish from the shallowest possible depths. Alternatively, fish caught at depth may be brought to the surface in stages to avoid too extreme a decompression. Most decompression damage occurs near the surface and by keeping fish at an intermediate depth for several hours, the change in volume and pressure of the swimbladder can be accommodated. Rates of removal of gas from the swimbladder are discussed by Tytler and Blaxter (1973), who give a decompression schedule for gadoid fish (Fig. 1). Jones (personal communication) recommends that haddock, *Melanogrammus aeglefinus*, be raised at a rate where the pressure is reduced by 10% every 2 h. Tytler and Blaxter (loc. cit.) suggest that though a fall in pressure of 60% usually results in swimbladder rupture, a change of 50% can be adapted to by gadoid fish in less than 5 h.

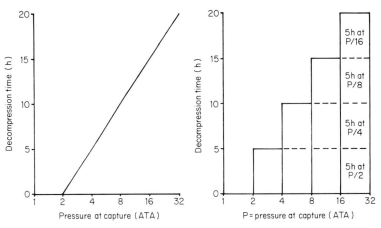

Fig. 1. (left) Aggregate time for safe decompression of gadoid fish; (right) decompression schedule showing steps required for safe decompression at different capture pressures. As an example, for a fish caught at 3 ATA (approximately 20 m depth) a single decompression halt of 5 h at a pressure of 1.5 ATA (5 m depth) is necessary. After Blaxter and Tytler (1973).

A variety of devices have been developed for catching and holding fish at depth to allow for subsequent gradual decompression. Detachable codends have been developed for trawls, which are released at completion of a haul, and close off. A float and small radio beacon are released to the surface. The codend and its contained fish can then be brought to the sea surface in stages. A much simpler device, which can be handled by one person, is a weighted cage which can be slid down a handline once a fish has been hooked to enclose the fish. The weight of the cage severs the cord connecting the fish hook to the main line, leaving the fish swimming freely inside the cage (Fig. 2). A variety of self-closing nets and tanks have also been developed for bringing smaller deep-water organisms to the surface (Brauer, 1972).

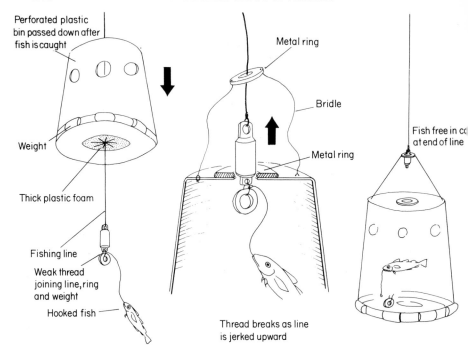

Fig. 2. Capture of fish inside a handline cage for subsequent slow decompression. Based on a design by R. Jones, the Marine Laboratory, Aberdeen.

The ambient pressure is of course not the only factor which may change when an animal is caught and brought to the surface. There may be substantial differences in temperature, salinity and oxygen level. Even washing the fish with surface water may result in thermal or osmotic shock, and be followed by death. Osmotic problems may especially be encountered if organisms from depths of 5 m or more are kept in water taken at the surface since the sea surface is often of low salinity especially near the coast. In addition, such factors as light level and ambient noise levels can be very different in a tank on the deck of a ship, and sensitive organisms may easily become stressed.

C. Methods of Capture

The choice of a particular fishing method will be dictated by many factors including the species sought, its density, the place and local legal restrictions. It is often sensible to employ the most common prevailing methods, which will generally have evolved to take account of specialized local conditions. Fishing expeditions can be expensive in manpower, and it is often worthwhile to investigate other sources. Such sources may include pet and scientific suppliers, commercial fish farms and marine stations. Some aquaria depend entirely on anglers and commercial fishermen for their fish.

(1) Netting

Fish caught by trawl or drag nets which are pulled along the sea bottom or through midwater, are often exhausted by swimming with the gear. They may be severely stressed, and their ability to withstand subsequent handling significantly impaired by this treatment. In addition, they may suffer much superficial damage and scale loss. To minimize these effects, towing times should be kept short and the net moved at slow speed. Ideally, the gear should also have a lined codend to minimize the effects of water flow on the fish and to retain water when the net is lifted out into the air. Fish caught in such a lined codend are much more lively than those caught in a net with a conventional codend, but many are often still poor in quality. Despite these disadvantages, towed nets often provide the only practical method of capture.

Gill-nets are generally hung in the water, and may drift with the current or be anchored. Fish are enmeshed by the head or gills as they swim into the net. The mesh size is generally chosen to trap fish of a particular size range, but some entangling nets like the trammel net or tangle net, are loosely hung or contain larger mesh sections, and the whole fish is enmeshed. A disadvantage of all these nets is that the fish are usually damaged on the head, gills or trunk, where they have been held by the netting. The damage is often especially severe with monofilament netting. Fish may also suffocate from forced closure of the gill chamber, exacerbated by fatigue. The net should be hung only for a short time, and should be carefully watched for fish hitting it. The fish should then be removed from the meshes quickly, taking care to minimize mechanical damage.

Cast nets are weighted pieces of netting which can be thrown over fish to entangle them. They are successful with fish which are not easily damaged and which are accessible to this form of fishing. Encircling nets, like the purse seine and beach seine are drawn around the fish to enclose them in a progressively smaller volume of water. The fish are rarely exhausted and the mesh size is usually too small for damage by entanglement. Healthy fish can be removed from the partially pursed net by brailing with a small lift or scoop net with a bucket. The chief damage is sustained by close contact with other fish, predators and harmful organisms like medusae. If the catch is large, the final pursing of the net may be so prolonged and involve a concentration of so many fish, that the oxygen level of the water is depleted. Crowding can be alleviated by slipping the net and allowing the bulk of fish to escape. With a beach seine, it is best not to draw the net right up to the shore, but to remove the fish while they are still immersed.

A dip-net, shaped like a bowl, can be very useful for catching fish at the surface. It can sometimes be very successfully applied at night, with fish immobilized or even attracted by means of a bright light. Where small nets are used to transfer fish from one tank to another, the netting should be soft and knotless to minimize mechanical damage. The mesh should be small enough to avoid entangling the fins, spines and gill covers, but not be so small that free passage of the net through the water is impeded. The bag of the net must be deep enough to retain the fish, especially when removed from the water, and for the more fragile species, it may need to be lined, so that the fish are always immersed in water. In very large tanks, netting partitions (which are easily made from plastic piping covering with synthetic netting or perforated polyethylene sheeting) can be used to shepherd or pen fish and to aid in their recapture. Alternatively, a netting lining placed inside the tank can be slowly pursed to enclose the fish.

(2) Trapping

Both baited and unbaited traps can be very effective in collecting live fish. Since the animal is enticed into the trap or enters of its own accord, it is rarely damaged or fatigued. However, the fish may later be damaged by other animals entering the trap, and is often injured when being extricated. Particularly delicate species are best removed underwater directly into a plastic bag. Alternatively, the lower part of the trap may be lined so that it retains water when hauled to the surface. Traps are especially useful for catching small fish on rocky shores or reefs, an example of such a trap being shown in Fig. 3a.

The design and operation of traps for adult salmonids are discussed by Allan (1965) and for salmon smolts by Mills (1964), while Clay (1961) and Hunter (1954) consider a variety of traps for other species. A range of specialized traps, sieves and screens prevent fish entering water extraction systems at industrial installations and may provide a good supply of live animals, though often they damage the fish.

(3) Electrical fishing

The capture of fish by electricity depends on maintaining an electrical field of adequate voltage and current flow in the water body. Salt and brackish waters are much more difficult to fish by this means than freshwater because the electrical conductivity is higher, requiring a substantial current to pass before fish are affected.

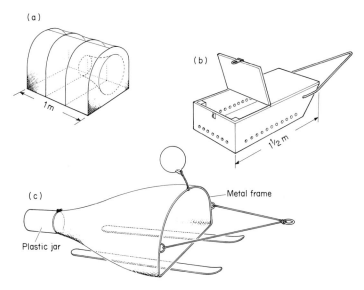

Fig. 3. Devices for the capture of small fish: (A) Simple fish trap, suitable for marine or freshwater species. (B) Floating keep-box of marine plywood. The shaped bow allows the box to be towed. The lid is normally closed.
(C) Small-fish trawl, with lined codend, float and skids.

Contributions in Vibert (1967) discuss the theory and practice of electric fishing. AC or DC can be used, but have different effects. AC stuns the fish, which may be collected by dip-nets, or by a downstream stop-net in running water. DC attracts fish to an anode by "galvanotaxis" (Chapter 9); the fish may be then collected with a dip-net or by a specially constructed scoop-shaped anode (e.g. Weiss and Cross, 1974). A refinement of DC fishing involves generating short pulses for a more economical use of power, enabling more portable DC generators to be used (Moore, 1955, Weiss, 1972). Other developments include the use of single or twin three-phase generators. Operator safety is considered by Hartley (1975). Methods of fishing are described by the authors already discussed and by Lagler (1968).

In most cases, if the apparatus is properly adjusted, fish recover very rapidly from the effects of electricity. However, an intense AC or pulsed DC electrical field can cause spinal fracture or haemorrhage. Electric fishing can be conducted by a small team in confined waters containing obstructions and where seine netting is impossible. All the apparatus can be carried in a small boat, making the unit very mobile. However, it is less efficient with small fish in large deep waters.

(4) Chemical methods

Rotenone (sometimes known as Derris) is an insecticide which, applied as an emulsion, inhibits the respiration of fish, bringing them to the surface where they may be collected. A procedure for small streams is described by Boccardy and Cooper (1963) and for pools by Meadows (1973a). Some fish are more susceptible to such asphyxiants than others; in general the elasmobranchs and eels are most resistant.

The emulsion is normally applied to give a final concentration of about 0.05 mg/l. Mixing can be a problem, especially in pools and Tate *et al.* (1965) suggest dispersal by the action of an outboard motor. Alternatively, the emulsion can be sprayed on to the water surface. An effective method of collecting fish by diver is to employ a flexible-sided bottle, with a small nozzle to squirt the asphyxiant into crevices and holes. The fish may then be netted or collected in polythene bags. Placing captured fish into fresh oxygenated or aerated water gives a high rate of recovery. Pools or streams downstream of a stop-net can be "neutralized" with potassium permanganate to prevent harm to other fish (Boccardy and Cooper, 1963), but this treatment is of little value in reviving fish. A 5% solution of methylene blue may revive some species. The toxicity of rotenone to some fish and invertebrates is discussed by Meadows (1973b).

In general, chemical collecting agents based on natural botanical substances like rotenone begin to degrade within a few hours of application and therefore do not have an extended effect. A variety of other chemicals may also be employed, including those listed later as tranquillizers. Their cost is generally prohibitive for large bodies of water, but they can be useful in enclosed waters. Gibson (1967) used a 20% solution of quinaldine in acetone, applied at a concentration of 20 ppm, to collect blennies from rock-pools. At the other extreme, MS 222 has been squirted over the gills of large sharks to subdue them (Clark 1962). With sodium cyanide, recovery of the fish is slow and often incomplete, and the material is exceedingly dangerous to handle. Another agent, isobornyl thiocyanoacetate, seems to be selective for certain species (Lewis 1968). Antimycin has also been applied with success. In some countries, the application of chemical agents to living animals is the subject of legislation, and only approved substances are permitted.

(5) Angling

Angling has several advantages over many other methods for obtaining small numbers of fish. Expertise is often available locally, and a collecting trip can be undertaken by one person with minimal equipment. The method can be species- and size-selective, and many fish can be obtained in excellent condition. A disadvantage is the relatively slow rate of catch.

Mechanical damage is often slight and is usually confined to the jaws, and can be minimized by the use of barbless hooks. In general, struggling by the fish can be minimized by using heavy tackle and by landing the fish quickly, preferably directly into water.

Long lines, set, or trot lines can provide larger numbers of fish. Suitable gear is described by Sainsbury (1971) and Nedéléc (1975), though it should be noted that some methods are illegal in freshwater in some countries. A disadvantage for many species is that the long-line hook may be swallowed, as the hook is not always "set" or "struck" into the jaw but is often swallowed with the bait. Fish with hard mouthparts can sometimes be hooked in the jaw with special hooks (e.g. the tuna circle hook). Hunsaker *et al.* (1970) have shown that trout caught by trolling with baited hooks are very likely to swallow the hook and sustain serious injury, whereas those caught on artificial flies and single treble-hooked lures are more often hooked in the jaw and show better subsequent survival.

(6) Eggs and young fish
Some eggs and very young fish may often be collected very easily, but identification can be a great problem if adult fish are not also in evidence. Finding the eggs and larvae is also a major problem. Many species have pelagic eggs and larvae, which may be taken in fine-mesh dip-nets or plankton tow nets. Eggs of nest-laying or demersal spawning species such as the salmonids, cottids and clupeoids may be collected from spawning sites either by divers or by dredges. Young fish may be collected in fine-mesh seine nets, purse seine or trawls, constructed of knotless netting, to minimize mechanical damage. Coles and Butterworth (1976) describe a beach seine 36.5 m × 4.8 m and a purse seine 36.5 × 6.6 m, both with 3 mm-diameter hexagonal mesh, which were effective at collecting small fish.

A design for a small fish trawl, given by Brown (1973), consists of a light metal framework, with a gape of about 50 cm, equipped with skids and floats. Most of the net is 4 meshes per cm, with a "codend" of 8 meshes per cm. Fish down to 15 mm were caught when towing at about 4 km/h. A somewhat larger small fish trawl (90 cm in diameter and 2 m long) is described by Johnson (1956) for catching juvenile sockeye salmon. Butterworth and Coles (1977) describe a small fish midwater trawl. With all towed gears, mechanical damage to the eggs and small fish is the major problem, which can be minimized by fishing the net for short periods. The fish caught may also be protected from the direct effects of water flow by lining the end of the net, as in Fig. 3c. If mechanical damage is a problem, then collecting by means of baited traps, or hand collection by a diver equipped with a bottle of strong anaesthetic solution and a polythene bag may provide a solution.

(7) Deep-water species

Though some deep-sea fish possess swimbladders which rupture when the fish are brought to the surface, many of the animals lack internal gas spaces and may be brought to the surface without sustaining serious damage. The enzymes of some deep-sea fish may be adapted to hyperbaric conditions but it seems that many deep-living fishes are relatively tolerant of large pressure changes, and need not be maintained under high pressures during collection. Much more serious problems may be created by factors unrelated to pressure. Deep-sea organisms are often stenothermal and stenohaline, and may need to be protected from warm, low salinity surface waters. Childress *et al.* (1978) have reported collecting living animals from depths as great as 1200 m off Southern California and attribute this success to the low prevailing surface temperatures in this region.

When collecting in other areas, it may be necessary to insulate and seal off the codend of nets for deep-sea species and to place the animals in refrigerated water as soon as they reach the surface. Childress *et al.* (1978) have constructed a thermally protecting bucket for use with midwater trawls. McCosker and Anderson (1976) have gradually acclimated deep-sea fish to temperatures 5–6°C above the capture temperature over periods of several days. Other factors which may be important are illumination (deep-sea organisms are familiar only with weak illumination, blue in colour) and oxygen level (many organisms come from oxygen-poor environments, though it is not clear whether high oxygen levels are undesirable).

Perhaps the most serious problem with many deep-sea fish, however, is their extreme fragility. Their bodies often show reduced structural support, so that the animals are flabby, often with an easily damaged integument. The sparse distributions of deep-sea organisms means that trawls and dredges are commonly employed to catch them, inflicting severe mechanical damage. Large volume grabs and water samplers, baited hooks and especially baited traps may offer a better chance of success. Traps in particular can be built so that they can later be sealed for transport to the surface. Nevertheless, deep-sea species have been captured with a large trawl fitted with a hyperbaric chamber towed at slow speed (3 km/h), the captured specimens being placed immediately into sea water barely above freezing. Some midwater fish may be captured in near-perfect condition by taking advantage of their epi-pelagic distribution while juveniles, or by capturing organisms at the peak of their nocturnal vertical migrations. They may even be attracted to the surface by means of lights and caught with a dip net. The capture, recovery and maintenance of deep-sea organisms in hyperbaric enclosures is discussed in a series of papers edited by Brauer (1972). Closing nets are described by Clarke (1969) and Davies and Barham (1969).

D. Handling and Holding

Handling fish during capture and transport should be kept to a minimum, ideally with fish being transferred in water, for example in a scoop, bucket or plastic bag. Where this is not possible, all surfaces coming into contact with the fish, such as cloths, nets and hands, should be thoroughly wetted. There is some advantage in wearing plastic surgical gloves. Large fish, especially gravid females, can be badly injured or killed by being lifted out of water while poorly supported. For such a fish a "stretcher" of canvas or netting, slung between two poles or on a hoop, allows lifting with minimum damage to the viscera. The fish should not be lifted by the caudal peduncle since this may result in spinal damage and haemorrhaging. Perhaps the best way of holding most fish is with one hand beneath the snout or jaw and the other supporting the belly. If fish need to be tagged or marked before transfer to a container for transport, the least damage is done to most species by placing them in a V-shaped trough lined with foam rubber. Additional restraint can be provided by webbing belts. Very large, or very delicate fish, can often best be transferred by swimming them into a tray or bag which is then removed from the water.

It is often necessary to hold fish for a period after capture, before placing them in a container for transport. Simplest is holding the fish in a net or cage in the water. Stott (1968) describes a keep-box and a floating net cage based on an inflatable life-raft. Anglers' keep-nets are satisfactory for short-term holding, but are usually of limited size, and considerable damage can arise from abrasion if fish are held in them for a long time. This damage can be reduced by the use of knotless mesh (Coles and Butterworth, 1976). Large sharks, caught on trot-lines, have been swum or slid into a live-car or barge with a slatted or perforated bottom which is then towed to the eventual destination (Clark, 1962).

When it is not possible or desirable to keep fish for an intermediate period in a netting enclosure or to tow them in a special keep box or barge, they may be placed in tank on the catching vessel or on shore. Such a tank may need to be baffled to prevent the water and fish slopping about, and may need to be thermally insulated. Fish are often less active in such a tank if there is a covering lid to exclude light. Black plastic bags, supported by a carrying box have been used successfully to hold large Atlantic salmon after capture. Many species regurgitate or defaecate immediately after capture, and an intermediate holding tank ensures that these materials are not carried into the transporting tank. Most commercial vessels have a clean-water pump which can be pressed into service to supply holding tanks. It should be noted that commercial fishermen seldom handle live fish gently; generally they require special training or instruction.

A very effective way of holding fish and then transporting them in bulk from the place of capture is by means of a barge. Such a vessel has been built by Ian Edwards of the Marine Laboratory, Aberdeen and is shown in Fig. 4. Fish caught by purse seine or ring net are transferred directly to the hold of the barge in large buckets and are then taken distances of up to 100 miles by towing the barge behind a fishing vessel or research ship. During the journey, fresh sea water is continually pumped into the hold and allowed to overflow. At their destination, the fish are shepherded to one end of the barge with a netting curtain and then transferred by bucket to a keep cage in the sea. Adult herring and mackerel, difficult and fragile pelagic species, have successfully been maintained in the barge at densities of up to 100 small fish per m³.

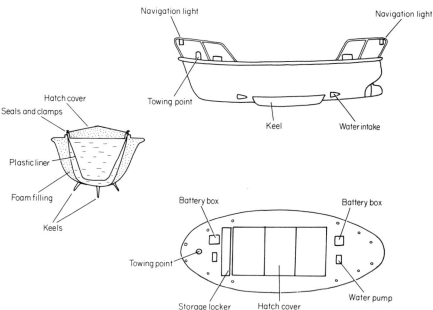

Fig. 4. A fish barge, made from a standard life-boat hull, designed by Ian Edwards of the Marine Laboratory, Aberdeen.

The vessel is constructed from a standard 8 m glass-reinforced plastic lifeboat hull. The hold, of 10 m³ volume, is constructed of plywood lined on the inside with glass-reinforced plastic and is separated from the hull by an injected layer of rigid plastic foam. This foam layer provides the buoyancy for the vessel. The hold is lined with a smooth nylon-reinforced PVC bag, supported by shock cords, and backed by water contained within the hold itself. Plastic foam hatch covers bolt in position over the hold and prevent water sloshing out of the tank, while still permitting some overflow. Water is delivered from the sea by duplicated pumps operating from DC batteries. Particularly important in the design of such a barge is the provision of a strong and stable towing point, a system of bilge keels to prevent the barge yawing when towed at high speeds (8–9 knots), duplication of the pumping system and a smooth lining to the tank. In the first few hours after introducing the fish, it is important to remove the considerable quantities of faeces and regurgitated food material which otherwise foul the water. This may be done with a suction pump or air lift. In the event of the barge entering a busy harbour or heavily polluted waters, the water circulation system can be closed down, and aeration substituted.

The advantage of such a barge is that it can be placed close to the point of capture of the fish, making transfer easy. Disturbance of the fish is also minimal. A similar vessel could be constructed with a perforated hull, doing away with the need for water circulation, but such a free-flooding barge could not be used in polluted waters.

II. FISH TRANSPORT

A. Introduction

A considerable literature exists on transporting live fish, mainly for food or restocking. The topic has recently been reviewed by Vollman-Schipper (1975). Such fish are often carried at very high densities with the minimum of water and equipment. However, the individual animals required for research are often very valuable in terms of the time taken to obtain them in good condition, and the numbers and weights are not usually large. It is often more important to maximize survival of the fish being carried, rather than to achieve high densities.

B. Containers

Large-scale commercial transport usually involves the use of specially constructed trucks and tankers fitted with a supply of compressed air or oxygen, but for small-scale operations, a simple trough or tank in a car or Land Rover is often adequate. Dimensions must be dictated by the numbers and size of fish to be carried (see page 211), and by the carrying capacity of the vehicle.

An important factor is that the tank or container should be well insulated to keep the water cool or warm, as the case may be. Fibreglass containers, from about 30 l capacity are widely available as general storage boxes or water cisterns. Clip-on lids are often also available. Perforated baffles, to stop water movement, are useful for road transport. They should be smooth to avoid damaging the fish, and removable to facilitate fish removal. Toxic materials should be avoided (Chapter 6). Polythene or PVC bags inside rigid containers are excellent at reducing water movement, covering sharp or abrasive surfaces and isolating the fish from toxic materials and are easily carried, but suffer from the disadvantage that they may easily be punctured. Small perforations are not a problem if the outside container is watertight or if two bags are used, one inside the other. The bags may be placed inside metal or polypropylene bins, or cardboard or polystyrene boxes, preferably fitted with strong carrying handles and lined with a suitable insulating material (Fig. 5). Ice can then be packed around the bag containing the fish. For air transport, the container must not only be lightweight but also sealed and leakproofed. The conventional plastic "ice-box" is very suitable for small fish. Design of containers for large batches of fish is discussed by Norris *et al.* (1960), Huet (1972) and Vollmann-Schipper (1975).

Where the container is being continually aerated during the journey, it can be designed to have maximum water volume. If the tank is aerated only at the beginning of the trip, the container must be designed to include a large gas space above the water to facilitate gas exchange. Indeed, for this form of transport the water volume must be kept to a minimum.

Some species of fish can be transported out of water for periods of several hours if immobilized with a suitable anaesthetic. After anaesthesia, the fish are packed in a mixture of a moist packing material e.g. sphagnum moss, and crushed ice in an insulated container. The packing material should be free-draining to prevent the accumulation of water around the fish and resultant hypoxia. The method will not work with many species whose gill filaments collapse out of water, preventing efficient oxygen exchange. Containers for transporting fish should be kept clean and should periodically be scrubbed with a sterilizing solution (Chapter 3).

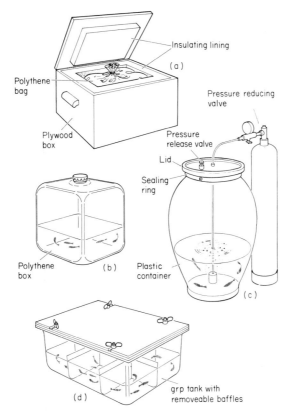

Fig. 5. Containers for transporting fish: (A) Insulated box, suitable for air-freighting small fish. (B) Simple container for small fish, note the low water volume to promote good mixing with the gas space above. (C) Simple transport tank made from a polypropylene drum, allowing a constant flux fo air or oxygen with minimal water loss. (D) Box with removeable perforated baffles.

C. Density of Fish

Under carefully controlled conditions, densities of up to 1 kg of fish per litre of water have been successfully transported (salmonids: Haskell and Davies (1958), Prevost and Piche (1939); carp: Bardach *et al.* (1972)). Densities of around one tenth of this are more usual and ensure that the health and well-being of the fish are preserved. As an approximate guide, 2 kg of fish can be placed in 20 litres of water inside a polythene bag, with a large oxygen-filled space above it, and at 10°C, can be carried for 5 h without the need for further oxygenation. However, the density chosen will in practice depend on the species, the type of tank, the temperature and many other factors, and must really be determined by trial and error for each specific situation. At high densities, fish become agitated, which increases oxygen consumption and risk of damage. Loss of mucus may also occur which can cause discomfort or choking of the gills. Foaming of mucus-laden water may occur with aeration, and may be suppressed by the use of a non-toxic anti-foaming agent.

D. Temperature

Temperature influences the activity and oxygen consumption of the fish, and also the oxygen-carrying capacity of the water. High temperature especially may also be directly lethal to fish. From all these aspects, a low water temperature, at least as cool as the water from which the fish were taken, is preferred. Cooling the fish has often been used successfully to calm fish for transport. Chipped or crushed ice is satisfactory for most journeys, but for long distance air freighting of fish, dry ice has a greater cooling capacity for its weight. However, caution must be exercised to prevent the evaporating CO_2 from dry ice coming into contact with the water. Deep frozen blocks of ice, or special cooling bags are safer and last a very long time.

With fish from warm tropical waters, water cooling can be a handicap. Heavy insulation reduces cooling to a minimum and chemical heating packs can be helpful. The problem is most pronounced when tropical species are being transported to temperate climes, especially if fish are trans-shipped from one aircraft to another and the container is left exposed to ambient conditions at the airport. Perhaps the best solution in this event is to arrange for someone on the spot to properly look after fish being trans-shipped (see p. 217).

In most cases, extreme temperature changes can be avoided by adequately insulating the fish container with plastic foam or expanded polystyrene and by travelling only at the most appropriate time of day. Temperature changes should be effected gradually, for example by switching on cooling gear or adding ice bags or dry ice containers after the fish have been placed in the transporting tank. On arrival at more permanent holding facilities, the temperature should be raised or lowered slowly over several hours if the difference is more than a few degrees.

E. Dissolved Gases

To maintain fish in a healthy state, there must be sufficient oxygen in the water. In addition, the build-up of carbon dioxide and ammonia must be prevented. Gas concentrations can become critical under transport conditions where the fish are stressed and their oxygen requirement greatly elevated. Oxygen concentrations can be maintained by bubbling compressed or pumped oxygen or air, or by surface agitation. For small quantities of fish transported for a short period, continual aeration is unnecessary. The fish are provided with well-aerated water with an air space above it, the vehicle movement providing the agitation. The effectiveness is increased by maximizing the surface area, or by providing an atmosphere of oxygen above the water. For this purpose, a large space of about 4 times the water volume must be left in the container to contain the air or oxygen. Where larger fish are being transported on especially long journeys, or where the animals have a high oxygen demand, it is necessary to bubble air or oxygen continually through the tank.

Pure oxygen is not harmful to freshwater fish (Winstone and Solomon 1976), but the cost of the gas and associated equipment may render compressed or pumped air a more attractive alternative. Medical air, or air for diving purposes is best, since compressed air for other purposes may contain oil or traces of noxious gases. If a gas cylinder is used, it is important to use a pressure regulator to meter the gas flow and to ensure that gas continues to flow at a constant rate regardless of cylinder pressure. Twelve-volt electric pumps can easily be run from a vehicle electrical supply to provide fish with air. In general, for transporting fish at high densities for long periods, the oxygen level can be best kept high, and CO_2 levels low, by ensuring that there is a continual flux of gas with the lid of the holding tank vented to the outside, either directly or by means of a pressure release valve.

Carbon dioxide is toxic to fish, both directly and by decreasing their ability to extract oxygen from the water (Alabaster, Herbert and Hemens 1957). With low fish densities and high aeration rates, it is unlikely to attain toxic levels. Where fish are transported without continual aeration, CO_2 does build up. Taylor and Solomon (1979a) describe a situation with high fish densities and low flows of oxygen where CO_2 concentration became a problem though the level of oxygen remained high. Loss of balance of fish occurs at CO_2 levels below lethal, so advance warning of a critical situation is given.

Ammonia is produced as the major nitrogenous excretory produce by most teleosts, and is very toxic. Oxygen concentrations and pH both affect ammonia toxicity. It is the un-ionized ammonia which is particularly toxic and the equilibrium is markedly influenced by pH; a shift from pH 8 to 7 produces a tenfold decrease in the quantity of un-ionized ammonia (Downing and Merkens 1955). Decrease in dissolved oxygen increases the toxicity of un-ionized ammonia (Merkens and Downing 1957). A change in pH ratio across a tissue barrier (e.g. gills) can also greatly influence the concentration of the un-ionized gas each side of the barrier (Spotte 1970). At low fish densities, the build-up of ammonia is unlikely to create problems during transport. The risk can be reduced further by holding fish without food for two days before transporting, as ammonia excretion rate drops rapidly in an unfed state.

Chemicals, either as solutions or tablets, are available from aquarium suppliers which when added to water, increase the oxygen content. These materials can be useful in an emergency, but care should be taken to ensure that they do not come into direct contact with the fish, and that they do not alter the pH of the water.

F. Salinity

The body fluids of both salt-water and freshwater fish have salt concentrations between those of freshwater and sea water. Thus, both are constantly under osmotic stress, and are having to work to maintain their internal ionic equilibrium. When a fish is physically damaged, the rate of exchange can increase and represent a greater stress. Alteration of the external medium has been used in the transport of both freshwater and sea fish to reduce this stress (Chapter 15).

Chittenden (1971) used a 5 g/l sodium chloride solution for carrying shad, *Alosa sapidissima*, while Wedermeyer (1972) used a 3 g/l solution for young coho, *Oncorhynchus kisutch* and rainbow trout. Smolts of chinook salmon, *O. tschawytscha*, have been successfully transported using a 15 g/l sodium chloride solution and threadfin shad, *Dorosoma peteneuse* using a 5 g/l solution. A useful secondary benefit of this procedure is that the risk of infection with the fungus *Saprolegnia* is much reduced by the use of as little as 3 g/l solution. Marine species, such as the clupeoids, which are very susceptible to water loss during capture, can be successfully transported in water of reduced salinity.

G. Tranquilizers

Greatly increased physical activity during transport can adversely affect the health of fish in two ways. Physical damage by abrasion with the tank and other fish has already been discussed. The second, less obvious way is by a physiological reaction to physical activity and other environmental factors such as low dissolved oxygen. Such a reaction is manifested in high blood lactate levels which can cause serious debilitation or death. Lactate levels may continue to rise for some hours after severe exercise, and it has been suggested that this may be involved in the so-called delayed planting mortality following transport of salmonids (Black 1957, 1958). A more detailed discussion of stress-induced changes in carbohydrate metabolism is given by Wendt and Saunders (1973) and the general topic of stress is discussed in Chapter 15. Thus, the level of physical activity of transported fish must be kept to a minimum. Low water temperatures can help, as can covering carrying tanks with light-proof material. A third possibility is the use of tranquillizers.

A considerable range of chemicals are potentially useful as tranquillizers, some being employed at higher concentrations as anaesthetics (Chapter 9). The ideal tranquillizer for fish transport reduces motor activity and oxygen demand. The substance should, however, be safe to the operator, have no side-effects upon the fish, and show a wide margin of safety between the effective dose and lethal dose. The substance must be cheap and easily administered, and the fish should show rapid induction to, and recovery from the tranquillized state.

McFarland (1960) concluded that tertiary amyl alcohol, methylpara-fynol and chloral hydrate were the most suitable materials, and considered that ethyl alcohol, tertiary butyl alcohol and MS 222 were the least suitable, the last tending to induce a progressively deeper anaesthesia. In reviewing fish anaesthetics, Bell (1964) listed seven as potentially useful for transport, viz. chloral hydrate, chloretone, methyl pentynol, MS 222, sodium amylobarbitone and tertiary amyl alcohol. Durve (1975) investigated thirteen anaesthetics for use in transporting young mullet and concluded that tertiary amyl alcohol and MS 222 offered fewest disadvantages, though several others were also considered effective. Taylor and Solomon (1979b) have investigated the three most widespread chemicals, MS 222, chloral hydrate and tertiary amyl alcohol.

Rainbow trout were examined at densities ranging from 75 to 400 g of fish to each litre of water, with a range of concentrations of anaesthetics. Physical activity was much reduced with all three chemicals, though periods of activity and hyperventilation occurred throughout with chloral hydrate. The oxygen flow required to maintain saturation appeared to be influenced only to a minor extent by MS 222 and chloral hydrate, but was markedly reduced with tertiary amyl alcohol. The decreased flow of oxygen possible with the latter substance, however, can result in the CO_2 level rising, a situation discussed by Winstone and Solomon (1976). From the point of view of other considerations, there is little to choose between the three. Costs for MS 222 and tertiary amyl alcohol are similar. Benzocaine may be substituted for MS 222, at a greatly reduced price and with more satisfactory results in freshwater, but it must first be dissolved in acetone or ethanol (Laird and Oswald 1975).

In view of the above considerations, tertiary amyl alcohol appears to be the most reliable of the available tranquillizers. Benzocaine offers the advantage of cheapness, but as with MS 222, the treated animal may develop hypoxia, induced by the lack of ventilation movements associated with progressively deeper anaesthesia (Chapter 9). Schoettger and Steucke (1970) suggested that some of the disadvantages of MS 222 for transporting fish could be overcome by using a synergic mixture of MS 222 and quinaldine.

The concentration of anaesthetic depends on the desired effect. McFarland (1960) suggests that the fish should be in a state of deep sedation but Durve (1975) preferred light sedation. Loss of equilibrium is undesirable since the animal may struggle to remain upright, but is not immediately lethal. Concentrations should be adjusted to just avoid this state. The concentration will vary with species and temperature, but suggested levels are:

(1) Tertiary amyl alcohol: 0.3–0.8 g (1.0 ml)/l
(2) MS 222: 10–30 mg/l
(3) Chloral hydrate: 250 mg/l
(4) Quinaldine: 5 mg/l, plus MS 222: 10–30 mg/l

These levels are well below those required for deep anaesthesia (Chapter 9). McFarland (1960) stresses the desirability of "pre-treating" the fish being tranquillized. The fish should be introduced to the tranquillizer an hour or so before gross handling or stimulation such as crowding or "joggling" in transport.

The most commonly used tranquillizer for terrestrial vertebrates, etorphine acetylpromazine is conventionally applied by direct injection as are several other anaesthetics (Chapter 9). This method of administration is not really suitable for transporting fish in water, but the method might be employed for special purposes, such as transporting large individual fish packed out of water in some moist material. There is a need for further tests on tranquillizers for the transport of fish.

H. General

It is important that the fish should be properly prepared for transport. Food should be withheld for at least one day beforehand, indeed for some cold water species with slow digestion rates, it is often better not to feed them for the preceding week to ensure that food cannot be regurgitated and excretion is minimal. Then the fish should be carefully transferred to their tank of newly aerated water for transport with a minimum of disturbance. If continuous aeration is not possible during the journey, a final topping up with oxygen or air will be necessary at the last possible moment, before the tank is finally sealed. If a polythene bag is in use, it should be inflated to provide a large gas space above the water, and the aerating tube withdrawn through a constricting neck before the bag is tightly tied (Fig. 6). The tank or bag, inside its container, should then be gently transferred to the vehicle and firmly secured in position so that it cannot move or topple over.

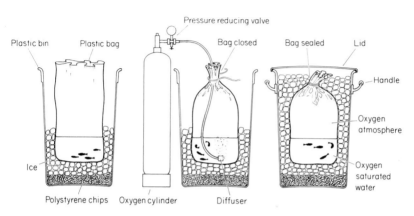

Fig. 6. Transport of fish in a plastic bag inside a waste bin. Only a small quantity of water is necessary. Such a tank has been used, unattended, to transport codfish from Scotland to the Netherlands by air.

Transport by air presents special difficulties, especially if frontiers must be crossed. The fish often have to be taken to the airport well before the flight leaves to permit inspection and weighing, and to enable a prodigious number of documents to be completed. Similarly, at its destination, the container may be subjected to further delays before it is handed over. Thus, it is not only the flight time that must be considered in planning transport by air. It is often useful to employ a specialist freight handler experienced in shipping livestock to help with the arrangements and complicated documentation. At stopover points, it may be necessary to employ someone to ensure that the fish are properly cared for, especially if flights are delayed. At London Heathrow, there is an animal welfare service to assist with this problem. As examples of the difficulties that can arise, it should be noted that not all aircraft are permitted to carry livestock, while even at certain international airports, special arrangements have to be made with customs officials if livestock arrive at weekends. One particular problem with air transport is that fish may be placed in an unheated cargo hold where the temperature may drop to very low levels during the flight. Tropical fish, especially, must be well insulated, and must be placed in a heated and pressurized part of the aircraft.

The various inspections of the fish which may have to be carried out are eased if the container has a small observation port which permits airline and customs officials to see the fish without completely unpacking everything. Sometimes, by special arrangement with the freight company, it is possible to stay with the fish until they are carried on board the aircraft. It is then possible to aerate the water at the last possible moment. Such adjustments may be forbidden after the container has been weighed or sealed, however. As an alternative for large fish on long journeys, it is possible to transport fish in a tank with an air or oxygen cylinder attached for continuous aeration. However, it is advisable to seek prior permission from the airline before this is done.

Where a customs inspection is obligatory, it is advisable to mark the container with a clear description of the number and nature of the fish, stating their country of origin and market value (so that any import duty can be swiftly levied, with a minimum of delay or fuss). Special documentation is sometimes necessary. For example, to enter some countries, fish must be certified by a veterinary surgeon as being free from particular diseases (salmonid fish, especially, must be certified as being free of certain virus infections). Sometimes the airline itself requires a certificate stating that the fish are free of parasites and infectious diseases, and fit to travel. Such certificates may have to be obtained from a government agency, and may involve a series of tests. It must also be remembered that international agreements restrict the importation of certain endangered species of fish, unless special licences are issued. Even within a country, legislation may not permit fish to be moved from one area to another without a certificate guaranteeing that they come from disease-free stock.

Having reached their destination, it is important to ensure that the fish are not simply dumped into a new tank. They must gradually be brought to the correct temperature before transfer. Gradually bleeding in water from the new holding tank is not advised (p. 164). If the fish are floated on to the surface of the new tank, it is often important that their bag or tank should continue to be aerated, since gas exchange even through a polythene bag is not sufficient. Finally, it is advisable that new stock are kept separate from existing stock for as long as possible to avoid the introduction of infection (see Chapter 10).

III. REFERENCES

Alabaster, J. S., Herbert, D. W. M. and Hemens, J. (1957). The survival of rainbow trout and perch, at various concentrations of dissolved oxygen and carbon dioxide. *Annals of applied Biology* **45**, 177–188.

Allan, I. R. H. (1965). Counting fences for salmon and sea trout and what can be learned from them. *Salmon and Trout Association Conference*, London.

Bardach, J. E., Ryther, J. H. and McLarnney, W. O. (1972). "Aquaculture", Wiley-Interscience, London.

Bell, G. R. (1964). A guide to the properties, characteristics and uses of some general anaesthetics for fish. *Bulletin of the Fisheries Research Board of Canada* **48**.

Black, E. C. (1957). Alterations in the blood level of lactic acid in certain Salmonid fishes following muscular activity. I Kamloops trout (*Salmo gairdneri*). *Journal of the Fisheries Research Board of Canada* **14**, 117–134.

Black, E. C. 1958. Hyperactivity as a lethal factor in fish. *Journal of the Fisheries Research Board of Canada* **15**, 573–586.

Boccardy, J. A. and Cooper, E. L. (1963). The use of rotenone and electro-fishing in surveying small streams. *Trans. American Fisheries Society* **92**, 307–310.

Brauer, R. W. (ed.), (1972). "Barobiology and the experimental biology of the deep sea". Proceedings of the 1st Symposium on high pressure aquarium systems. University of North Carolina.

Brown, D. J. A. (1973). The effects of power station cooling water discharges on the growth of coarse fish fry. *Proceedings of the 6th Coarse Fish Conference*. Janssen Services, London. 191–197.

Butterworth, A. J. and Coles, T. F. (1977). The use of a midwater trawl to sample lacustrine fish populations. *Fisheries Management* **8**, 35–42.

Childress, J. J., Barnes, A. T., Quetin, L. B. and Robison, B. H. (1978). Thermally protecting codends for the recovery of living deep sea animals. *Deep Sea Research* **25**, 419–422.

Chittenden, M. E. Jr. (1971). Transporting and handling young American shad. *New York Fish and Game Journal* **18**, 123–128.

Clay, C. H. (1961). "Design of fishways and other fish facilities". Department of Fisheries of Canada.

Clark, E. (1962). Maintenance of sharks in captivity. *1er Congrés international Aquariol. Monaco* **A**, Monaco. 1–19.

Clarke, M. R. (1969). A new midwater trawl for sampling discrete depth horizons. *Journal of Marine Biological Association of the UK* **49**, 945–960.

Coles, T. F. and Butterworth, A. J. (1976): The use of knotless netting in fisheries research. *Fisheries Management* **7**, 53–56.

Davies, I. B. and Barham, E. G. (1969). The Tucker opening-closing mechanism and its performance in a study of the deep-scattering layer. *Marine Biology* **2**, 127–131.

Downing, K. M. and Merkens, J. C. (1955). The influence of dissolved oxygen on the toxicity of unionised ammonia to rainbow trout (*Salmo gairdneri* Richardson). *Annals of applied Biology* **43**, 1–14.

Durve, V. S. (1975). Anaesthetics in the transport of mullet seed. *Aquaculture* **5**, 53–63.

Gibson, R. N. (1967). The use of the anaesthetic quinaldine in fish ecology. *Journal of Animal Ecology* **36**, 295–301.

Hartley, W. G. (1975). Electrical fishing apparatus and its safety. *Fisheries Management* **6**, 73–77.

Haskell, D. C. and Davies, R. O. (1958). Carbon dioxide as a limiting factor in trout transportation. *New York Fish and Game Journal* **5**, 175–183.

Huet, M. (1972). "Textbook of fish culture". Fishing News (Books) Ltd, London.

Hunsaker, D., Marnell, L. F. and Sharpe, F. P. (1970). Hooking mortality of cut-throat trout. *Progressive Fish Culturist* **32**, 231–234.

Hunter, J. G. (1954). A weir for adult and fry salmon effective under conditions of extremely variable run-off. *Canadian Fish Culturist* **16**, 5–8.

Johnson, W. E. (1956). On the distribution of young sockeye salmon (*Oncorhynchus nerka*) in Babine and Nilkirkqa Lakes B.C. *Journal of the Fisheries Research Board of Canada* **13**, 695–708.

Laird, L. M. and Oswald, R. L. (1975). A note on the use of Benzocaine (Ethyl *p*–aminobenzoate) as a fish anaesthetic. *Fisheries Management* **6**, 92–94.

Lagler, K. F. (1968). Capture, sampling and examination of fishes. *In* "Fish Production in Freshwater" (W. E. Ricker, ed.), IBP handbook No. **3**, 7–45.

Lewis, W. M. (1968). Isobornyl thiocyanoacetate as a fish drugging agent and selective toxin. *Progressive Fish Culturist* **30**, 29–31.

McFarland, W. N. (1960). The use of anaesthetics for the handling and the transport of fishes. *California Fish Game* **46**, 407–431.

McCosker, J. E., Anderson, M. E. (1976). Aquarium maintenance of mesopelagic animals a progress report. *Bulletin of the California Academy of Science* **75**, 211–219.

Meadows, B. S. (1973a). The use of rotenone in fisheries management. *Fisheries Management* **4**, 12–15.

Meadows, B. S. (1973b). Toxicity of rotenone to some species of coarse fish and invertebrates. *Journal of Fish Biology* **5**, 155–163.

Mills, D. H. (1964). The ecology of the young stages of the Atlantic salmon in the river Bran, Ross-shire. *DAFS. Freshwater Salmon Fisheries Research* **32**, 1–39.

Moore, W. H. (1955). A new type of electrical fish catcher. *Journal of Animal Ecology* **23**, 373–375.

Nédélec, C. (ed.), (1975). "Catalogue of small scale fishing gear". FAO Fishing News (Books) Ltd, London.

Norris, K. S., Brocato, F., Calandrino, F. and McFarland, W. N. (1960). A survey of fish transportation methods and equipment. *California Fish Game* **46**, 5–33.

Prevost, G. and Piché, L. (1939). Observations on the respiration of trout fingerlings and a new method of transporting speckled trout (*Salvelinus fontinalis*). *Trans. American Fisheries Society* **68**, 344–353.

Sainsbury, J. C. (1971). "Commercial Fishing Methods an Introduction to Vessels and Gears", Fishing News (Books) Ltd, London.

Spotte, S. H. (1970). "Fish and Invertebrate Culture", Wiley Interscience, New York.

Stott, B. (1968). Marking and Tagging. *In* "Fish Production in Freshwaters", (W. E. Ricker, ed.), IBP Handbook No. **3**, 78–92.

Tate, B., Moen, J. and Severson, B. I. (1965). The use of rotenone for the recovery of live fish. *Progressive Fish Culturist* **27**, 158–160.

Taylor, A. L. and Solomon, D. J. (1979a). Critical factors in the transport of living freshwater fish. I General considerations and atmospheric gases. *Fisheries Management* **10**, 27–32.

Taylor, A. L. and Solomon, D. J. (1979b). Critical factors in the transport of living freshwater fish. III The use of anaesthetics as tranquillizers. *Fisheries Management* **10**, 153–157.

Tytler, P. and Blaxter, J. H. S. (1973). Adaptation by cod and saithe to pressure changes. *Netherlands Journal of Sea Research* **7**, 31–45.

Vibert, R. (ed.) (1967). Fishing with electricity. Its application to biology and management. FAO/Fishing News (Books) Ltd, London.

Vollman-Schipper, F. (1975). "Transport lebender Fische", Parey, Berlin.

Wedemeyer, G. (1972). Some physiological consequences of handling stress in the juvenile coho salmon (*Oncorhynchus kisutch*) and steel head trout (*Salmo gairdneri*). *Journal of the Fisheries Research Board of Canada* **29**, 1780–1783.

Weiss, D. M. (1972). A high power pulse generator for electric fishing. *Journal of Fish Biology* **4**, 453–460.

Weiss, D. M. and Cross, D. G. (1974). A design for fishing electrodes for use in freshwater. *Fisheries Management* **5**, 114–116.

Wendt, C. and Saunders, R. L. (1973). Changes in carbohydrate metabolism in young Atlantic salmon in response to various forms of stress. International Atlantic Salmon Symposium, *ICNAF Spec. Publ.* **4**, 55–82.

Winstone, A. J. and Solomon, D. J. (1976). The use of oxygen in the transport of fish. *Fisheries Management* **7**, 30–36.

Chapter 8

The Food and Feeding of Captive Fish

C. B. Cowey

Institute of Marine Biochemistry, Aberdeen

I. INTRODUCTION

Until comparatively recent times, virtually all captive fish held for experimental or other purposes, have been maintained on natural food of one sort or another. To ensure continuity of supply this food has normally been stored deep-frozen, portions being thawed at appropriate intervals on demand. The type of food has to some extent, depended upon season as well as the location of the aquarium. In the UK, squid muscle, sand eels and sprats have frequently been favoured.

Underlying the use of these natural foods is the thought that as they form part of the diet of fish in the wild, they provide a complete diet.

While this may be true of the living food, it may not be so once this material has been deep-frozen for an indefinite period and then thawed. In particular, some of the fatty acids characteristic of marine animals are highly unsaturated and readily subject to autoxidation with deleterious consequences, while certain water-soluble vitamins are labile and therefore subject to degradation. Thus Blaxter *et al.* (1974) reported a mortality due to B vitamin deficiency, of cultured herring (*Clupea harengus*) given diets consisting of frozen mysids and minced mussel and squid. Besides the danger that natural food may deteriorate during storage, a second hazard is the possibility that transmissible diseases may be introduced into the aquarium stock; few establishments adopt procedures to eliminate this risk.

For reasons such as these (as well as, of course, the upsurge in fish farming) there has been an increasing interest in quantifying the nutrient requirements of various species of fish. Eventually these studies may result in the availability of pelleted food of reproducible quality, tailored to the needs of various species commonly held in aquaria. Controlled rations should help eliminate one of the variables (i.e. nutrition status) normally overlooked in experimental work. However, an effective ration is not just one that is nutritionally adequate; it must also be palatable to the fish. Thus the present chapter deals not only with the food requirements of fish, but also with compounds that when added to apparently bland but alien nutrients render the whole diet attractive (organoleptic compounds).

II. FOOD

A. Protein

Dietary proteins supply the amino acids necessary for growth and maintenance. Classically, amino acids are regarded as either essential (those which the animal cannot itself synthesize from non-specific sources of nitrogen and carbon and which must therefore be supplied in the diet) or non-essential. In a way, this distinction is artificial in that, were an animal supplied with only essential amino acids as nitrogen source, then some of these would have to be used to synthesize non-essential amino acids. Thus the quantitative requirements for essential amino acids would be greater than normal.

All species of fish so far examined require the same ten amino acids. These are arginine, lysine, histidine, threonine, methionine, valine, leucine, isoleucine, phenylalanine and tryptophan. The quantitative requirement of Pacific salmon (*Oncorhynchus tshawytscha*) for all these amino acids has been obtained from dose/response curves by Halver *et al.* (Mertz (1969) for summary). Data for other species, although incomplete at present, show marked differences between species (Cowey, 1979), differences that are related to the relative efficiencies with which digested amino acids are anabolized for protein synthesis or catabolized as sources of energy.

The protein component of the diet, then, must meet the needs of the fish for essential amino acids and at the same time supply enough non-essential amino acid nitrogen. Most experiments on the protein requirements of fish have been designed to evaluate the level of dietary protein necessary for optimal growth. Again, dose/response curves, in which a high quality protein has been fed at different dietary levels to groups of fish, have provided this information. Some of the values obtained for different species of fish are given in Table I. They show a high requirement for dietary protein. This is to be expected as many cold water fish are carnivorous, using protein not only for growth but also as an energy source. On the other hand, values for certain species generally accepted as being omnivorous such as carp (*Cyprinus carpio*), are also surprisingly high, much higher than those of omnivorous birds and mammals.

Table I. Estimated dietary protein requirements of certain fish.

Species	Crude protein level in diet for optimal growth (g/kg)	Reference
Rainbow trout (*Salmo gaitdneri*)	400–460	Satia (1976) Zeitoun *et al.* (1976) Tiews *et al.* (1976)
Carp (*Cyprinus carpio*)	380	Ogino and Saito (1970)
Chinook salmon (*Oncorhynchus tschwaytscha*)	400	DeLong *et al.* (1958)
Eel (*Anguilla japonica*)	445	Nose and Arai (1972)
Plaice (*Pleuronectes platessa*)	500	Cowey *et al.* (1970)
Gilthead bream (*Chrysophrys aurata*)	400	Sabaut and Luquet (1973)
Grass carp (*Ctenopharyngodon idella*)	410–430	Dabrowski (1977)
Brycon sp.	356	Saint Paul (1977)

No data appear to be available for herbivorous fish, although *Tilapia* are extensively cultivated in both Africa and South America and certain herbivorous species are maintained in both display and experimental aquaria.

Maximal growth rates are not always the main aim. There are several ways of limiting growth rate, one being to feed diets containing sub-optimal levels of dietary protein. Inspection of the relevant dose/response curves for the species in question (see Table I for references) will serve as a guide to the rates of growth obtaining at different dietary protein levels. The high protein requirement of many species of fish has meant a heavy reliance on a limited number of materials (all of high protein content) as ingredients of fish foods. Fishmeal or fish protein concentrate is almost ubiquitous. A variety of other animal (meat and bone meals, blood meals, beef greaves), vegetable (cotton seed, soyabean meals) and microbial sources of protein are also used. Currently, several single cell proteins are being evaluated and rainbow trout (*Salmo gairdneri*) have recently been successfully grown on a diet devoid of fishmeal, containing (as sources of protein) chicken by-product meal and hydrolysed feather meal together with supplementary methionine, lysine and tryptophan (Tiews, *et al.*, 1976).

B. Lipids

Lipids are important not only for their caloric contribution to the diet but also because certain fatty acids are essential components of biomembranes and cellular organelles. Fish given diets deficient in these essential fatty acids grow poorly, exhibit certain deficiency diseases and eventually die.

While lipid is an excellent energy source for most fish, a surfeit in the diet may lead to excessive deposition of lipid within the tissues of the fish and a gross alteration of carcass composition. For example, Lee and Putnam (1973) gave rainbow trout diets containing up to 24% herring oil. Excellent growth and feed conversion ratios were obtained, but the lipid level in the carcass rose from an initial value of 6.3% to 13.0% after eighteen weeks. Aquarium fish may be especially prone to such changes as they do not have to hunt or search for food. However, turbot (*Scophthalmus maximus*) given diets containing up to 9% lipid, added mainly as capelin oil (Adron *et al.*, 1976), had carcass lipid levels lower than or comparable to those of wild turbot.

Channel catfish (*Ictalurus punctatus*) have been successfully grown on diets containing up to 10% fat added either as beef tallow, olive oil or menhaden oil (Stickney and Andrews, 1971). Later experiments used diets containing up to 12% dry weight as lipid, the lipid being a mixture of 90% beef tallow and 10% menhaden oil (Stickney and Andrews, 1972). These experiments on catfish were conducted at water temperatures of 27–30°C, the high temperature probably aiding the digestion of the hard fat, beef tallow. High melting point animal fats have recently been shown to be a useful energy source for cold water fish as well. Trout rations containing 11% lard and 11% herring oil are as effective as similar rations containing 22% herring oil (Yu *et al.*, 1977).

Studies in a number of laboratories have shown that all fish so far examined require a certain minimal dietary intake of $\omega 3$ fatty acids (that is, fatty acids of the linolenic series, the higher members of which are commonly found in marine oils) for normal growth and good health. The absolute requirement of rainbow trout for linolenic acid was first demonstrated by Castell *et al.* (1972) and their findings have been amply confirmed by, among others, Watanabe *et al.* (1974).

Pathologies arising from a deficiency of linolenic acid in rainbow trout include caudal fin erosion, swollen pale livers and a shock syndrome or "fainting" (Castell *et al.*, 1972). The requirements of trout for linolenate was shown by Watanabe *et al.* (1974) to be between 0.83 and 1.66% of the diet. The 18 carbon linolenic acid is converted by the rainbow trout to longer chain, more highly unsaturated fatty acids (docosahexaenoic and eicosapentanoic) that are essential components of biomembranes. Recently, Takeuichi and Watanabe (1977) showed that smaller dietary concentrations of these two acids (0.25% of each of eicosapentanoate and docosahexanoate) were more effective in meeting the essential fatty acid needs than the higher levels of linolenic acid mentioned above.

Certain species of fish are not able to convert 18 carbon fatty acids such as linolenic acid to more highly unsaturated, longer chain members of the same fatty acid family with full essential fatty acid activity. Cowey *et al.* (1976a) observed that when the 18 carbon linoleic acid (a major component of corn oil) was given to turbot, the linoleic acid accumulated in the tissues without conversion to the 20 carbon arachidonic acid. Subsequently, Owen *et al.* (1975) showed that when ^{14}C-labelled oleic, linoleic or linolenic acids were given to turbot and the tissue fatty acids examined for radioactivity one week later, most of the radioactivity was located in the parent fatty acid fed. No further desaturation of any of the radioactive acids fed, and only a limited amount of chain elongation had occurred. This finding was fully substantiated (Cowey *et al.*, 1976b) by analysis of tissue fatty acids of groups of turbot given diets containing specific 18 carbon (oleic, linoleic, linolenic) 20 carbon (arachidonic) and 22 carbon (docosahexanoic) acids.

Thus, for normal growth and good health, turbot must be given long chain polyunsaturated fatty acids of the $\omega3$ series, preformed in the diet. Whether the metabolic capacity to convert 18 carbon fatty acids to longer chain more unsaturated acids is lacking in other fish remains to be seen. In the absence of such data, marine oils containing polyunsaturated acids of the $\omega3$ series should be included in the diet.

C. Carbohydrates

Many of the fish maintained as aquarium animals are carnivorous. The amylotic activity (capacity to hydrolyse complex carbohydrates) in their intestines is weak, a fact demonstrated by Shimeno *et al.* (1977) who compared amylase activity in carp and yellowtail (*Seriola quinqueradiata*); their results are shown in Table II. In line with this, it has long been known that in carnivores, the proportion of dietary starch that is digested decreases as the concentration of starch in the food is increased (Singh and Nose, 1967). Recently Tiews *et al.* (1976) have shown that pre-cooked starch is utilized much more readily by rainbow trout than is raw starch, possibly because physical changes in the starch during cooking render it more susceptible to amylotic attack. Whatever the reason, this finding should be exploited when starch is being used as a source of dietary energy.

Table II. Activities of amylase, pepsin and trypsin in the digestive organ of yellowtail, *Seriola quinqueradiata* and carp, *Cyprinus carpio*. Values expressed as μmole product formed/min, from the work of Shimeno *et al.*, 1977.

Enzyme	Yellowtail	Carp
Amylase		
per 100 g body weight	12.5	1040
per g organ	5.6	350
Pepsin		
per 100 g body weight	112	not detected
per g organ	73	
Trypsin		
per 100 g body weight	52	64
per g organ	23	21

Although cellulase activity has been detected in the gastro-intestinal tracts of some estuarine fish (Stickney and Shumway, 1974), presumably due to bacteria acquired from the environment, this activity is generally weak. Most fish have a short, relatively simple gastro-intestinal tract that does not lend itself to the development of an extensive bacterial fauna and so precludes the establishment of significant numbers of cellulolytic micro-organisms. Thus fish have little or no capacity to handle leafy materials containing cellulose; conversely, there is no requirement for a fibrous component in the food.

Another complex carbohydrate that features prominently in the natural diet of marine fish is chitin, a polymer of acetyl glucosamine and a component of the exoskeleton of Crustacea. There is no evidence that fish secrete a chitinase but recently, Goodrich and Morita (1977a) showed that chitinase activity was present in the stomach contents of a number of marine fish, the level of activity correlated directly with the nature of the stomach contents, being highest in those fish that had recently eaten large numbers of chitinaceous animals. The same authors (Goodrich and Morita, 1977b) also showed that stomach chitinase activity correlated directly with the proportion of chitinoclastic bacteria present. Immersion of *Enophrys bison* in water containing chloramphenicol (50 mg/l) killed all stomach bacteria and rendered chitinase activity undetectable. The use of sterile food also reduced chitinase activity.

Chitin is, of course, present in the crab and shrimp meals used in certain diets. At certain times, shrimp offal or meals are also used in salmon rations to provide astaxanthin, a pigment found in the flesh. The ability of fish to utilize the chitin in these materials clearly depends on the bacterial fauna present in the stomach or on whether any chitinoclastic bacteria are introduced with the food. Under normal conditions of pelleting, it seems unlikely that any such bacteria would survive.

D. Energy Density

Most nutritional studies on the energy density of diets have been concerned with the efficiency of energy and protein retention by the fish. The evaluation of an optimal protein/energy ratio in the diet (i.e. that ratio giving best protein retention or protein conversion) being a particular aim (Garling and Wilson, 1976).

In assessing the energy content of the diet and the contribution to it from the major compounds, the calorific values conventionally used are 9 kcal/g lipid and 4 kcal/g for both carbohydrate and protein. Some uncertainty surrounds the value used for protein because the main end-product of N metabolism in fish (ammonia) does not contain carbon whereas urea and uric acid excreted by mammals and birds respectively do. Thus it is arguable that the metabolizable energy of protein for fish is likely to be greater than that for birds and mammals (Cowey and Sargent, 1972).

When a restricted ration is fed, the concept of an optimal protein/energy ratio can apply only to those diets adequate in both protein and energy (i.e. diets with an identical protein/energy ratio but containing very different amounts of both protein and energy will give very different growth rates). Under conditions of restricted feeding (3% body weight/day), Garling and Wilson (1976) showed that food protein conversion by channel catfish was highest with diets containing 275 kcal/100g and 24% crude protein. If the ratio of protein/energy obtaining in this diet was maintained within the range 275–241 kcal/100g and 24–36% protein, then good growth resulted.

Lee and Putnam (1973), experimenting with rainbow trout, opted for satiation feeding 3–4 times/day. This procedure is frequently described as *ad libitum* feeding but because food is not available to the fish for a substantial part of each 24-h period, some restriction of food intake is implicit in the scheme. Nevertheless, Lee and Putnam showed that with this procedure "caloric intake regulated feed consumption", the fish apparently eats to satisfy its need for energy. Apart from diets low in both energy and protein (296 kcal/100g, 35.8% protein), weight gains were not significantly different in the range 368–440 kcals/100g; 35.6–53.6% protein. Within these ranges, different proportions of protein and non-protein energy in the diet did lead to variations in organ size (liver and intestine) and composition (carcass and liver); higher protein diets (53.3%) led to lower rates of protein retention.

Thus within limits, the balance of energy components in the diet may be designed with different ends in view, i.e. to maximize the utilization of (say) food protein or to ensure that the composition of the fish is not grossly altered from that pertaining in the wild or at the time of capture.

E. Vitamins

Those fish that have been studied have an absolute requirement for most water-soluble and fat-soluble vitamins (thiamin, riboflavin, pyridoxine, nicotinic acid, pantothenic acid, inositol, biotin, pteroylmonoglutamic acid, ascorbic acid, choline, α-tocopherol, cyanocobalamin, vitamin K, vitamin A and vitamin D). The quantitative requirement of several species of fish for most or all of these vitamins have been evaluated and deficiency diseases described. An excellent detailed review of these subjects is available (Halver, 1972) and will not be repeated here.

F. Minerals

There are obvious difficulties in assessing the mineral requirements of fish. Ions may be taken up from the water or lost to it via the gills; with marine fish there is the added complication that they drink sea water. In the absence of data on mineral requirements, the first test diets included a nutritionally balanced salt mixture together with a trace element supplement (Halver, 1957). Later, experiments with young trout and carp (Ogino and Kamizono, 1975) showed that weight gains were best when such a salt mixture comprised 4% of the dry diet. Of course, when dietary components containing relatively large amounts of ash are used (e.g. white fish meal), the requirement for several minerals may be more than satisfied from that source alone.

The requirement of freshwater fish for certain elements (Ca, P, Mg) has recently been examined. Andrews *et al.* (1973) showed that channel catfish grew best when given diets containing 1.5% Ca and 0.8–1.0% P. A similar requirement for P (0.6–0.7%) was demonstrated in carp by Ogino and Takeda (1976); in these, fish growth rate correlated with P intake but not with Ca intake probably because the water contained 20 ppm Ca but only 0.002 ppm P. Magnesium deficiency symptoms have been described for both carp (Ogino and Chiou, 1976) and rainbow trout (Cowey *et al.*, 1977). Both species require 0.05g Mg/100g diet for normal growth.

Sea water contains little or no phosphorus but comparatively large concentrations of Ca and Mg. In line with this (and in the knowledge that marine fish take salts directly from the water), Sakamoto and Yone (1973) showed that when red sea bream were given diets containing varying proportions of Ca and P, best growth occurred at a dietary Ca:P ratio of 1:2 with a dietary Ca level of 0.34%. Since then, Yone *et al.* (1974) have obtained good growth of red sea bream with their test diet (based on casein and other materials of low ash content) containing 8% of the mineral mixture shown in Table III that lacks both Ca and Mg.

Table III. Composition of mineral mixture (g or mg/100g) used in experiments with red sea bream, *Chrysophrys major* (from the work of Yone *et al.*, 1974).

KCl	5.2 g
$NaH_2PO_4 \cdot 2H_2O$	30.8 g
Fe citrate	1.5 g
$AlCl_3 \cdot 6H_2O$	9 mg
$ZnSo_4 \cdot 7H_2O$	178.5 mg
$MnSO_4 \cdot 4H_2O$	40 mg
CuCl	5.5 mg
KI	8.5 mg
$CoCl_2 \cdot 6H_2O$	52.5 mg
a-cellulose	62.2 g

G. Physical Form

One of the main properties needed in food for fish is a high degree of water stability. Without this property, considerable wastage may occur especially with fish that are not voracious feeders; in addition, the water will become badly contaminated with both particulate material and soluble organic matter.

For relatively small amounts of nutritionally defined diets, as may be used in research laboratories, gelatin, guar gum and carboxymethylcellulose have proven to be excellent binding agents. Gelatin (about 12% of the dry matter in the diet) is dissolved in cold water and the solution heated with stirring on a water bath to 80°; the gelatin solution is then removed from the heat source and other dietary materials added in turn with stirring. Thermolabile substances (vitamins) are added last as the temperature falls. The suspension is mixed well until the temperature falls to about 40° when it is poured into trays and placed in a refrigerator or cold room to set. The consistency of the diet depends on the volume of water in the final mix and on the duration and speed of stirring. Guar gum and carboxymethylcellulose are used at 2–5% of the dry matter in the diet, they are thoroughly mixed in a dry form with other dietary components in a mechanical mixer; water is then added slowly with continuous stirring until the consistency of the resulting paste or dough permits the formation of moist pellets (20–40% water) in a pelleting machine or mincing machine. Pellets may be air-dried or freeze-dried should a dry diet be required.

Several processes are used for the manufacture of dry feeds on a commercial scale. These include meals, flakes, pellets and extrusion cooking, different types of feed being appropriate for different sizes of fish and different feeding habits (bottom, demersal, surface etc.). The water stability of these products generally depends on the starches present in the diet formulation. The physical properties of the starch may change as a result of pressure or steam treatment during the manufacturing process giving improved binding characteristics.

Meals form the traditional starter feeds and consist of complete diets that have been ground and sieved to size ranges appropriate to the fish being reared. Flakes are made by treating a fine meal mixture with water and passing the resultant paste between large heated rollers. This treatment tends to gelatinize the starch and the thin flakes formed have a high water stability when dried. Pellets are probably the most widely used form of feed in cold water fish culture. They are made by pressurizing a meal-type feed in a die under the influence of steam, different sizes of die being used for different sizes of pellet. In the author's experience, many of the pellets so formed maintain their integrity in water for only a short time, but they are very good for fish that feed rapidly (rainbow trout, channel catfish). A variant on the pelleting process allows the production of expanded pellets which float at the water surface.

In extrusion cooking, a wet meal-type diet is heated, with or without steam, subjected to varying degrees of pressure and then extruded into a variety of shapes. When dried, this type of diet is said to have excellent water stability and has apparently been used successfully with certain invertebrate bottom feeders such as shrimp. Whether it will prove as successful with bottom feeding fish remains to be seen.

The bulk of commercially available feeds are dry and these have certain advantages, including ease of handling, elimination of necessity for deep-freezing and ready application to automated feeding. However, wet or moist feeds are used in a number of farming operations; one of the best known examples is the Oregon moist pellet (Table IV). This contains 30–40% wet fish (specifications for which are quite stringent) together with 70–60% of a meal mixture; the final moisture content of the diet is approximately 30%. Diets of this type may be particularly useful in weaning aquarium fish from natural food to artifical diets.

H. Feed Formulations

A number of dietary formulations are shown in Table IV. One of them is a nutrient test diet, the other three are practical diets formulated as a result of ongoing research in fishery experimental stations. As mentioned above, fishmeal is used as the principal source of high quality protein; lower levels of vitamin and mineral supplements are generally specified for these practical diets than for nutrient test diets because other constituents contribute significantly to these components. A larger selection of such diets which apply to a greater range of fish species is available in a recent article by Hastings and Cowey (1977).

It is not easy to say how these formulations compare with those produced by commercial manufacturers. Commercial producers have especial expertise in certain areas. Among them may be mentioned great knowledge of the available ingredients and a large ingredient purchasing power, a general understanding of nutrient availability in these ingredients, considerable experience in least cost formulation and in manufacturing rations economically. The diets listed in Table IV imply a fixed feed formulation; however, commercial practice encounters variation in both ingredient supply and ingredient price and as it attempts to combat price fluctuation in the finished product, on balance, it appears unlikely that fixed feed formulation would be strictly adhered to.

Table IV. Composition (%) of diets used in laboratory and large-scale rearing of fish.

Test diet for measuring nutrient requirements[a]		Oregon moist pellet[b]		Production diet for channel catfish[c]		Dry pellet rainbow trout diet[d]	
Casein or amino acid mixture	38	Wet fish	40	Fishmeal	12	Herring meal	35
Gelatin	12	Fishmeal	22	Soyabean meal	20	Soyabean meal	10
Dextrin	28	Shrimp or crabmeal	4	Blood meal	4	Wheat middlings	23
Corn oil	9	Wheat germ meal	3	Feather meal	3	Corn gluten meal	6
α-Cellulose/vitamin mixture	9	Dried distillers Solubles	3	Rice bran	40.5	Alfalfa meal	3
Mineral mixture	4	Vegetable oil meal	22	Rice dust	5	Brewers yeast	4
		Kelp meal	2	Dehydrated alfalfa meal	22	Corn fermentation extractives	8
		Vitamin mixture	1.5	Dried distillers solubles	4	Whey powder	4
		Choline chloride	0.5	Vitamin mixture	2	Vitamin and mineral supplement	3
		Vegetable oil	2			Marine oil	4

[a] Diet H-440, Western Fish Nutrition Laboratory, Cook, Washington.
[b] Crawford and Law (1972).
[c] Hastings and Dupree (1969).
[d] Formula PR4-25, Spearfish Fisheries Centre, Spearfish, South Dakota.

III. FEEDING SCHEDULES

The feeding regime adopted in the aquarium should meet the objectives for which the fish are being held. For most physiological, biochemical, behavioural or other experimental studies, the fish must have a complete, nutritionally balanced diet. For other purposes, including display, low or even zero growth rates may be desired and feeding rates may only need to match the maintenance needs of the fish.

In the experiments of Lee and Putnam (1973) mentioned previously, food intake of rainbow trout was related to the energy content of the diet, the fish apparently eating to satisfy their energy requirement. This relationship probably holds true for many species of fish and for them, satiation feeding 2–3 times/day should ensure energy and nutritional needs are met in full, and probably that maximal growth rates are obtained.

Some other species of fish have the capacity to ingest quantities of food far in excess of their energy requirement. Assimilation is largely incomplete and much undigested food passes out in the faeces. Thus, when attempting satiation feeding of fingerling gilthead bream (*Chrysophrys auratus*), the daily ingestion of food steadily increased, finally exceeding 20g dry diet (50% protein, 12% fat) per 100g biomass fish, with very low rates of digestion (unpublished data, Kissil, Cowey and Adron, 1977). Satiation feeding of species that can gorge themselves in this way is not only wasteful but also deleterious; quantities of organic matter that encourage bacterial growth being released into the water. Moreover, such a regime with such a species precludes certain types of experimentation such as determining the requirement for a given nutrient by a dose/response curve; much of the nutrient may be lost because passage through the gastro-intestinal tract is too rapid to allow assimilation. In the instance cited, satiation feeding had to be abandoned and a restricted ration given. For species such as the gilthead bream, a ration size or feeding regime that gives an optimal conversion (food or energy) rate, optimal growth rate or other characteristic should be determined by experiment for the prevailing environmental conditions (temperature, salinity, photoperiod, light intensity).

The use of suboptimal rations to control growth rate implies a knowledge of the interplay between food intake, metabolism, body size and growth rate. Paloheimo and Dickie (1965, 1966a and b) obtained a series of equations relating these parameters by analysis of the then existing data on food consumption and growth in fish. Their mathematical model has not, however, gained general acceptance (Warren and Davis, 1976; Gerking, 1971; Staples and Nomura, 1976) for a number of reasons including the fact that much of the data concerned a small size range of fish given supramaximal rations. Since then, Brett *et al.* (1969) have examined the relationship between ration size, temperature, growth rate and body composition. Groups of young sockeye salmon (*Oncorhynchus nerka*) were each given one of six different ration levels at six different water temperatures between 1° and 24°C; their growth rate and body composition were followed for several months. From the growth curves obtained, these authors were able to determine (1) the maintenance ration, which just maintains the fish without weight change; (2) the optimum ration, which provides for most efficient growth in terms of food conversion; and (3) the maximum ration, which gives the maximal growth rate. It was shown that as water temperature rose, there was a large increase in the size of ration necessary to meet these parameters. In particular, in the present context, maintenance ration increased rapidly above 12°C amounting to 2.6g dry diet/100g dry weight of fish/day at 20°C. The maintenance ration in fact increased seven-fold between 1°C and 20°C, and the optimum ration and maximum ration by five- and three-fold respectively over the same temperature range. Both ration level and water temperature affected gross composition of the body; it was especially noticeable that water content of the body increased with reduction in food intake.

The exact relationship among ration size, growth rate, temperature and body composition are likely to vary for different species of fish but the broad understanding achieved by Brett *et al.* should serve as a useful guide in maintaining at least cold water fish in aquaria at suboptimal levels of intake and growth rate.

IV. FEEDING BEHAVIOUR

A. Detection and Identification of Food

Feeding behaviour of fish is thought to follow a set pattern of sequential responses, namely (1) arousal to or awareness of the presence of food (2) location and identification of the food (3) intake to the mouth (4) acceptance of the food and ingestion to the gastro-intestinal tract or rejection from the mouth.

Many fish are sight feeders; they have a high visual acuity and they detect and locate food items by appearance and sometimes by movement. Other species rely on chemical stimuli. In terrestrial vertebrates, the olfactory organ detects volatile compounds in the inspired air, often with a high sensitivity. On the other hand, the gustatory cells sense dissolved molecules usually at comparatively high concentration. By contrast, all the chemical stimuli sensed by fish are present in solution in the water and although the olfactory organ may be the main site of long-distance reception, there can be little doubt that gustatory cells (which are frequently located externally) also serve in the detection and location of food.

However, this overlap does not signify a duplication in function, for the olfactory organ is anatomically distinct and may serve other specialized functions concerned with homing, mating and social behaviour. Even where the same group of compounds are the most effective stimuli for both receptor systems (as amino acids are in the channel catfish), a functional separation of the chemical senses is indicated because the olfactory and gustatory systems differ in sensitivity, specificity and electrophysiological response characteristics (Caprio, 1977).

Fish that rely heavily on chemoreceptors to locate food must sense the material very thoroughly before it is taken into the mouth, but when food pellets are rejected, it may be because their physical properties (texture, hardness) are inappropriate. Rejection of food pellets after entry into the oral cavity (observed by the author with turbot, cod and occasionally plaice and rainbow trout) is apparently much more common with sight-feeders. Olfactory acuity can be very great. The anatomy of the chemosensory receptors has been described by Bardach and Villars (1974), who mention that skipjack tuna (*Katsuwonus pelamis*) kept in a 75 000 litre tank engaged in a "frantic food search" when 100 ml sea water, in which one individual of their normal food had been rinsed for a few minutes, was put into the tank.

The morphology of taste buds is basically similar throughout vertebrates. They are composed of taste cells characterized by the presence of microvilli, supporting cells with apical protuberances and basal cells (Mackie, 1975). In fish, they may be present over the external surfaces as well as in the mouth. Certain species have high concentrations of taste buds on external appendages such as barbels and fins so that externally sited taste buds can numerically greatly exceed those present in the mouth. Present evidence is that the sensory thresholds of taste receptors are higher than those of olfactory receptors. Even so, Bardach and Villars (1974) demonstrate that for a series of sugars, taste thresholds of the minnow are much lower than those of man; channel catfish taste receptors yield thresholds of 10^{-9}M to 10^{-11}M for the most effective amino acids: L-alanine and L-arginine (Caprio, 1975).

A further sensory modality used in prey detection is an electric sense. Kalmijn (1971) has shown for certain sharks and rays, that at close ranges, electrolocation seems to dominate over olfaction in prey detection. Bioelectric fields generated by the prey are detected by the fish.

B. Taste Attractants

Both electrophysiological and whole animal techniques have been used to identify the nature of compounds with attractant taste properties for fish. The methods should be complementary, electrophysiological methods seeming particularly useful for screening large numbers of compounds at varying concentration and whole animal assays demonstrating in practice the value of these attractants in complete artificial feeds that often contain alien materials.

Several authors (Fujiya and Bardach, 1966; Sutterlin and Sutterlin, 1970) have shown that among other molecules, isolated taste fibres respond to inorganic ions, mineral and organic acids, but the significance of these findings in the context of food acceptability is not obvious. Fujiya and Bardach (1966) showed that although sensitivity to sweet substances is not widespread, several amino acids provoked a positive response from all the species examined (*Ictalurus natalis*, *Prionotus carolinus* and *Microgadus tomcod*), cysteine being the most effective. Among lipids, only charged molecules elicited any responses, cholesterol and inositides being the most effective. Aliphatic acids elicited discharges from the palatine nerve in Atlantic salmon (*Salmo salar*), (Sutterlin and Sutterlin, 1970) the compounds being increasingly stimulatory as chain length increased.

Few other studies have examined the role of lipids in taste perception, perhaps because hydrophobic molecules do not lend themselves easily to this type of experiment. On the other hand, a significant body of evidence points the importance of amino acids in taste appreciation. One of the most recent studies (Caprio, 1977) demonstrating that the taste system of channel catfish is very responsive to neutral amino acids, alanine being the most effective; branched chain amino acids, acidic amino acids and basic amino acids (other than arginine) being less active. Kreuger and Cagan (1976) have isolated a protein fraction from the barbel tastebuds of channel catfish that has high binding activity for alanine.

Another group of compounds eliciting electrical responses from taste receptors are the nucleotides. Kiyohara *et al.* (1975) showed that the lips of the puffer (*Fugu pardalis*) contain receptors excited by three types of molecule: (1) those responding to hydrochloric acid, (2) those responding to certain nucleotides and (3) those responding to amino acids; the quaternary amine betaine also stimulated receptors in groups (1) and (3). Recently, the same workers (Hidaka *et al.*, 1977) have shown that adenosine monophosphate, adenosine diphosphate, adenosine triphosphate, inosine monophosphate and uridine monophosphate at millimolar concentration elicited responses from the puffer fish facial nerve. Other ribonucleotides and deoxyribonucleotides were without effect as were the component structures (adenine, D-ribose, orthophosphate, adenosine and D-ribose-5-phosphate) of adenosine monophosphate when tested at millimolar concentration.

Whole animal experiments have involved a variety of methods including: (1) selection by the fish of one of a number of chambers or compartments arranged in a tank and serving as sources of mixtures under test (Hashimoto *et al.* 1967; Pawson, 1977), (2) observation by underwater television and photography of the reaction of fish in the natural environment to a source of possible attractants (Sutterlin, 1975), (3) growth and feed efficiency of fish given diets containing attractant mixtures (Yone *et al.*, 1974) and (4) number of pellets ingested by groups of fish (Mackie and Adron, 1978).

The bulk of these studies have again demonstrated that amino acids (either singly or combined together and perhaps acting synergistically) predominate as taste attractants. Only in the study of Mackie and Adron (1978) with turbot were they ineffective ("only very weakly active"). Hashimoto *et al.* (1968) experimented with extracts of short-necked clam that evoked feeding responses in *Anguilla japonica*; they fractionated this extract and showed that the active fraction contained taurine, aspartic acid, threonine, serine, glutamic acid, glycine and alanine (Konosu *et al.*, 1968). Pawson (1977) examined the responses of whiting (*Merlangus merlangus*) and cod (*Gadus morhua*) to extracts of lugworm. A fraction containing glycine, serine, alanine, glutamic acid, valine, leucine and threonine was active but only glycine and alanine were active when tested singly at the concentration present in lugworm. Sutterlin (1975) showed that glycine, γ amino butyric acid and alanine were the most potent amino acid attractants for *Pseudopleuronectes americanus*, *Fundulus heteroclitus* and *Menidia menidia*, respectively. Other amino acids had weaker activity.

Mackie and Adron (1978) began with a synthetic mixture simulating the water soluble, organic constituents of squid muscle. This was subdivided into groups of compounds of similar chemical structure that were tested in turn. By further fractionation, it was finally shown that inosine and inosine 5'-monophosphate are specific feeding stimulants for turbot.

Yone *et al.* (1974) used a synthetic diet based on casein and gelatin for their experiments on red sea bream (*Chrysophrys major*). A group of amino acids (phenylalanine, tyrosine, alanine, aspartic acid, lysine, serine and valine) stimulated food intake. Omission tests demonstrated that phenylalanine and aspartic acid were particularly important, food intake falling when they were omitted from the diet. Concurrent experiments showed that beef liver was a superior diet for red sea bream than a natural food, jack mackerel. By further experimentation with the amino acids added to their casein-gelatin diet, Yone *et al.* (1974) obtained growth rates equal to or even better than those obtained with beef liver while feed conversion efficiencies were only a little inferior to those with beef liver. The free amino acids added to the diet of Yone *et al.* (1974) were, g/100g: phenylalanine (0.6), arginine HCl (1.5), tryptophan (0.2), sodium aspartate (1.0) and valine (0.7). Of these, phenylalanine and aspartate were included for their attractant properties, the remainder to provide (together with the casein-gelatin) a complete quantitative spectrum of essential amino acids.

The results of Yone *et al.* (1974) are impressive because they translate into practice the findings of short-term experiments, giving effective proof that diets composed of alien materials can be rendered more or less permanently acceptable to a species of fish by inclusion of a limited number of compounds at quite low levels.

C. Inducing Fish to Eat

Difficulties may occasionally be encountered in persuading fish to take food even though the ration that is being offered is nutritious and contains known attractants in appropriate amount. This is especially true of fish that are being brought into an aquarium; such fish have usually been subjected to a variety of disturbing factors during transport. Those from the natural environment may have suffered the shock of being trawled, removed from the water at least twice during capture and transit and been confined temporarily in small volumes of water with little regard to changing temperature, oxygen tension and so on. Netting of captive (hatchery reared) fish ought to be less traumatic and considerable attention is now usually paid to the conditions obtaining during their transport. Even so, some reaction to the disturbance and change of surroundings is likely.

Thus, a period of 1–2 days is usually necessary before such fish will accept food. Should they continue to refuse food after this time, then certain steps are desirable. Water chemistry ought to be checked if this is not routinely done, water temperature ought to be as near as possible to that of the environment in which they recently lived. Many fish, newly introduced into an aquarium, display a fright reaction (darting to the peripheries of the tank in uncontrolled fashion) in response to unusual sounds and even when shadows move suddenly across the tank.

The effects of sound on fish behaviour in general and feeding behaviour in particular, have been examined in relatively few species. Blaxter and Holliday (1958), experimenting with herring, showed that noises with frequencies below 100 Hz caused a fright reaction and temporary cessation of feeding; sounds with frequencies greater than 100 Hz had no effect. Be that as it may, noisy disturbances in the aquarium should be avoided.

Light intensity may be another critical factor in feeding behaviour in fish, optimal light intensities are clearly likely to vary with species whether they are bottom, demersal or surface feeders. For herring, Blaxter and Holliday (1958) showed that there was a critical low light intensity (0.25 metre candles) below which feeding did not occur; the optimal intensity for feeding with this species was between 100–1000 m.c. Clearly a facility to vary the light intensity at the water surface above each tank is desirable in any aquarium system especially where it is planned to hold a number of species from different natural habitats.

For certain species, features that simulate or mimic natural conditions may be conducive to overcoming fright reaction and inhibition of the feeding response. Thus with marine flatfish, a sandy substratum placed temporarily in the tank has proved useful. Similarly, the provision of lengths of piping in a tank containing eels (*Anguilla anguilla*) appeared to aid induction of a feeding response, the eels secreting themselves within the piping.

Social factors and space (or restriction of space) may also be critical factors. For a full coverage of these the appropriate works should be consulted. Suffice it to say that we have observed the emergence of a dominant individual in a tank of a dozen or so rainbow trout. Removal of the said individual generally eliminated the problem i.e. dominance did not then become obviously characteristic of any other remaining individual.

These suggestions are aimed at overcoming fright reactions or similar inhibitions to feeding. Where fish are particularly recalcitrant, not having accepted food for several days despite all obvious steps having been taken to eliminate chemical, physical and behaviouristic inhibitory factors, there is something to be said for experimenting with texture, water content, size, shape and even colour of food. Other factors being equal an Oregon-type pellet, in which the wet portion of the feed is the natural food of the fish, is often conducive to the initiation of feeding. The natural food may then be eliminated from the ration over a period of days.

The literature survey on which this article is based was completed in February 1978, when the article was written.

V. REFERENCES

Adron, J. W., Blair, A., Cowey, C. B. and Shanks, A. M. (1976). Effects of dietary energy level and dietary energy source on growth, feed conversion and body composition of turbot (*Scophthalmus maximus* L.). *Aquaculture* **7**, 125–132.

Andrews, J. W., Murai, T. and Campbell, C. (1973). Effects of dietary calcium and phosphorus on growth, food conversion, bone ash and haematocrit levels of catfish. *Journal of Nutrition* **103**, 766–771.

Bardach, J. E. and Villars, T. (1974). The chemical senses of fishes. *In* "Chemoreception in Marine Organisms" (P. T. Grant and A. M. Mackie, eds), 49–104. Academic Press, New York and London.

Blaxter, J. H. S. and Holliday, F. G. T. (1958). Herring (*Clupea harengus* L.) in aquaria II. Feeding. *Marine Research* **No 6**, 22.

Blaxter, J. H. S., Roberts, R. J., Balbontin, F. and McQueen, A. (1974). B-group vitamin deficiency in cultured herring. *Aquaculture* **3**, 387–393.

Brett, J. R., Shelbourn, J. E. and Shoop, C. T. (1969). Growth rate and body composition of fingerling sockeye salmon, *Oncorhynchus nerka*, in relation to temperature and ration size. *Journal of the Fisheries Research Board of Canada* **26**, 2363–2394.

Caprio, J. (1975). High sensitivity of catfish taste receptors to amino acids. *Comparative Biochemistry and Physiology* **52A**, 247–251.

Caprio, J. (1977). Electrophysiological distinctions between the taste and smell of amino acids in catfish. *Nature, London* **266**, 850–851.

Castell, J. D., Sinnhuber, R. O., Wales, J. H. and Lee, D. J. (1972). Essential fatty acids in the diet of rainbow trout (*Salmo gairdneri*): growth, feed conversion and some gross deficiency symptoms. *Journal of Nutrition* **102**, 77–86.

Cowey, C. B. (1979). Protein and amino acid requirements of finfish. *In* "Finfish nutrition and fish feed technology" Vol. I (J. E. Halver and K. Tiews, eds), 3–16. H. Heeneman, Berlin.

Cowey, C. B., Adron, J. W., Owen, J. H. and Roberts, R. J. (1976a). The effect of different dietary oils on tissue fatty acids and tissue pathology in turbot *Scophthalmus maximus*. *Comparative Biochemistry and Physiology* **53B**, 399–403.

Cowey, C. B., Knox, D., Adron, J. W., George, S. and Pirie, B. (1977). The production of renal calcinosis by magnesium deficiency in rainbow trout (*Salmo gairdneri*). *British Journal of Nutrition* **38**, 127–135.

Cowey, C. B., Owen, J. M., Adron, J. W. and Middleton, C. (1976b). Studies on the nutrition of marine flatfish. The effect of different dietary fatty acids on the growth and fatty acid composition of turbot (*Scophthalmus maximus*). *British Journal of Nutrition* **36**, 479–486.

Cowey, C. B., Pope, J. A., Adron, J. W. and Blair, A. (1972). Studies on the nutrition of marine flatfish. The protein requirement of plaice (*Pleuronectes platessa*). *British Journal of Nutrition* **28**, 447–456.

Cowey, C. B. and Sargent, J. R. (1972). Fish Nutrition. *Adv. Marine Biology* **10**, 383–492.

Crawford, D. L. and Law, D. K. (1972). Mineral composition of Oregon pellet production formulations. *Progressive Fish Culturist* **34**, 126–130.

Dabrowski, K. (1977). Protein requirements of grass carp fry (*Ctenopharyngodon idella*). *Aquaculture* **12**, 63–73.

DeLong, D. C., Halver, J. E. and Mertz, E. T. (1958). Nutrition of salmonid fishes VI. Protein requirements of chinook salmon at two water temperatures. *Journal of Nutrition* **65**, 589–599.

Fujiya, M. and Bardach, J. E. (1966). A comparison between the external taste sense of marine and freshwater fishes. *Bulletin of the Japanese Society of scientific Fisheries* **32**, 45–56.

Garling, D. L. and Wilson, R. P. (1976). Optimum dietary protein to energy ratio for channel catfish fingerlings, *Ictalurus punctatus*. *Journal of Nutrition* **106**, 1368–1375.

Gerking, S. D. (1971). Influence of rate of feeding and body weight on protein metabolism of bluegill sunfish. *Physiological Zoology* **44**, 9–19.

Goodrich, T. D. and Morita, R. Y. (1977a). Incidence and estimation of chitinase activity associated with marine fish and other estuarine samples. *Marine Biology* **41**, 349–353.

Goodrich, T. D. and Morita, R. Y. (1977b). Bacterial chitinase in the stomachs of marine fishes from Yaquina Bay, Oregon, USA. *Marine Biology* **41**, 355–360.

Halver, J. E. (1957). Nutrition of salmonoid fishes III. Water soluble requirements of chinook salmon. *Journal of Nutrition* **62**, 225–243.

Halver, J. E. (1972). The Vitamins. *In* "Fish Nutrition" (J. E. Halver, ed), 29–103. Academic Press, New York and London.

Hashimoto, Y., Konosu, S., Fusetani, N. and Nose, T. (1968). Attractants for eels in the extracts of short-necked clam. I. Survey of constituents eliciting feeding behaviour by the omission test. *Bulletin of the Japanese Society of scientific Fisheries* **34**, 78–83.

Hastings, W. H. and Cowey, C. B. (1977). Fish diets and culture media. *In* "Handbook series in Nutrition and Food" (M. Rechcigle, ed), 279–290. CRC Press, Cleveland, USA.

Hastings, W. H. and Dupree, H. K. (1969). Formula feeds for channel catfish. *Progressive Fish Culturist* **31**, 187–191.

Hidaka, I., Kiyohara, S. and Oda, S. (1977). Gustatory response in the puffer. III. Stimulatory effectiveness of nucleotides and their derivatives. *Bulletin of the Japanese Society of scientific Fisheries* **43**, 424–428.

Kiyohara, S., Hidaka, I. and Tamura, T. (1975). Gustatory response in the puffer. II. Single fibre analyses. *Bulletin of the Japanese Society of scientific Fisheries* **41**, 383–391.

Konosu, S., Fusetani, N., Nose, T. and Hashimoto, Y. (1968). Attractants for eels in the extracts of short-necked clam. II. Survey of constituents eliciting feeding behaviour by fractionation of the extracts. *Bulletin of the Japanese Society of scientific Fisheries* **34**, 84–87.

Krueger, J. M. and Cagan, R. H. (1976). Biochemical studies of taste sensation. Binding of L-(^{3}H) alanine to a sedimentable fraction from catfish barbel epithelium. *Journal of biological Chemistry* **251**, 88–97.

Lee, D. J. and Putnam, C. B. (1973). The response of rainbow trout to varying protein/energy ratios in a test diet. *Journal of Nutrition* **103**, 916–922.

Mackie, A. M. (1975). Chemoreception. *In* "Biochemical and Biophysical Perspectives in Marine Biology" (D. C. Malins and J. R. Sargent, eds), 69–105. Academic Press, New York and London.

Mackie, A. M. and Adron, J. W. (1978). Identification of inosine and inosine 5′-monophosphate as the gustatory feeding stimulants for the turbot, *Scophthalmus maximus*. *Comparative Biochemistry and Physiology* **60A**, 79–83.

Mertz, E. T. (1969). Amino acid and protein requirements of fish. *In* "Fish in Research" (O. W. Neuhaus and J. E. Halver, eds), 233–244. Academic Press, New York and London.

Nose, T. and Arai, S. (1972). Optimal level of protein in purified diet for eel, *Anguilla japonica*. *Bulletin of Freshwater Fisheries Research Lab*. Tokyo, **22**, 145–155.

Ogino, C. and Chiou, J-Y. (1976). Mineral requirements in fish II. Magnesium requirement of carp. *Bulletin of the Japanese Society of scientific Fisheries* **42**, 71–75.

Ogino, C. and Kamizono, M. (1975). Mineral requirements in fish I. Effects of dietary salt mixture levels on growth, mortality and body composition in rainbow trout and carp. *Bulletin of the Japanese Society of scientific Fisheries* **41**, 429–434.

Ogino, C. and Saito, K. (1970). Protein nutrition in fish I. The utilization of dietary protein by young carp. *Bulletin of the Japanese Society of scientific Fisheries* **36**, 250–254.

Ogino, C. and Takeda, T. (1976). Mineral requirements in fish III. Calcium and phosphorus requirements in carp. *Bulletin of the Japanese Society of scientific Fisheries* **42**, 793–799.

Owen, J. M., Adron, J. W., Middleton, C. and Cowey, C. B. (1975). Elongation and desaturation of dietary fatty acids in turbot *Scophthalmus maximus* L. and rainbow trout, *Salmo gairdneri* Rich. *Lipids* **10**, 528–531.

Paloheimo, J. E. and Dickie, L. M. (1965). Food and growth of fishes I. A growth curve derived from experimental data. *Journal of the Fisheries Research Board of Canada* **22**, 521–542.

Paloheimo, J. E. and Dickie, L. M. (1966a). Food and growth of fishes II. Effects of food and temperature on the relation between metabolism and body size. *Journal of the Fisheries Research Board of Canada* **23**, 869–908.

Paloheimo, J. E. and Dickie, L. M. (1966b). Food and growth of fishes III. Relations among food, body size and growth efficiency. *Journal of the Fisheries Research Board of Canada* **23**, 1209–1248.

Pawson, M. G. (1977). Analysis of a natural chemical attractant for whiting *Merlangius merlangus* L. and cod *Gadus morhua* L. using a behavioural bioassay. *Comparative Biochemistry and Physiology* **56A**, 129–135.

Sabaut, J. J. and Luquet, P. (1973). Nutritional requirements of the gilthead bream, *Chrysophrys aurata*. Quantitative protein requirements. *Marine Biology* **18**, 50–54.

Saint Paul, U. (1977). Aspectos generales sobre la piscicultura en Amazonas y resultados preliminares de experimentos de alimentación con raciones peletizados con deferentes composiciones. *In* "Symposio de la Asociación Latino Americano de Acuicultura" (in press).

Sakamoto, S. and Yone, Y. (1973). Effect of dietary calcium/phosphorus ratio upon growth, feed efficiency and blood serum Ca and P levels in red sea bream. *Bulletin of the Japanese Society of scientific Fisheries* **39**, 343–348.

Satia, B. P. (1974). Quantitative protein requirements of rainbow trout. *Progressive Fish Culturist* **36**, 80–85.

Shimeno, S., Hosokawa, H., Hirata, H. and Takeda, M. (1977). Comparative studies on carbohydrate metabolism of yellowtail and carp. *Bulletin of the Japanese Society of scientific Fisheries* **43**, 213–217.

Singh, R. P. and Nose, T. (1967). Digestibility of carbohydrate in young rainbow trout. *Bulletin of Freshwater Fisheries Research Lab.* Tokyo **17**, 21–25.

Staples, D. J. and Nomura, M. (1976). Influence of body size and food ration on the energy budget of rainbow trout *Salmo gairdneri* Richardson. *Journal of Fish Biology* **9**, 29–43.

Stickney, R. R. and Andrews, J. W. (1971). Combined effects of dietary lipids and environmental temperature on growth, metabolism and body composition of channel catfish (*Ictalurus punctatus*). *Journal of Nutrition* **101**, 1703–1710.

Stickney, R. R. and Andrews, J. W. (1972). Effects of dietary lipids on growth, food conversion, lipid and fatty acid composition of channel catfish. *Journal of Nutrition* **102**, 249–258.

Stickney, R. R. and Shumway, S. E. (1974). Occurrence of cellulase activity in the stomachs of fishes. *Journal of Fish Biology* **6**, 779–790.

Sutterlin, A. M. (1975). Chemical attraction of some marine fish in their natural habitat. *Journal of the Fisheries Research Board of Canada* **32**, 729–738.

Sutterlin, A. M. and Sutterlin, N. (1970). Taste responses in Atlantic salmon (*Salmo salar*) parr. *Journal of the Fisheries Research Board of Canada* **27**, 1927–1942.

Takenichi, T. and Watanabe, T. (1977). Effect of eicosapentanoic acid and docosahexanoic acid in pollock liver oil on growth and fatty acid composition of rainbow trout. *Bulletin of the Japanese Society of scientific Fisheries* **43**, 947–953.

Tiews, K., Gropp, J. and Koops, H. (1976). On the development of optimal rainbow trout pellet feeds. *Archiv. Fischereiwiss. Beih.* **27**, 1–29.

Warren, C. E. and Davis, G. E. (1967). Laboratory studies on the feeding, bioenergetics and growth of fishes. *In* "The Biological Basis of Freshwater Fish Production (S. D. Gerking, ed), 175–214. Blackwell Scientific Publications, Oxford.

Watanabe, T., Ogino, C., Koshiishi, Y. and Matsunaga, T. (1974). Requirement of rainbow trout for essential fatty acids. *Bulletin of the Japanese Society of scientific Fisheries* **40**, 493–499.

Yone, Y., Sakamoto, S. and Furuichi, M. (1974). Studies on nutrition of red sea bream. IX. The basal diet for nutrition studies. *Report of the Fishery Research Laboratory, Kyushu Univ.* No. 2, 13–24.

Yu, T. C., Sinnhuber, R. O. and Putnam, G. B. (1977). Use of swine fat as an energy source in trout rations. *Progressive Fish Culturist* **39**, 95–97.

Zeitoun, I. H., Ullrey, D. E., Magee, W. T., Gill, J. L. and Bergen, W. G. (1976). Quantifying nutrient requirements of fish. *Journal of the Fisheries Research Board of Canada* **33**, 167–172.

Chapter 9

Vivisection, Anaesthetics and Minor Surgery

Peter Tytler[1] and A. D. Hawkins[2]

Biology Department, Stirling University[1] and Marine Laboratory, Aberdeen[2], UK

I. VIVISECTION

Various techniques described in this chapter are now performed routinely in many scientific aquaria, particularly those specializing in fish physiology and pathology. That pain and injury may result from the application of some of them must be considered before planning particular experiments, not only because the stress may affect the outcome and validity, but because moral problems are posed which are the concern not only of the scientist but of the general public. In many countries, experiments on animals are controlled by law. In the United Kingdom, for example, no painful or stressful experiment may be performed upon a vertebrate unless the experimenter first obtains a licence from the Home Office. This licence effectively authorizes only the conduct of experiments performed wholly under anaesthesia, since the animal must be killed before recovery from the effect of the anaesthetic, if it is likely to experience pain after recovery, or if any serious injury has been inflicted. When an anaesthetic would frustrate the object of the experiment, written certification by a president from certain Royal Societies and by a professor from specified medical veterinary or biological disciplines can be used to obtain exemption from the requirement to use an anaesthetic, but only for the performance of defined procedures of strictly limited severity. A similar certificate may be used to gain exemption from the requirement to kill an experimental animal before recovery from the anaesthetic when such killing would frustrate the object of the experiment.

A licence and appropriate certificates will only be issued if the experiments are to be carried out in premises considered by the authorities to be suitable. For fish, a conventional operating theatre is less important than a clean water supply and suitable holding tanks where fish can be permitted to recover with a minimum of disturbance. An operating table or shallow tank, perhaps supplied with recirculation facilities, is required for some work, but is by no means always necessary. A work bench, adequate lighting, a refrigerator for storing solutions and chemicals, a balance and an autoclave or small sterilizer complete the arrangements. The premises should not be open to the general public, and post-mortem work should be performed in a separate area or room and never on the operating table. Special facilities are required if infectious diseases are being investigated (Chapter 10).

A summary of the legislation pertaining to animal experiments in Sweden, Canada, the United States of America, the Netherlands and the United Kingdom is given by Porter (1975). A key feature of the law in the United Kingdom is that fish and other cold-blooded vertebrates are not exempt. Although certain techniques such as marking, tagging and the insertion of transmitters into the stomach of a fish can be performed without Home Office protection, it is advisable to consult the Inspectorate of the Home Office before attempting any procedure liable to inflict pain or suffering upon fish. By reducing stress and returning fish to normal behaviour quickly, the legal, humane and scientific requirements can all be satisfied.

II. IMMOBILIZATION AND ANAESTHESIA

Fish are difficult to handle. They are liable to struggle during capture and handling and this may have serious effects on their physiology and behaviour. Consequently it is often necessary to immobilize fish before attempting to perform even the most simple tasks, such as weighing and measuring.

A. Electrical Stunning

The simplest and safest technique of immobilizing fish electrically is by galvanonarcosis with an uninterrupted direct electric current. The fish move towards the anode, roll over on to one side and become immobile, with flaccid muscles (Halsband, 1967).

Galvanonarcosis is most effective with freshwater fish in small holding tanks. Kynard and Lonsdale (1975) immobilized yearling rainbow trout by subjecting them to 20 V DC between aluminium foil electrodes (20 cm × 20 cm) which were placed at either end of a perspex tank 36 cm in length. This technique produced rapid paralysis. After 1 min at 20 V, trout can be held immobile with 10 V, although there are occasional short bouts of disorientated movement. In this condition, it is possible to perform minor procedures such as marking, withdrawal of body fluids or injection of drugs, providing the fish is kept in the water with the head pointed towards the anode. In general, the fish treated recover almost immediately as judged by swimming behaviour and resumption of feeding activity. Galvanonarcosis appears to have no significant effect on the subsequent growth or behaviour of rainbow trout. Higher currents are needed for the galvanonarcosis of marine fish, because of the higher conductivity of sea water. Pulsed direct currents are effective, however, and can reduce the total power required.

An alternating current (220 volts, 350 mA), applied for 30 s will stop swimming, heart and respiratory activity for several seconds in rainbow trout. Most fish remain unresponsive to mechanical stimuli for 20 min during which they can be removed from the water and subjected to minor surgery. From the work of Madden and Houston (1976), it is clear that this treatment produces haematological changes similar to those from handling chemical anaesthesia, perhaps because hypoxia develops (Schreck *et al.*, 1976). Higher AC voltages and currents (Schreck *et al.*, 1976) result in greater physiological disturbance and require longer recovery times. Electro-anaesthesia or electronarcosis, as this technique is sometimes called, does have greater effects than chemical anaesthetics on some electrolyte levels and upon water content and distribution. Tissue oedema can persist for 24 h after shocking in rainbow trout.

The great value of electro-anaesthesia is that the fish can be immobilized rapidly in even relatively large aquaria without the need for netting. It may be applied in biochemical studies in which it is necessary to avoid chasing and fatiguing the fish before death. Sudden death of the animal can be brought about by applying an excess of electrical current, the muscles going into tetanus and often breaking the back.

B. Hypothermia

Low temperatures, either alone or in combination with chemical anaesthesia, can effectively tranquilize or immobilize fish. The technique is especially valuable in transporting fish and has been described by Ho and Vanstone (1961). The water temperatures may be lowered by refrigeration or by adding ice or dry ice (the latter in an isolating container vented to the atmosphere; Bell, 1964).

C. Chemical Anaesthesia

(1) Introduction

A wide range of drugs, some originally used to anaesthetize humans and other mammalian species, facilitate the handling, transport and surgery of fish. It is outside the scope of this chapter to review the properties and relative merits of all these drugs in detail. Reviews by McFarland (1959, 1960), Bell (1964), Klontz and Smith (1968), Smith and Bell (1967) and Oswald (1978) are recommended reading. In this chapter, we consider those drugs which are commonly used and whose properties, advantages and disadvantages are best known. Consideration will also be given to new drugs which show promise for future use.

Anaesthesia is a reversible intoxication of the nervous system, with several recognizable aspects which include narcosis or unconsciousness, sensory blockage, motor blockage and a reduction of reflex activity. By a judicious choice of the anaesthetic and its dosage, it is possible to emphasize selectively any of these components (McDonell, 1975). When massive surgery is to be performed and can be followed by a long recovery period, a total loss of overt sensory, motor and reflex activity can be tolerated. On the other hand, when physiological or pharmacological studies are desired, either on the anaesthetized fish or shortly after recovery, then the anaesthetic must be carefully chosen, perhaps to induce only a shallow analgesia, where the animal's sensitivity to pain is eliminated but other sensations remain intact. A light stage of anaesthesia is also useful if fish are to be transported long distances, where their reactivity to external stimuli must be curbed and their metabolic rate reduced to a basal level without drastically impairing cardiac and respiratory function.

The depth of anaesthesia can be recognized by various clinical signs. It has been supposed that fish follow a uniform sequence of behavioural change, as in the classification shown in Table I, the level reached being dependent upon the dosage. However, not all drugs or combinations of drugs will conveniently fit this scheme. The same criteria cannot be applied to the tranquillizers (or narcoleptics), the muscular relaxants and hypnotics like the barbiturates (which are inherently poor analgesics).

(2) Routes of drug administration

There are two routes for the administration of anaesthetic drugs to fish, either by inspiration or by injection. With inspiration, a drug previously dissolved in the ambient water is absorbed by the gills in the course of normal respiration. This method is the most common and is often considered the best since it allows closer control. The depth of anaesthesia can be quickly altered by adjusting the concentration of the drug in the water flowing over the gills. The uptake of inspired drugs can be affected by the pH of the water, though this is not a problem with sea water.

The alternative route is by intraperitoneal, intramuscular or intravascular injection. Intraperitoneal injection is probably the most common. The body wall is punctured, ventral to the lateral line and just anterior to the vent, with a short narrow gauge needle (2 cm, 23 G) so that the shaft moves rostrally between the scales into the peritoneum by way of the hypaxial musculature. The drug injected in this way is absorbed through the visceral blood vessels and perhaps by way of the lymphatic system. The time taken to induce anaesthesia by this method is relatively slow, between 10–25 min. The method is, however, simple. Relatively large volumes of drug can be administered, sometimes without preliminary immobilization.

Intramuscular injection is much less satisfactory since in many fish, the bulk of muscle has a poor blood supply. Consequently, only small

Table I. Classification of the behavioural changes that occur in fishes during anaesthesia (after McFarland, 1959).

Definable level of anaesthesia			Behavioural responses of fish
Stage	Plane	Word equivalents	
0		Normal	Reactive to external stimuli, equilibrium and muscle tone normal.
I	1	Light sedation	Analgesia, slight loss of reactivity to external stimuli (visual and tactile). Voluntary movement still possible. Opercular rate normal.
1	2	Deep sedation	Total loss of reactivity to external stimuli, slight decrease in opercular rate.
II	1	Partial loss of equilibrium	Partial loss of muscle tone, reacts only to very strong tactile and vibrational stimuli, rheotaxis present, but swimming capability seriously disrupted. Increase in opercular rate.
II	2	Total loss of equilibrium	Total loss of muscle tone, reacts only to deep pressure stimuli, decrease in opercular rate below normal.
III		Loss of reflex reactivity	Total loss of reactivity, opercular rate very slow, heart rate slow. The level of surgical anaesthesia.
IV		Medullary collapse	Respiratory movements cease, followed several minutes later by cardiac arrest. The level of overdosage.

volumes (less than 0.5 ml/kg of a drug) can be injected into the more vascular red muscle without causing blistering and haemorrhage. With the development of techniques for cannulating major blood vessels (page 272), it is possible to inject drugs directly into the blood to induce very rapid anaesthesia, but the fish must first be immobilized by some other method. Alternative intravascular methods, applied to an active fish, require considerable skill and may not always be successful. Suitable injection sites are the caudal artery and vein (both running inside the haemal canal), and the dorsal lymph vessel. With all forms of administration, the fish should be deprived of food for at least 24 h and preferably several days beforehand to avoid vomiting and defaecation during anaesthesia.

(3) The common anaesthetics

(a) Inspired drugs. The most common inspired general anaesthetics for fish were originally developed as local anaesthetics for administration to mammals. Analgesia and narcosis is produced by inhibiting neuronal transmission. Because of the complex nature of nervous organization however, the administration of a particular drug may produce widely different effects within the various parts of the nervous system, exciting some nerve cells and inhibiting others. Narcotic drugs diminish and abolish the excitability of nerve cells in the central nervous system, hence their value as general anaesthetics. Applied to particular nerve trunks however, they may abolish sensation from that part of the body supplied by the nerve, serving in this case as local anaesthetics.

Formerly, the most common fish anaesthetic was urethane (ethyl carbamate), which in solution at high concentrations produced a shallow anaesthesia with minimal effect upon heart and respiration. It is now known to have carcinogenic properties and should be used with great care. The most popular of the newer narcotic anaesthetics are derivatives of p-aminobenzoic acid, namely MS 222 (ethyl m-aminobenzoate methanesulphonate) and benzocaine (ethyl p-aminobenzoate). Both drugs have a high potency with short induction and recovery times (Table II). Although MS 222 has been more popular because it is very soluble in water and thus simple to administer, it may reduce the pH of freshwater (Wedemeyer, 1970, Laird and Oswald, 1975) and of the blood in freshwater fish (Soivio *et al.*, 1971). In the early stages of anaesthesia, the increased acidity of the medium agitates the fish, resulting in a higher heart rate than that shown by fish exposed to MS 222 in a buffered or seawater solution (Soivio *et al.*, 1977). Wedemeyer (1970) reported a progressive increase in blood urea nitrogen levels and a tendency towards hypercholesterolaemia and ACTH production in fish anaesthetized with unbuffered MS 222 in freshwater.

Benzocaine is not very soluble in water and has to be dissolved initially in ethanol or acetone (0.2 g in 5 ml) before being added to the anaesthetic bath. Its main advantages are its low cost, higher potency and in freshwater, the suppression of stress in stages I and II of anaesthesia. Because benzocaine is only weakly soluble, it is more difficult to apply an overdose. MS 222 can also be applied as an injection. It has also been

Table II. The dose levels required to induce deep anaesthesia (stage III) in fish and the range of induction and recovery times with commonly used inspired anaesthetic drugs.

Drug	Dose (mg/l)	Induction Time (min)	Recovery Time (min)	Complications	Supplier
MS 222 or Finquel (ethyl *m*-amino-benzoate methanesulphonate)	50–100	1–3[a]	3–15[a]	acid, toxic when exposed to light, promotes bacterial growth, asphyxiant	Sandoz Ltd, Basle, Switzerland. Ayerest Laboratories, New York
Benzocaine (ethyl *p*-aminobenzoate)	25–50 (first dissolved in acetone or ethanol)	3–4	5–20	promotes bacterial growth, asphyxiant	Aldrich Chemical Co. Ltd, Wembley
Quinaldine (2 methylquinolene)	0.01–0.03 cm³/litre (first dissolved in acetone or ethanol)	1–3	5–20	gill irritant, low analgesia, oxidized on exposure to air	Eastman Kodak Co.
Quinaldine sulphate	16	2–6	2–6	acidic, low analgesia	

[a] Induction and recovery rates vary inversely with weight; the influence of weight is particularly pronounced among smaller specimens (Houston *et al.*, 1969).

administered to large sharks and rays as a solution sprayed on to the gills at a strength of about 1 g/l. Both drugs have important side-effects which appear after recovery and persist for 4–7 days. The effects result mainly from a lack of oxygen or hypoxia, induced by insufficient water flow over the gills commencing in stage III of anaesthesia when gill ventilation is reduced by depression of the medullary respiratory centres (Figs 1 and 2;

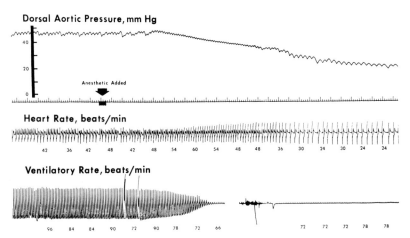

Fig. 1. Changes in blood pressure, heart rate (ECG) and ventilation during anaesthesia of a brook trout, *Salvelinus fontinalis*, with MS 222. (After Houston *et al.*, 1971.)

Houston *et al.*, 1971). The hypoxia is exacerbated by a marked slowing of heart rate or bradycardia (induced by the presence of de-oxygenated water at the gills), by an increase in resistance to blood flow through the gill lamellar pathways, and by a swelling of the erythrocytes which results in their accumulation in the gills (Fromm *et al.*, 1971; Holeton and Randall, 1967; Garey and Rahn, 1970). Forced irrigation of the gills with aerated anaesthetic solution immediately speeds up heart rate to more normal levels and slows the development of hypoxia (Fig. 3). Such a procedure is therefore advisable if the fish is to be kept in a state of maintained anaesthesia for more than a few minutes.

The main effects of hypoxia appear to be increased blood levels of glucose, lactate, K^+, Mg^{2+}, haemoglobin and haematocrit. Complete restoration of all blood parameters can require 7 days, but haemoconcentration, changes in blood pH, gas tensions and the respiratory movements may return to pre-anaesthesia levels within 4 h. One direct consequence of the vascular responses to hypoxia, particularly the fall in blood pressure, is increased urine flow and electrolyte loss (Hunn and Willard, 1970). In addition, observations of fish following handling, anaesthesia

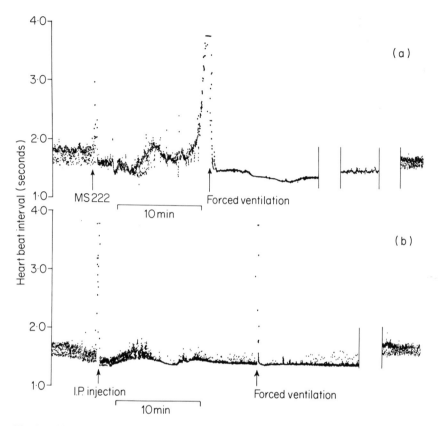

Fig. 2. Changes in heart rate of the cod, *Gadus morhua* during anaesthesia. (A) with 1:20 000 MS 222, (B) with intraperitoneal injection of 12 mg/kg Alphaxalone. Each dot on the record is a heartbeat interval. Note the pronounced bradycardia with MS 222, and the increase in heart rate following forced ventilation. With Alphaxalone, the fish retains its ventilatory movements and shows a reflex bradycardia when stimulated, but is effectively immobilized.

and minor surgery, have shown that behaviour is aberrant for at least 24 h, though the effects may be lessened if the fish is returned to familiar surroundings. In view of these physiological disturbances, it is advisable to delay measurement of behavioural and physiological parameters for at least 24 h after recovery from anaesthesia with *p*-aminobenzoic acid derivatives.

In spite of these complications, MS 222 and benzocaine are easily administered, and Bell (1964) considered MS 222 to be the best anaesthetic for surgical operations. Because of the marked bradycardia induced, these materials must be used carefully at only very light doses for transporting fish. Both materials should be protected from light in well closed containers.

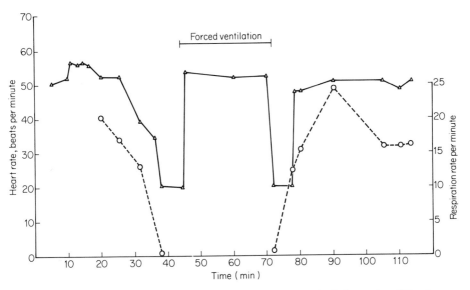

Fig. 3. Change in heart rate and ventilation rate of a cod, *Gadus morhua,* following anaesthesia by an intraperitoneal injection of sodium amylobarbitone. (After Wardle and Kanwisher, 1974.) The solid line is the heart rate.

The anaesthetic effect of quinaldine (2-methylquinolene) on fish was first reported by Muench (1968) who found that concentrations of between 2.5 and 20 ppm induced stage III anaesthesia in several species of freshwater fish in 0.5–4 min. It is a cheap, safe and effective anaesthetic for transporting, tagging, weighing and treating fish. However, it has several drawbacks. Although it produces a loss of equilibrium and depression of medullary centres in stage III, the fish do not completely lose reflex responsiveness which makes it unsuitable for elaborate surgery. Its efficacy is reduced by low pH and low temperatures, and because of its low solubility in water, it must initially be dissolved in ethanol or acetone. Perhaps the most serious of its drawbacks is that it releases a noxious irritant vapour harmful to the experimenter's eyes. Quinaldine in solution also causes copious secretion of branchial mucus by the fish and may induce cataracts in salmonid fish. These complications can be overcome with quinaldine sulphate which has the additional advantage of being very soluble in water. Like MS 222, quinaldine sulphate is acidic and in freshwater, must be buffered with sodium bicarbonate (0.45 g $NaHCO_3$/g $QnSO_4$, Blasiola, 1976).

Other inspired anaesthetics include carbon dioxide (as $NaHCO_3$), chloral hydrate, chloretone, ether, methyl pentynol, phenoxyethanol, amylobarbitone, pentobarbitone, propoxate, tribromoethanol, tertiary amyl alcohol and 2-amino-4-phenylthiazole.

(b) Injected drugs. To inject drugs, the fish may first need to be immobilized by electronarcosis, hypothermia or brief exposure to inspired drugs, which may later be flushed out. Great care must be taken to administer the correct dose of an injected drug since retrieval is impossible. Many of the drugs to be described have potent effects upon humans and an antidote should be at hand in case of accident. The effective dose of an injected drug is difficult to regulate and it is wise to administer the drug in two or three steps until the appropriate stage of anaesthesia is induced. Full recovery from a heavy dose of an injected drug may be prolonged because of the accumulation of the drug in non-nervous tissue and its slow subsequent release.

(i) Barbiturates: derivatives of malonyl urea, or barbituric acid, are hypnotic (sleep-inducing) drugs used extensively in human and veterinary medicine for sedation and both short- and long-term general anaesthesia. Barbiturates predominantly act upon the nerve synapses and are powerful depressants with only slight analgesic properties. In overdose, they may result in respiratory failure and reduced sympathetic tone which in turn results in a fall of blood pressure. Recovery is often prolonged.

Sodium thiopentone (Pentothal) and sodium methohexitone (Brevital) induce deep anaesthesia (stage III) only for short periods in both mammals and fish. In contrast, sodium pentobarbitone (Nembutal) and sodium amylobarbitone (Amytal) rapidly induce deep anaesthesia in fish for long periods (Keys and Wells, 1930) (Table III). During deep anaesthesia, the respiratory rhythm is slowed. The barbiturates result in bradycardia during suppression of the respiratory rhythm, but the reduction in heart rate develops only slowly compared with MS 222 anaesthesia. Heart rate can be restored to an acceptable level by forced ventilation of the gills, but this may be unnecessary while ventilatory movements persist. Barbiturates cause neuromuscular blockage and also inhibit the activity of sensory units in the central nervous system which limits their value for some physiological experiments. For surgical operations under conditions where forced ventilation is difficult, where the animal must be sedated for very long periods or where an inspired anaesthetic cannot be administered, the injection of barbiturates is satisfactory. However, the recovery period is long. Barbiturates can be purchased in the solid state or as aqueous solutions for injection; they can also be administered as inspired drugs.

Table III. Details of the dose and responses of fish to injected anaesthetic drugs (after Oswald, 1978; Keys and Wells, 1930).

Drug	Dose mg/kg	Site of Injection	Level of Anaesthesia	Duration (min)	Recovery Time (min)	Remarks
Sodium pentobarbitone (Nembutal)	30 48 72	intraperitoneal	II III IV	— 360 720	 720 1440	respiratory and cardiovascular depressant
Sodium amylobarbitone (Amytal)	20–30 40 40–54	intraperitoneal	III(1) III(2) III(2)	—	—	respiratory and cardiovascular depressant
Alphaxalone (Saffan)	12 19 24 36	intraperitoneal or intramuscular and intraperitoneal	II III(1) III(2) IV	— 60 60–180 240–360	— — 60–120 120	causes vasodilation, represses respiration, heart function nearly normal
Etorphine/acetylpromazine (Immobilan)	8–10	intramuscular	see text	30–60[a]		causes catatonia, loss of equilibrium; respiration and cardiovascular function remains nearly normal
Diprenorphine hydrochloride (Revivon)	8–10	intramuscular			1–5	revives fish after application of Immobilan

[a] The test run, however the anaesthesia lasts until the injection of Revivon.

(ii) Alphaxalone (Saffan, or Althesin): alphaxalone is a synthetic steroid anaesthetic lacking many of the side-effects of barbiturates or other steroid hormones (Child *et al.*, 1971). When the dosage is low, the fish loses equilibrium and muscle tone but respiration and circulation is maintained at approximately the basal level (Fig. 2). The gills appear bright red and engorged in contrast to the dull purplish colour associated with *p*-aminobenzoates and barbiturates. Electrocardiograms from fish injected with alphaxalone do not show the arrhythmia or extra QRS waves which can appear with other forms of anaesthesia, particularly barbiturates. Even with doses sufficient to stop respiratory movements, it is possible to record spontaneous activity in the lateral line nerve and to detect responses to water flow over the neuromasts. The duration of the anaesthesia is sufficiently long to perform complicated surgical techniques. With high doses, it is advisable to irrigate the gills artificially since respiration tends to be reciprocative. However, at low doses, respiratory movements persist and bradycardia develops only slowly. Alphaxalone is available as a solution, ready for injection.

(iii) Immobilon: etorphine acetylpromazine (Immobilon) is the transquillizer component of the syringe dart shot at large wild animals to immobilize them. A tranquillizer essentially depresses motor activity, though it may also induce mild analgesia and increase the animal's thresholds to stimuli. With acetylpromazine, there is a rapid loss of tone in skeletal muscle (catatonia) but a retention of normal respiratory and cardiovascular function (Blane *et al.*, 1967). Quick recovery is produced by injecting an equal dose of the antidote diprenorphine hydrochloride. Recently Oswald (1978) has established a suitable dosage for fish (Table III). Because of the small quantity required, intramuscular injection can induce rapid immobility. It has been shown to have minimal effect on the primary sensory pathways and there is no evidence of neuromuscular blocking.

(iv) Lignocaine: local anaesthetics such as Lignocaine (Xylocaine) or Procaine (Novocaine) which are rapidly absorbed through the skin, may be applied topically to reduce post-operative pain and trauma. Their action is to raise the threshold of sensory cells, to block neuronal conduction and to suppress spontaneous nervous activity. They can reduce post-operative disturbances in fish tagged conventionally or with transmitter tags. Lignocaine and Procaine can also be injected subdermally in a 2% solution to act as local anaesthetics, for example to reduce any inhibition or distress caused by contact of the fish with a clamp or holder, or they can be injected into the neural canal of the spinal cord between the 3rd and 4th vertebrae to immobilize the fish. The dosage must be limited to avoid any spread into the medulla and to prevent

visceral centres being affected. With extradural administration, the fish remains responsive to stimulation and the technique is therefore not recommended for sugical purposes unless used in conjunction with a light general anaesthetic. Both MS 222 and benzocaine may serve as mild local anaesthetics if applied topically or by injection. Local anaesthetics may be purchased with adrenalin added, the latter serving to restrict blood flow and confine the anaesthesia.

(c) Muscle relaxants. Muscle relaxants have no analgesic or narcotic properties and their action is simply to immobilize the fish. Some relaxants, like succinylcholine, exert their effect by depolarizing the motor end-plates; others, like curare, occupy the receptor sites at the motor end-plate. These two types may be administered to fish by intramuscular injection.

The most useful application of muscle relaxants is to eliminate movement during physiological studies, for example during the insertion of electrodes into the central nervous system, where any movement may destroy the unit whose response is being recorded. Relaxants may also be applied where the animal is to be immobilized, but sensory capacities are to remain intact. Relaxants may accompany light general anaesthesia or be applied alone. However, because the sensory capacities of the animal remain relatively unimpaired, their use is often under strict legal control. In the United Kingdom, no experiments can be performed under the effect of a curare-form substance except on a decerebrate animal or with special permission from the Home Office, even when a general anaesthetic is administered. A decerebrate fish is one in which the telencephalon (i.e. the corpora striata, olfactory lobes and olfactory tracts) is ablated or destroyed.

For general relaxation of the body musculature, d-tubocurarine (3–30 mg/kg) gallamine triethiodide (Flaxedil) (0.5–1 mg/kg), and succinylcholine (1–3 mg/kg) have been injected either intramuscularly or intraperitoneally. In sufficient dosage, these drugs stop ventilatory movements and forced ventilation may need to be applied to prevent the development of hypoxia. Gallamine also selectively abolishes activity in some efferent nerve fibres and may enhance apparent activity from sense organs.

As an alternative to employing a muscle relaxant, a teleost may be immobilized by severing the spinal column, behind the medulla. Similarly, ventilatory movements of the operculum can be halted by severing the appropriate motor nerves. In the United Kingdom, such a procedure is only permitted with a decerebrate fish.

III. HUMANE KILLING OF FISH

For most purposes, particularly if an anatomically undamaged fish is required, an overdose of MS 222, benzocaine or a barbiturate is perhaps the best method of killing fish. When it is essential to achieve an abrupt end, as for biochemical studies, electronarcosis followed by a sharp blow to the head is effective. Assurance that a fish is dead may be achieved by sectioning the spinal cord or medulla and destroying the more anterior parts of the central nervous system. It should be noted that an unanaesthetised elasmobranch treated in this way may show persistent rhythmic swimming movements for very long periods. In the United Kingdom, a decerebrate fish is considered by the Home Office to be dead (page 261).

IV. SURGERY AND SURGICAL EQUIPMENT

A wide range of surgical techniques may be applied to fish, ranging from simple injection or tag attachment, to extensive exploration of the central nervous system. For many procedures, it is only necessary to hold the fish for a short period in wet gauze or in a shallow water-filled trough lined with resilient plastic foam. However, where extensive surgery is to be performed or the animal is to be manipulated for a long period, more extensive facilities are called for.

A. Operating Table

Most operating tables for fish are based on or resemble an original design by Smith and Bell (1967) though alternative designs are available for more basic work, for example, that of Reinecker and Ruddell (1974) or for cephalic work, that of Goetz *et al.*, 1977). The table contains three basic parts:
  (a) a fish holder
  (b) a life support system
  (c) a light source.
Associated items like a microscope and micromanipulators may be added. It is also useful if the operating table incorporates a scale so that the fish may be measured.

(1) Fish holders
For much physiological and pharmacological work, the fish holder for round fish may consist of a vice, the jaws of which are padded with foam

rubber and overlaid with an adjustable muslin sling. All areas of fish outside that involved in surgery are covered with wet paper towelling or gauze. Cotton wool does not saturate well enough with water. For flatfish, or when round fish are to be held out of the vertical plane, a flat platform can be inclined at 30° to the horizontal plane and covered with flexible foam rubber. The fish can be secured with rubber bands hooked over pegs projecting from the edges of the platform or by metal or plastic clips.

For some experiments on the sense organs and nervous system, the holder must subject the fish to a minimum of body contact, the animal being held at a few isolated points. For example, the fish may be clamped rostrally by the snout Goetz *et al.* (1977) or by means of eyebars locking with the eye-sockets, the rest of the body being held by wire clips or adjustable bars and clamps (Figs 4, 5). Nervous inhibition as a result of the contact can be avoided by the topical application or injection of a local anaesthetic. In constructing the fish holder, it is important to ensure that respiratory movements are not obstructed and that forced ventilation of the gills is possible.

(2) Life support systems

After inducing deep anaesthesia in a holding tank containing a suitable inspired anaesthetic, or after injection of other drugs, the fish is transferred to the holder and fitted with a mouth-piece or branchial irrigator through which either clean water or an appropriate concentration of anaesthetic solution is passed. Forced irrigation of the gills is especially necessary with MS 222 and benzocaine anaesthesia (page 255). An anaesthetic delivered in this manner may often be more dilute than the original solution applied to the fish to prevent the fish entering a deeper stage of anaesthesia. The mouth piece can be a simple nozzle, or a specifically designed buccal tube equipped with lateral holes, producing fan shaped jets for irrigation of each branchial slit (Goetz *et al.*, 1977). The buccal tube may be designed to hold the head, or to facilitate surgery inside the buccal cavity, as in pinealectomy or aortic cannulation. The anaesthetic solution is pumped to the fish directly or via a constant head from a tank containing an aerator or oxygenator and perhaps a heat exchanger or ice bags for maintaining the temperature at or below the acclimation temperature of the fish. It is often useful if the tank has a graduated scale for measuring the water volume. Flow from the header tank may be monitored by passing it through a flow meter and can be adjusted by a needle valve on the supply to the fish. A two-way tap in the circuit allows changing from an anaesthetic solution to untreated water. A large drain or overflow must be provided to prevent the fish tank overflowing.

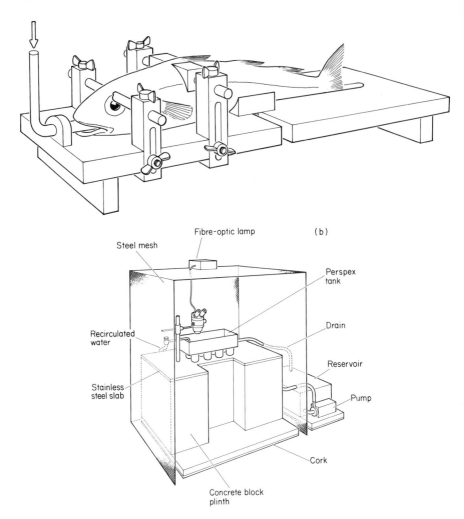

Fig. 4. Fish clamp, and operating table for cranial surgery and electrophysiological studies upon cod, *Gadus morhua*. (a) The fish is held in the perspex clamp by adjustable eye-bars and body wedges, and is placed inside a perspex tank (not shown), the water level being set by an overflow. (b) The tank is mounted on rubber tennis balls on an anti-vibration table and is enclosed within a wire mesh cage.

During surgery, the electrocardiogram of the fish may be monitored (page 269) to allow the state of the fish to be assessed. With freshwater species, the electrocardiograph electrodes can be built into the fish holder. With proper monitoring to avoid hypoxia, anaesthesia can hold a fish immobile for several hours. Recovery from anaesthesia is effected by

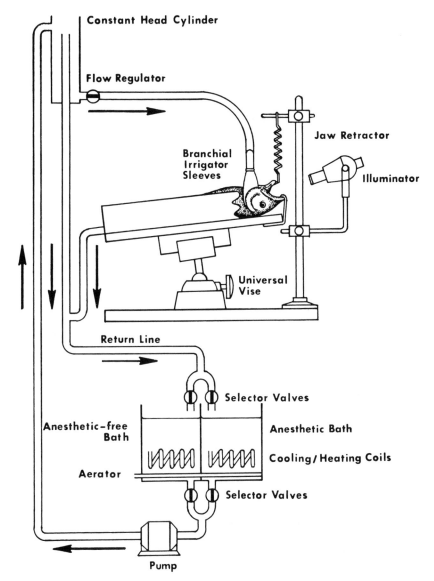

Fig. 5. Life support system for the maintenance of anaesthesia during catheterisation of the dorsal aorta (Houston *et al.*, 1969).

turning the appropriate selector valve from the anaesthetic bath to an uncontaminated water supply (Fig. 5). When the fish shows spontaneous rhythmic respiratory movements and sculling of the caudal fin, it can be released and returned to a holding tank for full recovery.

(3) Illumination

Adequate illumination for minor or superficial surgery can be provided by a 20 watt fluorescent adjustable desk lamp. However, for some electrophysiological work, discharge or thyristor controlled lamps must be avoided because they may introduce electrical interference. A focussing microscope lamp fitted with a heat filter may be employed for microsurgery or internal operations. A surgical or dental lamp will provide shadowless illumination. Where space is restricted, a fibre-optic lamp with removeable lenses may be used. Tt has the advantage of being cold and may be placed close to the preparation, even underwater.

All wiring and switches should be clear of the splash zone and preferably should be low voltage. A fibre-optic lamp has the additional advantage that the source can be placed well away from the experimental animal for electrical safety. It can be placed outside an isolating cage to reduce electrical interference.

B. Surgical Instruments and Surgical Technique

The choice of surgical instruments depends on the intended surgical procedure. The range of basic instruments commonly used in fish surgery includes dissecting and suturing equipment, forceps, needle holders, retractors, and injection and body fluid sampling equipment. For micro-surgical work, fine probes and hooks can be made by mounting small insect pins on small glass or wooden handles with sealing wax or quick-setting epoxy resin. Fine scalpels can be made immediately before they are required by breaking a razor blade (the more brittle non-stainless varieties are best). Fine cutting blades and chisels can also be constructed by shaping the ends of ordinary dissecting needles and probes on a grindstone and then sharpening them on a series of fine whetstones.

A major problem during surgery on the intact fish is bleeding from cut blood vessels. Care must be taken to avoid severing arteries. However, if major vessels are to be interrupted, they can be tied off with ligatures of fine thread before being cut, or sealed by means of electro-cautery or diathermy. It is often best to seal vessels by pressure with fine forceps, then applying heat by touching the forceps with the cautery or diathermy probe. Where conventional scalpels will not readily cut tissue, the surgery can be performed by diathermy. Should extensive bleeding occur with a preparation, haemostasis can be induced by means of coagulants, like gelatine foam, perhaps aided by the application of thrombin. Styptics or haemostatics like adrenalin will slow blood flow, but may have undesirable physiological effects. The clotted blood can later be removed with forceps. Blood and other fluids may be removed with a cotton bud or by means of a pipette operated by mouth suction or an aspirator. Where bleeding is extensive, a flow of sterile physiological saline can be introduced. Wounds may be closed with a variety of sutures, and bone may be sealed with a low melting point wax, vaseline, dental cement, or a special adhesive (for example Eastman 910 or a medically approved cyanoacrylate adhesive).

During surgery it must be remembered that neither sea water nor freshwater are iso-ionic or iso-tonic with fish body fluids, and care must be taken to irrigate wounds only with a suitable saline solution (page 274). Details of many useful surgical manipulations including abdominal laparotomy, urethal catheterization and neurophysiological preparation are given by Klontz and Smith (1968). A volume edited by Pavlovskii (1962) gives details of several surgical procedures while papers by Peter and Gill (1975), Peter *et al.* (1975) and Goetz *et al.* (1977) provide information useful for cranial surgery.

C. Ancillary Equipment

For fine surgery, it is often necessary to view the animal with a mounted lens, magnifying spectacles or a binocular dissecting microscope. In choosing the latter, particular attention should be paid to ensuring that the working distance of the instrument is sufficient. Ideally, the instrument should remain in focus at all magnifications. A zoom lens, where magnification can be varied continuously, is particularly advantageous. The base provided with a dissecting microscope is often unsuitable and it may be necessary to mount the instrument on a long pivoting arm, so that the microscope can be swung aside easily to allow the experimenter full access to the fish. With an extra-long arm, additional weight may need to be added to the microscope base and the arm itself may need to be heavily constructed to reduce tremor. Where electrodes or transducers are to be attached to the fish under the microscope, it is often essential that the microscope should be capable of being tilted out of the vertical. A special fitting may need to be constructed to permit this. Where micro-electrode work is being performed and the fish is mounted on an antivibration table, it is better if the microscope is not mounted directly upon the table but attached to a firm base elsewhere.

A wide variety of micromanipulators and electrode holders are available for animal work and are perfectly suitable for use with fish. In general, such aids are mounted directly on the base carrying the fish. If this base is made of steel, it can be an advantage to mount the micromanipulator on a magnetic plate, so that it may easily be repositioned while remaining stable. A suitable heavy flat base can be made from a marking out table (used in engineering workshops) mounted on felt, rubber tubing or tennis balls. Lumps of soft non-toxic aquarium putty or plasticine, are useful aids for holding instruments or for temporarily fixing cables and other pieces of equipment during surgery. Magnetic plates and clamps which can be switched on and off are available from engineering suppliers. Because of the risk of electrical shock to the experimenter, it is advisable to connect all electrical apparatus to the main supply by means of an earth-leakage circuit breaker.

Operating tables and fish holder can be cleaned with sodium hypochlorite or a proprietary brand of sterilizing agent, but should be washed with clean water before allowing the fish to contact their surface. Instruments may be sterilized by autoclaving (15 min. at 120°C) or by placing in hot water or alcohol and flame. If an anti-rust preparation is used to cleanse surgical instruments, the substance must be thoroughly removed or it may contaminate tissues.

V. MARKING FISH

The simplest way to identify fish is to isolate individuals in well labelled tanks but where this is not possible, then one must resort to marking or tagging techniques of which there are many (Gerking, 1963). Ideally, the form of identification should give the maximum amount of information with the minimum effect on physiology or behaviour. The simplest method is fin clipping which gives wide scope for individual marking, but may interfere with normal swimming. Other popular techniques involve attaching numbered tags by metal clips, monofilament or braided nylon, inert metal traces and plastic tubing, but puncturing the integument may lead to the development of lesions or fungal infections (Roberts et al. 1973a, b, c; Morgan and Roberts, 1976). Nevertheless, such techniques are widely applied to fish which are released into the open sea.

Freeze branding is particularly useful since it provides an easily recognizable mark which can be detected for up to 12 months. It is simple, quick and the brand does not become infected. In this technique, the dorsum of an anaesthetized fish is brought in contact for 2 s with a numbered brass, aluminium or copper stamp which has been pre-cooled by immersion in liquid nitrogen (Laird et al., 1975). Forty-eight hours after branding, a distinct outline of the number can be seen, particularly in fish kept in a light coloured environment. It has been successful with salmonid fish but in some marine species, the brand is recognizable for only 1–2 months. Cooling of the stamp may also be achieved by means of a slurry of solid CO_2 and ethanol, or by a volatile refrigerant like Freon. The coolants are kept in a vacuum flask, the stamp immersed until effervescence stops, wiped clean and applied to the fish.

Hot brands can be applied by immersing the stamp in boiling water, but the cold marking technique is considered to be less traumatic. Dye-marking techniques have been introduced which employ a jet in-noculator. The jet of dye punctures the integument and leaves a coloured spot in the dermis which can persist for several months. A binary code on the fins or dorsal surface of the fish can identify individuals. Coloured latex rubber can also be injected beneath the skin by means of a conventional syringe. Fish may readily be marked by means of a silver nitrate pencil, though with some species, the mark is not permanent.

VI. ELECTROCARDIOGRAPHY

Electrocardiography is often useful for monitoring the depth of anaesthesia and the level of hypoxia which the fish may be experiencing during an operation (Houston *et al.*, 1971; Ross and Wiewiorka, 1977). Recovery from an anaesthetic can also be closely monitored. Electrocardiography is widely used to assess the condition, activity and metabolic rate of both captive and free-swimming fish (Priede and Tytler, 1977; Priede and Young, 1977).

The electrical potentials generated by the heart during the cardiac cycle may be detected either by implanted or external electrodes. If the former, two electrodes are implanted subcutaneously and midventrally, either both in the heart region or one in the pectoral region and the other near the anus. Alternative loci are the axillary pits of the pectoral fins from which a standard ECG can be obtained, suitable for detecting cardiac malfunctions. The electrodes normally consist of narrow (18–30 SWG), short lengths of silver or stainless steel wire insulated with Teflon, Diamel or some other material, bared at the tips and soldered to each of the insulated leads of a twisted pair or twin screened cable. With stainless steel wire, it is necessary to use a high temperature solder and concentrated phosphoric acid as a flux. The solder joints can be insulated with a silicone rubber sealer, quick-setting epoxy resin or shrink-fit tubing. Ideally, the water-proofing material should serve as a slightly elastic bed on which to tie the sutures which secure the electrodes in place. The insulated wires are then led around the body and anchored elsewhere by a simple suture (Priede and Tytler, 1977).

The ECG signals from the two implanted electrodes may be fed into the input of a high-gain, AC-coupled, differential input pre-amplifier, with the common line or earth connected to the water by a third electrode or plate. Ideally, the pre-amplifier should be fitted with high and low frequency "noise" filters. Such filters are commonly incorporated into suitable monitoring or recording instruments, but they can be bought or made separately from relatively simple circuits. A filter bandwidth of 2–150 Hz gives a full waveform but a narrower bandwidth of 40–100 Hz filters out respiratory and swimming movements and is often more useful (Fig. 6). The electrocardiogram can be monitored aurally simply by connecting a loud speaker to the output of an audio amplifier. The audible monitor is particularly useful for checking the condition of fish during a single-handed surgical operation.

A visual display of the ECG can be obtained by placing a cathode ray oscilloscope across the output of the pre-amplifier. It is advisable to use a CRO with a slow-sweep speed of 1 cm/s or even less and with a long persistence screen or storage facility so that the wave-form is retained. Permanent records can be made by photographing the CRO screen or by feeding the signal to a pen recorder. A particularly useful form of display is shown in Fig. 2 and was obtained by feeding an analogue signal proportional to the heart beat interval to a pen recorder. "Hardwire" electrocardiography has the disadvantage of restricting the movements of the fish as a result of the length of cable connecting it to the monitor. A way around this has been found by the use of miniature ultrasonic (Priede and Young, 1977; Wardle and Kanwisher, 1974) or frequency-modulated radio transmitters (Frank, 1968; Nomura *et al.*, 1972). Some transmitters relay the processed ECG as a complete wave-form and others as a pulse triggered by the QRS complex, to a receiver and monitor. The transmitter is either attached dorsally or inserted into the stomach with the leads issuing from a gill slit.

It is possible to dispense with implanted electrodes when using freshwater fish (for example see Spoor and Drummond, 1972). A pair of submerged silver stainless steel or carbon electrodes are placed on opposite sides, or above and below the holding tank, immersed in the water and not touching the tank. The electrodes are connected by screened wires to a high-gain AC coupled pre-amplifier and thence to a suitable monitor. Since the system detects all external changes in electric potential produced by the fish, it is also possible to discriminate between the activity of locomotor and respiratory muscles and the ECG. These signals are shunted by sea water and cannot readily be detected from marine species. The advantage of external electrodes is that the ECG can be detected without handling, anaesthetizing or stressing the fish, though the fish must be confined in a tank. It should be noted that when the fish is

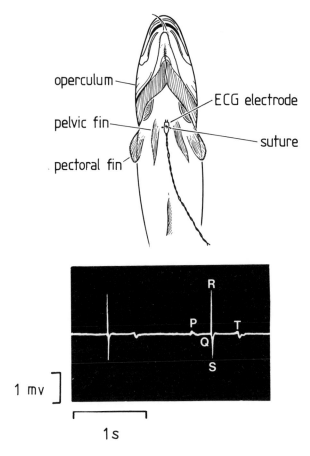

Fig. 6. Electrocardiogram of cod, recorded with a filter bandwidth of 40–100 Hz.

very active, it is often very difficult to separate the ECG from electrical noise and movement artefacts.

The relative magnitude of the various components of the electrocardiogram vary with the position of the electrodes and the filter bandwidth employed. With most fish, a peak amplitude of about 1 mV can be expected for the QRS component, but much lower amplitude signals can readily be handled provided that the preparation is suitably earthed and screened from noise. In general, the heart rate lies between 1 and 4 beats per second for unanaesthetized fish, with occasional longer intervals, but the rate varies from species to species and with temperature; it is also faster in stressed or swimming fish. Anaesthetized fish generally show a faster and less variable heart rate (Fig. 2). Fish in a state of hypoxia at first show an increase in heart rate, but this is followed by a marked slowing of the rate or bradycardia, which is reversible. Severe hypoxia is characterized by an irregular or a rhythmic beating of the heart and an increase in the T component of the electrocardiogram.

VII. BLOOD SAMPLING

Blood can readily be drawn from fish by puncture of the heart, bulbus or conus arteriosus, ventral or dorsal aorta, branchial arteries, caudal artery or caudal vein (running in the haemal canal ventral to the vertebral column) or subintestinal vein, but because of the relatively low blood volumes in fish (5–7 cm^3/kg) and the difficulty of access to these structures, the process can be traumatic. Samples may be taken repeatedly from individual fish by dorsal aorta cannulation, as well as singly from freshly killed specimens.

Dorsal aortic cannulation was described by Smith and Bell (1964) who passed a polythene cannula through the snout into the buccal cavity where it was inserted through the roof of the mouth into the dorsal aorta at the confluence of the efferent branchial arteries (Fig. 7). The physiological consequences of this operation are discussed by Houston *et al.* (1969). Soivio and Oikari (1976) found that the time for recovery from handling and surgery was shortened if the fish was shielded from visual stimuli. By restricting the fish in an opaque tube, they showed that it was possible to extract blood samples (0.06 cm^3/100 g of fish) without obvious discomfort. With this technique, there is the added bonus that it is possible to monitor changes in blood pressure (Randall *et al.*, 1965), and it provides a useful route for the injection of anaesthetics and drugs.

In addition to those techniques mentioned above, fish can be bled rapidly by cutting through the branchial arches or caudal peduncle. It is essential to reduce the time and severity of handling before killing because of the changes in the properties of the blood, particularly the reduction in blood clotting time reported by Casillas and Smith (1977). Because of the risk of blood clotting, it is advisable to use heparinized instruments. Methods in fish blood analysis are described by *Soivio et al.*, 1977, and Schreck *et al.*, 1976. Samples may be taken from the lymphatic system of fish by way of the dorsal lymph vessel, which runs along the vertebral column, above the spinal cord. The location of the vessel in several teleosts is described by Wardle (1971).

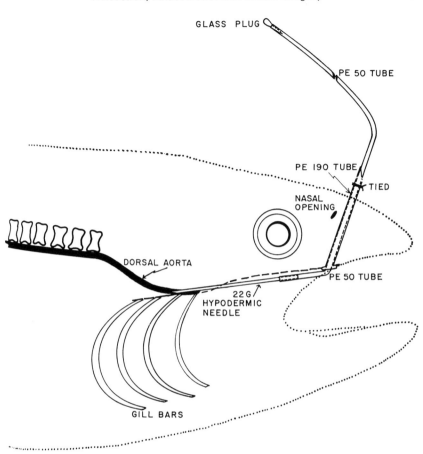

Fig. 7. Saggital section of a cannulated salmon (Smith and Bell, 1964).

VIII. PHYSIOLOGICAL SALINE SOLUTION

During surgical interference with a fish, it is often necessary to bathe or wash tissues. A saline medium may also be required for the injection of drugs. Neither freshwater nor sea water, nor solutions isotonic with these media are suitable because of undesirable osmotic and ionic effects. Natural plasma from the animal can be employed, but must be prepared immediately before use by centrifuging the blood of an animal killed without anaesthesia. Alternatively, a saline solution can be prepared which is isotonic or iso-ionic with the blood of the species concerned. A series of physiological saline media for fish, based largely on the organic composition of the blood serum, are listed in Table IV. It should be noted that the blood composition of many fishes may be closer to that of man than of the frog, and that frog "Ringer" may contain lower levels of chloride, sodium and calcium ions than fish serum.

For those physiological applications where an isotonic solution of sodium chloride is adequate, a solution of between 0.85 to 1.0% is satisfactory. For most applications, saline solutions should be air-saturated and sterilized (by filtration through a 0.22 μm millipore filter, which can be conveniently attached to a hypodermic syringe) or autoclaved (15 min at 120°C).

IX. GENERAL

In this chapter, we have described a range of techniques which can be applied successfully to fish. For the researchers who use them routinely they are simple and easy, but to the newcomer they may seem formidable. Skill only develops through practice and yet more practice, and there can be no substitute for trying out a particular technique. Preferably, this experience should be gained by working under supervision with cadavers to develop the manual dexterity and confidence necessary with the living animal. It is important to remember, however, that there are major ethical as well as practical differences between working with a corpse and with its living counterpart.

X. REFERENCES

Blane, G. P., Boura, A. L. A., Fitzgerald, A. E. and Lister, R. E. (1957). Actions of Etorphine Hydrochloride (M99) a potent morphine-like agent. *Journal of Pharmacology and Chemotherapy* **30**, 11–22.

Blasiola, G. C. (1976). Quinaldine sulphate, a new anaesthetic formulation for tropical marine fishes. *Journal of Fish Biology* **10**, 113–120.

Bell, G. R. (1964). A guide to the properties and uses of some general anaesthetics for fish. *Fisheries Research Board of Canada, Bulletin* **148**, 4.

Casillas, E. and Smith, L. S. (1977). Effect of stress on blood coagulation and haematology in rainbow trout (*Salmo gairdneri*). *Journal of Fish Biology* **10**, 481–492.

Child, K. J., Currie, J. P., Davies, B., Dodds, D. R., Pearce, D. G. and Twissle, D. J. (1971). The pharmacological properties in animals of CT 1341—A new steroid anaesthetic agent. *British Journal of Anaesthesia* **43**, 2.

Dijkgraaf, S. (1973). A method for complete and selective surgical elimination of the lateral-line system. *Experientia* **29**, 737–738.

Table IV. The composition of physiological saline media for a variety of freshwater and marine fish. The quantities of constituents are given as millimoles except where stated otherwise. To convert millimoles into milligrams multiply by the molecular weight.

Constituents (mmole)	Molecular weight	General freshwater teleost (a)	Brown trout, *Salmo trutta* (b)	Cutthroat trout, *Salmo clarki clarki* (b)	Freshwater eel, *Anguilla anguilla* (c)	Electric eel, *Electrophorus electricus* (b)	General marine teleost (a)	Saithe, *Pollachius virens* (d)	Cod, *Gadus morhua* (e)	Cod, *Gadus morhua* (h)	Marine eel, *Anguilla anguilla* (c)	Bullhead, *Cottus scorpius* (f)	General Elasmobranch (g)	Dogfish, *Scyllium canicula* (a)	Cuckoo ray, *Raja naevus* (h)
$NaCl$	58.4	93.96	124.06	126.88	114.0	169.06	232.2	174.88	154.0	142.0	150.0	142.0	291.6	270	312.0
KCl	74.6	1.89	5.1	4.96	2.0	4.96	8.1	6.17	5.63	2.6	0.2	2.6	3.24	11.34	4.0
K_2SO_4	174.3	—	—	—	0.4	—	—	—	—	—	0.11	—	—	—	—
$(NH_4)_2SO_4$	132.1	—	—	—	—	—	—	—	—	—	—	—	—	—	—
$NaH_2PO_4 \cdot 2H_2O$	156.0	—	2.63	2.56	—	0.26	—	—	—	3.2	—	3.2	—	—	—
$Na_2HPO_4 \cdot 2H_2O$	178.0	—	—	1.12	—	1.18	—	—	—	—	—	—	—	—	—
$NaHCO_3$	84.0	—	11.9	3.69	20.0	—	—	0.6	—	18.5	20.0	18.5	—	—	—
$NaOH$	40.0	—	—	—	3.0	—	—	—	—	—	2.4	—	—	—	—
Na_2SO_4	142.0	—	—	—	—	—	—	—	—	—	—	—	3.52	3.96	—
KH_2PO_4	136.1	—	—	1.25	—	—	—	—	—	—	—	—	—	—	—
$MgCl_2 \cdot 6H_2O$	203.3	—	—	—	0.2	1.48	1.8	0.43	—	1.0	0.2	1.0	2.16	6.84	—
$MgSO_4 \cdot 7H_2O$	246.5	—	0.93	1.26	—	—	—	—	—	—	—	—	—	—	5.0
$CaCl_2 \cdot 2H_2O$	147.0	1.08	1.56	—	0.63	2.99	1.08	1.91	1.7	2.7	0.63	2.7	1.8	4.68	—
Tris-maleate	237.2	—	—	—	—	—	—	—	—	—	0.25	—	—	—	—
Urea	60.1	—	—	—	—	—	—	—	—	—	—	—	450.0	394.2	450.0
Heparin		—	1 g/l	—	5000 IU/l	—	—	—	—	—	5000 IU/l	—	—	—	—
Glucose	180.2	—	—	—	1 g/l	—	—	—	—	—	1 g/l	60.75	—	—	—
Lactic acid	90.1	—	—	—	5.0	—	—	—	—	—	5.0	—	—	—	—
Polyvinyl pyrrolidone		—	—	—	20 g/l	—	—	—	—	—	20 g/l	—	—	—	—
HEPES	238	—	—	—	2.5	—	—	—	—	—	2.5	—	—	—	10.0
Water (ml)		to 1000	1000	1000	to 1000	1000	to 1000	975	to 1000	to 1000	to 1000	to 1000	to 1000	to 1000	to 1000
Mean freezing point (°C)		—	−0.58	−0.54	—	−0.69	—	—	—	—	—	0.617	—	—	—
pH		—	—	—	7.65	—	—	—	7.4	7.4	7.65	—	—	—	7.4

(a) Pantin (1948), (b) Wolf (1963), (c) Girard *et al.* (1977), (d) Tytler (unpublished), (e) Dijkgraaf (1973), (f) Hudson (1967), (g) Roberts and Ryan (1971), (h) Johnston (1980). *Marine Biology Letters*, **1**, 323–328.

Frank, T. H. (1968). Telemetering the electrocardiogram of free-swimming *Salmo irideus*, *I.E.E.E. Trans. Biomed. Eng. BME* **15**, 111–114.

Fromm, P. O., Richards, B. D. and Hunter, R. C. (1971). Effects of some insecticides and MS 222 on isolated perfused gills of trout. *Progressive Fish Culturist* **33**, 138–305.

Garey, W. F. and Rahn, H. (1970). Normal arterial gas tensions and pH and breathing frequency of the electric eel. *Resp. Physiology* **9**, 141–150.

Gerking, S. D. (1963). Non-mutilation marks for fish. *I.C.N.A.F. Spec. Publ.* **4**, 248–254.

Girard, J-P., Thomson, A. J. and Sargent, J. R. (1977). Adrenalin induced turnover of Phosphatidic acid and Phosphatidyl inositol in chloride cells from the gills of *Anguilla anguilla*. *Febs Letters* **73**, 267–270.

Goetz, F. W., Hoffman, R. A. and Pancoe, W. L. (1977). A surgical apparatus for fish and its use in the pinealectomy of salmonids. *Journal of Fish Biology* **10**, 287–290.

Halsband, E. (1967). Basic principles of electric fishing. *In* "Fishing with Electricity—its application to biology and management" (R. Vibert, ed.), 57–64. Fishing News (Books) Ltd, London.

Ho, F. C. and Vanstone, W. E. (1961). Effect of estradiol monobenzoate on some serum constituents of maturing sockeye salmon (*Oncorhynchus nerka*). *Journal of the Fisheries Research Board of Canada* **18**, 859–864.

Holeton, G. F. and Randall, D. J. (1967). Changes in blood pressure in the rainbow trout during hypoxia. *Journal of experimental Biology* **46**, 297–305.

Houston, A. H., De Wilde, M. A. and Madden, J. A. (1969). Some physiological consequences of aortic catheterization in brook trout (*Salvelinus fontinalis*). *Journal of the Fisheries Research Board of Canada* **26**, 1847–1856.

Houston, A. H., Madden, J. A., Woods, R. J. and Miles, H. M. (1971). Some physiological effects of handling and tricaine methane sulphonate anaesthetization upon the brook trout (*Salvelinus fontinalis*). *Journal of the Fisheries Research Board of Canada* **28**, 635–642.

Hunn, J. B. and Willord, W. A. (1970). The effect of anaesthetization and urinary bladder catheterization on renal function of rainbow trout. *Comparative Biochemistry and Physiology* **33**, 805–815.

Keys, A. B. and Wells, N. A. (1930). Amytal anaesthesia in fishes. *Journal of Pharmacology and Experimental Therapeutics* **39**, 115–128.

Klontz, G. W. and Smith, L. S. (1968). Fish as biological research subjects. In *Methods of Animal experimentation*. Vol. 3. (W. I. Gay, ed.), Academic Press, London and New York.

Kynard, B. and Lonsdale, E. (1975). Experimental study of galvanonarcosis for rainbow trout (Salmo gairdneri) immobilization. *Journal of the Fisheries Research Board of Canada* **32**, 300–302.

Laird, L. M., Oswald, R. L. (1975). Benzocaine (Ethyl p-aminobenzoate) as a fish anaesthetic. *Fisheries Management* **64**, 92–93.

Laird, L. M., Roberts, R. U., Shearer, W. M. and McArdle, J. F. (1975). Freeze branding of juvenile salmon. *Journal of Fish Biology* **7**, 167–172.

Madden, J. A., Houston, A. H. (1976). Use of electroanaesthesia with fresh water teleosts, some physiological consequences in the rainbow trout, *Salmo gairdneri* Richardson. *Journal of Fish Biology* **9**, 457–462.

McDonell, W. (1975). Sedation, analgesia and anaesthesia. In *An Introduction to Experimental Surgery* edited by J. De Boer. J. Archibald and H. G. Downie Excerpta Medica, Amsterdam.

McFarland, W. N. (1959). A study of the effects of anaesthetics on the behaviour and physiology of fishes. *Institute Marine Science* **6**, 24–35.

McFarland, W. N. (1960). The use of anaesthetics for handling and the transport of fishes. *California Fish Game* **46**, 407–431.

Morgan, R. I. G. and Roberts, R. J. (1976). The histopathology of salmon lagging. IV The effects of severe exercise on the induced lesion in salmon parr at two temperatures. *Journal of Fish Biology* **8**, 289–292.

Muench, B. (1968). Quinaldine, a new anaesthetic for fish. *Progressive Fish Culturist* **20**, 42–44.

Nomura, S., Ibaraki, T., Hirose, H. and Shirahata, S. (1972). Application of back pack cardiotelemeter for fishes. 1 Heart rate and cardiac reflex in fishes during unrestrained swimming. *Bulletin of the Japanese Society of Scientific Fisheries* **38**, 1105–1117.

Oswald, R. L. (1978). Injection anaesthesia for experimental studies in fishes. *Comparative Biochemistry and Physiology* **60c**, 19–26.

Pantin, C. F. A. (1948). "Notes on Microscopical Technique for Zoologists", .Cambridge University Press.

Pavlovskii, E. N., ed. (1962). *Techniques for the Investigation of Fish Physiology*. Academy of Science USSR. (Translated by the Israel Program for Scientific Translations. Jerusalem 1964).

Peter, R. E. and Gill, V. E. (1975). A stereotaxic atlas and technique for forebrain nuclei of the goldfish. *Journal of Comparative Neurology* **159**, 69–102.

Peter, R. E. and Macey, M. J. and Gill, V. E. (1975). A stereotaxic atlas and technique for forebrain nuclei of the Killi fish. *Journal of Comparative Neurology* **159**, 103–128.

Porter, A. R. W. (1975). The law and animal experimentation. *In* "An Introduction to Experimental Surgery", (J. De Boer, J. Archibald and H. G. Downie, eds), Excerpta Medica, Amsterdam.

Priede, I. G. and Tytler, P. (1977). Heart rate as a measure of metabolic rate in teleost fishes, *Salmo trutta* and *Gadus morhua*. *Journal of Fish Biology* **10**, 231–242.

Priede, T. G. and Young, A. H. (1977). The ultrasonic telemetry of cardiac rhythms of wild-living brown trout (*Salmo trutta L.*) as an indicator of bioenergetics and behaviour. *Journal of Fish Biology* **10**, 302–318.

Randall, D. J., Smith, L. S. and Brett, J. R. 1965 Dorsal aortic blood pressures recorded from the rainbow trout *Salmo gairdneri*. *Canadian Journal of Zoology* **43**, 863–872.

Reinecker, R. H. and Ruddell, M. O. 1974. An easily fabricated operating table for fish surgery. *Progressive Fish Culturist* **36**, 111–112.

Roberts, A. L. and Ryan, K. P. (1971). The fine structure of the lateral line sense organs of dogfish. *Proceedings of the Royal Society London B.* **179**, 157–169.

Roberts, R. J., MacQueen, A., Shearer, W. M. and Young, H. (1973a). The histopathology of salmon tagging. I The lesion in newly tagged parr. *Journal of Fish Biology* **5**, 497–503.

Roberts, R. J., MacQueen, A., Shearer, W. M. and Young, H. (1973b). The histopathology of salmon tagging. II The chronic tagging lesion in returning adult fish. *Journal of Fish Biology* **51**, 615–619.

Roberts, R. J., MacQueen, A., Shearer, W. M. and Young, H. (1973c). The histopathology of salmon tagging. III Secondary infection associated with taggin. *Journal of Fish Biology* **5**, 621–623.

Schreck, C. B., Whaley, R. A., Bass, M. L., Maughan, O. E. and Solarzzi, M. (1976). Physiological responses of rainbow trout *Salmo gairdneri* to electroshock. *Journal of the Fisheries Research Board of Canada* **33**, 76–84.

Smith, L. S. and Bell, G. R. (1964). A technique for prolonged blood sampling in free swimming salmon. *Journal of the Fisheries Research Board of Canada* **21**, 711–717.

Smith, L. S. and Bell, G. R. 1967 Anaesthetic and surgical techniques for Pacific salmon. *Journal of the Fisheries Research Board of Canada* **24**, 1579–1588.

Soivio, A. and Oikari, (1976). A technique for repeated sampling of the blood of individual resting fish. *Journal of Experimental Biology* **63**, 207–217.

Soivio, A., Nyholm, K. and Huhti, M. (1977). Effects of anaesthesia with MS 222, neutralised MS 222 and benzocaine on the blood constituents of rainbow trout, *Salmo gairdneri. Journal of Fish Biology* **10**, 91–101.

Spoor, W. A. and Drummond, R. A. (1972). An electrode for detecting movements in gradient tanks. *Trans. American Fisheries Society* **101**, 714–715.

Wardle, C. S. (1971). New observations on the lymphatic system of the plaice and other teleosts. *Journal of the Marine Biological Association of the UK* **51**, 977–990.

Wardle, C. S. and Kanwisher, J. W. (1974). The significance of heart rate in free swimming cod, *Gadus morhua*. Some observations with ultrasonic tags. *Marine Behaviour and Physiology* **2**, 311–324.

Wedemeyer, G. (1970). Stress of anaesthesia with MS 222 and benzocaine in rainbow trout. *Journal of the Fisheries Research Board of Canada* **27**, 909–914.

Wolf, K. (1963). Physiological salines for freshwater teleosts. *Progressive Fish Culturist* **25**, 135–140.

Chapter 10

Fish Disease: Its Prevention, Diagnosis and Treatment

A. H. McVicar[1] and R. H. Richards[2]

Marine Laboratory, Aberdeen[1] and the University of Stirling,[2] UK

I. INTRODUCTION

Because of the largely unpredictable nature of disease outbreaks and their frequently serious pathogenic effects, diseases rank among the more important constraints to holding fish captive. The appearance of disease in fish can be attributed to both the action of infectious agents and to other more general environmental factors including water quality, inadequate diet and stress. Although in this chapter, emphasis will be placed on the prevention, diagnosis and treatment of infectious disease, it is also necessary to consider the role of the environment. Outbreaks of disease can seldom be attributed to a single causative factor, and it is common for sub-clinical infections of endemic disease agents to progress to overt disease in direct response to particular handling or holding conditions. As many pathological changes can be symptomatic of both infectious and non-infectious disease, an awareness of both is essential for accurate diagnosis and selection of treatment procedures.

Detailed information of disease outbreaks in aquarium systems is scanty. Some information of relevance to the research aquarist can be derived from numerous reports of experiences in commercial fish culture establishments and in hobby aquaria, but it is not intended here to review disease in these areas. Detailed reviews of fish pathology with particular reference to disease, have been made by Amlacher (1970), Reichenbach-Klinke (1974), Ribelin and Migaki (1975) and Roberts (1978), all of which contain data applicable to the research aquarium.

II. SOURCE OF DISEASE AND SUSCEPTIBILITY OF AQUARIUM FISH

It has been frequently recorded that fish held in captivity are much more prone to outbreaks of disease than are fish in their natural environment. Undoubtedly, many aquarium disease problems can be directly attributed to physical damage and traumatic shock which may be associated with (a) capture and transportation, (b) handling during and after experimentation or (c) following some deterioration in the holding conditions, for example, after mechanical failures in the aquarium system. However, infectious disease can also occur in apparently previously healthy stock fish. New infections are often introduced when fish, plants and live food are added to an aquarium while new stocks may themselves succumb to the differences in water quality and the range of infectious organisms already present. Whenever possible, appropriate steps should be taken by using quarantine and disinfection procedures (see below) to prevent the introduction of infectious agents into an aquarium system.

Obviously water is a major source of introduction and dissemination of disease, but sterility can only be achieved under very specialized conditions and although filtration and treatment of water may limit spread of some conditions, most aquarium systems have a high risk of fish being exposed either continuously or intermittently to a range of infective organisms. Most of these seldom or never cause disease in the host in the wild, but several can become highly pathogenic in the particular conditions of an aquarium. This change in pathogenicity can be attributed to an upset of the often finely balanced relationship (mutual adaptation or tolerance) between host and parasite. In practical terms, this appears as an increased susceptibility of the fish to disease, an enhanced success of reproduction and transmission of the infectious agent and the outbreak of diseases not normally associated with a particular host. Consequently, by developing an aquarium environment as similar as is practically possible to the natural environment of the fish, especially regarding water quality and feeding, many disease conditions may be avoided or the incidence and severity of any particular outbreak reduced.

III. DIAGNOSIS OF DISEASE

The diagnosis of aquarium fish disease should be based on a consideration of the history of the affected stock, careful observation of any behavioural changes and clinical signs and on post-mortem examination. Early detection and treatment of a disease is obviously desirable as establishment of the disease may cause difficulty in treatment and lead to a higher mortality rate.

A. History

A study of the previous history of the fish and the development of the disease conditions will often give some idea as to the type of disease involved. Many conditions commonly arise as a sequel to factors causing stress in the stock and it is important to identify these to achieve successful and lasting control.

Records of water quality, especially temperature, pH, dissolved oxygen, ammonia and specific gravity should be carefully considered for the period leading up to and during an outbreak (note Chapter 3). Flow-through type systems are less likely to be at fault than a recirculated or static system unless there is some mechanical fault or contamination of the supply. Stocking fish at densities too high for the type and efficiency of an aquarium system commonly leads to the outbreak of disease.

The original source of the fish and the length of time they have been in the system often provides information as to the cause of disease. While aquarium-bred fish are usually well adapted to a life in captivity, readily take artificial foods and adapt to small volumes of tank space, fish from the wild are often traumatically injured during capture, frequently damage themselves against tank sides and fittings and may not feed. As discussed above, infectious agents are also often introduced with new stocks. From the length of time over which disease signs have appeared and the number of individuals affected with a particular condition, it is possible to separate chronic disease, such as fish tuberculosis (TB), which progressively affects a stock, from acute conditions (for instance by water pollution), which occur suddenly and affect the entire stock. There is often species-specificity in terms of response to tank conditions or particular disease agents.

B. Behavioural and Clinical Signs

Once a history of the fish stock has been established, behavioural abnormalities and other signs of disease should be noted: common signs are summarized in Table I but are seldom characteristic of one disease only. They may include loss of appetite (usually the first sign of ill health), abnormal swimming movements or speed of gill ventilation, changes in colouration or clamping of fins against the body. "Flashing" or flicking of the fish against plants and rocks are signs of irritation commonly seen in association with parasitic disease. Also visible may be other gross signs of disease including ulcerations (Fig. 1), swellings, fin-rot (Fig. 2), skeletal deformities, exophthalmos (Fig. 3) and emaciation or abdominal dropsy (Fig. 4). Such a history and gross examination will often enable one to determine whether some husbandry factor, usually including water quality, or some infectious disease is occurring, though it must again be stressed that the latter often follows the former. Detailed post-mortem examination including histology will then be necessary to confirm original suppositions.

C. Post-mortem Examination

Fish may be killed with a variety of anaesthetic agents, detailed in Chapter 9, but it is often preferable to kill by decapitation when carrying out parasitological examinations to avoid possible anaesthetic effects on the parasites themselves. It is imperative that live fish are examined, preferably a sample of apparently healthy as well as moribund fish. Fish tissues and many parasites degenerate very rapidly after death, many parasites will leave a dead host and free-living saprophytic organisms often accumulate so that examination of any but recently dead carcases is seldom fruitful. Damage to the fish skin should be avoided at this stage

Table I. Signs of disease in fish. Note that the signs are seldom specific to any single disease.

Sign	Disease
Inappetance/abnormal swimming or colouration	All
"Flashing", flicking the fins or body against a surface	Parasitic agents, especially protozoa. Chemical irritants, e.g. copper
Greyish skin blotches (excessive mucus production)	Protozoan infections. Chemical irritants
Skin haemorrhages	Larger ectoparasites. Bacterial infection. Cannibalism/self-inflicted trauma
Skin ulcerations	Ectoparasites/cannibalism/bacterial disease/TB
Cotton wool-like skin growths	*Saprolegnia* fungal infections. Certain bacterial infections, especially *Flexibacter* spp
Small white spots up to 2 mm in diameter, raised above skin surface	*Ichthyophthirius* in freshwater; *Cryptocaryon* in marine systems
Larger swellings/lumps on skin surface	Tumours/parasitic cysts. Bacterial lesions. TB
Fin erosion	Poor water quality. Fin-nipping. Physical irritation. Bacterial infections
Exophthalmos	Any conditions affecting heart/liver/kidney. Eye fluke infections. Supersaturation of water with dissolved gases
Internal haemorrhages	Bacterial infections. *Ichthyophonus*/TB/parasites visible on further examination
Internal lumps and swellings	*Ichthyophonus*/TB/parasite cysts
Ascites	Liver/kidney/heart disease. Bacterial septicaemia

Table I. (continued)

Sign	Disease
Emaciation	TB/some nematodes/*Octomitus*
Skeletal deformities	TB/nutritional defects/congenital problems
Bubbles in vessels in fins and eye	Gas bubble disease from supersaturation with dissolved gases or from pressure damage during capture
Opacity of lens	*Diplostomum*/nutritional deficiency

and a careful examination of the external surface of the fish should be made for any gross abnormalities and the presence of larger parasites. Lesions are usually more easily detected if this examination is carried out with the fish in water when careful observation with a low-power stereo microscope will often reveal parasites on the skin and gills.

Although some parasites such as leeches, monogeneans and copepods

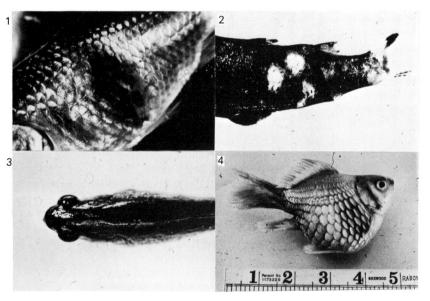

Fig. 1.   Ulceration of goldfish skin.
Fig. 2.   Fin rot in salmon.
Fig. 3.   Exophthalmos in rainbow trout.
Fig. 4.   Ascites in goldfish.

are visible to the naked eye, smears of mucus and superficial cells must be made from skin and gills to detect and identify many parasites, especially the protozoa. A temporary slide preparation should be made and examined microscopically up to a magnification of $\times 250$. Several smears from each fish and several fish should be examined. In addition, gill squashes should be prepared by cutting out a gill arch, dissecting soft tissues off the bone and cartilage and teasing out on a slide. These often reveal larger parasites as well as evidence of telangiectasis (a breakdown of blood vessel walls to produce cystic dilations containing blood and restricting gill blood flow) or epithelial hyperplasia. After noting the results of the examination of external surfaces, the fish is dissected open and the internal organs examined for any gross signs of disease such as any cysts or swellings or the presence of parasites, before being carefully cut open and examined microscopically. Squashes of pieces of internal organs, prepared between slides and coverslips should again be examined for parasites. The intestine should be opened and scrapes of the mucosal surface again examined for parasites.

Bacteriological examination of internal organs may be carried out by taking samples aseptically and streaking them on to a variety of media. These techniques, and those involving virological examination should be carried out by specialist laboratories. Live specimens are usually required but freshly dead fish sent on ice or even deep-frozen may be suitable for certain isolations.

A particularly suitable technique for the diagnosis of fish diseases is that of histopathology, but this must once again be carried out by specialists. Sample fish should preferably be delivered live but if this proves impossible, live specimens should be killed, the organs carefully dissected out, and small pieces of each organ (no larger than 0.5 cm^3) should be placed into 10% neutral buffered formalin, with a ratio of at least 10 volumes of fixative to one of tissue and sent on to the laboratory concerned together with a detailed history of the case. The formulation of the fixative is given below:

Neutral Buffered Formalin:

Formalin (40% formaldehyde)	100 ml
Tap water	900 ml
Na H$_2$ PO$_4$ H$_2$O	4 g
Na$_2$ HPO$_4$	6.5 g

Taxonomic keys for the identification of parasites include those of Kudo (1966) and Kreier (1978) for protozoa, Yamaguti (1958–1963) for helminths, acanthocephala and nematodes, Mann (1962) for leeches and Kabata (1970, 1979) for parasitic copepods. The general parasitology of fish is dealt with by Bykhovskaya—Pavlovskaya *et al.* (1964), Hoffman (1967) and Hoffman and Meyer (1974) and the systems of Glorioso *et al.* (1974) and Shotts and Bullock (1975) may be used to aid in the diagnosis of bacterial pathogens.

Following the procedures outlined above, many of the disease agents may be identified and then adequate control and future preventative measures instigated. The cardinal rule in any other than the most simply diagnosed diseases should be to "consult an expert".

IV. DISEASE OF FISH IN THE RESEARCH AQUARIUM

A. Non-infectious Disease

Most disease conditions and losses in aquarium systems are associated with faults in husbandry or management of the fish and usually involve either water quality, nutrition or tank design.

(1) Disease due to tank design and physical damage
Design problems are usually obvious to those with experience in such matters and are frequently associated with physical trauma in the fish. The tank surface may be abrasive and sharp angles may be present within the tank; netting may cause trauma though knotless netting is probably the least damaging. Any handling of the fish will cause loss of skin surface and possible secondary infection or osmotic loss. This becomes a particular problem when fish are used in long-term experiments involving, say, repeated use of intraperitoneal injection. In such cases, judicious use of anaesthetics may be particularly helpful (see Chapter 9). Stocking density is another important factor to consider, not only because of obvious problems with the maintenance of water quality, but also because crowding of fish often leads to cannibalism and resultant fin-rot (Fig. 2) or secondary infectious diseases. Similarly, if irritant parasitic infections or certain faults in water-quality are not rapidly corrected, then self-traumatization often results from efforts to remove the irritant.

(2) Disease from poor water quality
Perhaps the most common problems occurring in aquarium systems are those of poor water quality and there are many records of associated disease conditions, especially involving the gills. Many water quality parameters can be regularly monitored and controlled by system design, variation in flow rate or efficient filtration. If infectious disease is found, primary problems with water quality should always be considered.

(a) Incoming water. The need to ensure the high quality of water entering an aquarium system is discussed in Chapter 3. Gill disease is often a result of irritation by a variety of chemicals in the water supply. Copper is highly toxic and any system utilizing even a small quantity of copper piping is likely to produce excessive levels of copper in the water (Chapter 6). Other heavy metals such as lead or zinc may also be toxic to fish but usually at much higher levels and over more prolonged periods than copper. pH and hardness of the water supply affect the toxicity of many heavy metals, and changes in pH, especially if they occur rapidly, may themselves be fatal. Marine fish in particular require constant pH conditions of between 7.8 and 8.3. Gills may also be severely affected by free chlorine which is included as a sterilizing agent in many household water supplies, but this may be removed either by charcoal filtration, rigorous aeration or the use of sodium thiosulphate at 1 g/10 l water.

Elevated carbon dioxide levels, though seldom fatal unless very high and accompanied by low dissolved oxygen levels, after prolonged exposure, may lead to the condition of nephrocalcinosis. This syndrome is usually seen as a grossly swollen kidney containing numerous gritty calcium deposits, often visible as worm-like structures in the ureters. Supersaturation of the water supply with gases, particularly nitrogen, is commonly encountered in pumped systems and leads to "gas-bubble" disease. The dissolved gas concentrations within the fish are partially a reflection of those in the outside aqueous environment and sudden pressure changes may lead to gases coming out of solution into the gas phase. In this way, bubbles of gas are formed in the blood stream and are grossly visible in the vessels in the fins or in the eyes. The fish may be killed outright or suffer a variety of deformative or other pathological organ changes. Leaking pumps and rapid temperature changes are often responsible for the development of the condition (Chapter 3).

(b) Fish metabolism and recirculation. Overstocking will lead to a decrease in the level of dissolved oxygen and a rise in the level of waste products in the water. Such wastes generally include ammonia or nitrites, increased CO_2 levels and an increase in solid suspended material, all of which regularly lead to the development of gill disease. In early stages, mucus production is increased and this eventually develops into hypertrophy or hyperplasia of gill epithelia (Fig. 5) so that a considerably greater distance has to be covered from gill blood vessel to outside water by respiratory gases during gaseous exchange. This considerably stresses the fish, leading to retardation of growth, abnormal behaviour and often the development of a variety of disease conditions. The condition known as

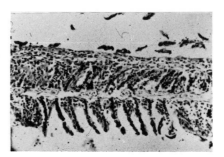

Fig. 5. Hyperplasia of rainbow trout gill.

telangiectasis may also result from such adverse water conditions. The particular problems associated with water treatment are discussed in Chapters 3 and 4.

(c) Treatment of fish and equipment. A rather bizarre way in which fish are damaged or killed is by over-treatment with a variety of chemicals such as formalin or copper sulphate. Chemotherapy commonly depends on a substance being more toxic to the disease organism than to the host but the threshold levels are often only marginally different. In high concentrations, they cause sloughing of respiratory lamellae and at lower doses, particularly with prolonged use, they will lead to the chronic changes in gills described above. Detergents or disinfectant compounds used in sterilizing tanks and equipment are also often toxic and contamination of the water supply should be avoided. If ultraviolet sterilization of water is employed, direct illumination of fish with ultraviolet light must be avoided as blindness frequently results.

(3) Dietary disease

Dietary problems as a whole are often difficult to diagnose without specialist assistance. It is generally difficult to wean wild fish on to dry diets and even if this is achieved, there may be a particular deficiency syndrome which then leads to the development of other disease conditions, or it may in itself be fatal. Dietary disease still occurs in salmonids, on which considerable research has been carried out, and it is thus hardly surprising that dietary imbalance is commonly encountered in some of the more exotic species used in experimental aquaria. Gross imbalance in protein : carbohydrate : fat ratios may occur, but even more common are vitamin deficiencies. The water-soluble vitamins in particular are rapidly lost from the body, and if not replaced, their loss will result in a variety of disease conditions. Vitamin E deficiency leads to muscle and liver lesions and the condition of pansteatitis, especially if associated with high dietary levels of unsaturated fat. Such high fat levels also often lead to lipoid liver degeneration, a particularly common problem in aquarium fish. Overfeeding readily contaminates the water supply and will lead to a deterioration in water quality.

Heavy metals have also been implicated in nutritional disease when their over-use in feed binders has led to the so-called "hepatorenal syndrome" in which liver and kidney lesions develop. Histopathology is, however, necessary to diagnose this disease. High levels of magnesium in the diet have also led to nephrocalcinosis. Hepatoma has been caused in a number of fish species by fungal toxins contained in contaminated food and food source and freshness should always be carefully checked. However, not all tumours are dietary in origin. Many appear to be virus-induced and others have no known cause. Many non-infectious tumours usually affect only single fish and destruction of affected fish is often the only remedy though surgery may sometimes be performed on particularly valuable specimens. Foodstuffs may transmit disease, especially parasitic disease if live feeds are used. Dried foods or freeze-dried foods partially remove this problem but are seldom themselves "complete" diets. The diet selected will depend on the fish species and the availability of different foods.

B. Infectious Disease

Disease in aquarium fish may result from infection by any one of a wide range of organisms (viruses, bacteria, fungi, protozoa, metazoa). The type of organism involved and the severity of the resulting condition may vary according to the species of fish held, their origin, the source of water supply and the location and design of the aquarium. It is therefore not realistic to attempt to produce a comprehensive list of disease-causing agents for aquarium fish in general, but by reference to some of the more troublesome infectious agents, it is possible to draw attention to the characteristics of the more common and severe diseases. Frequently, overt disease results from simultaneous infection by more than one type of organism, often with an associated husbandry fault.

(1) Skin, fins and gills
The external surfaces of fish are vulnerable to physical and chemical damage. Most disease conditions of the skin, fins and gills occur indirectly, particularly as a result of bacterial or fungal invasion of small skin lesions or abrasions of fin margins. Certain infectious agents, themselves not fatal, can cause lesions which then allow secondary infection with other more pathogenic organisms.

Saprolegnia and other fungal agents are common infective agents of fish wounds in fresh and brackish water appearing as grey or white cotton wool-like patches on the skin (Fig. 6). Concurrent bacterial infections of

Fig. 6. Saprolegnia infection in brown trout.

such lesions are also common, particularly involving the genera *Pseudomonas* and *Aeromonas* in freshwater and *Vibrio* in sea water. In addition to extensive inflammatory change and necrosis at the initial infection site, a generalized septicaemia may result. Such infections, and the clinically similar *Cytophaga* (agent of "cold water disease") and *Flexibacter* (agent of "columnaris disease") are typically associated with poor holding conditions such as high stocking densities, organic pollution and abnormal temperatures. Vibriosis is probably the single most significant bacterial disease of marine aquarium fishes (and some freshwater fish fed diets containing marine fish) occurring in a very wide range of species. Affected fish may suddenly die showing few signs, but dermal haemorrhaging is common, especially in the lateral and ventral areas of the body, at fin margins and around the anus. Characteristic deep skin ulcers with dark red margins develop in severely diseased fish and internally, the spleen is typically enlarged and small haemorrhages occur throughout the viscera. The bacteria are found commonly in the gut of healthy fish and the disease condition normally only develops in adverse environments (particularly at high temperatures, the critical level varying with different species of fish).

Small skin lesions are also believed to be the main site of entry of the virus *Lymphocystis* which causes wart or pearl-like growths mainly on the fins and skin. This disease can cause significant mortalities in many marine and some freshwater aquaria. At present, no treatment is effective with the possible exception of minor surgery. Fortunately, many affected fish recover spontaneously and the problem largely becomes one of isolating the infection to restrict its spread.

A range of protozoan parasites is known to cause skin and gill disease in captive fish and many illustrate how normally harmless organisms in the wild can become serious pathogens in the aquarium. Free-living ciliates and algae often abound in nutrient-rich substrates such as aquarium water, and cases have been reported both in marine and freshwater where various species have invaded fish tissues to produce disease. Stalked ciliates such as *Apiosoma, Scyphidia* and *Epistylis* usually have an ectocommensal form of relationship with fish using the skin only as an attachment surface, but in tank fish, they can become pathogenic probably initially by causing skin irritation. Similarly, the trichodinid ciliates (*Trichodina, Tripartiella, Trichodinella*, Fig. 7) are normally browsers on detritus and occur in small numbers on the skin and gills of wild fish, but they can multiply rapidly and become a major problem in both marine and freshwater aquaria. Signs of infection include respiratory distress, skin irritation and the appearance of grey mucus-covered patches on the skin surface (Fig. 8) which rapidly degenerate to form large open lesions.

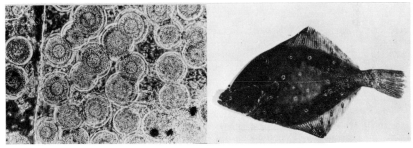

Fig. 7. (Left)   *Trichodina* infection of plaice skin.
Fig. 8. (Right)   Plaice showing thickening and greying of dorsal skin surface in response to *Trichodina* infection.

Increased mucus production, whitening and thickening of the epidermis or erosion of the epithelial surface, opening the site to secondary infection, are characteristics of several serious skin and gill protozoan infections. Many species of marine fish, especially in tropical aquaria, are susceptible to "velvet disease" (also termed "rust disease" and "coral fish disease") caused by the flagellate *Amyloodinium*, while freshwater fish in tropical aquaria are prone to infection with a related organism, *Oodinium*. The gills are principally affected, with hyperplasia of the respiratory epithelia and occasional haemorrhaging. A similar host reaction occurs in response to *Ichtyobodo* (= *Costia*) (Fig. 9) feeding on epithelial cells and heavy mortalities have often been attributed to this common disease in a wide range of freshwater fish species. Young and debilitated fish are particularly affected. *Chilodonella* in freshwater and the similar marine genus *Brooklynella* are ciliates which also feed directly on epithelial cells and cause severe lesions in aquarium fish. Probably the most significant of all protozoan parasites of aquarium fish are the ciliates *Ichthyophthirius* in freshwater and its marine counterpart *Cryptocaryon*. The term "white spot" refers to the feeding stages of the parasites (up to 1 mm in size) embedded in the epidermis. Serious irritation of the skin and gills occurs and when the parasite matures, it escapes to the exterior by rupturing the epithelium, resulting in either osmotic loss through skin lesions or in skin thickening. High temperatures, crowding and other adverse tank conditions encourage this disease, epizootics of which have been commonly reported from aquaria throughout the world, especially following a recent fish introduction.

Although many species of sporozoa have been recorded from the skin and gills of fish, few have yet proven to be of significance to aquarium fish. The microsporidan *Glugea anomala*, infecting the stickleback and *Nosema hertwigi*, infecting *Osmerus* and other species in both fresh and sea water invade the subcutaneous connective tissue (and other organs) producing large cysts up to several millimetres in size. Epidemics are also seen in wild fish. Such parasites, when introduced into aquarium populations may result in many deaths.

Metazoan ectoparasites causing disease in aquarium fish are fewer in number but associated mortalities may be equally severe. Monogenean flukes have direct life cycles and several species, through the clasping action of their attachment organs on the epithelial surfaces and their habit of feeding on tissue and blood, cause irritation and abrasion leading to the formation of open lesions. The gyrodactylid and dactylogyrid groups are common on the gills and skin of a wide range of marine and fresh water fish, but each parasite species tends to be specific to one host species. Gyrodactylids are viviparous and are capable of rapid multiplication, particularly when tank conditions are poor.

Increased pathogenicity of both *Gyrodactylus unicopula* (Fig. 10) and *Trichodina* sp. was noted when both species were present together on plaice. Monogenetic disease problems of captive fish have been identified with *Benedenia* and mullet, *Heteraxine* and yellowtail, *Discocotyle* and rainbow trout, *Entobdella* and sole and numerous others. Most infections can be seen with the naked eye or low-power magnification, and affected fish often show respiratory distress and "flashing". Larval digenean flukes may invade the eyes of fish causing blindness (e.g. *Diplostomum* "eyefluke" in rainbow trout) or the skin (e.g. *Cryptocotyle* "black spot" of marine fish) causing local nodule formation or death in young fish when infection is heavy. These problems are normally relatively easy to avoid in aquaria

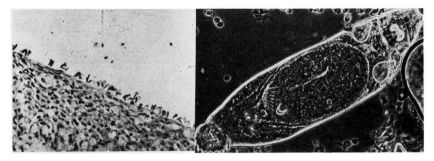

Fig. 9. (Left)   *Ichtyoboda* (*Costia*) infection of rainbow trout gill.
Fig. 10. (Right)   *Gyrodactylus* sp. from plaice showing enclosed fully developed embryo.

through interrupting the life cycle by removal of the specific mollusc intermediate host from the water supply.

Although ectoparasitic crustaceans e.g. *Argulus, Lernaea, Ergasilus, Lepeophtheirus* (Fig. 11) and leeches (*Piscicola, Hemibdella*) have been associated with mortalities in both marine and freshwater-cultured fish, the parasites are large enough to be seen without magnification on the skin and gills and are relatively easily controlled in tanks, so that they should not present too serious a problem in a well managed aquarium. Leeches have been implicated as the vector of several pathogenic blood protozoa.

(2) Internal organs
Several highly pathogenic diseases, produced by both viruses (e.g. Infectious Pancreatic Necrosis, Viral Haemorrhagic Septicemia) and bacteria (e.g. Enteric Redmouth Bacterium, Bacterial Kidney Disease) are known to affect the internal organs of farmed fish. The clinical signs and gross pathology of the more important are described in the treatise on fish pathology edited by Roberts (1978), but as specific diagnosis is difficult without specialist techniques and as legislation is in existence throughout the world designed to restrict the distribution of some diseases, it is recommended that a recognized fish disease laboratory be consulted if these are suspected in an aquarium. Care should be taken to obtain either non-diseased stocks from fish culturists, or wild fish from areas where such diseases are absent.

In general, infectious diseases of the internal organs are probably of lesser significance than external diseases of aquarium fish, but they do present their unique problems. They are often not easy to diagnose, so that the disease is often well established before any problem is apparent. Therapy is difficult as it is common for sick fish to stop feeding (most

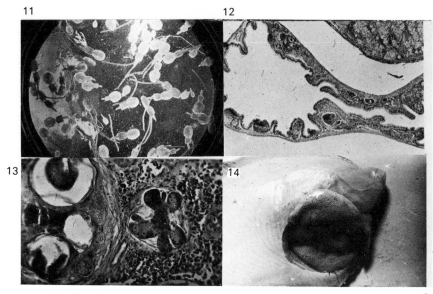

Fig. 11.   Salmon louse *Lepeophtheirus*. (By courtesy of Dr R. Wootten.)
Fig. 12.   Section of *Mycobacterium* infected intestine (TB).
Fig. 13.   Section of *Ichthyophonus* infected liver.
Fig. 14.   Plaice infected with *Glugea*.

recognized treatments are oral), and it can be a problem achieving suitable tissue levels of chemotherapeutants without causing toxicity problems in the fish. As was discussed above, a generalized infection with characteristic internal signs often arises from infection of external lesions with a variety of bacteria. Tuberculosis, caused by the bacterium *Mycobacterium marinum* has been reported to be one of the most common diseases of aquarium fish. The disease is contagious, frequently leading to mass mortalities in a very wide range of fish species. Affected fish show general debilitation, internal haemorrhages, necrosis of internal organs and the formation of tubercles throughout the body (Fig. 12). Some of the gross signs of the disease due to the systemic fungus *Ichthyophonus* are similar (Fig. 13) and it is possible that the two have been confused in the past. *Ichthyophonus* is primarily a disease of sea fish throughout the world with localized high levels of infection reported to cause occasionally high mortalities in some wild populations. Freshwater fish may be affected through feeding on diseased marine fish and several serious epidemics in rainbow trout cultivation have occurred in this way. Infection has been recorded in most families of fish kept in freshwater and marine aquaria. Infection is oral and the fungus rapidly spreads throughout all soft tissues of the body with groups of spores and the host inflammatory reaction appearing macroscopically as white spots and streaks. Accurate diagnosis is made by allowing germination of the spores to occur after death of the host. There is no known cure.

Cysts and nodules in the musculature and internal organs could also indicate infection by microsporidan or myxosporidan protozoa, but few have been found to cause problems in aquaria. Diagnosis is made by the microscopic appearance of spores enclosed in the cysts. In cyprinids and other freshwater fish outbreaks due to the genera *Myxobolus* and *Henneguya* have been reported and problems with *Ceratomyxa* have been experienced with salmonids. Probably the best known fish sporozoan is *Myxosoma cerebralis* which causes "whirling disease" in salmonids by eroding skeletal cartilage, but this disease is a problem of earth pond culture rather than aquaria. Members of the microsporidan genus *Pleistophora* are common parasites of the muscle in marine and freshwater fish, *P. hyphessobryconis* being a serious pathogen of characids and cyprinids causing "neon tetra disease", in aquaria. Blood protozoa (*Trypanosoma*, *Cryptobia*) have been reported from various fish, and blood flukes (*Sanguinicola*) may produce thrombosis and necrosis from destruction of the blood supply of carp and trout gills, but the spread of both groups may be readily controlled in the aquarium as they require vector or intermediate hosts which are easily eliminated.

The gut of fish often has an extensive range of micro-organisms and parasites, but few with the exception of the bacteria mentioned previously, have been found to cause problems in aquaria. Although not considered by many to be a pathogen, the flagellate *Hexamita* (= *Octomitus*) shows massive increases in numbers in debilitated fish and may contribute to host death. Various coccidia occur in the intestinal walls of fish, but only one group, *Eimeria* spp, have been reported to cause problems in captive fish. Heavy mortalities of young carp have been associated with this disease which appears clinically as submucosal nodular formation with associated enteritis. In plaice infected with the microsporidan protozoan *Glugea stephani*, the intestinal submucosa is progressively invaded (Fig. 14) with resulting mortalities in aquarium and cultivation tank environments. The disease can usually be prevented by lowering water temperatures to 12°C. Helminth parasites are common in the gut lumen and viscera of fish, but disease conditions have seldom been attributed to them in research aquaria. All have complex life cycles and in an aquarium environment, have little chance of completing this. However, care should be taken regarding possible infection in live food as, for example, *Daphnia*, *Tubifex* and marine copepods may harbour intermediate stages of parasites.

Serious disease conditions in aquarium fish can thus result from infection by a wide range of organisms. When a disease breaks out, three things must be determined as rapidly as possible: (a) the cause of the disease, so that a suitable treatment can be initiated immediately, (b) the source of the disease, so that infection and reinfection can be prevented, and (c) aquarium conditions or associated handling procedures which have made the fish susceptible to disease, such as crowding, poor tank conditions, poor water quality and damage to external surfaces. With regard to the source of disease, newly introduced stocks must always be prime suspects, whether of the same or different species (emphasizing the need for quarantine). Disease is often present sub-clinically in the natural environment but can develop into overt disease in the aquarium. The water supply must similarly be considered as a potential source of infective organisms.

V. CONTROL

The control of fish disease in aquarium systems depends on the prevention of fish disease in wild and experimental fish stocks, good husbandry of experimental fish stocks and rapid diagnosis and treatment of any problems as they arise.

A. Prevention

Detailed control measures to avoid the introduction of diseases into any country are outside the scope of this book, but the prevention of contaminated fish imports and the introduction of quarantine procedures are measures utilized by many countries. Similar measures may be undertaken in an experimental aquarium system. Fish should, wherever possible, be obtained from apparently disease-free stocks and new introductions should be quarantined for a period of at least a month during which careful observation and sampling should be carried out. The design of experimental facilities is also often controlled by legislation (for example the Cruelty to Animals Act in Britain) and experimentation and aquarium functioning are designed to avoid the pain and stress that often leads to a variety of secondary infections.

As mentioned earlier, maintenance of good water quality is of paramount importance and in order to prevent the introduction of pathogens via the water supply, systems involving ozonization or ultraviolet irradiation of water are recommended. Chlorine in water supplies may have some beneficial effects but the concentration should be monitored to ensure that toxic levels are not reached. Disinfection of aquaria and equipment may be routinely carried out with a variety of iodine-based disinfectants. Again, the fish must not be allowed to come into contact with these materials, and any application should be followed by thorough washing. Problems of waste disposal are obviously much greater with a large volume of water in a flow-through system. Disposal of carcasses by incineration is preferred, though a variety of other methods are available.

B. Treatment

Should preventive measures fail, a variety of treatments are available, depending very much on the aquarium system in use and the disease being treated. Medicaments may be given orally either by stomach-tube in anaesthetized fish so as to administer an exact dosage, or by mixing with food. Antibiotics are commonly used in this way but the latter method is difficult to apply as sick fish do not feed or may vary their food intake and therefore the dosage received. The other common method of treatment is external treatment via the water supply. This may involve a bath in the medicament for varying lengths of time dependent on the system and the disease. Similarly, especially if active fish species are densely stocked in a flow-through system, a "flush" treatment of chemical may be applied. The latter treatment usually involves use of a higher concentration of treatment compound and still more concentrated solutions are used for dip treatment (i.e. very short duration of exposure in a net to the treatment compound).

Probably the most satisfactory treatment in a flow-through system is a "flowing" treatment where a known quantity of compound is passed continually through the system (by drip-feeding) over the required length of time. Dose-rate in this method is much more easily controlled than by the "flush" system. Individual fish treatment may also be undertaken by intraperitoneal or intramuscular injection or even by painting the medicament on to the skin with a soft brush. Any method involving handling of the fish causes more stress and the likelihood of traumatic skin damage. As well as problems associated with handling fish, many compounds used have direct toxic or irritant effects on skin and gills, especially with repeated treatment or overdosage. Single treatments are often sufficient for fish ectoparasites but repeated treatments are often necessary for parasites with a cyst stage or a stage embedded in host tissues. A major problem with the treatment of internal ailments is actually ensuring that the treatment compounds reach the site of action. They may be prevented from doing so by, for instance, the presence of necrotic tissue, excessive fibrous tissue or a blood-brain barrier to the drug.

Whatever the treatment, a small group of the animals should be treated first and then observed, if possible, over a 24-h period. Adverse reactions should be obvious by this time and these may occur as many medicaments have really only been well tested on the rainbow trout. Any treatment usually involves some form of arithmetical calculation and such figures should always be checked. Death or ineffective treatment may result from errors in calculating the concentration of the drug. Adequate dissolved oxygen levels are also particularly important and aeration during treatment is often indicated. Oxygen levels should be monitored during treatment, if possible. Many chemicals are rapidly inactivated by organic debris and tanks should be cleaned prior to usage. If biological filtration is in use, water should be run to waste during treatment to avoid effects on the filter. If at all feasible, starvation of fish prior to treatment may help by reducing oxygen demand and waste production. Similarly, decreasing stocking densities and increasing water flows often helps to improve the general condition of fish during and after treatment.

Table II. Treatment of fish diseases.

(1) External protozoa	Formalin ⎫ often as a Malachite Green ⎭ mixture Quinine hydrochloride Salinity change Acriflavine Copper Sulphate Chloramine T
(2) Monogenean Flukes	Organophosphates Formalin
(3) Crustacea	Organophosphates ? Formalin

(4) Bacteria
  (External infections)
  (Systemic infections)
	"Fin-rot"—QAC
	Nifurpirinol
	Range of antibiotics

(5) Fungal Infections	Salinity change Malachite Green Phenoxethol
(6) Nematodes	Piperazine
(7) Cestodes	Various vermifuges—Note CAB Annotated Bibliography No. 26, Anthelmintic Control of Parasites of Fish

Treatment of organisms by taxa is given in Table II. Relatively few compounds are available at the present time and the need for a product licence to be issued for new medicaments in many countries limits expansion of the range of compounds. Perhaps the simplest treatment of all is a variation in salinity from fresh to salt water or vice versa. This method relies on the fact that many parasitic agents have a much narrower salinity range than their fish hosts but efficacy does vary depending on the particular parasite or host fish. Parasites with a complex life cycle are often excluded by removing a stage in the parasite life cycle (e.g. killing off snails to prevent *Diplostomum* infection). Formalin (40% formaldehyde) is widely used to treat external protozoa and monogenetic flukes and may have some affect on certain crustacea. It works well at dose rates of 167–250 mg/l for an hour, the smaller dose being applied in soft acid water where formalin shows an increased toxicity. Half-hour treatment at 500 mg/l is more likely to be effective against crustacean parasites. Oxygenation is often required during treatment and filtration of the formaldehyde prior to use may be required to remove any white deposits of toxic paraformaldehyde.

Malachite green (analytical grade) is a dyestuff commonly used to treat fungal infections and ectoparasitic protozoa and monogeneans. A 1% solution of the chemical may be painted directly on to fungal infections in larger fish. It may also be used as a 1-minute dip at 67 mg/l or as a bath, flush or flowing treatment at 1–2 mg/l for an hour. Prolonged bath treatment may also be successful with a dose of 0.1–0.15 mg/l. Forms of the compound containing excessive quantities of zinc should be avoided. It may be used in persistent infections (e.g. with *Ichthyophthirius* infection) in combination with formalin at the normal strength for 1-hour bathing. Phenoxethol (2-phenoxyethanol) is used for external fungal infections as well as for "fin-rot". It forms a 1% saturated aqueous solution and may be used at 10 ml of this solution/l for a 1-hour bath. Methylene blue is useful in static aquarium systems as a long-term bath at a concentration of 3 mg/l and neutral acriflavine may similarly be used at 0.02 mg/l for up to 3 days. Chloramine T (May & Baker Ltd) kills a variety of ectoparasitic protozoa and monogeneans by liberating chlorine and is effective at 10 mg for 24 h while quinine hydrochloride has been used at 30 mg/l for prolonged baths to treat external protozoa. Organophosphates are particularly useful against crustacea and monogenetic parasites in a 1% dip for 2 min or as a prolonged bath at 0.1 mg/l. A variety may be available e.g. Neguvon and Dipterex (Bayer Agrochemicals) or Bromex but they are toxic to man by absorption through the skin and are also highly toxic to fish and should be used with extreme care.

Bacterial infections often rapidly develop and may take the form of surface infections, e.g. "fin-rot" or systemic disease. Treatment of the former with quaternary ammonia compounds such as Roccal (Bayer) and Hyamine 3500 (Lennig Chemicals) is usually effective at dose-rates of 1–4 mg/l for an hour. These compounds do have a relatively narrow safety margin and should be used with caution. Nifurpirinol is used in many countries for the same purpose at a dose-rate of 1 mg/l. General husbandry and water-quality parameters should also be checked if "fin-rot" becomes a problem. Copper sulphate may also be used as a "fin-rot" treatment at approximately 500 mg/l for a 1-minute dip, but this compound is particularly toxic to gills, especially in soft water. It is also occasionally used in longer-term baths at a concentration of approximately 0.0001 mg/l. These dose rates will vary with the hardness of the water being treated.

Most systemic bacterial diseases (with the exception of corynebacterial kidney disease of salmonids) are caused by Gram-negative bacteria and respond to oral broad-spectrum antibiotic therapy. Dose rates suggested for trout are: Sulphadiazine at 22 g/100 kg fish/day, the first day followed by 5–10 days at half-dosage; nitrofuran compounds at 11 g/100 kg fish/day for 5–10 days; oxytetracycline at 7.5 g/100 kg fish/day for 5–10 days and trimethoprim/sulphonamide mixtures of 1:5 ratio at 5.5 g/100 kg fish/day for 5–10 days.

In bath form, nitrofurans have been used at 20 mg/l and oxytetracycline at 13 mg/l. This may be especially useful for treatment of small fish or larvae suffering from bacterial disease. Antibiotics are only available on veterinary prescription in Britain and many other countries except for research purposes and the full course of treatment should always be applied to try to reduce the development of resistant strains of bacteria. Many new compounds are continually being tested for use in fish medicine but their use is as yet experimental and reliance must be placed on the few available compounds mentioned here. Specialist advice should be sought if preliminary treatment proves ineffective.

VI. REFERENCES

Amlacher, E. (1970). "Textbook of Fish Diseases" (translated by D. A. Conroy and R. L. Herman), TFH Publications, New Jersey.

Bykhovskaya-Pavlovskaya, I. E., Gusev, A. V., Dubinina, M. N., Izyumova, N. A., Smirnova, T. S., Sokolovskaya, I. L., Shtein, G. A., Shulman, S. S. and Epshtein, V. M. (1964). "Key to parasites of freshwater fish of the USSR", IPST, Jerusalem.

Glorioso, J. C., Amborski, R. L., Larkin, J. M., Amborski, G. F. and Culley, D. C. (1974). Laboratory identification of bacterial pathogens of aquatic animals. *American Journal of Veterinary Research* **35**, 447–450.

Hoffman, G. L. (1967). "Parasites of North American Freshwater Fishes", University of California Press, Berkeley and Los Angeles.

Hoffman, G. L. and Meyer, F. P. (1974). "Parasites of Freshwater Fishes". A review of their control and treatment. TFH Publications, New Jersey.

Kabata, Z. (1970). "Diseases of Fishes", Book 1: Crustacea as Enemies of Fish. TFH Publications, New Jersey.

Kabata, Z. (1979). "Parasitic Copepoda of British Fishes", Ray Society, London.

Kreier, J. P. (ed.) (1978). "Parasitic Protozoa", Vols 1–4. Academic Press, New York and London.

Kudo, R. R. (1966). "Protozoology", Thomas, Springfield Illinois.

Mann, K. H. (1962). "Leeches (Hirudinea): Their Structure, Physiology, Ecology and Embryology", Pergamon Press, New York.

Reichenbach-Klinke, H.-H. (1974). "Fish Pathology. A guide to the recognition and treatment of diseases and injuries of fishes, with emphasis on environmental and pollution problems", TFH Publications, New Jersey.

Ribelin, W. E. and Migaki, G. (eds) (1975) "The pathology of Fishes". The University of Wisconsin Press, Madison, Wisconsin.

Roberts, R. J. (ed) (1978). "Fish Pathology". Bailliere Tindall, London.

Shotts, E. B. and Bullock, G. L. (1975). Bacterial diseases of fishes. Diagnostic procedures for gram-negative pathogens. *Journal of the Fisheries Research Board of Canada* **32**, 1243–1247.

Yamaguti, S. (1958–1963) "Systema Helminthum". Vol. I–V., Interscience Publishers Inc., New York and London.

Chapter 11

The Rearing of Larval Fish

J. H. S. Blaxter

Dunstaffnage Laboratory, Oban, Argyll, Scotland

I. INTRODUCTION

The young stages of marine fish are, with the exception of the sharks and rays, usually very small. The floating eggs are of the order of 1 mm in diameter, the females being very fecund. The larvae (fry) of many species (Figs 1 and 2) are often only 3–5 mm in length at hatching. At first, they live on a yolk supply for a period of hours or days depending on the species and the temperature of the surrounding water. During this yolk–sac stage, the larvae develop organs such as the eyes and jaws which are vital for the subsequent phase when the larvae switch from yolk to external food sources. It has often been thought that the larvae enter a critical stage (see May, 1974, for a discussion) at first feeding, that there are often very high mortalities as the larvae first seek food and that the success of a brood (and in the case of commercial fish, subsequent recruitment to the fishery) may thus be determined in the space of a few days.

After first-feeding, most species undergo a further phase of development sometimes called a "post-larval" stage. Since this phase ends in metamorphosis, it seems more appropriate to refer to "yolk–sac larva(e)" prior to first feeding and "larva(e)" as a general term for all stages from

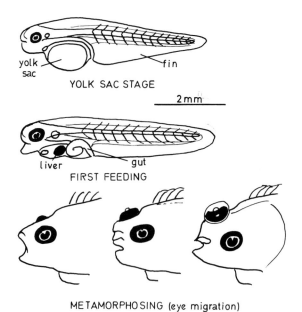

Fig. 1.   Stages in development of plaice larvae; the three lower drawings are of stage 4 plaice.

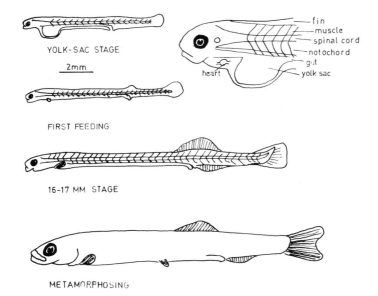

Fig. 2. Stages in development of herring larvae.

hatching to metamorphosis. During the later larval stages, there is an elaboration of the body structures, especially the development of gills, as the larvae change from cutaneous to branchial respiration. The alimentary canal becomes more complex from the simple larval tube to the later elaborations of stomach, pyloric caecae and gut, the skeleton ossifies and the primordial fin fold of the larva differentiates to the median and especially the caudal fin. Other internal organs like kidney, liver and swimbladder may also develop. Together with these processes of differentiation, the larva grows, becomes more active and less vulnerable to predation.

Metamorphosis takes place some days to months after hatching depending on the species. At metamorphosis (see Figs 1 and 2), the larva gains its adult shape, pigment and scales develop in the skin and the distinctive larval transparency is lost. Larval flatfish undergo the characteristic eye migration to come to lie on one or other side. Schooling species collect together and generally the stages near and after metamorphosis live inshore in nursery areas.

Exceptions to this general pattern are found in the sharks and rays which often produce few large yolky eggs attached to the substratum. The young are large at hatching but nevertheless swim for a considerable time with a large yolk sac and undergo a rather less distinctive metamorphosis after some months. Other species are ovoviviparous, giving birth to live young. Among the bony fish, there is a wide variability in the life history. A few of the more offshore fish like herring and capelin lay their eggs on the seabed. Many shore fish attach their eggs to the substratum and also build nests, guard their eggs and even brood the eggs and young in the mouth. A very good general account of the development of the young of British marine fish species is given by Russell (1976).

From the early days of marine science, interest in rearing marine fish has arisen from three needs:

(1) Identification of the young stages of well-known adult fish provides information on life histories and helps to solve various fisheries' problems (Russell, 1976).

(2) Successful rearing provides new and interesting material for a wide range of experimental research. This has been developed especially in Norway, the UK and the USA (see Blaxter 1969, 1974 for further reading).

(3) Holding and rearing provides the possibility of "farming the sea" (see account by Shelbourne, 1964). The Norwegians, British and Americans were among the first to build hatcheries in which the eggs and yolk-sac larvae of commercial fish were kept free of predators. Before first feeding, they were transferred to the sea. Sad to relate, subsequent monitoring of the success of the brood never revealed unequivocal evidence of an improved recruitment.

In the 1960s, later attempts to transfer much older larvae or newly metamorphosed fish, especially plaice, to the sea as established feeders also ended in failure. Early life in the hatchery was not sufficiently rigorous and a disastrously high mortality of the transferred fish resulted from poor viability, inadequate behavioural responses to predators or inability to transfer to wild food.

The improvement in hatching techniques of the 1960s led to a different approach to mariculture where the young fish would be held in the hatchery until they became of marketable size. A technology for plaice was developed first but was not cost-effective. It seems that this type of mariculture is only economically viable for more valuable "luxury" species like lemon sole, sole and turbot. At the time of writing, all three species are being reared in the UK and the marketing of turbot is imminent. Improvements in early feeding and accelerated growth in the cooling water effluents of power stations are mainly responsible for this success. In other countries, especially France, turbot and sea bass are being investigated for similar purposes quite apart from a wide range of freshwater species.

II. REARING PROBLEMS

Why is it that marine fish have been difficult to rear? Is it possible to predict whether a particular species will be more difficult than another? What preliminary investigations could be made to identify future difficulties?

Houde (1973) discusses many of the problems of rearing but the main problem seems to be one of size. Once fertilized eggs, adequate aquarium facilities and sea water are available, the problem is to provide sufficient food of the right size and nutritional content in surroundings which are suitable for feeding, not overcrowded and generally optimal in other ways. The main and early checks have always been in the provision of small food organisms for small larvae with even smaller mouths. The factors to be dealt with in turn are then:

(1) Provision of suitable water supplies and aquaria
(2) Collection of the fertilized eggs
(3) Feeding
(4) Growth and mortality

Kinne (1976) gives a good general account of the rearing techniques and problems to be discussed in the next few pages.

III. WATER SUPPLY

Recirculated sea water or a constant supply of fresh sea water is acceptable for larval rearing, both having advantages and disadvantages (Chapter 1). A well managed recirculation system may lack natural food organisms, may show a gradual accumulation of metabolites, and may be contaminated by other users, but it is more often more stable in water clarity, pH, salinity and oxygen saturation. Fresh sea-water, pumped from a near-surface inshore site, may be low in salinity, supersaturated with dissolved gases, and is more subject to fluctuation of the chemical and physical conditions.

IV. OPTIMUM WATER CONDITIONS

In designing the optimum conditions for rearing without prior knowledge of the requirements of a particular species, it seems prudent to follow the temperature and salinity regime found in the sea under natural conditions. It should be borne in mind, however, that young stages may survive for a short time in conditions far outside this optimum. The question of optimum conditions remains something of a mystery. For example, conditions well within the lethal limits are often not optimal. It is also true that recent rearing experiments using combinations of temperature and salinity followed by a sophisticated "response–surface" analysis have shown an apparent optimum *outside* the natural range.

A. Water Flow

Rates of flow must be adjusted not only to suit the egg or larval population but also to prevent the accumulation of organisms at the outflow end. Turbulence in the tank should not exceed the swimming ability of the larvae nor should it disturb larval feeding. Other considerations are the importance of flow in temperature control, in flushing out metabolites and unwanted micro-organisms and in preventing undesirable aggregations of eggs, larvae or food. A desirable flow rate is of the order of 10% of the tank volume/hour.

B. Mixing and Aeration

At slow flow rates of about 10% of the tank volume/hour, the water is poorly mixed. Vertical temperature gradients and "dead" spaces may occur. In fact if mixing by means of the inflowing water *is* adequate, it indicates that the flow rate is too high. Mixing can be achieved by gentle aeration although this is not suitable for the longer clupeoid type of larva which is damaged by rising bubbles. A jet of air directed obliquely at and *above* the surface can be effective as can sub-surface gently-rotating paddles or rising and falling plates on the plunger jar principle.

C. Temperature

High temperatures accelerate and low temperatures retard development. Some examples of this are shown in Fig. 3 for the incubation stage. In larval life, the rate of yolk resorption is also influenced by temperature but temperature effects are less marked once the larvae start to feed. As a guide, it would seem acceptable to use rearing temperatures within ± 2 deg. C of the natural sea temperature.

Quantitative information on the influence of temperature on rate of development is useful for predicting times of hatching and other events in development. A simple rule is to calculate the number of "day-degrees", that is the product of incubation time in days $(D) \times$ temperature in °C (T) which is approximately constant if T is near the natural temperature, that is:

$$T \times D = k$$

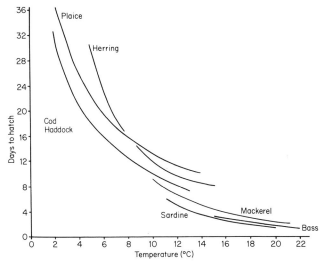

Fig. 3. The effect of temperature on incubation time in seven species of marine fish.

This assumes, however, that at $0°C$ the days to hatching are infinite which is not necessarily true. A better relationship incorporates the biological zero (T_o), the temperature at which incubation does take infinite time, that is:

$$(T - T_o) \, D = k$$

Having established D for one temperature $T°C$, D can be estimated for other temperatures. T_o, where it has been ascertained (by extrapolation) from a plot of D against T, is usually between $0°C$ and $-2°C$ in temperate species (see Blaxter, 1969).

D. Salinity

At least some teleosts like herring and plaice show a remarkable ability to withstand different salinities in the early stages (see Holliday, 1969). Fertilization may be possible in salinities from 5 to 55‰. Osmotic regulation by the egg is not fully functional until the blastopore closes. Before this, the developing egg may be able to withstand salinities from 5 to 45‰ for short periods. Later, the egg can tolerate salinities from 5 to 45‰ for long periods. The late-stage eggs and larvae seem to regulate their body fluids at a level equivalent to a salinity of about 12‰. For much marine fish rearing, it is probably acceptable to use salinities between about 12 and 35‰.

E. pH

Sea water is fairly well buffered with a pH near 8.0. Changes in pH are a sign that the water supply is not being properly managed. Although larvae are likely to tolerate values between 6.5 and 8.5, it is simple to control pH in a recirculating system by the use of marble chips in the filter.

F. Oxygen

The oxygen-carrying capacity of water falls with increased salinity and temperature. Oxygen is rarely limiting near the surface of the sea except in areas of red tides or other unusual phenomena. Marine fish larvae are likely to withstand a drop in oxygen to 40% of the air saturation volume (about 2.5 ml/l at 10°C in sea water) for a long period, and even withstand 30% saturation for an hour or more (de Silva and Tytler, 1973). There is no clear evidence that larvae are more resistant to hypoxia after development of the gills, which are not present in the earlier larval stages. After metamorphosis, when haemoglobin appears, there is some evidence that lower oxygen levels can be tolerated.

Once water becomes supersaturated as a result of warming or the entrainment of air, a very undesirable situation may arise. Gas can come out of solution in the gut or tissues of the larvae which cannot compensate for the increased buoyancy and float helpless upside down at the surface. The cure is pressurize the larvae to about 2 atm, which causes diffusion of the gas into solution. Another symptom of supersaturated water is intense activity of larvae which may result in clumping under bright lights or swimming up the meniscus at the tank walls.

G. Heavy Metals

Copper is the most likely contaminant in marine aquaria as a result of using brass, bronze or copper fittings in the sea water system. What little is known suggests that concentration of even 30 μg/l copper may be harmful in the egg stage of herring. (Cadmium, on the other hand, was not harmful at 1000 μg/l to herring and flounder eggs.) After hatching, herring and plaice larvae were found to be sensitive to concentrations around 1000 μg/l copper. The copper concentration of unpolluted sea water is normally 1–2 μg/l. It is obviously desirable to keep all substances containing copper out of contact of rearing tanks especially if the copper level is likely to rise above 20 μg/l.

H. Light

Rearing tanks should be shaded from ultraviolet light and from the heating effects of infra-red light. Overhead daylight with appropriate shading allows a natural daylength with appropriate slow changes in illumination at dusk and dawn so avoiding sudden shock changes of light or dark. It also gives an even spread of illumination over the tank surface. Artificial light should be provided by fluorescent tubes giving even illumination, ideally with a dimming system to simulate dusk and dawn. (See also section VII. Feeding.)

I. Micro-organisms

Very little is known of the susceptibility of eggs and larvae of marine fish to disease. Some measurements in tanks have shown "total viable" bacterial counts of several thousand per ml. Herring larvae showed no enhanced mortality in counts of up to 1000/ml although the more normal levels were 200–400/ml.

Without aeration, rearing tanks will develop an oily surface scum which is probably a mixture of bacteria and fat from the food. The only sure way to remove it is by running it off daily into a small beaker at the surface. Bacterial levels can be controlled by the addition of a mixture of 50 iu/ml of crystalline sodium penicillin and 0.05 mg/ml streptomycin sulphate. Erythromycin at 0.01 mg/ml is also effective. Ultraviolet sterilization of the inflowing water is also practised. In general, even with these controls, rearing tanks tend to act as traps for bacteria especially on the walls and floor and in dead spaces.

In some instances of high mortality, it has been found effective to remove the larval population larva by larva to a clean tank of fresh sea water. Hypotrichous ciliates are a very common contaminant of rearing tanks. There is no evidence that they attack live healthy larvae but they certainly scavenge and destroy dead larvae very rapidly. Since dead larvae disappear quickly, a false impression of survival may be obtained.

J. Summary

A summary of the rearing conditions discussed in the last few pages is given in Table I.

Table I. Acceptable environmental conditions for marine fish larvae.

Temperature	± 2 deg. C of natural sea temperature
Salinity	12–35‰
pH	7.0–8.5
Oxygen	40–100% saturation
Copper	< 20 μg/l
Light	Avoid direct sunlight. Use natural day length at 100–500 lux; with artificial light, ensure even illumination over surface
Bacteria	200–400 viable count/ml (not pathogenic)

V. TANK DESIGN

A. Shape and Size

Many workers use black plastic circular tanks of various sizes (Fig. 4). The black walls give high contrast between the food and background, so enhancing visual feeding. The circular shape prevents the aggregation of larvae in corners. Black plastic tubs used in the UK as expansion or cold water roof cisterns for domestic water supply ranging in volume from 20 to 5υυ ἰitres are ideal. Square or rectangular tanks occupy less space and may be suitable for some species. In general, large tanks are ideal for reducing the surface/volume ratio, so reducing the interaction between the larvae and the tank walls; small tanks are better for maintaining high food density.

B. Inflow and Outflow

The usual practice is to take the inflow to the bottom of the tank. Because larvae are rheotactic it may be necessary to attach gauze over the end to prevent the larvae swimming up the inflow. The edge of the end of the inflow tube, if glass, should be rounded by heat. The outflow is usually taken from the surface but must be protected to prevent loss of larvae (Fig. 4). If gauze is used, it should be selected to retain the food as well as the larvae. Even a coarse mesh will prevent the outflow of the oily surface film and this must be removed in other ways (see above, page 311).

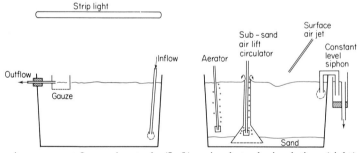

Fig. 4. Arrangement for rearing tank. (Left) a simple tank circulation; (right) some possible modifications to create circulation or to provide a siphon outflow in a tank which cannot be machined to bore a hole in the wall.

VI. COLLECTION AND TREATMENT OF MATERIAL

A. Eggs and Sperm

These can be obtained from a spawning fishery when the fish can be "stripped" or gonads dissected followed by artificial fertilization. It is quite a common practice to induce spawning in tanks by the injection of chorionic gonadotropin followed by stripping or artificial fertilization. The results are not always as good as with natural spawning, and there may be a heavy "fall-out" of inviable eggs even after an apparently successful fertilization.

An investigation is needed of the size of eggs produced by different females. Older females as well as winter–spring spawners may produce larger eggs than younger fish or summer–autumn spawners (see discussion by Bagenal (1971). This is well exemplified by the herring (Fig. 5) where winter-spring spawners have large eggs and low fecundity and summer–autumn spawners small eggs and high fecundity. If the species under investigation has a variety of spawning seasons and egg size, large eggs should be chosen since they will yield larger larvae with better prospects of feeding.

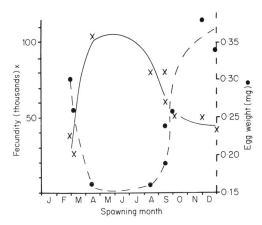

Fig. 5. Inverse relationships between fecundity and egg dry weight in different spawning races of herring.

B. Storage

Dissected gonads may be stored dry in jars at a temperature of around 4°C and remain fertile for at least 24, or even 48 h.

Sperm but not eggs may be stored for several months in liquid nitrogen or air or solid carbon dioxide after the addition of an antifreeze agent like glycerol or dimethyl sulphoxide. This is a specialized technique and authorities such as Horton and Ott (1976) should be consulted before attempting such a procedure.

C. Fertilization

The eggs may be fertilized by mixing with sperm in sea water, allowing about 10 min for fertilization to occur. It is also possible to fertilize eggs without the addition of sea water. The fertilized eggs should be well washed before incubation to prevent bacterial growth on dead sperm. The demersal attached eggs of species like herring which stick to a substratum may be incubated on glass plates.

D. Incubation

Pelagic eggs tend to collect at the surface around the sides of a tank and should be carefully redistributed each day by a glass rod or gentle aeration. The antibiotic treatment described on page 311 may also be used to cut down bacterial growth on the eggs. The glass plates for attached eggs may be stacked vertically back-to-back to prevent detrital settlement. Such eggs are more easily counted and re-distributed than pelagic eggs. During gastrulation prior to closure of the blastospore mechanical disturbances, especially vibration, should be kept to a minimum and the eggs should not be transported. This is in part a delicacy of the process of differentiation and may be partly a question of shell strength. For a while following fertilization, the chorion is more easily burst than in later stages of incubation.

E. Stocking Density

Pelagic eggs may be kept at a density of 10–50/litre. Eggs attached to a substratum should not be allowed to touch each other. On hatching, the larvae will often tend to aggregate near the surface. The early stages can be kept at a maximum density of 50/litre but more space must be provided as they grow. There may be some social facilitation during feeding so that stocking density should not be too low. Single larvae rarely thrive.

Survival will be improved by the progressive transfer of growing larvae to larger tanks but it must be borne in mind that it is more difficult to obtain high food densities in larger tanks and so a compromise must be reached where food is sufficiently dense yet the larvae have sufficient space. A density of 3–10 larvae/litre is probably optimal in tanks of 100–500 litres volume. To some extent, the problem of space depends on distributing the larvae throughout the tank. Gentle aeration with hardy species, above-surface air jets and diffuse light will help as will slowly moving paddles or plunger jar plates. Changes in behaviour also influence decisions about tank shape and volume. Clupeoid larvae become extremely active as they grow and need a large volume; flatfish larvae start to settle on the floor of the tank so that a large shallow tank is more desirable.

F. Transfer

Most species can be transferred by pipettes with the sharp edge at the tip rounded by heat. Larvae can also be caught at the surface by beakers or other containers. Nets should not be used.

VII. FEEDING

A. Food Supply

Hunter (1981) discusses the general feeding behaviour and ecology of marine fish larvae. A good account of food used for marine fish rearing is given by May (1970). The problem is that inanimate food is taken less readily than living and moving food. This live food must be small enough to be taken by larvae as small as 3–4 mm in body length. Some species seem to have especially small jaws in the early stages e.g. turbot, lemon sole and some gadoid fish; others such as plaice, sole and herring present less of a problem. In predicting the success of a particular rearing method or food for a new species, the gape of the jaw should be measured. Figure 6 gives some information of the size of gape that may be found.

The main types of food and the minimum dimension of the organism concerned (e.g. diameter if cylindrical) is given in Table II as a guide to first feeding. Thus the nauplii of the anostracan *Artemia salina* can be used in the early stages of feeding herring, plaice and sole, as can the nauplii of the cirripede *Balanus*. The rotifer *Brachionus plicatilis* is much smaller and caused a significant improvement in the rearing of smaller larvae like turbot and anchovy. The naked dinoflagellate *Gymnodinium splendens*, which is even smaller still, has allowed greater success in the very early rearing of anchovy.

May lists the great range of living and inanimate food used by earlier workers. In general, algae and diatoms alone have not proven successful foods. A bloom of the alga *Chlorella* was necessary for the rearing of tuna larvae although it was not eaten. Crustacean larvae, as well as bivalve trochophores and gastropod veligers, have been successful as invertebrate prey. Natural plankton, sieved to give food of the appropriate size, has been commonly used with excellent results, as have collections of copepods such as *Tigriopus* from rock pools or *Tisbe* which often occurs

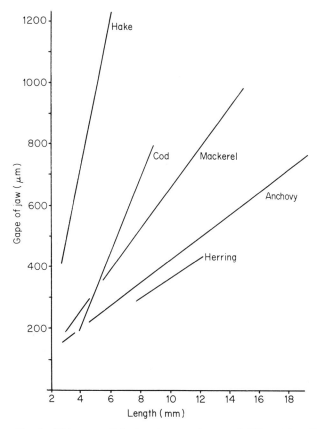

Fig. 6. The gape of the jaw in some larvae of different length.

naturally in aquaria. However, the use of natural plankton requires a suitable boat to make daily collections and the quality and quantity are often unpredictable. In addition, potential predators may be introduced in their young stages and grow in the rearing tanks to become a danger. Inanimate proprietary foods, liver, egg yolk, minced invertebrate meat (mussel) have in general been unsuccessful. A major breakthrough in larval rearing could be the development of an encapsulated diet of very small size, neutrally buoyant and of optimal nutritional value.

In general, then, most species at first-feeding require food 50–100 μm wide (Fig. 7). Such small food items should be at densities of 10–50 ml or even up to 100/ml for *Gymnodinium*. The normal practice is to increase the size of food as the larvae grow, often with *Artemia nauplii* as the basic diet. A density of 1–2/ml is then adequate but levels up to 5/ml may be beneficial. There is evidence that some species, e.g. anchovy and herring, do not thrive on *Artemia nauplii* alone so that a mixed diet is safer. Later "weaning" from planktonic food to prepared pellets or pastes usually results in some mortality. This weaning is particularly difficult in sole at metamorphosis. In general, later stages will continue to take the smaller

Table II. Larval first feeding.

Food species	Width μm	Source	Rate fed no/ml	Fish reared
Artemia nauplii	250–350	Sold commercially	1–3	herring, plaice, sole
Balanus nauplii	250	Collected from adults on shore March/April	1–3	herring
Brachionus plicatilis	60–180	cultured on algae	20–50	anchovy, lemon sole, sea bass, turbot
Gymnodinium splendens	50–60	cultured on enriched sea water	50–100	anchovy
Mollusc trochophores and veligers	50–120	spawned from adults	1–5?	anchovy, herring
"Wild" copepod nauplii	50–100	plankton net	1–3	anchovy, herring, sardine and other species

plankton organisms fed in the early larval stage. This is a wasteful process and some workers "on-grow" *Artemia* with yeast or algal cultures and feed it when larger. Other workers have set up balanced tanks with algal cultures, herbivorous copepods or rotifers and the predatory larvae together. Thus *Chlorella* added to such a tank probably improved the survival of tuna larvae by feeding their prey. On-growing of metamorphosed stages usually involves their transfer to synthetic food or pellets. The formulation of these and nutritional requirements are fully discussed by Kinne (1976). However, it is worth giving the details of a diet used by Adron *et al.* (1974) for rearing plaice to metamorphosis (Table III). The particle size ranged from 180 to 355 μm and survival to metamorphosis was 20%.

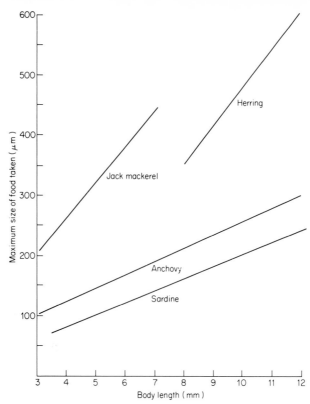

Fig. 7. Maximum width of food taken by some larvae of different length (cf. Fig. 6).

Table III. Artificial diet used by Adron *et al.* (1974) for rearing plaice larvae to metamorphosis.

Component	Weight g/100 g dry diet
Freeze-dried cod muscle	53.4
Freeze-dried whole hen's egg	10.0
Shrimp meal	10.0
Cod-liver oil	4.0
Encapsulated vitamin mixture	3.3
Vitamin mixture	2.8
Mineral mixture	1.0
Glucose	5.0
α tocopherol	0.4
Sunset yellow F.C.F.	0.1
Furanace	0.8 mg
Gelatin	10.0
Water (removed finally by freeze-drying)	150.0

B. Light and Feeding

Almost all teleost larvae investigated are "visual" feeders, especially in the young stages. They may take in some small organisms by swallowing sea water as part of the process of osmoregulation; especially when the food density is very high. Experiments (Fig. 8) show that a threshold for feeding is around 0.1 lux. It is desirable to keep the illumination above 100–200 lux but perhaps not more than 1000 lux (equivalent to outside light in the early evening or on an overcast day).

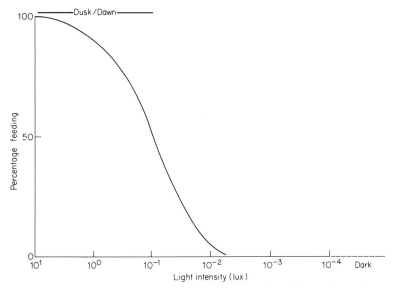

Fig. 8. Effect of light intensity on feeding success, a generalised threshold curve based on a number of species.

VIII. MORTALITY AND GROWTH

A. Initial Mortality

An initial mortality will occur at fertilization as a result of some eggs being infertile. The stage up to closure of the blastopore is always considered very delicate and eggs should not be subjected to vibration or transported in the gastrula stage. Overcrowding of eggs laid on a substrate is to be avoided; owing to lack of oxygen or cramping of development, the central eggs in a mass or spread on a plate often die.

At hatching, some premature larvae are often bent and non-viable. If hatching is delayed, it can be stimulated by light or warming, a very long period for hatching itself being undesirable. A non-viable hatch is often a sign of poor quality eggs or high bacterial levels, naturally spawned eggs often being more viable than artificially fertilized eggs.

B. Starvation

Mortalities at first feeding can be avoided by attention to food size, distribution and larval density. Starving larvae tend to float head down in the water. This increased buoyancy is maintained until the body fluids become more concentrated ionically as osmotic imbalance sets in; the larvae then sink to the floor of the tank. The term "point of no return" (PNR) has been coined to represent the stage when larvae are still alive but too weak to feed even if food becomes available. Some information on the PNR is given in Table IV, from which it can be seen that older larvae can withstand substantial periods of complete starvation.

Table IV. Time to reach "point of no return" (PNR).

Species	Age, days from hatching or stage	Temp. °C	Days to PNR
Anchovy	newly hatched	15	5.5
		22	3
Bream	newly hatched	22	3.4
		30	2.4
Haddock	newly hatched	7	6
Herring	newly hatched	8–12	8.5–20[a]
	6	9	6
	30	9	8
	50	9	8
	74	9	12
	88	9	15
Plaice	newly hatched	8–12	11
	Stage 3a	8–12	15
	Stage 4a	8–12	23

[a] Depends on egg size.

C. Predation

Mortality due to predation can be avoided by checking the tanks for predators like medusae or amphipods which may have grown in the tank after being introduced with small natural plankton as food. Concentrations of dead larvae at one point in a tank are often due to predation by sessile hydroids. Weak larvae may be sucked against the outflow and drop to the bottom of the tank once the flow becomes occluded, giving the appearance of high mortality from some other cause.

D. Abnormalities

One of the main abnormalities found in tanks is a high body-weight for a given length compared with wild fish (Fig. 9). The larvae appear shorter

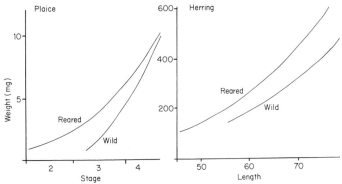

Fig. 9. Body weight plotted against larval stage (see Fig. 1) in plaice and body length (mm) in herring, showing the difference between reared and wild fish.

and fatter and have a high condition factor. Flatfish are prone to fin-biting and also pigment abnormalities, some being completely albino, others "piebald". This probably arises in part from the stress of overcrowding. Clupeoids suffer from abnormalities in the dermal bones. Many species tend to have a high fat content but this is a feature of all tank-held fish, not just the young stages.

E. Growth

Food quality and quantity and larval density determine growth as does the size of tank. There is a common trend for a size-hierarchy to develop, that is, the range in length of the larvae increases with age (Fig. 10). It is not known whether this phenomenon occurs in the sea; it is likely that slow growers are preyed on selectively and that the wild larval populations represent the fast growers. This is partly borne out by tank experiments where it is sometimes difficult to match the mean natural growth rate.

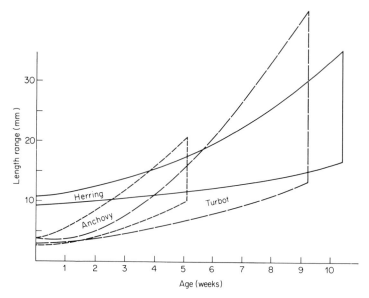

Fig. 10. Typical change in range of length with age (in weeks post-hatching) in three species, showing the "size-hierarchy" effect.

IX. REFERENCES

Adron, J. W., Blair, A. and Cowey, C. B. (1974). Rearing of plaice (*Pleuronectes platessa*) larvae to metamorphosis using an artificial diet. *Fishery Bulletin US.* **72**, 353–357.

Bagenal, T. B. (1971). The interrelation of the size of fish eggs, the date of spawning and the production cycle. *Journal of Fish Biology* **3**, 207–219.

Blaxter, J. H. S. (1969). Development: Eggs and larvae. *In* "Fish Physiology" (W. S. Hoar and D. J. Randall eds), **3**, 177–252. Academic Press, New York and London.

Blaxter, J. H. S. (ed.) (1964). "The Early Life History of Fish". Springer Verlag, Berlin.

Holliday, F. G. T. (1969). The effects of salinity on the eggs and larvae of teleosts. *In* "Fish Physiology" (W. S. Hoar and D. J. Randall, eds), **1**, 293–311. Academic Press, New York and London.

Horton, H. F. and Ott, A. G. (1976). Cryopreservation of fish spermatozoa and ova. *Journal of the Fisheries Research Board of Canada* **33**, 995–1000.

Houde, E. D. (1973). Some recent and unsolved problems in the culture of marine fish larvae. *Proceedings of the World Mariculture Society* **3**, 83–112.

Hunter, J. R. (1981). The feeding behaviour of marine fish larvae. *In* "The physiological and behavioural manipulation of food fish as production and management tools". ICLARM, Manila. (In press.)

Kinne, O. (ed.) (1976). "Marine Ecology. Cultivation". **3(2)**, 968–1035. Wiley. Chichester.

May, R. C. (1970). Feeding larval marine fishes in the laboratory: A review. *California Maritime Research Commission* CalCOFI Rep. **14**, 76–83.

May, R. C. (1974). Larval mortality in marine fishes and the critical period concept. *In* "The Early Life History of Fish" (J. H. S. Blaxter, ed.) 3–19. Springer Verlag, Berlin.

Russell, F. S. (1976). "The Eggs and Planktonic Stages of British Marine Fishes". Academic Press, London and New York.

Shelbourne, J. E. (1964). The artificial propagation of marine fish. *Advances in Marine Biology* **2**, 1–83.

Silva, C. de and Tytler, P. (1973). The influence of reduced environmental oxygen on the metabolism and survival of herring and plaice larvae. *Netherlands Journal of Sea Research* **7**, 345–362.

Chapter 12

Rearing Salmonids in Freshwater

J. E. Thorpe

Freshwater Fisheries Laboratory, Pitlochry, Scotland

I. INTRODUCTION

Ideally, for successful rearing of wild animals in captivity, the advantageous features of their natural habitats should be maximized and the disadvantages minimized. With salmonid fishes, some progress has been made towards such goals, but this has often been hampered by the development of large-scale systems for the farming of these species, where the design of holding facilities and husbandry methods has been tailored more to the convenience of manufacturing processes and operator requirements than to the basic needs of the fish. These designs (for example, see Huet, 1972), while they have been relatively successful for production systems where the physiological process of interest is somatic growth, are not necessarily ideal for the study of finer biological details of these fishes. It is pertinent therefore to review briefly the main features of salmonid biology which must be considered in designing adequate holding facilities for these fishes.

II. CHARACTERISTICS OF SALMONID FISHES

A. General Life History

The salmonids are lithophil spawners. They excavate shallow depressions in gravel beds of streams, rivers or lakes, into which they deposit relatively large yolky eggs (3–9 mm in diameter) and cover them with loose gravel. The coregonines and thymallines broadcast their eggs over gravel substrates, where they remain unprotected until hatching. Most species spawn in autumn or winter, but some *Salmo, Coregonus* and *Thymallus* spp. spawn in spring and developmental rate depends primarily on temperature. After hatching, the eleutheroembryo stage (Balon, 1975) of salmonines is spent buried in the gravel bed environment until the young fish requires an external food source. Emergence into open water usually occurs in the spring, and the young of stream-dwelling forms take up station headed into the water currents. The subsequent residence time in freshwater varies between species, from almost immediate downstream emigration to the sea to completion of the entire life span there, with a range of intermediates between, and sometimes within species. Emigration downstream implies subsequent return immigration to the spawning area, so that those species which leave freshwater as juveniles also spend a variable period in freshwater again as mature adults. Characteristic life span varies between species and between populations within species, from about 2 years in some *Oncorhynchus* spp. to over 40 years in some *Salvelinus* spp.

B. Egg Stage

To support embryonic development within the chorion, the egg requires an adequate surface for oxygen acquisition and the removal of metabolic wastes. The selection of a gravel substrate by the spawner ensures that eggs are deposited in an area where they are unlikely to become covered in silt, which could impede gaseous exchange. Among salmonines, continual percolation of water currents through the gravel interstices of the redd ensures the oxygen supply, and Stuart (1953) claimed that the spawner selected its site such that sufficient interstitial flow was available.

C. Larval Stage

At hatching, the larvae have large yolk sacs, and the embryo to whole larval dry weight ratio varies between species and thus, the characteristics of post-hatching embryonic development vary between species, and within species by environmental temperature. The principal advantages of larval development within the gravel bed appear to be protection from predators, and the minimizing of locomotor activity (Marr, 1963). The latter advantage assures the maximum availability of yolk for the formation of body tissue, and thus the maximum size of fish at emergence from the gravel at the first-feeding stage. Retention of the larvae within the gravel is ensured by strong photonegative behavioural responses which wane or are briefly reversed at the time of emergence.

D. Feeding Juveniles

To ensure continued growth and development, the larva must obtain external food by the time its own yolk supply has fallen to the level of its maintenance needs. Therefore, for salmonines, emergence from the gravel is necessary at this time, which has been defined experimentally among Atlantic salmon (*Salmo salar* L.) as occurring at a dry weight embryo: total larva ratio of about 0.85 (Marr, 1966).

Once emerged, the so-called fry show species-specific behavioural differences. Hoar (1953) has noted that for fishes to maintain station in a river, they must possess behavioural mechanisms that ensure that they are not displaced passively by the current. Those which migrate to sea promptly (e.g. *Oncorhynchus gorbuscha*) show sheltering behaviour orientated toward the stream bed until they encounter a conspecific. Then, this shelter response is replaced by shoaling. The fry group in mid-water, and are passively displaced downstream at twilight when their optomotor orientation responses fail temporarily, due to retinal responses which are slower than the rate of change of light intensity. The shelter response breaks down less rapidly in species which later migrate seawards and in these species, it may be reinforced by territorial aggression, retaining individual fishes in very precise sites on the stream bed. Such territoriality also has to break down to allow these fish to leave the streams, and this is often a concomitant of the physiological changes that occur at the so-called parr-smolt transformation in the months prior to departure to sea. In the fully freshwater stream forms, these changes are less intense. Although minor migrations may take place, the animal may maintain its station through the retention of territorial, rheotactic and thigmotactic responses.

Intermediate behaviour is evident in the sockeye salmon (*O. nerka*) which spends part of its immature feeding stages in lakes, and shows gregarious feeding behaviour there similar to that of the fully lacustrine coregonines and some char species. Feeding during this period is primarily on drift or surface foods in streams (Rawson, 1950; Wankowski, 1977), or on mid-water or benthic animals in lakes (Scott and Crossman, 1973; Thorpe, 1974b; Ware, 1972 and 1973). The energy spent in acquiring food seems to be minimal. Fish in streams adopt stations which allow them to intercept food particles of optimal size reaching them on the current. Fish in lakes cruise gently, with little evidence of bursts of rapid activity.

E. Parr-Smolt Transformation

In the period prior to emigration to sea, juvenile salmonines show morphological changes (silvering, elongation of body proportions) which are the consequences of physiological change. The disproportionate length increase, possibly at the expense of weight, implies a change in endocrine control processes over growth. Parallel changes in behaviour distinguish the emigrants from those remaining in freshwater.

In Atlantic salmon at this time, the fish show an unwillingness to stem currents over 2 body lengths/s (Thorpe and Morgan, 1978), whereas the non-migrants have been shown to maintain station at speeds up to 8.3 b.l./s. Such high current speeds are also withstood by several *Oncorhynchus* species during the freshwater phase (Brett and Glass, 1973; Glova and McInerney, 1977). This behaviour would enhance downstream displacement among active fish, bringing them ultimately into brackish and then fully saline marine waters. Sodium and potassium ATP-ase activity increases at this time, thus facilitating the switch in osmoregulatory processes from those appropriate to a hypo- to those of a hyper-osmotic environment (Conte *et al.*, 1966).

Sometimes fully freshwater forms may show analogous changes, even producing silvered smolt phases, associated with displacement from streams to lake habitats. The periods of tolerance of marine salinity levels show a circannual rhythm (Hoar 1976), but it is evident from recent work (Clarke and Blackburn, 1977) that the induction of these physiological states is dependent on a lengthening photoperiod, and their maintenance on the temperature regime.

F. Subadults

Among those forms which remain in freshwater, basic habitat requirements from the first-feeding stage to sexual maturation change in scale, an increase in body-size requiring an increase in food intake, and very probably an increase in food particle-size. The means by which these changed requirements are obtained may be through modest movement (Thorpe, 1974a), or through increased territorial behaviour directed at conspecifics of comparable size. Sexual maturation as in other vertebrates, is influenced by photoperiod, but the initial triggering mechanisms remain obscure. In general, higher temperatures are preferred at the fry stage, and decrease gradually through development to maturity (Hokanson 1977). These thermal optima differ between species, and this is reflected in their geographical distribution. For example, several *Salvelinus* spp. are found far to the north of the natural limits of *Salmo* spp., and this is apparently attributable to a comparatively high growth efficiency of the former at temperatures of 10–13°C, too low for growth in the latter which thrive at temperatures in the range 12–16°C.

III. AQUARIUM DESIGN

In view of the particular characteristics of salmonid fishes, it is clear that special holding facilities are desirable for each developmental stage, perhaps most critically so among the migratory salmonids. In the following paragraphs, some of the facilities developed for holding Atlantic salmon (*Salmo salar*) are described, with supplementary comments on variants for other species.

A. Egg Stage

Water must be continually exchanged at the egg surface to achieve adequate oxygenation. The conventional solution has been to place the eggs on a slatted or perforated tray (Figs 1 and 2) through which a gentle flow of water can percolate with minimal mechanical disturbance to the egg. The deposition of silt is avoided by filtration of the water supply. This simple holding system is preferable to a gravel-filled tank since the eggs can be inspected at will and without disturbance. Infertile, dead or damaged eggs can be removed quickly before they provide a focus for proliferation of fungal hyphae which, once established, can quickly invade and kill neighbouring eggs. Slatted trays allow the hatching fish to drop through on to the aquarium floor and provide a simple means of removing the ruptured choria. For incubation of eggs by the million, stacking tray systems have been designed which are used widely in the aquaculture industry (e.g. Menzies and Curtis, 1966); for small-scale

Fig. 1a.   Incubation baskets for salmonine eggs, in use at Almondbank Smolt Rearing unit, for Atlantic salmon eggs. The basket shown has a corrugated insert, (see also fig. 4b), and egg tray.

Fig. 1b. The incubation basket in use.

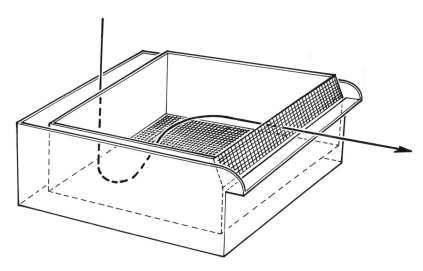

Fig. 2. Diagram of a "Californian Box" incubator. (After Huet, 1972.) Arrow shows direction of water flow.

laboratory purposes, these units have no great advantage over simple trays. For the smaller, freely broadcast coregonine eggs, incubation jars are preferable (Fig. 3), the water flow adjusted so that the eggs are continually gently agitated. This ensures that the lighter dead eggs are easily siphoned from the top of the batch.

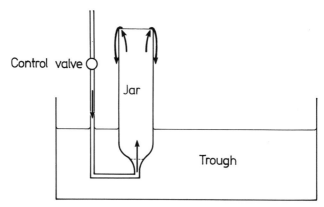

Fig. 3. Jar for incubating Coregonine eggs. Water flow is controlled at the valve, the eggs being gently agitated in the upward flow through the jar. The hatching fry are carried out over the lip of the jar into the trough below.

B. Alevin Stage

The requirement is for minimal disturbance of the developing larva, to permit maximal conversion of yolk into body tissue, and minimal wastage of this energy supply through locomotion. Marr's experiments (1966) identified light, temperature, water flow and surface contour as factors influencing the efficiency of yolk conversion in Atlantic salmon alevins, and showed that at first-feeding, the largest embryos were those reared in the dark on a corrugated surface. Corrugations were provided by laying 2 cm diameter glass rods side-by-side over the whole floor of a lidded black perspex aquarium trough. Such a system is expensive and wasteful of space (Fig. 4a); a cheaper and less wasteful alternative has a simple plastic moulding (Fig. 4b) sealed into the floor of a perforated hatchery basket (Fig. 1). The hatching alevins fall through the slatted egg trays into the furrows of this material, whose inclined walls provide sufficient vertical support to inhibit swimming. These baskets are held in simple troughs through which a flow of about 5 l/min of filtered water is maintained, in darkness, or in low-intensity red light, beyond the visible spectral range of salmon (i.e. >690 nm). Low red light is preferable to full darkness, as it allows frequent inspection of the troughs without disturbance to the developing larvae. Coregonine larvae are ready to

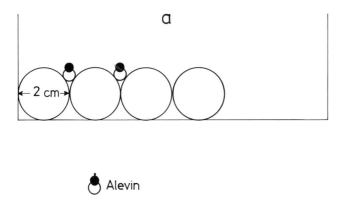

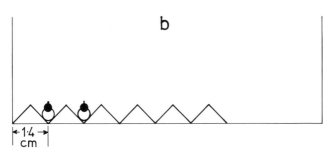

Fig. 4.   Grooved surfaces, for alevin baskets: (a) glass rods, laid parallel across floor of basket, (b) plastic moulding cemented into floor of basket.

accept external food within 3–5 days of hatching and therefore it is desirable to transfer them from the incubation jars to feeding aquaria promptly after hatching.

C. Feeding Juveniles

The right food must be presented to the young fish, in an appropriate way and in the right environment. Dietary composition is dealt with extensively in Chapter 8 and will not be considered here. The salmonids are morphologically best suited to feed on moving particles in open water; thus lacustrine species require small zooplankton organisms as first food, and the riverine ones, small particles of organic drift. Recent experimental work (Wankowski, 1977) has shown that among Atlantic salmon juveniles, the first-feeding fry respond to, ingest and retain a wide range of particle sizes, but rapidly become much more selective. Optimum response, retention and growth is achieved when the food items have a breadth of 2–2.5% of the fish's fork length. In the wild, these fry orient into the stream flow, remain in close contact with the substrate and move forward or to the side to intercept potential prey items in the drift. Efficient partitioning of the drift resources is achieved among stream-dwelling salmonids through territoriality, and the spatial mosaics of individual feeding stations are maintained through a repertoire of aggressive behaviour.

It has been established by experiment that an increase in the opportunities of obtaining food particles is correlated with a reduction in aggressive interactions. Thus, ideally food particles for Atlantic salmon fry must travel horizontally towards the fishes and be presented close to their resting stations as frequently as possible along as many separate trajectories as there are fish to reduce fighting. The radial flow tank was designed in an attempt to achieve these goals (Fig. 5). Inflowing water is directed perpendicularly to the centre of the tank floor, so that it is carried away radially, and flows out of the tank by a circular peripheral drain. Adjustable drain pipes set the water level at whatever height is required (15 cm depth in 1 and 2 m diameter tanks), and this leads to a cellular flow-pattern within the water body in the tank. Food particles are introduced into the water inflow before it reaches the tank so that feed is distributed radially across the tank floor. The fish, orientating into the current, range themselves around the periphery of the tank, pointing inwards, but their position can be manipulated easily using their pronounced responses to over-head cover. The fish will congregate under a ring-shaped cover suspended in the tank, with their heads at the inner perimeter, so that their position in the tank can be determined by the appropriate choice of diameter of ring (Fig. 6). For first summer fish (up to c. 8 cm fork length), such covers work best if the fish has to close the dorsal fin to shelter below the ring. At this stage, as noted earlier, juvenile salmon occupy stations at water flows up to 8.3 body lengths/s. The young fish also show preference for resting on a non-reflecting dark surface. The regular radial pattern of resting fish forms most readily if the tank walls are light. Thus the tanks should have black floors and white walls.

Since the location of the fish in the radial tanks can be controlled quite precisely, the current speed that they experience can also be controlled easily, as the linear flow across the tank base can be calibrated against a volume flow-meter on the tank inflow. As flow-rate influences the rate of smoltification, and as swimming performance changes during the parr-smolt transformation (Thorpe and Morgan, 1978), it is desirable to retain

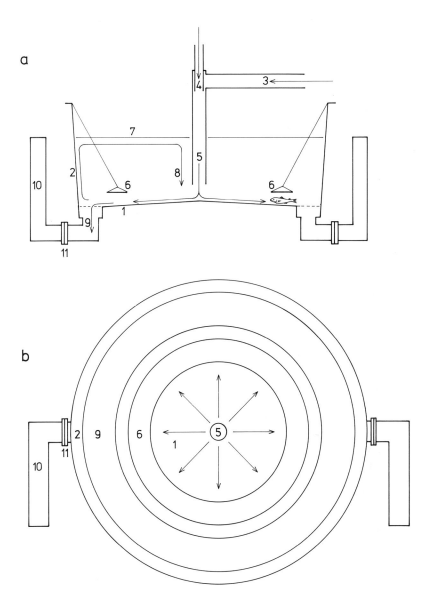

Fig. 5. Radial flow tank: (a) side view, (b) top view. (1) Tank base. (2) Tank side. (3) Main water input. (4) Food input. (5) Central water inlet. (6) Cover ring suspended from tank rim. (7) Water surface. (8) Current cell. (9) Peripheral drain, with perforated cover. (10) Adjustable standpipe. (11) Swivel joint.

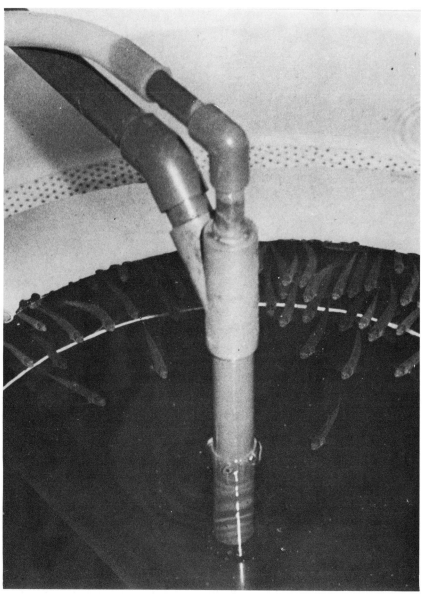

Fig. 6. Atlantic salmon parr (0 +) under a ring cover in a 1 m diameter radial flow tank.

such flexibility and control over flow. With perspex wall or floor panels, these tanks can also be used as observation units. The design is preferable to the conventional circular or square tangential-flow aquaria, as it can provide an environment more appropriate to a territorial fish. While such requirements can also be met in long narrow stream tanks, the radial tanks have the added advantage that surplus food particles and faeces are voided from the tank quickly, without this material passing other individuals downstream (Fig. 7).

For laboratory experiments, it is important that automatic feed-dispensers should be controllable precisely. Numerous feeders are available for the commercial production of salmonids, but laboratory devices tend to be individually developed for specific needs. The basic requirements are for a dispenser from which a measured ration of dry food can be delivered at a precise time, and for a time-controlled system which allows great flexibility in the setting of feed regimes. Two simple systems have been used with the radial tank. First, the "Caddymatic" feeder (Fig. 8) (see Minaur, 1971), which is versatile enough to use in production systems, and which consists of a mass-produced tea-dispenser operated by a solenoid, with a range of precision-drilled inserts for the delivery drawer to define the ration size. The firing of the solenoid is controlled by a short-interval electric time-switch, allowing firing at multiples of 5-min intervals, and that switch is itself governed by a long-interval time-switch, so that the period within 24 h during which feeds are available, is controllable.

Secondly, an elegant little feeder was designed by Wankowski (1977) for use in an experiment where total ration in relation to fish size and food-particle size had to be controlled very precisely (Fig. 9). This consists of a horizontal tube containing the feed, through which a close-fitting piston is drawn very slowly by a wire attached to an electric motor making 1 revolution per 24 h. By varying the positions of the pin attachments, and the diameter of the tube and piston assembly, the rate of delivery of feed can be altered, and the whole system is again controlled by a time-switch. With both these feeders, the food particles are delivered into a funnel receiving a subsidiary water flow, which is then mixed with the main flow before it enters the tank.

Some salmonid species adapt quickly to self-feeding devices, in which the animal is "rewarded" with food when it pushes a bar or lever. This propensity has been exploited by commercial trout farmers, but Atlantic salmon seem to be less trainable. Miller, working with *Salmo gairdneri*, has recently used "Campden" single pellet feeders designed originally for feeding mammals and birds in laboratory experiments. These promise to be useful in some small-scale experiments.

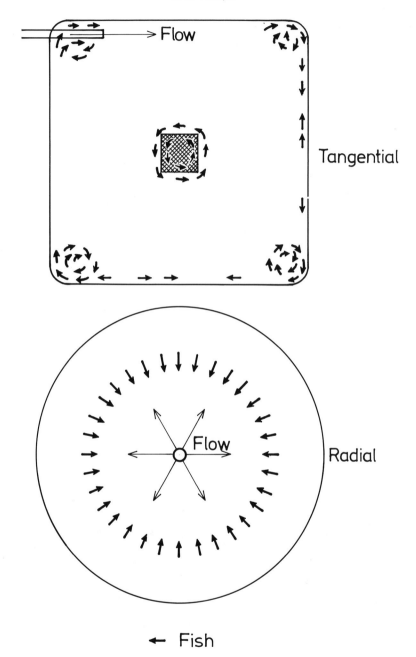

Fig. 7. Comparison of spatial distribution of young Atlantic salmon fry in a conventional tangential-flow tank, and a radial-flow tank.

Fig. 8. "Caddymatic" feeder (Crown Copyright).

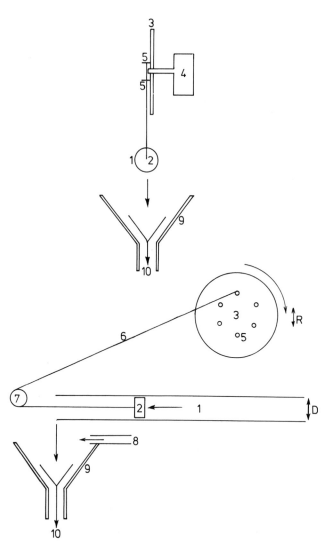

Fig. 9. Wankowski feeder: (Top) end view, (Bottom) side view. (1) PVC cylinder, internal diameter D. (2) Piston, external diameter D. (3) Pulley wheel. (4) Geared electric motor. (5) Pulley pins (six), adjustable to give radius R. (6) Steel monofilament wire. (7) Secondary pulley. (8) Water input. (9) Funnel, top diameter 25 cm. (10) Water and feed outlet to experimental tank.

D. Parr-smolt Transformation

With change in behaviour at the parr-smolt transformation, changes in holding facilities may be required by migratory salmonids. For example, current speeds tolerated by smolting fish are less than those by non-smolts, and thus flow rates will need adjustment. But in the wild, territorial behaviour must decline if the fish are to relinquish their attachment to a particular site. Thus the radial tank system becomes a less appropriate environment at this time and incipient smolts may be housed better in annular tanks which mimic endless streams (Fig. 10). In these, the fish may take up station or drift with the current. As with the radial tanks, these flume channels can double as observation chambers or experimental units.

E. Subadults

By the subadult stage, individual salmonids are greater than 15 cm long, greater than 50 g in weight and require large-scale holding aquaria. By this stage, the tanks and net pens developed for the commercial users become more appropriate holding devices.

F. Adults

Mature adult salmonids do not feed, but may be very active around spawning time. Therefore, to ensure successful retention, the aquarium facilities must be designed to allow the individual fish adequate space for continual gentle swimming but should discourage them from vigorous activity such as the wild fish exhibit at falls and rapids (Stuart, 1962). These needs can be met in large ponds or channels with low water velocity, and preferably a sub-surface intake to inhibit leaping behaviour. Some overhead cover is desirable to shade the fish and to reduce their activity.

G. General

Salmonid fishes are found chiefly in clear, cool, well oxygenated oligotrophic waters, and therefore water quality is a prime consideration for their successful rearing. This subject is dealt with fully in Chapter 4.

Fig. 10. (a) Endless flume, for holding Atlantic salmon during the parr-smolt transformation, (b) drainage system from flume.

IV. REFERENCES

Ali, M. A. and Hoar, W. S. (1959). Retinal responses of pink salmon associated with its downstream migration. *Nature* **184**, 106–107.

Balon, E. K. (1975). Terminology of intervals in fish development. *Journal of the Fisheries Research Board of Canada* **32**, 1663–1670.

Brett, J. R. and Glass, N. R. (1973). Metabolic rates and critical swimming speeds of sockeye salmon (*O. nerka*) in relation to size and temperature. *Journal of the Fisheries Research Board of Canada* **30**, 379–387.

Clarke, W. C. and Blackburn, J. (1977). A seawater challenge test to measure smolting of juvenile salmon. *Fisheries Research Board of Canada Technical Report* **705**.

Conte, F. P., Wagner, H. H., Fessler, J. and Gnose, C. (1966). Development of osmotic and ionic regulation in juvenile coho salmon (*Oncorhynchus kisutch*). *Comparative Biochemistry and Physiology* **18**, 1–15.

Glova, G. J. and McInerney, J. E. (1977). Critical swimming speeds of coho salmon (*Oncorhynchus kisutch*) fry to smolt stages in relation to salinity and temperature. *Journal of the Fisheries Research Board of Canada* **34**, 151–154.

Hilliday, F. G. T., Tytler, P. and Young, A. H. (1974). Activity levels of trout (*Salmo trutta*) in Airthrey Loch, Stirling, and Loch Leven, Kinross. *Proceedings of the Royal Society of Edinburgh B* **74**, 315–331.

Hoar, W. S. (1953). Control and timing of fish migration. *Biological Reviews* **28**, 437–452.

Hoar, W. S. (1976). Smolt transformation. Evolution, behaviour and physiology. *Journal of the Fisheries Research Board of Canada* **33**, 1234–1252.

Hokanson, K. E. F. (1977). Thermal requirements of percid fishes. *Journal of the Fisheries Research Board of Canada* **34**, 1524–1550.

Huet, M. (1972). *Textbook of Fish Culture*. Fishing News (Books) Ltd, London.

Marr, D. H. A. (1963). The influence of surface contour on the behaviour of trout alevins, *S. trutta* L. *Animal Behaviour* **11**, 412.

Marr, D. H. A. (1965). The influence of light and surface contour on the efficiency of the salmon embryo. *Report of the Challenger Society* **3**, No. 17.

Marr, D. H. A. (1966). Influence of temperature on the efficiency of growth of salmonid embryos. *Nature* **212**, 957–959.

Menzies, W. J. M. and Curtis, G. R. (1966). A new type of hatching tray. *Salmon Trout Magazine* **178**, 221–223.

Minaur, J. (1971). A simple electrically operated feeder for use in salmon rearing. *Journal of Fish Biology* **3**, 413–415.

Rawson, D. S. (1950). The grayling (*Thymallus signifer*) in Northern Saskatchewan. *Canadian Fish Culturist* **6**, 3–10.

Scott, W. B. and Crossman, E. J. (1977). Freshwater Fishes of Canada. *Fisheries Research Board of Canada Bulletin* **184**.

Stuart, T. A. (1953). Water currents through permeable gravels and their significance to spawning salmonids. *Nature* **172**, 407.

Stuart, T. A. (1962). The leaping behaviour of salmon and trout at falls and obstructions. *Freshwater and Salmon Fisheries Research* **28**, 1–46.

Thorpe, J. E. (1974a). The movement of brown trout, *Salmo trutta* L., in Loch Leven, Kinross, Scotland. *Journal of Fish Biology* **6**, 153–180.

Thorpe, J. E. (1974b). Trout and perch populations at Loch Leven, Kinross. *Proceedings of the Royal Society of Edinburgh B* **74**, 295–313.

Thorpe, J. E. and Morgan, R. I. G. (1978). Periodicity in Atlantic salmon smolt migration. *Journal of Fish Biology* **12**, 541–548.

Thorpe, J. E., Morgan, R. I. G., Ottaway, E. M. and Miles, M. S. (1980). Time of divergence of growth groups between potential 1 + and 2 + smolts among sibling Atlantic salmon. *Journal of Fish Biology* **17**, 13–22.

Thorpe, J. E. and Wankowski, J. W. J. (1979). Feed presentation and food particle size for juvenile Atlantic salmon, *Salmo salar*, L. *Finfish Nutrition and Fishfeed Technology* **1**, 501–513.

Wankowski, J. W. J. (1977). The role of prey size in the feeding behaviour and growth of juvenile Atlantic salmon (*Salmo salar* L.) Ph.D. Thesis, University of Stirling.

Wankowski, J. W. J. and Thorpe, J. E. (1979a). Spatial distribution and feeding in Atlantic salmon, *Salmo salar* L. juveniles. *Journal of Fish Biology* **14**, 239–248.

Wankowski, J. W. J. and Thorpe, J. E. (1979b). The role of food particle size in the growth of juvenile Atlantic salmon (*Salmo salar* L.). *Journal of Fish Biology* **14**, 351–370.

Ware, D. M. (1972). Predation by rainbow trout: the influence of hunger, prey density, and prey size. *Journal of the Fisheries Research Board of Canada* **291**, 1193–1201.

Ware, D. M. (1973). Risk of epibenthic prey to predation by rainbow trout (*Salmo gairdneri*). *Journal of the Fisheries Research Board of Canada* **30**, 787–797.

Chapter 13

Culture of Shellfish

P. R. Walne

Fisheries Experiment Station, Conwy, Wales

I. INTRODUCTION

This chapter deals with the culture of commercially important bivalve molluscs and decapod crustaceans. Other important groups of invertebrates which have been studied in culture, notably copepods, other small crustaceans and annelids, are beyond the scope of this book.

II. BIVALVES

A. General Considerations

A characteristic of bivalves, important for their culture, is that they continually pump sea water through their mantle cavity where it is filtered before being discharged back to the sea. They are dependent on this current for their food supply, for oxygen and for carrying away the products of respiration and excretion. One can unwittingly culture bivalves in apparently clean water which is devoid of food, contains only a fraction of the oxygen contained in normal sea water and includes an unhealthy concentration of excretory products.

The maintenance of bivalves largely revolves around solving the difficulties raised by their filtering behaviour. A recent review (Winter, 1973) showed that many bivalves filtered 0.5–10 l/h/g dry meat weight. Small bivalves filter proportionately more than large specimens and increased temperature will also increase filtration. A mussel 50 mm in length contains about 1 g dry meat, and requires between 1 and 10 litres of new water per hour. Mussels retain 3–10% of the oxygen in the sea water that passes through the mantle cavity (Bayne et al., 1976a). Excretion varies with size and condition, but according to Bayne et al. (1976b), a mussel of 1 g dry meat weight can excrete 0.074–1.9 mg ammonia/h. It has been suggested that the filtration rate of clams and mussels is reduced when the ammonia concentration reaches 3–7 mg/l.

The rate at which food is depleted in a static tank can be illustrated by calculating the food left when one 50 mm mussel is kept in a tank holding 1, 5 or 10 litres of sea water. Let us assume three rates at which the mussel filters the water, 0.5, 1.0 and 2.0 l/h. It may *pump* at a greater rate, but these are the rates at which it filters.

The filtration rate is given by the equations:

$$F = V.G.$$

$$G = \ln C_1/C_0$$

where F is the filtration rate in litres per hour, V is the volume per animal in litres, G is the grazing coefficient and C_0 and C_1 are the food in the water at the beginning and end of one hour respectively. Table I has been calculated from these formulae for a period of one hour. If the same data are used for 24 h, the bottom line becomes 30%, 9% and 1% respectively. A mussel in 10 litres of water will have little food left after 24 h if filtering at 1 to 2 l/h.

While some bivalves will have periods of inactivity, for practical purposes, it can be assumed that bivalves filter continuously and that the

Table I. The percentage of food left after 1 h when one mussel of 50 mm shell length is kept in three different volumes of water and filters at three different rates.

Volume	Filtration rate l/h		
	0.5	1.0	2.0
1	61	37	14
5	90	82	67
10	95	90	82

food concentration in the water will decline exponentially. Figure 1 shows the changing food concentration with a mussel kept in 10 litres of

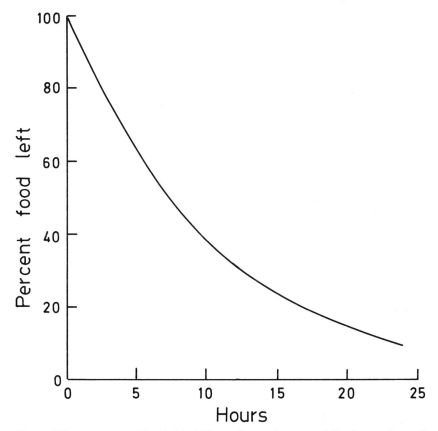

Fig. 1. The percentage of food left in 10 litres of water by a mussel filtering continuously at 1 litre per hour.

water. Even with this comparatively generous volume, half the food is gone after 7 h and half the day is spent with a food concentration less than a third of the original. At the same time, the oxygen content of the sea water will have been declining and ammonia and other excretory products will have been accumulating. Clearly, a good water supply is essential for bivalve culture.

B. Algal Culture

Bivalves fed in the laboratory are usually offered living unicellular algae as food and although some trials have been made with artificial foods, they are no substitute. There is a wide variation in food value between algal species and unfortunately, many that grow well in laboratory culture are poor foods. However, there are several species which appear to be generally satisfactory for bivalves and whose laboratory cultivation is well defined (Table II). For most feeding purposes at the Fisheries Experiment Station, Conwy, we find three species adequate for larval, spat and adult culture, they are the green flagellate *Tetraselmis suecica*, the yellow-brown flagellate *Isochrysis galbana* and the small diatom

Table II. Algae which are widely used as food for bivalves. The cell volumes give a comparative index of size.

Class and Species	Approximate cell volume (μm^3)
HAPTOPHYCEAE	
Dicrateria inornata Parke	21
Isochrysis galbana Parke	57
CHRYSOPHYCEAE	
Pavlova (Monochrysis) lutherii Droop	32
PRASINOPHYCEAE	
Tetraselmis suecica (Kylin) Butch.	335
Pyramimonas virginica	30
BACILLARIOPHYCEAE	
Skeletonema costatum (Greville) Cleve	170
Chaetoceros calcitrans (Paulsen) Takano	40
Cyclotella nana Hustedt	40

Chaetoceros calcitrans. It is likely that various combinations of these species will suit most purposes and most of the comments in the following paragraphs relate to them. Details of many methods of culturing algae, a variety of formulae for media, and details of various techniques are given by Stein (1973). At Conwy, we find that it is only necessary to cultivate bacteria-free algae for special experiments. For normal feeding, the presence of bacteria is not troublesome but it is important that the cultures are kept free from other algae and protozoa. Suitable media for all the species listed in Table II are given in Table III.

Erd-Schreiber medium is very satisfactory for maintenance since frequent sub-culturing of the cultures is not necessary. A soil extract is prepared by autoclaving together 1 litre of water and 1 kg of soil for about 30 min. After cooling, the extract is clarified by filtering or by decanting after a period of standing, sterilized again and allowed to stand. To prepare the medium, filtered sea water is sterilized by auto-claving. The required amounts of phosphate and nitrate are dissolved in a little hot fresh water and added to the cooled sea water. The soil extract is then added aseptically.

The preparation of soil extract is laborious and for routine culture, the artificial medium is easier to prepare. It contains more components than some species require but it is often convenient to use one medium for all the species being cultured. Filtered sea water is sterilized by autoclaving or pasteurization, and after cooling, the salts are added aseptically. Alternatively, the salts can be added to the filtered sea water and the prepared medium sterilized by passing it through a sterilizing filter. Better growth of *Tetraselmis* and *Isochrysis* is obtained if the salinity is adjusted to 25‰. *Chaetoceros* is a little more difficult to culture. We obtain the most successful results using a medium sterilized by autoclaving which is then allowed to stand for 48 h. The salinity should be adjusted to 15–25‰ and the enrichment should be double the quantities shown in Table III. In addition, 2 ml of a solution containing 4 g of sodium metasilicate ($Na_2 SiO_3.5H_2O$) per 100 ml should be added to each litre of medium. This gives an enrichment of 12 mg silica per litre. Further improved growth can also be obtained by increasing the level of iron.

Stock cultures are satisfactorily maintained in 250 ml of Erd-Schreiber medium in 500 ml flat-bottomed round flasks. Natural north light will provide adequate illumination unless rapidly growing cultures are wanted. For the preparation of food cultures, a 250 ml culture can be used as the inoculum for a 2 litre culture of either medium in a 4 or 5 litre conical flask. Sufficient of the original inoculum should be retained to inoculate a new stock culture, thus maintaining the cycle. The 2 litre culture should be given some artificial illumination by ordinary white

Table III. (1) The composition of Erd-Schreiber medium (2) The stock solutions for a general algal medium.

---

(1) Erd-Schreiber medium

$NaNO_3$	0.10 g
Na_2HPO_4	0.02 g
Soil extract	50 ml
Sea water	1 litre

(2) Stock enrichment solutions

    (i)

$FeCl_3$ $6H_2O$	2.60 g
$MnCl_2$ $4H_2O$	0.72 g
H_3BO_3	67.20 g
E.D.T.A. (Na salt)	90.00 g
NaH_2PO_4 $2H_2O$	40.00 g
$NaNO_3$	200.00 g
Trace metal solution	2.0 ml
Distilled water	to 2 litres

    1 ml is added to each litre of sea water

    (ii)   The trace metal solution has the following composition

$ZnCl_2$	2.1 g
$CoCl_2$ $6H_2O$	2.0 g
$(NH_4)_6Mo_7O_{24}$ $4H_2O$	0.9 g
$CuSO_4$ $5H_2O$	2.0 g
Distilled water	to 100 ml

    It is necessary to acidify this solution with HCL to obtain a clear liquid

    (iii)   Vitamin stock solution

B_{12}	10 mg
B_1 (Thiamine)	200 mg
Distilled water	to 200 ml

    10 ml is added to each 100 litres of sea water

---

fluorescent strip lighting in order to promote rapid growth. This culture is suitable for feeding directly to larvae or small spat where the requirements for food are small. We have found 1 litre and 2 litre Roux flasks very satisfactory for small quantities of rapidly growing culture for larval and spat trials. They are readily autoclaved and can be closed with a cotton wool plug or a silicone bung drilled for an aeration line. Standing in a shallow water bath (for cooling) in front of a white or cool white fluorescent strip light gives excellent illumination. Aeration should control the pH at 7.9–8.0. It is easy to remove aseptically a proportion of the culture when required and replace with fresh media. Thus the cultures are run on a semi-continuous basis and a daily harvest of 25–33% of the total volume can be obtained. Under these conditions, the three major species used at Conwy should reach the following cell densities:

Isochrysis galbana   10 000–15 000 cells per μl
Chaetoceros calcitrans   20 000–40 000 cells per μl
Tetraselmis suecica   1 000– 1 500 cells per μl

The lower concentration is about the lowest that we find acceptable for feeding and the higher concentration is reached or exceeded by many cultures.

For larger quantities, more elaborate systems are required. A method based on 20 litre round flasks has been used for many years at Conwy (Walne, 1974). In recent years, we have obtained an average weekly yield per flask of: *Isochrysis galbana* (at 10 000 cells/μl) 20–30 litres, *Tetraselmis suecica* (at 1000 cells/μl) 35–45 litres. To obtain these yields, the flasks are continually illuminated, cooled to about 20°C, aerated with an air/CO_2 mixture and in some cases, mechanically stirred as well. They are run on a semi-continuous basis and aeration, medium and harvesting lines are regularly steam sterilized. The quantities of algae required for culturing bivalves of various sizes are discussed later.

C. Sea-water Systems

The sea water requirement of all except the smallest bivalves is considerable. Adult bivalves the size of oysters or mussels are much more easily studied where a plentiful supply of raw sea water is continuously available from the sea, although it is possible to study smaller numbers using a recirculation system. Borehole sea water, or that obtained from sub-beach filters, has the disadvantage that the phytoplankton has been removed and all food has to be provided by cultured algae.

With raw sea water, the pipe runs should be as short as possible and generally the water should be used soon after collection. Continuous pumping is ideal since it minimizes storage but with an estuarine source, it may only be possible to pump at some stages of the tide. For bivalve culture, especially breeding and larval culture, the seawater must be very clean. Any initial holding tank and the pipes leading from the tank to the laboratory should be cleansed regularly. In summer, at Conwy, the storage tank and pipes are cleaned on a 14-day schedule, the tanks being sprayed with a hypochlorite solution and the pipes rodded.

It is generally best to filter the water when culturing bivalve larvae and early spat. For large quantities, an all-plastic plate or candle filter using diatomite as a filter-aid gives good results. Small quantities may be filtered through cellulose or glass filter papers, membrane filters or disposable filter candles. The first portion of water should be rejected. A very fine porosity is not required as the aim is to reduce the number of particles over 2 μm in size and largely eliminate those over 5 μm.

For heating small quantities of water, an electric system is usually the most satisfactory, with a glass or titanium-sheathed immersion heater and thermostat in a header tank. For larger quantities, indirect heating through a heat exchanger may be cheaper. It is less easy to obtain fine control from the latter in conditions of variable flow, due to the time taken for the heat exchanger to warm up or cool down. Discharging into a header tank, which contains electric heating, for final temperature control will provide water with a more even temperature. Water will supersaturate with air if it is heated rapidly. This does not seem to harm embryos, larvae or adult bivalves, but difficulties can be encountered with small spat. A large air bubble accumulates in the mantle cavity, the spat are unable to free themselves, and many may die. The remedy is either to allow the water to trickle down a filter column containing plastic rings or spacers, or better still, to aerate vigorously with fine bubbles in a column or tank before use.

Recirculation systems requiring continuous treatment of the water have not been used for bivalves at Conwy. Their use would pose the normal problems (see Chapters 1 and 3) with the additional difficulty of avoiding the loss of the unicellular algae used for food. Percolating filters, pressure filters and foam towers are all likely to remove the algae and other particulate food from the water.

D. Culture of Adults

Adult bivalves may be grown in tanks as breeding stock or for various experimental purposes. If the animals are at normal temperatures for growth and gonad development, then a good test of the environment is whether such activities occur. It is difficult to prevent loss of tissue weight.

Ostrea edulis kept at a breeding temperature of 18–21 °C with a flow rate of 0.6–2.5 litres of raw sea water per oyster per hour, plus supplementary feeding of 2 cells of algae per μl, decreased in dry flesh weight from 1.61 to 1.20 g over six weeks (Gabbott and Walker, 1971). In another experiment, *O. edulis* was kept at a flow rate of 1.2 litres of raw sea water per hour, with an enrichment of 10 cells per μl of *Tetraselmis*. If the algal culture had a cell concentration of 10^3 cells per μl, this was equivalent to feeding 288 ml of algal culture per oyster per day. There was a decline in dry meat, but it was less than that experienced by control oysters which received no supplement. It was noticeable that many of the broods of larvae liberated by oysters receiving this extra food were liberated sooner, and the larvae grew at an enhanced rate and provided more spat than the broods from the control stock (Helm *et al.*, 1973). It is a general experience at Conwy that stock which have been conditioned for a long period do not produce good quality larvae.

For breeding purposes, the period of conditioning prior to the first liberation of larvae is dependent upon the time of year and initial condition of the stock. Between December and May at Conwy, it varies between 22 to 71 days for *O. edulis*, and is about 28 days for *Crassostrea gigas*. From June onwards it is only a few days. For *O. edulis* we usually obtain about 10 broods of larvae per 100 adults and we recover $0.5–0.7 \times 10^6$ larvae at each liberation.

Since adult bivalves need a good deal of algal culture (or raw sea water) to keep them in good condition, it is worth ensuring that the conditions of water flow in relation to the animals ensure the maximum uptake of particles. We use rectangular tanks fed by a splash jet at one end with an overflow fed from the bottom of the tank at the opposite end. The bivalves are laid on a plastic mesh tray held at about mid-water depth. With 50 oysters in a 90 litre tank, more than 80% of particles are removed with flow rates up to 60 ml/min. per oyster. Less than 2% of particles settle on the tank bottom. When the tank is cleansed, the tray is lifted out causing little disturbance to the animals.

Burrowing bivalves may require a substrate because the adductor muscles of mature animals are not strong enough to hold the shells together for long periods of time. Bivalves are very sensitive to light and to vibration, and the tanks should be quiet and dark. In a busy laboratory, bivalves spend a high proportion of their time closed.

Bivalves can carry either on their shells or in their bodies, pests and diseases of commercially important bivalves. In some countries, a licence is required for the import, deposit or holding of exotic species of marine molluscs in open or closed sea water systems. A licence may also be required for the transfer of marine molluscs to pest-free areas from specified areas where pests occur. In these circumstances, quarantine measures are required. Details can be found in Spencer *et al.* (1977).

E. Spawning and Fertilization

There are many ways of inducing spawning in oviparous species. Quite different methods often suit individual species, circumstances and experimenters.

The induction of natural spawning is often accomplished by holding the animals in a tray fed for alternate periods with warm and cold water. Additional stimuli may be provided by adding a suspension of sperm obtained from a sacrificed animal. Mechanical shock such as rattling in a bucket or pricking the adductor muscle can be effective inducements. Once spawning has begun, it is remarkably persistent and spawning individuals can be removed to separate vessels filled with several litres of filtered sea water where they will continue to liberate gametes. Sometimes animals, although ripe, cannot be stimulated to spawn. Small quantities of gametes for research purposes can be obtained by drilling through the shell and sucking small quantities from the gonad with a pipette. Larger quantities are obtained by opening the animal, slitting the gonad and gently squeezing the gametes into sea water. Some authors have either injected the animal with potassium salts or held the gonad in ammonia solution to hasten the liberation of gametes. After spawning, the eggs are allowed to settle in 10 cm of water for about an hour after which the supernatant is discarded.

Fertilization of *C. gigas* is normally accomplished by mixing about 10 ml of sperm with 1 litre of egg suspension and allowing to settle for 1–2 h before discarding the bulk of the water. The fertilized eggs are finally cleansed by passing them through a 124 μm sieve into 125 litres of filtered sea water at 24°C. Fertilized eggs will develop to the D-larval stage within 24 h. We find with *C. gigas* that we obtain equally good results with ratios of 100 to 1000 sperm per egg, and egg densities of 10–100/ml. Poor fertilizations can be correlated with increase in age of gametes. Crosses made within 1 h of release will give a good yield of normal D-larvae but delays of 3 h and 5 h reduce the yields to 50% and 25%. Some males and females consistently produce poor yields of D-larvae. To avoid poor yields and possibly reduced vigour of larvae and spat, it is good practice to use eggs and sperm from a number of oysters in pooled fertilizations.

The early embryonic stages are easily influenced by the environment. For example, the proportion of *C. gigas* eggs which develop into D-larvae have been used as a bioassay test to measure the distribution of industrial effluents in north-west United States. Recent work at Conwy has used this technique routinely to bioassay water quality in the hatchery. Development of replicate samples in an artificial sea water (Zaroogian *et al.*, 1969) has been used as a standard. These tests have shown that the water at Conwy shows seasonal and occasional fluctuations in quality for both embryonic development of *C. gigas* and the larval development of *O. edulis*. This aspect of culture is developed further in Chapter 3.

F. Culture of Larvae

Bivalve larvae can be grown in a wide variety of sizes of vessels. For small-scale experimental purposes, hard-glass beakers holding 1–5 litres of water are excellent. Smaller glass vessels, for example 100 ml boiling tubes, yield good results. Larger glass vessels also yield good results, but are heavy and cumbersome. For this reason, larger vessels are now invariably of plastic.

The normal behaviour of oyster and many other bivalve larvae is to swim vertically up in the water column and then sink down for a period before again swimming upwards. To accommodate this behaviour, it is advantageous to have the culture vessel taller than its diameter. To take an extreme case, we have had excellent results in vertical 10 cm diameter glass tubes 180 cm long. Square or rectangular vessels are not satis-factory as the larvae, particularly as they mature, collect in large numbers in the corners. Vessels the shape of a bucket are satisfactory. Not all plastic vessels are non-toxic (Chapter 6) and tests should be made to compare the growth, survival and metamorphosis of replicate samples of larvae grown in glass and in the untested plastic vessels. Vessels made of pure plastic such as white polyethylene, polypropylene, clear polystyrene or polycarbonate are usually suitable. Moulded fibreglass vessels are widely used especially in large-scale culture.

Sea water for larval culture must be prepared carefully if consistent results are to be obtained. Some workers obtain good results if the natural food is left in the water, but the value of this varies with place and time. If the natural phytoplankton is not very abundant, or the species unsuit-able, it is better to filter the water and start again. At Conwy, all water for larvae is filtered. Feeding by filter feeders depends on the particle density in the water and if many of the particles are not food items, then food intake and hence growth will be reduced. An excessive degree of filtering is not required and may indeed be harmful as it may lead to an unbalanced bacterial flora which will result in a higher density of bacteria than if the original inoculum had been larger. A method which removes most particles over 2 μm will be satisfactory. Where large quantities of sea water are required, plate or candle filters using diatomite as a filter-aid, give good results. For smaller quantities, GFC filter paper, filter candles and small disposable fibreglass filter tubes are appropriate.

The filtering method should be either cheap enough for disposal or suitable for thorough cleansing at the end of each day's run. Removal of the collected material should be by washing and scrubbing, followed by either heat sterilization or cold sterilization in hypochlorite. If the organic material is left on the filtering medium, it will be the site of intensive bacterial activity and these bacteria will contaminate the water when the filter is used the next day. It should be the aim to keep bacteria numbers low throughout the sea water system. Natural sea water normally only contains a few hundred bacteria per ml, and this is the number which should be present in the treated water used for larval rearing. The avoidance of the build up of bacteria will greatly lessen the likelihood of disease among the larval cultures.

After filtration, we pass the water through an ultraviolet sterilizer which consists of a 44 W low-pressure mercury discharge tube in a quartz envelope. The outer jacket is made of hard glass. Units of this type have a fairly large through-put. Germicidal tubes can also be used over static pans of water or over a glass trough through which the water flows slowly. Alternatively, tubes of this type can be made into a flow-through sterilizer by sealing the discharge tube into an outer PVC jacket and passing the water through the annular space between the two.

Artificial sea waters, either from commercial sources or made up to a known fomulation, have been used for culturing larvae for short periods. The problems that may arise over longer periods are unknown. In general, they offer no special advantages and for longer term studies, the quantities required generally make the use of natural sea water more attractive.

(1) Starting a larval culture

Taking either a batch of D-larvae arising from an earlier fertilization, or a brood of recently liberated larvae, the first step is to wash them and then estimate the number of larvae. The batch of larvae is passed through a larger mesh sieve to remove large particles and then on to a smaller mesh to retain the larvae: 35 µm mesh for the 70 µm larvae of *C. gigas* and 90 µm mesh for the 170–180 µm larvae of *O. edulis*. The larvae are thoroughly washed on the sieve with clean sea water, rinsed for not more than 30 s in 3 ppm chlorine, rinsed again in clean sea water, and finally suspended in a graduated cylinder. The larval suspension can then be thoroughly dispersed by a stirrer made from a perforated plastic plate attached to the end of a rod. Three 0.5 or 1.0 ml samples are withdrawn with an automatic pipette and counted on a squared slide. The appropriate quantity of suspension to give the required number of larvae can then be withdrawn from the cylinder. For *O. edulis*, a larval density of 1000–1500/litre is satisfactory. For *C. gigas*, where the larvae are much smaller, 7000–10 000/litre can be used.

(2) Stirring and aeration

Larvae reared to maturity in small vessels have a better growth rate if some agitation is provided. Successful early experiments in the 1920s and 1930s on the culture of bivalve larvae and many other marine invertebrates were made with the aid of plunger plates. Glass discs with a diameter a little less than that of the culture vessel oscillated at intervals through the water column. Although now largely discarded, it is possible that the technique could be useful for some species adapted to vigorous water movement such as on open coasts.

Compressed air is very easy to use and we find it beneficial in most work with larvae. A series of trials (Helm and Spencer, 1972) showed that in 1-litre beakers, aeration rates from a capillary jet below 5 and over 12.5 litre/h led to reduced growth rates of *O. edulis* larvae. Larger vessels had their own characteristics, with larvae grown in the better aeration conditions showing an earlier development towards metamorphosis. In small squat vessels, aeration can lead to the larvae concentrating in one place on the bottom. In tall vessels, like test-tubes, very gentle aeration from a jet gives excellent mixing.

(3) Water change
It is not absolutely necessary to change the water during the rearing of bivalve larvae. The writer was able to obtain several hundred to over a thousand spat in 1 litre beakers in trials testing the effect of antibiotics (Walne, 1958). In those experiments, the larvae were grown rather slowly and at low food levels. Now larvae are grown more rapidly (and probably nearer to their normal rate in the sea) and water changes are advantageous. It is our usual practice to transfer the larvae to clean water every 48 h. With small vessels, this can be accomplished by tipping the culture through a plastic sieve made from a short section of PVC pipe with a nylon mesh stuck across one end with PVC adhesive. A series of similar sieves allows particles larger than the larvae as well as debris, faeces and small moribund larvae to be screened out. The larvae are well washed, rinsed for not more than 30 s in 3 ppm chlorine, rinsed in sea water and returned to a clean vessel filled with freshly filtered and sterilized sea water. It may be necessary to adjust the salinity. For *O. edulis*, we use the ambient salinity (28–34‰); for *C. gigas*, it is adjusted to 25‰ with filtered tap water which has been aerated overnight.

Part of the value of a water change is to reduce the build-up of an undesirable bacterial flora. It would appear that a dense bacterial flora can have an undesirable effect on larvae as well as specific species or strains which can cause rapid mortality. Antibiotics and other controlling agents for bacteria, for example Sulmet, were frequently used in larval cultures. In recent years, it would seem that their use has declined. This decline has been brought about by the increasing recognition of the dangers of using antibiotics routinely and by their cost, coupled with the recognition that good standards of hygiene in the culture laboratory and in obtaining sea water, made their use unnecessary. For a number of years, we used to add routinely a mixture of 50 units penicillin G and 0.05 mg streptomycin per ml and this dosage may be useful elsewhere. It is now several years since we used any antibiotics at Conwy for larval rearing.

(4) Feeding and larval numbers

The maximum growth rate of many larvae is obtained when they are kept in a cell density of about 100 cells per μl of *Isochrysis galbana*. To keep them at this level with daily feeding, it is necessary to have the larvae sufficiently sparse so that they do not significantly alter the concentration of food in the water from one day to the next. There is only a small reduction growth when larvae are kept at 50 cells per μl. Below this level, growth is increasingly affected by the diminished food supply. It is therefore possible to cultivate larvae at about their maximum growth rate when the food level oscillates daily between about 100 cells and 50 cells per μl. Larval concentrations are fixed on this basis. It is a mistake to suppose that the problem of larger concentrations of larvae can be overcome by increasing the food level fed. This leads to wasteful feeding or even to inactivity and to unfavourable physical conditions in the sea water.

We find that three species of algae are sufficient for most work. The following schedule shows the concentrations in cells per μl to which the larval cultures are raised daily by the addition of sufficient algae:

		Chaetoceros	*Isochrysis*	*Tetraselmis*
C. gigas	To day 10	50	50	
	After day 10	33	33	3.3
O. edulis	(i)		50	5
	(ii)	33	33	3.3

Small *C. gigas* larvae cannot take *Tetraselmis*. The two rations for *O. edulis* are alternatives; the first was used for many years. When *C. gigas* larvae reach 120–140 μm, they are large enough to take *Tetraselmis*.

Experiments have shown that as a general rule, larvae regulate their feeding rate and food intake according to the total volume of algae per unit volume of water rather than to the number of particles. This means that if it is wished to construct another diet by using a different species or combination of species, a suitable feeding level is given by providing a total volume of algae approximately equivalent to 100 cells of *Isochrysis* per μl. Any alga varies in cell volume from time to time and we take this density of *Isochrysis* as equivalent to 5000–6000 μm^3 algal material per μl.

(5) Settlement

The time of settlement is critical to bivalves because at that period, a habitat is selected to which the animal is likely to be restricted for the rest of its life. Oysters are unusual in cementing themselves permanently to the substrate at the time of metamorphosis. Other species use a more flexible connection in the form of a byssus which may be used for a few weeks only or which may persist throughout life.

Laboratory studies have shown a variety of factors to encourage the settlement of larvae. In practice, many species of well grown bivalve larvae will metamorphose on the side or bottom of the vessel without any special provisions being made. We have found that the burrowing species *Venerupis* and *Mercenaria* metamorphose at the bottom of a bin, *Mytilus* and *Choromytilus* will fix to the bottom and side of a bin, and species of oysters will attach preferentially to collector sheets of plastic (e.g. PVC) or glass with a matt surface either lying on the bottom of the tank or suspended in the water column. Shells of oyster, mussel or cockle are also good collectors and may be suspended in the water on a plastic thread passing through a small hole drilled in each shell. The shells must be clean or the culture will become fouled. The artificial collector can be made more attractive by painting with an aqueous extract of the flesh of the same species of oyster and allowed to dry before placing in the culture tanks. Growing larvae appear to be indifferent to whether they are kept in the light or the dark, but at the time of settlement, some illumination stimulates metamorphosis.

Species attached by a byssus can be readily removed from the culture container, by careful brushing or by a jet of water, and subsequently cultured in sieves (see below). Species which cement to the substrate present a different problem, the answer to which depends on their subsequent fate. If only small spat are required for experimental purposes, it is convenient to allow them to remain attached to a matt-surfaced glass plate which can be conveniently moved about and allows microscopic examination of the live animals. If the spat are to be grown to a larger size, then they can be removed from their settlement surface within 24 h of metamorphosis by scraping with a sharp razor blade and cultured in sieves (see below). If the spat are allowed to remain attached to the substrate, it may be necessary to thin them carefully to avoid overcrowding.

G. Culture of Spat

The principles of culturing very young spat are similar to those adopted for larvae, the main difference being that as spat are larger, their requirements are correspondingly greater. Temperature and salinity will depend on the species concerned. If it is a species which has not been previously studied, it would be as well to use the average conditions found in its natural environment at the appropriate time of the year. We use about 24°C for both species of oysters and for clams and reduce the salinity to about 25‰ for *C. gigas*.

Unattached spat are conveniently kept in boxes fitted with a mesh base. Many that we use are polystyrene boxes 34 × 20 × 12.5 cm deep from which the bottom has been removed and 210 μm nylon mesh bases glued on in place. These boxes are partially immersed in a glass-fibre tank containing filtered sea water enriched with 5 cells per μl of *Tetraselmis*. The water is recirculated by a centrifugal pump which continuously distributes the water through the boxes via splash jets. These should provide a flow of about 2 ml per spat per minute. Spat density in the trays should not exceed 20 per cm² and will need reducing as the spat grow. A useful research sized model which has been used extensively at Conwy uses a 50 litre polypropylene tank holding four polystyrene trays with a base size of 17.5 × 11.5 cm. The water is circulated by an aquarium plastic centrifugal pump which sucks 4 l/min of water from the bottom of the tank and delivers it through a perforated distribution pipe to the trays (Walne and Spencer, 1974). Good growth is obtained if the vessel is stocked with 20 spat per litre and fed sufficient *Tetraselmis* culture daily to restore the concentration to 10 cells per μl.

Burrowing species will grow in these systems but they will grow much better if allowed to bury in a substrate appropriate to the species. This is not difficult to arrange on a small scale but on a large scale, the problems of cleansing and changing the substrate have not been solved. Whatever system is adopted, it is recommended that the water is changed twice a week. If high densities of spat and feeding are used, then more frequent changing will be beneficial. The spat should be well cleansed but not so vigorously as to damage the shell margin. Cleansing with hypochlorite is not necessary. As the spat get larger, their requirements for food and clean water rise rapidly, and except in specific experiments, economy dictates that they should be kept in natural sea water at ambient temperature. This may be achieved by keeping them in trays through which fresh sea water is continuously passed. Better still is to place them in shallow trays or bags made with a mesh just small enough to retain the animals, and either hang the containers from a raft or attach them to racks fixed to the seabed.

(1) Food supply for spat

After metamorphosis, the quantity of food required by bivalves increases rapidly if a reasonable rate of growth is to be maintained. We find that *Tetraselmis suecica* is an adequate food for several species of bivalves.

Although not nutritionally the most valuable, it is the most reliable in culture, and can be produced in large quantities. To obtain a 1–3 mg increase in live weight, it is necessary to feed an oyster spat 10^6 cells of *Tetraselmis* over a 21-day period. Put another way, to grow to a live weight of 10 mg in 21 days after settlement, a spat will need to eat 10^7 cells. As a good culture of *Tetraselmis* will contain 1500 cells per μl, this 21-day ration can be obtained from 6.7 ml of culture. This is about the feeding rate that we normally employ, but it could be improved by feeding more in the third week. Investigations of food requirements have shown that in oysters, an excellent ration over 7 days is 5×10^6 cells *Tetraselmis* per mg wet weight of spat at the beginning of the week. Thus, a spat weighing 5 mg at the beginning of the week will require 25×10^6 cells spread over the week. This will be given by a ration of 2.4 ml of culture containing 1.5×10^6 cells *Tetraselmis* per ml per day per spat.

Although the concentration of food can change considerably during the day, it should not rise too high to lead to wasteful feeding. We find that the peak should not exceed 10–15 cells per μl. About 20 spat per litre of water is satisfactory at the smaller sizes, but as they grow, feeding may be required several times a day if the recommended peak concentration is not to be exceeded. If an excessive frequency of feeding is required, the problem can be eased by reducing the number of spat per litre.

III. DECAPOD CRUSTACEA

A. Holding Adults

The methods which are used for the storage of lobsters are suitable for storing most crustaceans. Since these animals are expensive, simple but effective methods have been well described. The major requirements are water of the correct salinity, a reduced water temperature to increase the solubility of oxygen and to reduce consumption by the lobsters, and a system which does not include heavy metals in its construction. The reduced temperature used should be equivalent to the average winter temperature normally experienced by the species. It is suggested that 1 kg of lobsters requires 5.3 litres of well aerated sea water per hour at 4.4°C, 10.5 litres at 12.8°C and 15.8 litres at 17.2°C. This water can be either in a flow-through system or recirculated and well oxygenated. It can also be either natural or artificial sea water.

A simple formulation for artificial sea water which has been found suitable for lobsters is:

NaCl	23.51 g
$MgSO_4.7H_2O$	5.74 g
$MgCl_2.6H_2O$	4.55 g
$CaCl_2.2H_2O$	1.19 g
KCl	0.56 g
Water	1 litre

This gives a salinity of about 30‰.

Lobsters and other crustaceans kept in this way should have their claws bound to stop fighting and should not be fed because the contamination of the water will increase the oxygen demand. In a recirculation system, there will still be a gradual accumulation of excretory products which will have to be kept in check with biological and mechanical filters (Ayres and Wood, 1977; Wood and Ayres, 1977) or with periodic changes of water. Such a system is suitable for holding crustaceans for short periods but is not sufficient for normal growth.

B. Breeding

Larval or juvenile crustaceans may be obtained from female specimens which have already been fertilized and in the case of many decapods, are already carrying eggs. Penaeid prawns do not carry their eggs and the great majority of studies on them have been based on catching ripe impregnated females from the wild which will usually spawn at night one or two days after capture.

To avoid egg loss from decapods, good aeration and water flow must be maintained. The sign of unduly stressed conditions is often a steady loss of eggs so that by the time they are ripe for hatching few are left. Eggs can become infected with a variety of organisms. These difficulties suggest that there is a case for removing the eggs from the female and rearing them separately in more aseptic conditions. In practice, this seems to be less successful than leaving the job to the female whose continual attention, particularly in the removal of dead eggs and in continuous aeration, is better than more artificial methods.

Successful attempts have been made with the removed eggs of *Palaemon serratus* which had passed through 50–75% of their development. Development was successfully completed when the eggs were held in a mesh sieve through which a water current was maintained by an air lift (Wickins, 1972a). Another technique successful for some crabs involves removing the egg mass from the female by cutting the strands from the pleopods and then dissociating the strands with glass needles into groups of 100–1000 eggs. These groups are then washed in clean water and placed in compartments measuring 9 cm² in a plastic box. The box is then placed on a shaker in an incubator. These species have a rapid development and hatch within a week or two (Costlow and Bookhout, 1960). The technique may be less successful with species which incubate for 6–9 months.

Mating is difficult to achieve in the laboratory because the right physical environment must be provided and the male and female must be introduced at the right time to avoid fighting and cannibalism. If a population will live together, fertilized females can be isolated as required. If not, a male and female have to be introduced at the correct stage of the moulting cycle. In most decapods, the female is receptive soon after moulting while still soft; the male has to be in the hard-shelled condition. Considerable success with *Macrobrachium* (a large freshwater prawn) has been achieved by introducing a hard-shelled male to an isolated female within a few hours of the latter moulting. In some crabs, the male recognizes when the female is about to moult and keeps in attendance. The female will not spawn until her exoskeleton becomes hard and even then, spawning may be delayed. In the lobster, spawning may be delayed for several months. Fertilized females can be selected in the field since they may be recognized by the presence of a plug in the mouth of the oviduct in crabs and lobsters, spermatophores in the female thelycum in penaeid prawns, and spermatophores deposited near the base of the fifth pair of pereiopods in carideans.

C. Hatching

Hatching of the eggs occurs at night in many species which incubate their eggs. The larvae are negatively geotactic and positively phototactic to unidirectional light. These behavioural traits may prevent predation by larger animals in the hatching tank. The larvae are attracted to the vicinity of the overflow and are separated from the waste water by the water flowing through a sieve kept partially submerged in a bowl of water.

D. Larval Culture

The larvae of all decapod crustaceans have some common characteristics which make them difficult to culture. They are all planktonic and at some stage go through a metamorphosis to the adult form. To maintain an equable and appropriate environment, the food has to be kept suspended in the body of the water. Many larvae have delicate spines and setae which are damaged by contact with surfaces. The water should be free of small particles which might be trapped on such setae. A further problem is that in the soft condition immediately after moulting, the larvae are subject to cannibalism by other larvae. This can be overcome or alleviated by growing the larvae in isolation or by ensuring that food particles are abundant in the water.

In decapods, there is variation in the proportion of development which takes place within the egg and the proportion in the planktonic phase. In the Euphausiaceae and in the Penaeidae, the eggs hatch into a nauplius larva which moults several times but does not feed. This moults into a protozoea larva which after several moults, changes into a mysis larva before developing into the final adult form. At the other extreme, in the lobster, most of these stages take place in the egg and only four planktonic stages precede the bottom-living form. It seems likely that most species with eggs hatching at an early stage produce larvae requiring algal food initially while those which hatch later produce fully carnivorous larvae. Decapod larvae can be reared in small or large containers, in still or moving water, in recirculated or running water, depending on the requirements of the investigator and the characteristics of the larvae. Compartmented transparent plastic boxes can be used and are obtainable in a wide variety of sizes. Small versions are available as divided petri-dishes or tissue culture equipment, while larger trays are stocked by general merchants. The water has to be changed every day or two and new food introduced. The technique seems particularly suitable for crab larvae (Costlow and Bookhout, 1959). One litre hard glass beakers are suitable for caridean prawns (Reeve, 1969a, b; Wickins, 1972b). Twenty to fifty larvae per beaker are suitable densities. Some stirring from gentle aeration is helpful and a food level of 5–20 *Artemia* per ml is a satisfactory level of food (see below).

These techniques in static water can be readily adapted to provide a continual exchange of water. The solid base of the culture vessel is removed and replaced with a suitable mesh. The container is then floated in a larger tank which is stirred or aerated. The turbulence ensures an exchange of water through the mesh base and the water in the tank can be continually changed. Suitable small containers can be made from short lengths of plastic tube. Care in selecting a suitable mesh is required since some species of larvae can become entangled during the moult. Larger containers may be required for delicate species or when large numbers of post-larvae are required. Cultures in 60–70 litres of water in plastic bins have given good results with *Palaemon serratus* (Wickins, 1972a). It made no difference whether flowing or standing water was used. About 50% of the larvae reached post-larvae if the tank was stocked with 75–100 larvae per litre. At 200/l, the yield fell to 10–20 post-larvae/l.

The Hughes bin is a rearing system specifically developed for lobster larvae (Hughes *et al.*, 1974). This is a cylindrical fibreglass bin with a domed bottom. It holds 38 litres of water which overflows through a central standpipe made from PVC and which is surrounded by a screen to retain the larvae. Water is returned from the reservoir at 10 l/min through a specially constructed boss at the base of the standpipe. Outlets drilled into the boss return the water tangentially so that there is a circular and an upward flow to the water in the bin. It is possible to rear 3000 to 5000 lobster larvae per bin. A method which has been used very successfully in the past is the plunger jar (Rice and Williamson, 1970). Circulation in the culture vessel is maintained by a plate alternately rising and falling through the water column. Traditionally, the plate is moved by a counter-balancing tipping bucket.

(1) Food for Larvae
The early larvae of the Penaeidae and Euphausiaceae require planktonic algae as food. Species of *Tetraselmis*, *Skeletonema*, *Phaeodactylum* and *Cylindrotheca* have given satisfactory results for Penaeidae at 50–450 cells per μl depending on larval density. It is also usual to use a dense culture of phytoplankton along with *Artemia* in the culture of *Macrobrachium* larvae; *Isochrysis* and *Tetraselmis* are suitable species. In this case, the alga is probably not a food item for the *Macrobrachium* but may improve water quality and keep the *Artemia* in good condition while awaiting capture by the predator (Maddox and Manzi, 1977; Wickins, 1972b).

Otherwise, decapod larvae are carnivorous, and feeding is therefore a matter of providing an adequate level of live or dead food in suspension in the water column. Freshly hatched *Artemia* is widely used since compared with other cultured foods, it is readily available from stored dry cysts. The advantage over a dead food which can also be stored, is that it remains live and free from decomposition (until it dies) in the culture vessel. However, it is not entirely free from trouble. Different strains with various origins are on the market and these differ in food value from time to time. It is also possible that brine shrimps from the same source may vary in value because of natural variations in conditions. Examples have been given by Bookhout and Costlow (1970) and by Wickins (1972c). In the case discussed by the latter author, the early stages of *Palaemon* grew well but as metamorphosis approached, the larvae became deformed. The problem could be overcome by feeding the brine shrimps on cultured algae before offering them to the prawn larvae.

The consumption of *Artemia* nauplii by *Palaemon* larvae rises from 20 to 400 per day during larval development (Reeve, 1969b). The mysis stage of a penaeid will consume 18–75 nauplii per day. Lobster larvae consume at least eight adult *Artemia* per day (Carlberg and Van Olst, 1976). If brine shrimp nauplii are not fed, they will be using their food reserves and hence be less nutritious. For example, there is a 20% loss in weight between the first and each of the next two instars. Nauplii should be hatched and used daily if they are not fed with algae. *Artemia* may not be suitable for some decapod larvae, in which case other readily obtainable live species can be tested, for example, rotifers, mollusc larvae, polychaetes and their larvae and freshly caught plankton. Dead food, cut or crumbled to a suitable size, can be used. Chopped *Mytilus*, fish, egg yolk and deep frozen *Artemia* and mysids have all proved successful. They are not as good as live food because they are more difficult to keep in suspension, and if not eaten quickly will start to decompose. Further rations can be added every few hours by mechanical means (Serfling *et al.*, 1974), but it is not practicable to keep them frozen while in the hoppers. Studies are in progress on encapsulated diets for crustacean larvae but the work is not yet sufficiently advanced for them to be used routinely.

E. Juvenile and Adult Culture

After metamorphosis, the adult form is assumed but it may be several moults before adult habits are fully taken up. For example, it may be a little while before prawns accept all their food off the bottom of the tank rather than some from the water column. A period of weaning may be required.

The systems used for the culture of juveniles are essentially the same as those used for adults. The differences come from question of scale and the greater acceptance of losses by cannibalism among juveniles than among adults. The ideal system, and one which is likely to lead to the greatest survival, is to keep each animal individually. This can be achieved with individual containers of adequate size, by aerating and changing the water periodically. This system is cumbersome if a number of animals have to be kept, and in experiments, it is difficult to ensure comparable conditions in each container. Lobsters have been kept by many experimenters in boxes or pots with a mesh base and which stand in a larger tank of water. The size of the container has to be increased as the animal grows, and it is advantageous to keep the mesh size as large as possible. In this way, waste food and faecal material more readily falls through into the circulation water. It is not necessary to handle the animals since daily servicing and routine changing of the water can be carried out without disturbance.

Some crustaceans, for example *Palaemon*, do not do well in compartments with mesh bases because appendages tangle with the mesh. Plastic compartments with a few holes drilled in the side to permit circulation are suitable and can also be used in feeding trials as food is not so readily lost. The success of community tanks depends very much on the species and the area offered to each animal. Five to fifty *Palaemon serratus* can be kept in a 25 litre tank at a constant level of mortality, but this increases rapidly at higher levels of stocking (Forster, 1970). Penaeid shrimps can be reared at high stocking densities giving a standing stock of 1.5–2.0 kg live weight per m². The useful space can be increased by providing shelves in the tank. For example, netting hung vertically or horizontal shelves will extend the area for prawns; a layer of shells on the bottom provides many niches for small lobsters.

Whichever system is used, the water must be changed periodically. With compartments standing in an outer tank, exchange will occur through the mesh if there is some turbulence in the water in the larger tank. This can be aided by using a syphonic overflow so that the water rises and falls a few centimetres in the compartments. The water in the outer tank or that in a community tank will either receive a continuous flow or periodic change of new water, or will be part of a recirculation system in which the water is continually treated to keep it in condition (see Chapter 3).

(1) Food for juveniles and adults
A very wide variety of foods will successfully rear decapods to adult size. For shrimps, prawns and lobsters, the flesh of bivalve molluscs is satisfactory provided that some crustacean flesh, for example shrimp, mysids, krill or shore crabs, is added periodically. The advantage of bivalve molluscs is that if they are freshly opened, the flesh will remain live in the water for some hours. Hence decomposition and the loss of natural juices which leads to fouling are considerably reduced. Dead fish or meat should be avoided. The size of the daily ration should be adjusted so that only a very small amount is left after 24 h. This is discarded and replaced by a new ration. Artificial diets are being developed for the commercial cultivation of prawns, shrimps and lobsters. Background research is revealing many of the dietary requirements of some decapods. Artificial diets are commercially convenient in that they have a standard composition, can be stored, and are easy to feed in automatic equipment. On a small-scale, they do not offer any growth or survival advantages over fresh foods. Several recent reviews discuss the composition of recent formulations (Forster, 1976; New, 1976 and Wickins, 1976).

IV. REFERENCES

Ayres, P. A. and Wood, P. C. (1977). The live storage of lobsters. *Laboratory Leaflet, MAFF Direct. Fish. Research, Lowestoft*, **37**.

Bayne, B. L., Thompson, R. J. and Widdows, J. (1976a). Physiology: I. Chapter 5. *In* "Marine Mussels: their Ecology and Physiology" (B. L. Bayne, ed.), 121–206. Cambridge University Press, Cambridge.

Bayne, B. L., Widdows, J. and Thompson, R. J. (1976b). Physiology: II. Chapter 6. *In* "Marine Mussels: their Ecology and Physiology" (B. L. Bayne, ed.), 207–260. Cambridge University Press, Cambridge.

Bookhout, C. G. and Costlow, J. D. (1970). Nutritional effects of *Artemia* from different locations on larval development of crabs. *Helgoländer wiss. Meeresunters* **20**, 435–442.

Carlberg, J. M. and Van Olst, J. C. (1976). Brine shrimp (*Artemia salina*) consumption by the larval stages of the American lobster (*Homarus americanus*) in relation to food density and water temperature. *Proceedings of the Seventh Annual Meeting World Mariculture Society, San Diego*, 379–389.

Costlow, J. D. and Bookhout, C. G. (1959). The larval development of *Callinectes sapidus* Rathburn reared in the laboratory. *Biological Bulletin*, **116**, 373–396.

Costlow, J. D. and Bookhout, C. G. (1960). A method for developing brachyuran eggs *in vitro*. *Limnology and Oceanography*, **5**, 212–215.

Forster, J. R. M. (1970). Further studies on the culture of the prawn, *Palaemon serratus* Pennant; with emphasis on the post-larval stages. *Fishery Investigations, London*, Ser. 2 **26**.

Forster, J. R. M. (1976). Studies on the development of compounded diets for prawns. *Proceedings of the First International Conference on Aquaculture Nutrition, Delaware*, 229–248.

Gabbott, P. A. and Walker, A. J. M. (1971). Changes in the condition index and biochemical content of adult oyster (*Ostrea edulis* L.) maintained under hatchery conditions. *Journal du Conseil permanent international pour l'Exploration de la Mer* **34**, 99–106.

Helm, M. M., Holland, D. H., and Stephenson, R. R. (1973). The effect of supplementary algal feeding of a hatchery breeding stock of *Ostrea edulis* L. on larval vigour. *Journal of the Marine Biological Association of the UK* **53**, 673–684.

Helm, M. M. and Spencer, B. E. (1972). The importance of the rate of aeration in hatchery cultures of the larvae of *Ostrea edulis* L. *Journal du Conseil permanent international pour l'exploration de la mer* **34**, 244–255.

Hughes, J. T., Shleser, R. A. and Tchobanoglous, G. (1974). A rearing tank for lobster larvae and other aquatic species. *Progressive Fish Culturist* **36**, 129–132.

Maddox, M. B. and Manzi, J. J. (1977). The effects of algal supplements on static system culture of *Marobrachium rosenbergii* (de Man) larvae. *Proceedings of the Seventh Annual Workshop on World Mariculture Society. San Diego*, 677–687.

New, M. B. (1976). A review of dietary studies with shrimp and prawns. *Aquaculture* **9**, 101–144.

Reeve, M. (1969a). The laboratory culture of the prawn *Palaemon serratus*. *Fishery Investigation London Ser.* 2, **26**, 38 pp.

Reeve, M. (1969b). Growth, metamorphosis and energy conversion in the larvae of the prawn, *Palaemon serratus*. *Journal of the Marine Biological Association of the UK* **49**, 77–96.

Rice, A. L. and Williamson, D. I. (1970). Methods for rearing larval decapod Crustacea. *Helgoländer wiss. Meeresunters* **20**, 47–434.

Serfling, S. A., Van Olst, J. C. and Ford, R. F. (1974). An automatic feeding device for the use of live and frozen *Artemia* for culturing larval stages of the American lobster, *Homarus americanus, Aquaculture* **3**, 311–314.

Spencer, B. E., Helm, M. M. and Dare, P. J. (1977). Recommended quarantine measures for marine molluscs. Technical Report MAFF Direct. Fishery Research Lowestoft, **32**.

Stein, J. R., ed. (1973). "Handbook of phycological methods". Cambridge University Press.

Walne, P. R. (1958). The importance of bacteria in laboratory experiments on rearing the larvae of *Ostrea edulis* (L.). *Journal of the Marine Biological Association of the UK* **37**, 415–25.

Walne, P. R. (1974). "Culture of Bivalve Molluscs: 50 years' Experience at Conwy". Fishing News (Books), West Byfleet.

Walne, P. R. and Spencer, B. E. (1974). Experiments on the growth and food conversion efficiency of the spat of *Ostrea edulis* L. in a recirculation system. *Journal du Conseil permanent international pour l'exploration de la mer*, **35**, 303–318.

Wickins, J. F. (1972a). Developments in the laboratory culture of the common prawn *Palaemon serratus* Pennant. *Fishery Investigation London Ser.* 2, **27**.

Wickins, J. F. (1972b). Experiments on the culture of the spot prawn *Pandalus platyceros* Brandt and the giant freshwater prawn *Macrobrachium rosenbergii* (de Man). *Fishery Investigation London Ser.* 2, **27**.

Wickins, J. F. (1972c). The food value of brine shrimp, *Artemia salina* L., to the larvae of the prawn, *Palaemon serratus* Pennant. *Journal of experimental marine Biology and Ecology* **10**, 151–170.

Wickins, J. F. (1976). Prawn biology and culture. *Oceanography and Marine Biology: an Annual Review* **14**, 435–507.

Winter, J. E. (1973). The filtration rate of *Mytilus edulis* and its dependence on algal concentration, measured by a continuous automatic recording apparatus. Marine Biology **22**, 317–328.

Wood, P. C. and Ayres, P. A. (1977). Artificial sea water for shellfish tanks. *Laboratory Leaflet, MAFF Direct. Fishery Research, Lowestoft*, **39**.

Zaroogian, G. E., Pesch, G. and Morrison, G. (1969). Formulation of an artificial sea water media suitable for oyster larvae development. *American Zoologist* **9**, abstract No. 549.

Chapter 14

Keeping Sharks for Research

Samuel H. Gruber[1] and Raymond S. Keyes[2]

Rosentiel School of Marine and Atmospheric Science[1],
University of Miami, Florida and Sea World, San Diego, California[2]

I. INTRODUCTION

Historically, the maintenance of sharks in captivity has been relatively unsuccessful. While certain sharks such as *Ginglymostoma*, *Heterodontus*, *Odontaspis* and *Negaprion* have lived for several years in the laboratory (Davies, 1960; Clark, 1963a) the usual survival period, especially for the large pelagic sharks, has been short. In spite of this, sharks and their allies are being increasingly utilized as subjects in biochemical, physiological and behavioural experiments (Hodgson and Mathewson, 1978). The biological literature of 1979 listed well over 100 studies on captive elasmobranchs.

In the nineteenth century, a few shark species, particularly members of the bottom-dwelling families were kept in European aquaria (Gruber and Myrberg, 1977). Clark (1963a), reviewing the distribution and longevity of sharks in captivity, reported that over 50 species had been held in aquaria for periods of up to several months. A carpet shark, *Chiloscyllium plagiosum*, apparently survived a record 25 years (Clark, 1963b). Despite these successes, the consensus has been that most species are difficult to collect and transport, and that once captive, they frequently refuse to feed and eventually die (Clark, 1963a, b; Essapian, 1962; Gohar and Mazhar, 1964; Martini, 1974).

Over the years, attempts have been made to study sharks in their natural habitat, but because the shark is shy and prone to flight when disturbed, and because of the concealing nature of the marine environment, many workers have turned to the laboratory and aquarium for the detailed study of shark behaviour and physiology (Myrberg, 1976). However, the fragility of most sharks in captivity and the lack of information on maintaining them in an adequate physiological state means that in many cases, critical data are being gathered from abnormal specimens. This has been emphasized by Martini (1974, 1978) who demonstrated acute haematological changes in certain sharks upon capture. Because of the past difficulties in keeping sharks and the increasing interest in this group, researchers will require information on the basic techniques for maintaining sharks if they expect to study healthy specimens.

The purpose of this chapter, then, is to bring together our personal experiences in keeping sharks and to present some principles which will increase the chances of providing healthy sharks as laboratory subjects. The details will refer to the maintenance of the lemon shark, *Negaprion brevirostris*, a species with which we have worked for many years. However, with suitable modification, these techniques should be adaptable to other species of cartilaginous fishes.

II. SPECIAL CHARACTERISTICS OF SHARKS

That sharks differ considerably from bony fishes is well known to scientist and layman alike. Some of the characteristics that differentiate elasmobranchs from teleosts are: the lack of true bone (see Moss, 1977), possession of placoid scales, retention of urea (shared with coelacanths), special attachment of the body musculature to the skin (Wainwright *et al.*, 1978) and separation of the gill openings. Certain of these features are irrelevant to shark maintenance while others have importance for their successful husbandry.

As a group, sharks are anatomically and physiologically diverse. In this regard, the choice of a species that readily adapts to the conditions of the laboratory and a knowledge of its natural history are among the more important factors in keeping healthy sharks. The physical size of adult sharks presents difficulties in husbandry, many of which are shared with other large aquatic animals. Large sharks require large aquaria, particularly horizontal distances, if normal swimming behaviour is to be maintained. This is critical, because proper metabolic functioning of sharks may be linked to their ability to swim normally. The effect of a shark's excretory products on water quality is also a concern; the concentration of ammonia excreted by a large shark may reach toxic levels if bacterial nitrification is inadequate. The size and complexity of an aquarium system needed to supply adequate oxygen and maintain acceptable water quality for a shark 2 m in length may be economically prohibitive. However, an understanding of the biological requirements of the subject species coupled with knowledge of aquarium design can, in most cases, reduce capital outlay while assuring successful maintenance of these delicate animals.

Probably the most important problems of biological origin which affect the survival of sharks in captivity arise from their cardiovascular and respiratory systems. Many species must swim for efficient oxygen exchange (Clark and Kabasawa, 1977). Until recently, the respiratory countercurrent system of teleosts, so important for the efficient extraction of oxygen by the gills, was said to be missing in sharks. The primary evidence was anatomical; septa associated with the gill structure apparently interfered with the countercurrent flow. However, Grigg (1970) was able to demonstrate a countercurrent flow (possibly of low efficiency) in the respiratory cycle of the bottom-dwelling Port Jackson shark (*Heterodontus portus-jacksoni*). Still, the relatively meager gill surface (11 times less than in the mackerel) and the low oxygen-carrying capacity of the blood (Hughes, 1965) suggest that sharks may not be particularly efficient at extracting oxygen from the water, especially when at rest. For example, Brett and Blackburn (1978) reported that some species of sharks possess metabolic levels that are among the lowest of all fishes. In addition, metabolic rates will decrease further as an individual animal grows (Pritchard *et al.*, 1958). Yet other elasmobranchs have developed the streamlined body shapes and elevated body temperature of some highly evolved teleosts (Carey *et al.*, 1971). Since metabolic rates in sharks are so variable, it is difficult to generalize about them.

The venous system of sharks has several sinuses which may hinder the efficient return of blood to the heart. The caudal veins of sharks are provided with valves, and muscular movement assists in venous return. Therefore, best oxygenation at the tissue level in many species may occur at some optimum swimming velocity rather than at rest. The importance of this will be evident during our discussion on transportation of sharks. Keep in mind that some species can rest on the sea floor while respiring normally, although ram ventilation is requisite to the survival of other sharks (Hughes and Umezawa, 1968). The efficiency of shark respiration and circulation may be much lower than that of teleosts. In practice, we have observed that bony fishes tend to survive for a time in oxygen-depleted water, while sharks in the same aquaria perish. Clearly, the research aquarium should provide adequate space and water circulation for both normal swimming and respiratory function. This will minimize physiological problems associated with insufficient gas exchange.

Elasmobranchs possess an array of sensory systems of extreme sensitivity (Gruber and Myrberg, 1977). Although serving these predators well in the wild, they can cause some difficulties in captivity. For example, the ampullae of Lorenzini (subdermal sensory cells abundant on the head and snout) function in the detection of weak electric fields (Boord and Campbell, 1977). However, together with the olfactory rosette, they are quite sensitive to metallic ions such as copper. Although copper is a common therapeutic agent for bony fishes, exposure of sharks to the metallic ion may cause the ampullae of sharks to become clogged with mucus. The loss of environmental information and increased chances of infection will decrease the likelihood of the shark's survival.

Finally, behavioural problems connected with the active habits and propulsive mechanisms of sharks can reduce the chances of successful maintenance. Unlike most bony fishes, all sharks lack a swim bladder. They must generate lift by forward motion or else sink to the bottom. Many sharks, particularly the more pelagic species, rarely contact solid barriers during their normal activities. However some, such as the nurse shark *G. cirratum* and reef whitetip *Triaenodon obesus*, spend much of their time resting on the bottom or in underwater caverns. Unlike the benthic sharks, the more active species are difficult to keep, particularly if their "normal" swimming strategies are interrupted.

Klay (1977) has provided a possible explanation for past difficulties in the keeping of large pelagic sharks. The key to Klay's hypothesis is a swimming pattern which he terms the "glide/rest period". He defines this as the distance an "efficiently" swimming shark covers without muscular contraction. He believes that the primary cause of mortality in captive pelagic sharks is that their living space is not large enough to permit a complete swimming cycle including the glide/rest period. Thus, in a small tank, the shark does not swim normally and stalls when encountering a wall. Such a shark uses more energy to swim and eventually becomes exhausted. Klay's hypothesis is a reasonable explanation of some of the problems associated with keeping large sharks and it should be possible to test this hypothesis. Some of our observations seem to support Klay's theory. We have found that large lemon sharks significantly reduce their food consumption when moved to a larger pool. This suggests that swimming performance may be coupled with metabolic efficiency.

III. CAPTURE AND TRANSPORT OF SHARKS

Sharks must be treated with great care during capture and transport to the laboratory facility if trauma is to be avoided. The first critical phase in the keeping of sharks is the method of capture. Mazeaud *et al.* (1977) point out that capture and transportation can result in several types of stress which may induce struggling, hypoxia, and thermal and osmotic shock. All of these may have lethal consequences. Moreover, the effect of such stress can be delayed and thus the relation of subsequent death of the specimen to capture trauma will not be apparent.

As stated, metabolic disturbances brought about by a short period of stress can be of relatively long duration. Martini (1974) demonstrated that prolonged struggling during the capture of the spiny dogfish, *Squalus acanthias*, deleteriously affects blood serum protein. Lactate accumulates and the oxygen-carrying capacity of the blood declines. Such animals often become immobile, and as their condition deteriorates, they eventually stiffen and die. Over the centuries, a number of methods have been used for the capture of sharks, such as angling by handline, surface or bottom trotline, gill netting, trawling and trapping. Not all of these techniques lend themselves to collection of live specimens. Trapping and trawling are to be avoided, and care must be taken in all capture methods to minimize the length of time the shark is restrained.

In relatively clear shallow water, where a shark can be approached by the collector, one of the least traumatic techniques is cast netting (Fig. 1). When trapped in a cast net, small lemon sharks (as well as nurse and bonnethead sharks, *Sphyrna tiburo*) offer little resistance. While the sharks are entangled in the net, they can be safely moved to the collecting boat. A handline has many of the advantages of a cast net. The time of struggling is short and the shark's protective mucus remains intact, while skin and eyes are not injured as is often the case with trap or trawl. Trotlines may be used if they are checked frequently and are particularly effective in capturing large deep-living sharks.

When storing sharks in a holding tank, care should be taken in placing the newly acquired specimen, especially if it is being added to those

Fig. 1. Capturing a lemon shark by cast netting. (1a) Collector tracks shark until he gets within throwing distance. (1b) The 3 m diameter monofilament net is cast over the shark (1c) which is trapped in the folds of the net as the centre line is hauled in. Both struggling by the shark and physiological trauma are minimized with this collecting method. Photos: J. Galindo.

previously collected. If possible, the shark should be held in a horizontal position and quietly lowered into the tank. Commotion created by the new specimen often stimulates the other sharks to dash around and even bite each other. This is particularly important when dealing with large sharks since if frightened, they may damage one another severely. This principle applies to most captive sharks; strong, unexpected stimuli usually evoke strong responses in which sharks may pose a danger to handler as well as to each other. Care must also be taken when moving the potential research specimen from collection site to laboratory aquarium. Those species capable of respiring normally while resting on the bottom (e.g. lemon shark, nurse shark, tiger shark *Galeocerdo cuvieri*, leopard shark *Triakis semifasciata*, and others) can be shipped with fewer problems than those that must swim constantly.

A simple transportation technique best suited for the smaller benthic species (less than 1 m in total length) utilizes an inexpensive styrofoam ice chest and double 0.25 mm polyethylene bags. After the shark is fasted for several days to reduce the production of faecal matter, the animal is placed in a bag containing enough sea water to cover its back. Pure oxygen is bubbled into the bag to a pressure of about 0.35 kg/cm^2 greater than that of ambient. Pure oxygen is desirable not only because of the increased O_2 exchange at the gill surface, but also because of a slight anaesthetic effect on the shark. The neck of the bag is then twisted and sealed tightly with a large elastic band (Fig. 2b). Prepared in this manner, a shark can easily survive a trip of at least 10 to 15 h. Care must be taken when placing the animal in the container to minimize thrashing and the chance of puncturing the bag. For small sharks prone to biting, a pressurized polyester resin-coated tank (Fig. 2a) may be substituted for the plastic bags. The interior of this tank must not be abrasive and all protrusions must be removed. The dimensions should be such that the shark cannot easily turn (as is true of the previous method) or else large enough that it may swim gently. A transport tank which allows gentle swimming has been successfully used with small individuals of species considered difficult to transport, such as the brown shark, *Carcharhinus plumbeus*.

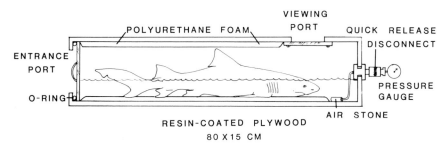

Fig. 2a.   Diagram of a compact life–support system used for transporting several species of small elasmobranchs. Under only 7 litres of cooled sea water, sharks have survived periods of several hours provided that the tank is pressurized with pure oxygen to 0.35 kg/cm^2.

Fig. 2b.   Simplified version of the tank is a polyethylene bag inflated with pure oxygen and sealed with an elastic band. Note the level of water just above the gills of this lemon shark. Photo: N. Chitty.

Moving large bottom-dwelling species (greater than 2 m total length) of the pelagic sharks that must swim constantly requires greater care and planning. The transport of large animals is expensive. Equipment and transportation costs, particularly with air transport, increase dramatically as the volume of the water grows. Thus we have designed containers only slightly larger than the shark and with low water volume. In these containers we have successfully transported large bull, *C. leucas*, brown, tiger, lemon and white sharks, *Carcharodon carcharias*, over great distances (Fig. 3). Twenty-four-hour transits have been successful when

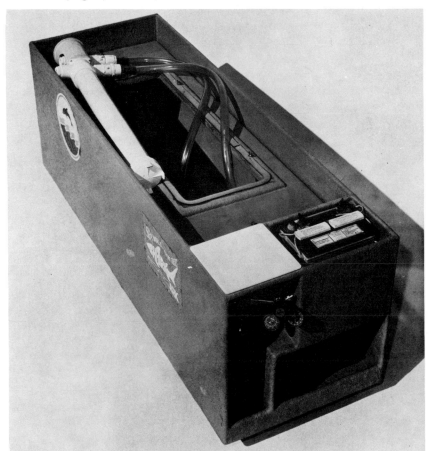

Fig. 3. Photograph of a polyester coated wood and fibreglass transport container showing oxygen supply, cartridge filter for removing particulate material and 12 volt power source. This self-contained and portable device is useful for boat, truck or air transportation of most species of shark. The overall length of the box is about 2.5 m. Photo: Sea World.

the proper equipment is used and an attendant carefully monitors the transport system.

In this transport box, the shark's respiratory demands are met by slowly bubbling pure oxygen into the impeller of a 12 V DC submersible bilge pump placed near the shark's head. The transport container should have dry compartments for the storage of small oxygen bottles and 12 V batteries. A 1.0 m^3 bottle will supply sufficient oxygen for a 12-h trip (Fig.

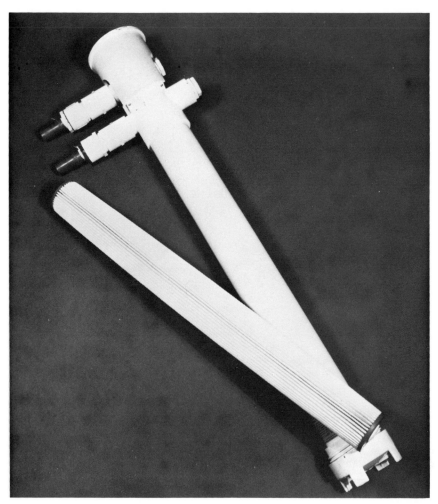

Fig. 4. Detail of the cartridge filter (Rainbow Lifeguard Products) showing the paper element which will remove particulate matter of 35 μm. We recommend use of such a filter if transport time exceeds several hours. Photo: R. Keyes.

3). During transit, the sea water should be continuously filtered to remove particulate matter. We suggest use of a cartridge-type filter (Fig. 4) receiving water from an independent pump and battery. This redundancy also assures that the shark's oxygen supply is not interrupted.

Every few minutes, the attendant should gently stimulate the animal by slowly flexing its caudal peduncle or by firmly palpating and stroking alternate sides of the animal's dorsal musculature from the pectoral region to the second dorsal fin. This manipulation should evoke slow swimming movements lasting for several seconds. If an animal such as the bull or brown shark is allowed to lie motionless for 5 min, tissue damage from improper blood circulation will occur. This manifests itself in increasing rigidity progressing anteriorly from the caudal area. If the body musculature can be vigorously flexed and extended, this stiffness can be reversed, especially with smaller sharks, and the specimen will revive. The buildup of the shark's waste products in the water may be controlled with ion exchange resins (i.e. Mesco-ecolyte, Mesco Corp.). Recirculating the sea water through such resin maintains water quality, a major limiting factor for time of transit in the past.

In conclusion, transportation of sharks, particularly the large or pelagic species, is difficult at best. The foregoing suggestions will not guarantee success, but should give the research aquarist a foundation on which improved techniques may be built and greater success in the transportation of sharks achieved.

IV. TYPICAL AQUARIUM SYSTEMS FOR SHARKS

A. The Aquarium System

Design of the water circulation system and the aquarium habitat of the shark are the most important considerations in the long-term maintenance of research specimens. Only with proper environmental conditions can the researcher expect to keep healthy sharks, which is a prerequisite for collecting reliable data.

There are a few basic water system designs (Spotte, 1973). We recommend the use of closed or semi-closed recirculating sea water systems for keeping sharks in the laboratory. The major drawback of an open or flow-through system is the experimenter's inability to control environmental factors such as salinity, temperature and environmental contaminants. In addition, it is often not possible to achieve effective levels of medication in a flow-through system because of dilution.

Pathological infection is also a problem with open systems. For example, within the geographical range of the lemon shark, the infection and reinfection of captive specimens with the monogenean fluke *Dermopitherius* sp. can become an isoluble problem in an open system. Such infections can easily be controlled in recirculating sea water systems. A high efficiency 2000 litre closed aquarium system (Honn and Chavin, 1975) and 1 500 000 litre semi-closed system (Keyes, 1979) have been described which allow the long-term maintenance of sharks.

B. Environmental Control

We have found a particular set of environmental conditions conducive to keeping young lemon sharks in the laboratory. The following comments will refer to this species, but may suit the needs of some other elasmobranchs.

Bower and Bidwell (1978), Buckley (1978), Collins *et al.* (1975), Hampson (1976), Smart (1978) and Srna and Baggaley (1975) have described nitrification in recirculating aquatic systems. They have pointed out the deleterious effects of improper reduction of metabolic waste products, particularly toxic un-ionized ammonia, by biological filters. Thus, standard aquarium techniques should be followed to assure sufficient nitrification and concomitant detoxification of metabolic waste before valuable specimens are placed in the research system. Nitrification may be speeded by installing a biological filter (Huisman and Wood, 1974) and by inoculating that filter with pure cultures of *Nitrosomonas* sp. and *Nitrobacter* sp. The bacterial colony can be maintained on ammonium chloride when animal waste products are unavailable.

In general, water quality is maintained by recirculation through mechanical and biological filters. In addition, 10–20% of the system's water volume is replaced monthly, maintaining the aquatic environment within the prescribed limits. During water replacement, the necessary volume is removed and new sea water is pumped through a sterilizer (Fig. 5) and into the aquarium. Recirculation differs slightly depending upon the system but follows the same general pattern as shown in Fig. 5. Each tank is provided with either a cartridge filter for removal of fine particles or a sand filter, both of which increase nitrification in the system. Biological filtration may also occur in the carbonate gravel bed provided that circulation through the bed is adequate. Finally, specially fabricated environments (i.e. Actifil Bio-Rings, Norton Pollution Control Products) conducive to the growth of *Nitrosomonas* can be placed in the recirculation system for added nitrification (Fig. 6). Such "bio-rings" are designed to greatly increase surface area available for nitrifying bacteria while not decreasing flow rate, a common problem in gravel beds.

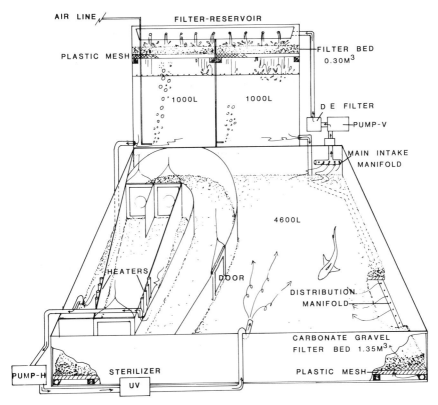

Fig. 5. Perspective diagram of an aquarium and underwater "Y-maze" used in testing for colour vision in the lemon shark. There are two circulation patterns in this 6600 litre system. For vertical circulation, water enters the intake manifold of pump "V" at mid-level where it is pumped at 75 l/min. through a diatomaceous (DE) filter and up to a filter reservoir. From there it flows by gravity through an 18 cm (in depth) carbonate filter bed into the reservoir where it is aerated, and then flows into the main tank via distribution manifolds running the length of either side. These manifolds lie under a false bottom so recycled water is channeled first under then up through the gravel on the tank bottom to return to the intake manifold, thus completing the vertical cycle. For the horizontal pattern, pump "H" takes water from areas of reduced circulation in the maze, pumps it through the sterilizer (UV) and finally out on the surface of the main tank. This sets up a slowly rotating current which the sharks often swim against.

With proper nitrification and the entire volume recirculating at least twice every hour, it is possible to keep up to 1 kg of lemon shark in as little as 100 litres of water. For example, to save space we have constructed a two-tiered tank (Fig. 7), the combined volume of which does not exceed 800 litres. We routinely keep three sharks in each tank. However, this is

Fig. 6. Photograph of a variety of plastic "bio-rings". (Norton Pollution Control Products) which furnish a large surface area for growth of nitrifying bacteria. These surfaces will not reduce the rate of flow through filter beds, a problem usually found in gravel biological filters. Photo: Sea World.

clearly the limiting case, for if a single component fails even slightly, the sharks become seriously stressed within a few hours. In the small research aquarium, we prefer a ratio of 1 kg of shark to 500 litres of sea water.

Water temperature, a critical factor in the keeping of sharks, especially tropical species, should be continuously controlled and monitored. Temperature is easily maintained by thermostatically controlled water heaters working in concert with space heaters, dehumidifiers and air conditioners. Water is maintained at $25 \pm 2\,^{\circ}\mathrm{C}$, a temperature at which healthy tropical sharks will feed normally but not become so active as to bite one another in competition over food.

Salinity of the aquarium water is maintained at 28–31‰ by diluting full strength sea water (36‰) with distilled or deionized freshwater. Tap water is not recommended because of the possibility of contamination, especially with toxic copper ions from the plumbing. The rationale for maintaining the salinity at approximately 28‰ is that ectoparasites

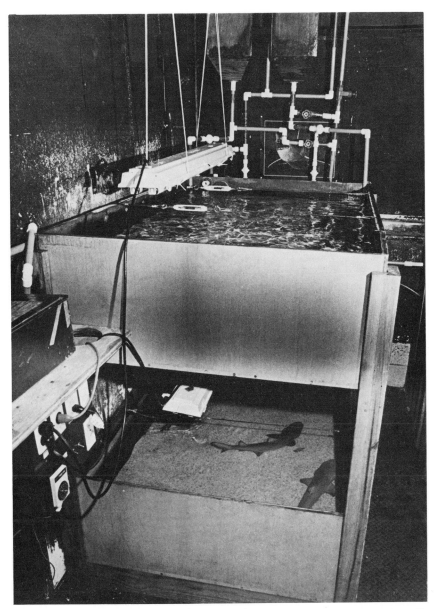

Fig. 7. Photograph of a two-tiered laboratory aquarium used to house up to six juvenile lemon sharks. Screen tops have been removed to show sharks which can clearly be seen in the lower tank. The tanks are nested to save floor space. Circulation patterns in this system are very similar to those shown in Fig. 6. This is a high-efficiency system since up to 10 kg of sharks are routinely maintained in only 800 litres sea water. Photo: N. Chitty.

Fig. 8.   Lemon shark, *Negaprion brevirostris*, in the shark tank at Sea World, San Diego. This species is susceptible to pathogenic infection which, if left untreated, will develop into large secondary infection. Photo: Sea World, Terry Roberts.

succumb at low salinity while the weakly euryhaline lemon sharks do quite well at these levels. Trematodes, often a serious problem with captive lemon sharks, can be controlled in this way. However, most sharks subjected to lower salinities experience metabolic difficulties (Chan and Wong, 1977; Lewiston *et al.*, 1979) and do not seem as tolerant to diluted sea water as do lemon and bull sharks. The hydrogen ion concentration of sea water does not vary much unless aquarium conditions deteriorate significantly. Small changes in pH may be buffered by a carbonate gravel bed for a short period. Additions of sodium hydroxide and calcium carbonate also stabilize falling pH.

Illumination should be controlled so that the cyclic activity patterns of sharks are maintained, in so far as possible. Lighting fixtures may be placed on electromechanical timers to give sharks 12 h of light per day. Allowance for seasonal changes does not seem necessary. Continuous bright illumination damages the photoreceptors and pupillary function and should thus be avoided.

Mechanical damage to the animals is one of the major problems faced by the shark aquarist. Young lemon sharks are animals of the flats and are not as well adapted to confinement as, for example, the nurse shark, a more benthic species. If the enclosure is not large enough, lemon sharks tend to move about the periphery of the tank with fins touching the wall, occasionally bumping protruding objects. This is especially true when they are frightened, as they may dash straight ahead into the wall, injuring their tail, fins and most important, their snout (Davies, 1960). Fish pathogens (usually gram negative bacteria) quickly infect the open wounds, and the animal stops feeding and dies if the infection is not arrested. The installation of germicidal lamps in the flow system can reduce such bacterial infection (Fig. 5). Ozone is also utilized as a bacteriostat in some aquarium systems and appears to be useful in the husbandry of sharks (Keyes, 1979). However, empirical studies should be undertaken when employing ozonation since chronic gill pathology and haematological changes have been shown in trout exposed to ozone levels of 5 mg/l (Wedemeyer *et al.*, 1979).

We recommend that researchers keep specimens small enough to swim unhindered in the laboratory. To avoid mechanical damage to fins, snout and body, all exposed tank surfaces should be covered with resilient, closed-cell polyurethane foam to act as a "shock absorber". All equipment placed in the water should also be located behind foam barriers. Research aquaria should have a source of continuous aeration in addition to that furnished by the pump and filter, because oxygen deprivation is usually the primary cause of death should there be a pump failure. If a filtration system is designed that produces more than one atmosphere of pressure, the water should be tumbled to eliminate the possibility of air embolism or gas bubble disease (Fickeisen and Schneider, 1976).

V. MAINTENANCE OF THE LEMON SHARK

Lemon sharks, along with nurse sharks, are popular experimental elasmobranchs because they are relatively easy to handle, readily available and can be maintained in captivity. Lemon sharks are members of the Carcharhinidae and are distributed worldwide in tropical and subtropical oceans. They are found in shallow tropical marine and brackish waters. In the northwest Atlantic, the young are born in the spring and are especially common on flats and shallow passes in the waters of south Florida.

Although they are relatively easy to keep, problems have arisen with their maintenance. As we have emphasized, sharks are more fragile than most teleosts, and require careful husbandry if they are to be useful research subjects. For example, Graeber (1974 and personal communication) had to drop the lemon shark from his visual discrimination studies because his specimens did not survive in an open system long enough to learn the required tasks. The problems Graeber and others have encountered in keeping lemon sharks have now been solved for the most part, and it is possible to maintain lemon sharks in the laboratory for prolonged periods.

A. Food and Feeding

The difficulties of developing a comprehensive nutritional plan for elasmobranchs are compounded by lack of careful studies. At this time, our dietary concepts are based on comparison between sharks and bony fishes and the established nutrient requirements of commercial species (Halver, 1972).

Halver (1976) feels that formulas for balanced fish diets must include an energy source plus adequate essential amino acids, essential fatty acids, vitamins and minerals to promote normal growth. Obviously, nutrient requirements vary with species, size, water temperature and stress. For proper growth, all fish examined to date require the same ten amino acids: arginine, histidine, isoleucine, leucine, lysine, methionine, phenylalanine, threonine, tryptophan and valine. These must be in the diet in nearly balanced amounts to furnish an acceptable amino acid pattern before fish tissue can be formed.

Vitamin excess and deficiency diseases have also been described for fishes. In fishes, as in other vertebrates, the water-soluble vitamins function as co-enzymes. Unfortunately, requirements and function for fat-soluble vitamins are less well known. It is known, however, that storage of the fat-soluble vitamins is cumulative and hypervitaminosis can occur when the diet contains large amounts of the fat-soluble vitamins for prolonged periods. To further complicate the formulation of an adequate diet for sharks, Halver (1976) mentions that symptoms for mineral deficiency have been reported for fish, yet little is known about mineral requirements, for example, as enzyme activators. In this regard, thyroid hyperplasia, discussed below, has been observed in sharks.

Food and feeding patterns of sharks will vary between field and laboratory. Although captive sharks, i.e. *Odontaspis* and *Heterodontus*, have been known to fast for months (D. Nelson and F. Carey, personal communication) the usual effects of starvation are catastrophic. Histological and biochemical deterioration has been documented in many tissues, including the kidney, spleen and muscles (Martini, 1974). Young lemon sharks lose about 1% of their in-air body weight per day when experimentally fasted. As the shark falls below about 80% of its *ad libitum* weight, physiological changes become irreversible (Gruber, unpublished results). Baldridge (1972) demonstrated that an 89 kg lemon shark starved for 84 days fell at death to 79.6% of its original weight-in-air.

Unlike some elasmobranchs, lemon sharks can easily be induced to eat cut frozen fish. This allows for routine vitamin and mineral additions to a shark's normal ration (Table I). The levels given in Table I are based on requirements of other marine organisms and have been modified for sharks. This is but a first approximation and should be refined when adequate dietary levels for sharks have been established. However, long-term maintenance of lemon, nurse, bull and brown sharks has been successful using the vitamin supplements we give in Table I. Geraci (1972) demonstrated thiamine (vitamin B_1) deficiency in marine mammals maintained on food fish containing large amounts of the naturally occurring enzyme thiaminase. Captive lemon sharks may be affected by

Table I. Dietary supplements for captive sharks. Many of the vitamins and minerals are furnished in a single multivitamin tablet. Vitamins A, B_1, C, E and ferrous gluconate were separate tablets. These supplements have been used successfully for four years on lemon sharks and nurse sharks, and for two years on bull sharks and brown sharks.

Dietary addition	Dosage (per kg animal weight per week)
A	3570 I.U.
B_1	210.0 mg
B_2	0.39 mg
B_6	0.23 mg
B_{12}	0.9 mg
C	37.5 mg
Calcium pantothenate	0.6 mg
Choline	Trace
D	150 I.U.
E	37.5 I.U.
Ferrous gluconate	11.25 mg
Folic acid	Trace
Inositol	Trace
Kelp (iodine)	18 μg
Niacin	0.6 mg

thiaminase and show signs we interpret as hypovitaminosis B_1. One condition involves the body becoming laterally curved, the head slightly elevated and the animal swimming in circles. These signs disappear rapidly with an increase of vitamin B_1 in the shark's diet. Although the success of this therapy has not been confirmed for other sharks, the similarities of vitamin utilization by other vertebrates suggests that the treatment will generally be efficacious. Feeding frozen fish minimizes the transmission of disease organisms from the food to the shark, but the vitamins and minerals lost during the freezing are particularly important. The loss of these nutrients can prevent autoxidation of lipids, which may lead to microcytic anaemia and lipoid degeneration of the liver when the food fish are frozen improperly (Smith, 1979). Thus it is desirable to feed fresh fish when possible or, if unavailable, freshly frozen fish.

Graeber (1974) demonstrated that short periods of deprivation enhanced feeding in the lemon shark. He also noted a cyclical pattern of food intake apparently unrelated to physical changes in the environment. During a 3-year period, Gruber (unpublished data) observed food consumption and resultant motivational changes in confined lemon sharks. They consumed about 25% of their body weight per week under his conditions. As we mentioned earlier, swimming space may be related to metabolic efficiency. Keyes (unpublished data) found that food consumption of large lemon sharks declined to less than 8% of their body weight per week when they were placed in a large tank. Keyes suggested that the greater freedom permitted unhindered swimming and thus higher metabolic efficiency. Therefore, the sharks required less food to survive. With such favourable environmental conditions, motivation remains high and most sharks will perform experimental tasks well and remain healthy at these levels of consumption.

Lemon sharks will stop eating when they become satiated, leaving unwanted food on the bottom of the tank. Decomposing fish can quickly foul a closed system. Deteriorating water quality associated with poor husbandry, such as failure to remove uneaten food, has been a primary cause of death in captive sharks. The ensuing bacterial bloom rapidly depletes oxygen, stressing the animals and causing them to regurgitate previously ingested food, thus providing a further energy source for continued bacterial growth. Therefore all uneaten food must be removed after feeding.

If given a relatively large piece of food a lemon shark will, with lateral oscillation and twisting of its head, remove bite-size pieces. As it does so, small scraps torn from the food enter the water and induce bacterial growth. Accordingly, individual bite-size pieces of fish should be fed to the sharks so that they ingest the entire food in one movement. It has become apparent that lemon sharks will consume the flesh of many fish species, but prefer certain types, such as the Carangidae. The local availability of food fish will influence selection, but food similar to the shark's natural diet is probably best.

B. Growth

The growth rates of captive fishes are known to vary according to such factors as crowding, confinement and competition (Magnuson, 1962), and may differ significantly from wild specimens of the same species. The growth of many species of sharks has been reported to be exceedingly slow. Free-ranging tagged juvenile lemon sharks and dogfish grow only a few centimetres over periods of up to 18 months (Jensen, 1965; Starck, unpublished data). Gruber (unpublished data) found that lemon sharks captured in the spring usually average 61 cm total length and during three years in captivity, grew only 5 cm in total length per year.

In contrast to these slow growth rates, Kistnasamy (1974) recorded an average increase of 17.5 cm per year in sand tiger sharks, *Odontaspis taurus*, after eight years in captivity. Similarly, we have studied carcharhinid sharks maintained in pools large enough to allow unrestricted swimming and have recorded rapid growth. Five juvenile lemon sharks grew approximately 26 cm per year, four small Galapagos sharks, *C. galapagensis*, grew approximately 36 cm per year and six young Pacific blacktip sharks, *C. melanopterus*, increased approximately 24 cm per year. We suggest that swimming behaviour, as it perhaps affects metabolic efficiency; and differences in diet and water quality, all influence the growth rate of captive sharks.

C. Prophylaxis

Sharks are a phylogenetically "old" group and many parasites have evolved with them. Thus host specificity is expected and not unusual in the elasmobranchs (Croll, 1966). This is especially true with tapeworms (cestodes), several orders of which are restricted to sharks. Infection may be compounded since sharks live for many years and consume a variety of parasitized prey. Even before capture, sharks are probably under some stress from parasitic infection. In the laboratory, the possible elimination of natural immunity that normally limits parasitic invasion may allow endemic diseases to reach epidemic proportions. One of the best methods to reduce disease in captive sharks is to avoid the introduction of pathogens. Because of this, pathological conditions which frequently arise in captive sharks kept in open systems are largely eliminated when an environmentally controlled recirculating water system is used.

The most common lemon shark disease seen in our laboratory aquarium involves haemorrhage combined with the appearance of numerous white punctiform lesions of about 1 mm diameter distributed over the animal's body (Fig. 9). If left untreated, the lesions usually erupt and become infected and the shark ceases feeding. If the specimen is not properly isolated and treated, the disease will rapidly spread throughout the study colony. The etiology of this disease is uncertain, but histological analyses utilizing the electron microscope suggest a viral invasion (Gruber and Udey, unpublished observations) with secondary bacterial infection. Dingerkus (personal communication) has identified *Vibrio* organisms in these lesions.

Wild lemon sharks are occasionally infected with the monogean flukes (*Dermopitherius* sp.) which will rapidly spread through a

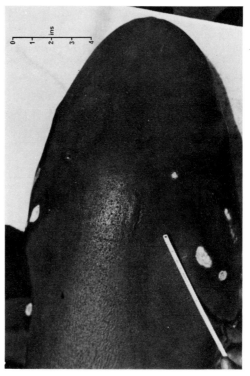

Fig. 9. Head of a 2.95 m lemon shark showing white lesions of unknown aetiology. These are analogous, but much larger (approximately 250 mm²) than the spots on juveniles (1–5 mm²) described in the text. Note the symmetry of the affected areas. Note also the small translucent organisms distributed over the head. These are monogean flukes (*Dermopitherius* sp.) mentioned in the text. Photo: S. Gruber.

captive shark colony. The initial signs of the infection are scratching on the bottom and yawning, as well as skin discoloration, together with the appearance of opaque, elliptical organisms 2 mm long over the shark's body. If untreated, the foci of infestation will develop into large lesions open to secondary bacterial invasion. This condition, along with the one described in the preceding paragraph, is readily controlled by addition of dimethyl (2,2,2-trichloro-l-hydroxethyl) phosphonate (trade names Masoten, Dylox, Neguvon). At a water temperature of 24°C, three treatments with this chemical at 0.50 ppm at five-day intervals are effective in controlling the disease in a semi-closed system. A single exposure at 2.0 ppm is effective in a closed system. The toxicity of Dylox seems to increase as water temperature increases; sharks show increased respiration and other signs of stress at higher dosages and temperatures. This chemical, although moderately toxic, is pH-labile and degrades in sea water after 24–36 h.

Occasionally a lemon shark will stop feeding, and after several days, body coloration, which is usually dark yellow-grey, will become very pale and the animal will stop swimming. Animals which have been well adapted to captivity and apparently healthy for more than 30 months may succumb in 5–10 days. Post-mortem examination in at least three such cases has revealed internal bleeding combined with septicaemia due to complete rupture and severing of the small intestine (spiral valve) near the cloaca. One possible explanation is that the shark accidentally ingested sharp carbonate substrate which mechanically severed the tissue while passing through the gut.

Two cases of hyperplasia of the thyroid (goitre) have been positively identified (Fig. 10). Both lemon sharks were in captivity for at least two years and occupied the same tank with several other specimens but none of the other sharks were affected. The goitre developed over a period of several months and due to its location, just behind the lower jaw, interfered with feeding. The gut of one of the sharks contained gravel from the tank bottom, reflecting problems with control of feeding movements. Both specimens were sent to the US Registry of Tumors in Lower Animals for histological study. Thus, Harshbarger (personal communication and unpublished results) identified the lesions as goitres and suggested from the histology that they were possibly the result of nitrogenous toxicity and not iodide deficiency.

Topical and systemic bacterial invasion is common in newly collected specimens, particularly when the animal receives rough handling or when collection materials (nets, hooks, live wells, shipping boxes) have not been sterilized between usages. Such infection often results in the death of the specimen. One type of infection known as fin or tail rot (Keyes, 1977)

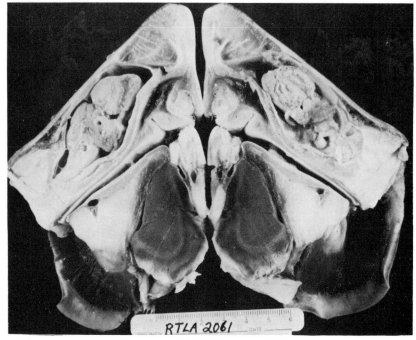

Fig. 10. Median sagittal section of the head of a 3.4 kg, 73 cm (fork length) female lemon shark (*Negaprion brevirostris*) RT LA 2061 which died on 9.III.79 from complications caused by a large (5 × 3 cm) goiter. The goiter is the dark mass just below the tongue and seen on both halves of the lower jaw. Scale is in cm. Photo: J. Harshbarger.

is easily controlled by dissolving the antibiotic nitrofurazone to 9 ppm in the aquarium water. This concentration could damage the nitrifying bacteria living in the filter.

If a sick animal is still feeding, antibiotics such as tetracycline can be given orally at a rate of 250 mg/kg each day. If it is not feeding, intraperitoneal injection at 30 mg/kg can be administered. The efficacy of antibiotics and other medication in the treatment of shark diseases is not well described, but the therapeutic value of such agents in fish disease is well known (Herwig, 1979). Obviously the type of medication and method of application are important factors in the successful treatment of shark disease. In all cases, stress due to handling should be kept to a minimum and, where possible, non-invasive techniques should be used. Biological control of certain diseases of sharks may be possible. For example, we have observed the cleaner wrasse *Labroides dimidiatus* enter the mouth and search the buccal chamber of lemon sharks resting on the bottom.

It is advisable to quarantine all newly captured sharks for a period of several days to allow the expression of any disease. During this period, attention and medication may be given to the recently collected shark while it acclimates to the research aquarium.

D. Miscellaneous Observations

We recommend keeping small crustacean scavengers with the sharks and providing some sort of cover (i.e. rocks, tiles, etc.) that will not interfere with the shark's movement. Crabs will effectively remove small uneaten pieces of food. They must be removed, however, during routine Dyloxing since the required concentration is lethal to most crustaceans.

The tank should be built so that sharks cannot become wedged between objects suspended in the water. Lemon sharks as well as other species will explore the environment and will suffocate if trapped. When designing a shark aquarium, it is best to ensure all surfaces are smooth with no submerged objects the shark may strike. When building a rectangular pool (particularly if it is small), corners should be rounded. We do not recommend round pools when dealing with the more difficult species. Sharks seem to prefer to follow the pool's circumference and do not use the glide/rest swimming mode described earlier. The reason for this is unknown. Although an animal will rarely jump out of the tank, all aquaria with low sides should be covered.

Captive juvenile lemon sharks usually do not act aggressively towards one another. We have not observed fighting in these animals, and on only a few occasions have we found apparently healthy juvenile sharks dead with marks of attack. Adult lemon sharks will occasionally bite one another; mating activities in sharks frequently result in badly wounded females (Gruber and Myrberg, 1977). Fortunately, sharks have good regenerative abilities and replace lost tissue quickly. Conflict between individuals may increase when species and sizes are mixed. For example, some species such as the bull shark prefer to eat other sharks and rays. For the most part, however, non-aggressivity may be a general feature of shark behaviour (Gruber and Myrberg, 1977).

Both quinaldine and MS-222 (tricaine) have frequently been used as general anaesthetics for sharks. We have also used Nembutal, pentothal sodium and tubocurare as immobilizing agents. The most satisfactory has been MS-222 because of ease of control over depth of anaesthesia and apparent lack of side-effects (see chapter 9 on anaesthesia). It is possible to immobilize small lemon sharks without drugs by turning them over and holding them in an inverted posture until they relax. After a few minutes the animals will fall into a "trance-like" state. When so immobilized, they will not struggle and can be placed in an underwater holder and manipulated. While inverted they continue to respire and when righted will swim away without apparent damage. This phenomenon, called tonic immobility, is well known in other animals and has been recently reviewed by Carli (1977) and others.

One final point concerns security for captive sharks. A number of workers have reported acts of vandalism in connection with keeping these animals (i.e. Clark, 1969; Nelson, personal communication). The general public is beginning to appreciate the highly evolved and adaptive qualities of this marine predator, but man still suffers from many of the attitudes that have led to the decimation of terrestrial predators such as the wolf, mountain lion and eagle. Thus captive sharks must be effectively isolated from the general public. Intrusion alarms may be combined with water-level indicators and flow sensors that continuously monitor these functions in the research aquarium. Thus, if accidental or purposeful interruption to water flow should occur, an alarm is activated that may be connected to an automatic telephone dialing machine.

VI. CONCLUDING REMARKS

Admittedly, it is difficult to assess the physiological condition of animals like captive sharks for which baseline data from natural populations are not available. Martini (1974) recommends the use of previously established haematocrit values as an indicator of physiological condition. Stable haematological values would be taken as a favourable indication, while a dynamic value would possibly indicate deleterious physiological changes.

We prefer to use non-invasive behavioural measures combined with the external appearance of the shark to assess physiological condition. A normally swimming lemon shark, whose motivation for food is high and that feeds well, is usually considered to be healthy. This is especially so if body coloration and skin appearance are good. These last factors are unfortunately subjective and require experience with the particular experimental species.

While keeping sharks for scientific research presents certain problems (see Rasmussen and Rasmussen, 1967), it is possible to maintain some species in apparently good condition for long periods. Success largely depends upon two factors: (1) choice of species, and (2) reduction of stress associated with capture and captivity. A key factor in choosing a shark species for research purposes may be whether it can efficiently maintain respiration without swimming. These species (orectolobids, some carcharhinids, etc.) seem to survive the rigours of captivity better than those that have high oxygen demands, or those that require constant swimming motion. Once the shark is in captivity, the major goal should be to maintain a healthy subject for experimentation and observation.

ACKNOWLEDGEMENTS

Advances in the art of keeping sharks have resulted from efforts of many people at Sea World and other oceanaria, and from the academic community. To these workers we give our thanks. We are grateful to the following for critically reviewing part or all of this manuscript: V. Carpenter, L. Garibaldi, A. Hawkins, G. Klay, A. Myrberg, P. Murphy and M. Shaw. We thank Ms Marie Hirata-Gruber for the line drawings. Mobay Corporation kindly supplied Dylox^R for evaluation as a prophylactic agent and Chas Pfizer Co. supplied tetracycline as a therapeutic agent. We are grateful to J. Harshbarger, Director, US Registry of Tumors in Lower Animals, for providing the pathology report and photographs of thyroid hyperplasia shown in Fig. 9. Preparation of this article was supported in part by NSF Grant OCY-78-26819 and ONR contract N00014-C-0175 to Samuel H. Gruber, and supported by Sea World Incorporated.

VII. REFERENCES

Anon. (1976). School sharks recaptured after 25 years. *Australian Fish. Newsletter* **30**, 3.
Baldridge, H. D. (1972). Accumulation and function of liver oil in Florida sharks, *Copeia* **2**, 306–325.
Boord, R. L. and Campbell, C. B. (1977). Structural and functional organization of the lateral line system of sharks. *American Zoologist* **17**, 431–441.
Bower, C. E. and Bidwell, J. P. (1978). Ionization of ammonia in sea water: effects of temperature, pH and salinity. *Journal of the Fisheries Research Board of Canada* **35**, 1012–1016.
Brett, J. R. and Blackburn, J. M. (1978). Metabolic rate and energy expenditure of the spiny dogfish, *Squalus acanthias*. *Journal of the Fisheries Research Board of Canada* **35**, 816–821.
Buckley, J. A. (1978). Acute toxicity of un-ionized ammonia to fingerling coho salmon. *Progressive Fish Culturist* **40(1)**, 30–32.
Carey, F. G., Teal, J. M., Kanwisher, J. W. and Lawson, K. D. (1971). Warm-bodied fish. *American Zoologist* **11**, 137–145.
Carli, G. (1977). Animal hypnosis in the rabbit. *Psych. Rec.* **1**, 123–143.

Chan, D. K. O. and Wong, T. M. (1977). Physiological adjustments to dilution of the external medium in the lip shark, *Hemiscyllium plagiosum* (Bennett) III. Oxygen consumption and metabolic rates. *Journal of Experimental Zoology* **200**, 97–102.

Clark, E. (1963a). Maintenance of sharks in captivity. Part 1. General. *Institut Oceanographique Monaco Bulletin* **1A**, 7–13.

Clark, E. (1963b). Maintenance of sharks in captivity with a report on their instrumental conditioning. *In* "Sharks and Survival", pp. 115–149 (P. W. Gilbert, ed.), D. C. Heath & Co., Lexington.

Clark, E. (1969). "The Lady and the Shark", Harper and Row Co., New York.

Clark, E. and Kabasawa, H. (1977). Factors affecting the repiration rates of two Japanese sharks, *Triakis scyllia* and *Heterodontus japonicus*. *O.N.R. Tokyo Scientific Bulletin* **1**, 1–11.

Collins, M. T., Gratzeks, J. B., Shotts, E. B. Jr, Dawe, D. L., Campbell, L. M. and Seen, D. R. (1975). Nitrification in an aquatic recirculating system. *Journal of the Fisheries Research Board of Canada* **32(11)**, 2025–2031.

Croll, N. A. (1966). *Ecology of Parasites*. Heinemann Inc., London.

Davies, D. H. (1960). Sharks. *Bulletin of the South African Association of Marine Biological Research* **1**, 15–19.

Essapian, F. S. (1962). Notes on the behavior of sharks in captivity. *Copeia* **1962(2)**, 457–459.

Fickeisen, D. H., Schneider, M. J. (1976). Gas Bubble Disease, Technical Information Centre ERDA, *Oak Ridge, Tennessee*.

Geraci, J. R. (1972). Experimental thiamine deficiency in captive harp seals, *Phoca groenlandica*, induced by eating herring, *Clupea harengus*, and smelts, *Osmerus mordax*. *Canadian Journal of Zoology* **50(2)**, 179–195.

Gilbert, P. W. (1977). Two decades of shark research: a review. *BioScience* **27**, 670–673.

Gilbert, P. W. and Heath, G. W. (1972). The clasper-siphon sac mechanism in *Squalus acanthias* and *Mustelus canis*. *Comparative Biochemistry and Physiology* **42A**, 97–199.

Gohar, H. A. F. and Mazhar, F. M. (1964). Keeping elasmobranchs in vivaria. *Publications Marine Biological Station, Al-Ghardaga* **13**, 242–245.

Graeber, R. C. (1974). Food intake patterns in captive juvenile lemon sharks, *Negaprion brevirostris*. *Copeia* **1974(2)**, 554–556.

Grigg, G. C. (1970). Water flow through the gills of the Port Jackson shark. *Journal of Experimental Biology* **52**, 565–568.

Gruber, S. H. and Myrberg, A. A. Jr (1977). Approaches to the study of the behavior of sharks. *American Zoologist* **17**, 471–486.

Halver, J. E. (1972). *Fish Nutrition*. Academic Press, New York and London.

Halver, J. E. (1976). Formulating practical diets for fish. *Journal of the Fisheries Research Board of Canada* **33**, 1032–1039.

Hampson, B. L. (1976). Ammonia concentration in relation to ammonia toxicity during a rainbow trout rearing experiment in a closed freshwater-sea water system. *Aquaculture* **9**, 61–70.

Herwig, N. (1979). *Handbook of Drugs and Chemicals Used in the Treatment of Fish Diseases.* C. C. Thomas, Springfield, Illinois.

Hodgson, E. S. and Mathewson, R. F. (1978). *Sensory Biology of Sharks, Skates and Rays.* Office of Naval Research. US Government Printing Office, Washington, D.C.

Honn, K. V. and Chavin, W. (1975). Prototype design for a closed marine system employing quaternary water processing. *Marine Biology* **31**, 293–298.

Hughes, G. M. (1965). *Vertebrate Respiration.* Harvard University Press, Cambridge.

Hughes, G. M. (1966). The dimensions of fish gills in relation to their function. *Experimental Biology* **45**, 177–195.

Hughes, G. M. and Umezawa, S. (1968). Oxygen consumption and gill water flow in the dogfish, *Scyliorhinus canicula* L. *Journal of Experimental Biology* **49**, 559–564.

Huisman, L. and Wood, W. E. (1974). *Slow Sand Filtration.* WHO, Geneva.

Jensen, A. C. (1965). Life history of the spiny dogfish. *Fisheries Bulletin* **65**, 527–554.

Keyes, R. S. (1977). Some methods for the control of topical bacterial infection of marine fish. *Drum and Croaker* **172**, 5–7.

Keyes, R. S. (1979). Description of live shark exhibit and research center, Sea World San Diego. Sea World, San Diego Shark Research Center Report 79–1.

Kistnasamy, N. (1974). Ragged tooth sharks in the aquarium: the tale of Bess and George. *Bulletin of the South African Association of Marine Biological Research* **11**, 27–30.

Klay, G. (1977). Shark dynamics and aquarium design. *Drum and Croaker* **17**, 29–32.

Lewiston, N., Newman, A., Robin, E. and Holtzman, D. (1979). Shark heart mitochondria: effects of external osmolarity on respiration. *Science* **206**, 75–76.

MacCallum, G. A. (1926). Deux nouveaux trematodes parasites de *Carcharhinus commersoni: Philura orata* et *Dermopitherius carcharhini. Annales de parasitologie humaine et comparée* **4**, 162–171.

Magnuson, J. J. (1962). An analysis of aggressive behavior growth and competition for food and space in Medaka (*Oryzias latipes* (Pisces, Cyprinodontidae)). *Canadian Journal of Zoology* **40**, 313–362.

Martini, F. H. (1974). Effects of capture and fasting confinement on an elasmobranch *Squalus acanthias.* Unpublished dissertation, Cornell University.

Martini, F. H. (1978). The effects of fasting confinement on *Squalus acanthias. In* "Sensory Biology of Sharks, Skates and Rays" (E. S. Hodgson and R. F. Mathewson, eds.), Office of Naval Research. US Government Printing Office, Washington, D.C.

Mazeaud, M. M., Mazeaud, F. and Donaldson, E. M. (1977). Primary and secondary effects of stress in fish: some new data with a general review. *Transactions of the American Fisheries Society* **106(3)**, 201–212.

Moss, M. L. (1977). Skeletal tissues in sharks. *American Zoologist* **17**, 335–342.

Myrberg, A. (1976). Behavior of sharks—a continuing enigma. *Naval Research Review* **29(7)**, 1–11.

Pritchard, A. W., Florey, E. and Martin, A. W. (1958). Relationship between metabolic rate and body size in an elasmobranch (*Squalus suckleyi*) and in a teleost (*Ophiodon elongatus*). *Journal of Marine Biology* **17**, 403–411.

Rasmussen, R. A. and Rasmussen, L. E. (1967). Some observations on the protein and enzyme levels of fractions in normal and stressed elasmobranchs. *Transactions of the New York Academy of Science* **29**, 397–413.

Smart, G. R. (1978). Investigations of the toxic mechanisms of ammonia to fish —gas exchange in rainbow trout (*Salmo gairdneri*) exposed to acute lethal concentrations. *Journal of Fish Biology* **12**, 93–103.

Smith, C. E. (1979). The prevention of liver lipoid degeneration (ceroidosis) and microcytic anemia in rainbow trout *Salmo gairdneri* Richardson fed rancid diets: a preliminary report. *Journal of Fish Diseases* **1979(2)**, 429–437.

Spotte, S. (1973). *Marine Aquarium Keeping*, J. Wiley and Sons, New York.

Srna, R. F. and Baggaley, A. (1975). Kinetic response of perturbed marine nitrification system. *Journal of Water Pollution Control* **47(3)**, 472–485.

Wainwright, S. A., Vosburgh, F. and Hebrank, J. H. (1978). Shark skin: function in locomotion. *Science* **202**, 747–749.

Wedemeyer, G. A., Nelson, N. C. and Yasutake, W. T. (1979). Physiological and biochemical aspects of ozone toxicity to rainbow trout (*Salmo gairdneri*). *Journal of the Fisheries Research Board of Canada* **36(6)**, 605–614.

Weihs, D., Keyes, R. S. and Stalls, D. M. (1981). Voluntary swimming speeds of two species of large carcharhinid sharks. *Copeia* **1**, 219–222.

Chapter 15

Physiological Stress in Captive Fish

C. S. Wardle

Marine Laboratory, Aberdeen, Scotland

I. INTRODUCTION

When performing experiments on fish, it is nearly impossible to avoid interaction between the experimenter and subject. Unless the fish has been reared in the laboratory, it is first necessary to capture it from the wild and to confine it. The fish must then be handled to inject or extract samples or attach a transmitting device and may have to be transferred from tank to tank. Some workers argue that a group of control fish may be treated in exactly the same way, omitting only the test treatment. However, it must be realized that both the control and the test fish are at least one stage, and often further removed from the state of wild fish and the relevance of these other changes must be considered in relation to the experimental results and conclusions.

Ideally, one would perform all experiments remotely on wild fish in their own environment without touching or interfering in any way. Since this ideal is unattainable, and some handling of the fish is necessary, we must find out what happens to the physiology of fish caught from the wild, transferred to an aquarium tank and subsequently handled. The dramatic changes that do occur underline the problems of experimenting with fish in aquarium tanks. At first sight, it seems improbable that the act of carefully transferring a fish from one mass of water to another should result in serious physiological change. Yet, even when this second water mass has been carefully regulated to match the original in all its physical and chemical properties, pronounced changes in many of the measurable physiological features of the transferred fish occur and persist for long periods so that the captured fish may never again be the same as the wild fish.

Some of the physiological reactions observed are clearly due to exhaustion or physical damage. Other reactions are classified as stress reactions because of their similarity to reactions so called in mammals and man. It is inevitable that much of our interpretation and understanding of what happens in fish is derived from the more substantial work on the physiological and stress reactions of mammals and man. The aim of this chapter is to consider some of the qualitative differences between wild and captive fish, to understand the basic changes that occur when fish are caught and handled, and how they might be avoided. The relatively simple changes of exhaustion and superficial damage are considered first and the more complex and less well defined stress reactions examined later.

II. DAMAGE DURING CAPTURE AND HANDLING

Catching fish from the wild or from a tank will always involve some exercise of the swimming muscles. A fish taken by a trawl net, seine net or a baited hook may be exhausted to a considerable degree by the time it is transferred to its first holding tank. Wriggling of the fish in nets and bumping against tank walls can seriously damage the skin structure and fin edges. An experimenter restraining a wriggling fish can add to the muscular exhaustion as well as crushing the internal organs. Some of these difficulties are discussed in Chapter 7.

A. Physical Exhaustion and Lactic Acid

Many workers do not realize how rapidly a fish becomes exhausted and how long it takes to recover. Nearly all species of fish have a substantial proportion of their body weight as anaerobic white swimming muscle. When made to use this muscle, a substantial glycogen store (0.3–1.0 g glycogen/100 g muscle) is rapidly converted to a similar weight of lactic acid which, without using oxygen, releases energy for the escape attempt. Half of the muscle glycogen store can be converted to lactic acid during 2 min. of active evasive swimming (Black *et al.*, 1961). Once the glycogen store in the anaerobic muscle has been converted to lactid acid, the fish must seek and maintain shelter for up to 24 h while the glycogen store is replenished. This anaerobic white swimming muscle is normally reserved for escape reactions and other active bursts of swimming. In practice, the exhausted fish is easily caught and handled.

Most fish have about 3% of their body weight as circulating blood while up to 30% may consist of white muscle. If all the lactic acid was transferred from the muscle to the blood following active swimming, very high levels of lactic acid would result. In general, fish do not have the same capacity as warm blooded mammals to use large amounts of lactate as a substrate for other aerobic reactions. Some protective reactions do exist in the fit fish; a large part of the lactate may be used to reform glycogen without leaving the muscle cell (Batty and Wardle, 1979; Wardle, 1978). Adrenaline released into the bloodstream causes capillaries in the white muscle to increase in volume, yet the lactate is actively held by the muscle cells (Wardle, 1978). However, any weakening of the active metabolism of the muscle cells, possibly from a stress reaction during capture, can cause the lactate to pass into the bloodstream and hasten death. It is likely that the reports of the lethal effect of lactic acid in exhausted fish have arisen for this reason.

It seems unreasonable that use of the anaerobic muscle should by itself lead to death. It is important to realise that when a rested fish is caused to wriggle or is startled, it will use up some of the muscle glycogen store, leaving a lactate pool in the muscle. The lactate pool creates a greater demand for oxygen and constitutes a hazard if there is any weakening of general metabolism. It is interesting that chasing a group of fish on one day will ensure that the muscle lactate is not released to the blood when the fish are chased the next day (Wardle, 1978). The first chase primes the lactate retaining mechanism of the fish and can therefore protect the fish prior to transport or transfer from salt to freshwater, where any lactate release would add to the other disturbances in the fish's physiology.

Sudden unexpected visual or auditory stimulation can startle a fish into very rapid escape motion. The Mauthner cells have been shown to cause more or less synchronized contraction of the anaerobic swimming muscle on each side of the fish in turn, causing the fish to make an initial powerful tail sweep. The startle reaction results in a substantial proportion of the glycogen store being converted to lactic acid. The large energy output is seen as a pronounced acceleration of the body.

B. Physical Exhaustion and Increased Oxygen Requirements

Some fish species can tolerate shortage of oxygen whereas others cannot. In general, the tolerance is related to a commitment to maintain aerobic tissue and the degree of commitment is indicated by the relative amount of the red swimming muscle.

Fish species which rest near the bottom (e.g. cod and plaice), use their white muscle to sprint when catching prey, tend to have small amounts of red muscle and have a low maximum oxygen intake capacity (below 400 mg O_2/kg/h). Fish which normally swim continuously have more red cruising muscle (e.g. Salmonidae) and are able to take in up to 800 mg O_2/kg/h from the water (Brett and Glass, 1973). The warmer ocean cruising fish like the Scombroidei, including mackerel and tuna, are able to take in oxygen continuously at rates between 600 and 1000 mg O_2/kg/h even when inactive (Stevens, 1972). These fish have large relative gill area, high haematocrit and large quantities of red swimming muscle. The more aerobic tissue a fish has, the greater is its commitment to a minimum continuous supply of oxygen; the aerobic tissue must receive oxygen to survive.

Following capture of all types of fish, the white muscle may be completely exhausted and for long periods of up to 24 h the oxygen intake may be well above the resting level and possibly near its maximum uptake level. The resting level of oxygen intake can be as low as 50–150 mg O_2/kg/h depending on temperature and size, so that a tank which seems adequately aerated for 20 resting fish may be entirely inadequate when 20 exhausted fish are introduced. Exhausted fish may have oxygen uptakes of 5 times the resting level in small fish and up to 10 times the resting level in larger fish (Brett, 1972).

C. Physical Damage

Often, the protective mucous layers, scales and essential skin structures are damaged in capture (Chapter 7).

Adult mackerel *Scomber scombrus* and herring *Clupea harengus* are especially sensitive to skin damage and any chance of survival in aquaria is destroyed within seconds by the slightest touch of a hand or tank wall against their skin. Elmhirst (1908) discovered that herring survived better in a mixture of equal parts sea water and freshwater. Parrish, Blaxter and Holliday (1958) found that loss of scales and damage to the epidermis lead to osmotic dehydration, loss of equilibrium and death, which could only be prevented by avoiding skin contact. Initial survival was increased by keeping the fish in dilute 17‰ sea water but there was no evidence that there were long-term advantages. The problems in keeping and experimenting with herring and other clupeoids are discussed by Blaxter and Holliday (1963).

Some reactions to capture are contagious. A pheromone is released by special cells in the skin of many cyprinids and other Ostariophysan and the Gonorhynchiform fish when the skin is damaged and has a dramatic effect on the individuals of the same species in the same mass of water. The species shown to have this alarm system are listed by Pfeiffer (1977).

Marine species such as the cod, saithe, haddock and many of the flatfish are commonly selected for experiments because they tolerate handling. Avoiding capture by rearing fish in the laboratory has been an alternative and successful approach. Blaxter (1975) compares and indicates some of the differences between wild and reared fish and outlines the problems inherent in both approaches for a number of species.

III. THE STRESS REACTION

After capture or transfer, fish can recover from the exhaustion of their anaerobic swimming muscle. Fish can also survive physical set-backs such as skin abrasion and can show adaptation to the new circumstances of captivity. However, during the adaptation phase, other symptoms can be detected which are not obviously linked directly with the exhaustion cycle or physical damage. Why do captive fish show major changes in red blood cell count, increased eosinophil counts, long-term elevation of glucose, onset of diuresis and numerous other changes in their physiological and endocrinological status that are considered by many workers to be stress reactions? What properties are peculiar to wild fish or long-term aquarium inhabitants that are missing in newly caught or transferred fish?

A. Comparing Wild and Captive Fish

When we transfer a wild fish to captivity, we can match all the physical and chemical properties of the water but cannot match the familiar home ground and its role in the life of the fish. Recent experiments with trout and cod have shown that fish caught, labelled with an ultrasonic transmitter and returned to their place of capture, remain within a definable home range for periods of weeks. The fish show daily patterns of movement from place to place within this limited area. If a fish is moved from where it was caught to another position outside the home range, then, within a day or so, it will return to the area where it was caught.

Priede (1978), using a heartbeat transmitting tag, showed that the fish replaced where it had been caught had a high heart rate which reduced to expected resting levels within 24 h. A fish replaced some distance from the point of capture maintained an elevated heart rate until it had found its way back to its home ground, three days later. It is worth considering what happens if the fish is not allowed to return to its home ground. Fish behave in a particularly sensitive fashion when caused to move away from their familiar home ground to explore new areas. A detailed study by Kleerekoper *et al.* (1974) demonstrated that a goldfish exposed to new ground makes a careful progression area by area, resulting in a gradual displacement of its centre of activity. In a 10 m diameter circular tank at Aberdeen, cod familiar with one side of the tank will race along an 8 m race track in response to feeding lights (Wardle and Kanwisher, 1974). The introduction of a length of rope across the race track causes a halt to further racing until this new feature has been explored. The same fish allowed through a fence to another half of the tank will explore every square metre before freely racing between lights through the new area.

On its home ground or area, the fish is familiar with its food sources, its enemies and its safe resting place. The fish may spend much of its time maintaining its presence in this area and the size of the space and the pattern of use within it may have taken weeks or months to become established. Loss of this home ground, or change in the familiar environment of a more mobile fish, may stimulate non-specific adaptation responses. In experiments, the imposition of continuous darkness or physical shock such as rapid temperature change can also stimulate a physiological stress reaction.

B. The Stress Reaction in Teleost Fish

Selye (1936) suggested that the reaction to non-specific stressors was a general adaptation, mediated by the release of adrenaline from the adrenal medulla and cortico-steroids produced by the adrenal cortex. Adrenaline had previously been recognized as the hormone released in emergency fight or flight reactions (Cannon, 1911). A review of the general-adaptation syndrome or stress reaction was published by Selye (1950) in which, with an accumulated knowledge of endocrine mechanisms, he was able to describe a general theory of the stress reaction in mammals and man. Stress reactions have been observed in many different vertebrates transferred from their home grounds to zoos (Martin, 1976; and Snyder, 1975).

The diagram (Fig. 1) shows the anatomical and physiological

apparatus necessary to generate a stress reaction as they occur in the teleost fish. The diagram is designed around the requirements suggested by Selye (1950 pp. 371–382). The essential features include a nervous system with a sensory system that receives stimuli from the environment. The brain acts as an interpreter, allowing a new situation to be related to past experience, so that stimuli are recognized as compliments or insults. There is an internal monitoring system, providing the feedback necessary for the maintenance of the composition of the circulating body fluids. There are neural connections via the hypothalamus to the autonomic

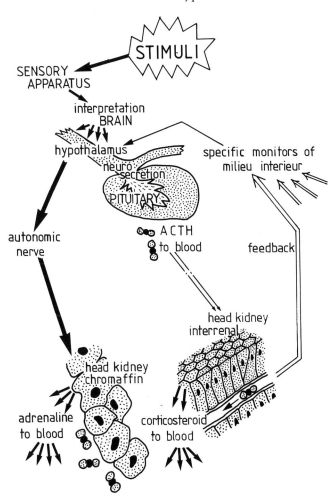

Fig. 1. The diagram outlines the apparatus necessary for the development of the stress reaction in fish.

innervation of the chromaphin tissue which secretes adrenaline and is found in the head-kidney of fish. There is a neurosecretory pathway from the hypothalamus to the pituitary gland and the secretion of adrenocorticotropic hormone (ACTH) to the blood stream. The ACTH controls secretion of corticosteroids by the adrenocortical cells of the interrenal gland in the head-kidney. This is a feedback-regulated system, perhaps with an adjustable threshold, controlling the blood levels of corticosteroids circulating through the tissues. There are many reviews that support the existence in fish of the apparatus outlined in Fig. 1 (for example see Chester Jones, 1969).

Brett (1958), while discussing stress in fish, pointed out the difficulty of separating those mechanisms involved in adaptation to a stressor and those involved in homeostatic adjustments that constantly occur during the preservation of the *milieu interieur*. The different components of the stress reaction can clearly function in many different combinations in the general maintenance of homeostasis within the body. There is no doubt that fish are sensitive to their immediate surroundings via a number of sense organs and the hypothalamus contains many of the sensory regions which monitor and cause reaction to changes in the *milieu interieur*. There have been a great many studies examining the stress reactions in fish since its proposal by Selye (key references include Mazeaud *et al.*, 1977; Mezhnin, 1978; Strange *et al.*, 1977; Soivio *et al.*, 1977; Wydoski *et al.*, 1976).

C. Experiments on Tank-adapted Fish

It is safe to assume that tank adaptation of a fish caught from the wild will always induce some form of physiological stress reaction. One can also assume that once a stress reaction has been induced, then measurement of any property of the animal will indicate a change. When examining a selected feature of the animal's physiology by experiment, it is important to know how rapidly and by how much it will change due to the stress reaction.

For example, a seasonal cycle in haematocrit does exist in fish and can be measured in plaice, *Pleuronectes platessa*. As the gonad ripens, the female red blood cell count gets lower reducing from 25% to somewhere near 15% and the male count gets higher, rising from 25% to 35%. However, when the fish are caught from the wild, a stress reaction characterized by a rapid increase in red cell count occurs in both sexes over a 20 min. period and this is followed by a slow lowering of cell count during the next 4 h. A diuresis then occurs causing the bladder to fill with hypotonic urine and haemodilution is checked (Wardle, 1968). It is therefore important to take the haematocrit samples with the knowledge of the stress reaction in order to find the sex difference and seasonal change. And vice versa, it is important to know the sex differences when looking at the tank adaptation reaction.

One of the possible functions of the corticosteroids in fish is in initiating a seasonal change from a state where the fish is actively feeding to a state where the fish is not feeding and is releasing and transporting material from storage areas and body tissues to maintain substrate levels for body metabolism (Chester Jones *et al.*, 1969). Normally in temperate fish species, a marked annual cycle takes place with the building of a large reserve during the summer feeding months and the depletion of this reserve through the winter. This cycle is often exaggerated by the building of the gonad during the winter non-feeding months.

In the stress reaction following capture, the raised blood levels of corticosteroids may cause release of the substrates for metabolism from the body storage areas and the appetite of the animal will be lost. Fish in captivity are able to survive starvation for very long periods and it is often difficult to initiate feeding in many marine species in aquaria. It seems that the process of initiating feeding in captive fish could be one of breaking this state of body catabolism initiated by the corticosteroid secretions. Some species are much more difficult to start feeding than others following capture or a transfer to a new tank. It has been shown that mixing the newly caught or transferred fish with fish already feeding speeds up the establishment of feeding (Verheijen, 1956; Parrish *et al.*, 1958; Blaxter and Holliday, 1958).

IV. DECREASING STRESS AND AIDING RECOVERY

We have examined some of the differences between the wild and tank fish and outlined the sorts of mechanisms that have been shown to be involved in the reactions observed. As the experimenter is always involved in handling and sampling his fish, he must be aware of the exhaustion and stress cycles in order to make proper interpretation of his results. The more control he has achieved in both these cycles, the more chance there is that his experiment will be meaningful. The outline of the stress reaction in Fig. 1 indicates a number of points where the initiation and development of the reaction might be interrupted. Substances such as tranquillizers might destroy the recognition of stimuli as insulting, although practical results with fish have not yet been demonstrated. Attempts to replace the essential features of the home ground may be worthwhile, or training tactics may be developed to distract fish from some part of the distressing sensory input.

Training has shown elimination of some of the more obvious stress symptoms in cod, saithe and haddock in experiments in large aquaria at Aberdeen. When these fish, which are perhaps some of the easier marine species to keep in aquaria, are introduced to a tank, their first activity is to explore carefully the whole area of the tank in small stages and during the first days of captivity, they will tend to establish a preferred region of the tank. During this period, measurements show serious physiological disturbance within the fish. Outwardly, the fish may show odd colour patterns and will not feed. Eventually, 4–7 days after capture—perhaps less in warmer water—repeated administration of food will lead to initial nervous feeding by some of the individuals and once feeding is established, the fish might be considered to be tank-adapted. During this same period, fish seriously damaged during capture will usually become obviously sick and they can be discarded. The selected fish can be kept for long periods in tanks and they will typically move slowly around the tank showing typical but unnatural behaviour patterns such as swimming close to the surface or swimming along endless repeated routes.

Further degrees of adaptation and training seem to be beneficial to these fish. The racing experiment designed to make fish voluntarily sprint between two feeding points appears to improve the tolerance of the fish to further handling. In the race, fish are trained from their initial feeding to take food at a small flashing light. The light flashes when food is presented and the fish within 2 or 3 days will learn to race from any point in the tank to this flashing light. If when fish have gathered at the light, it is extinguished and an identical light flashed some distance away, the fish will swim immediately to the new light. Fish can be raced back and forth between lights for a dozen times during a feeding session, repeated each day.

If one of these trained fish is caught from the tank, anaesthetized, treated in some way and returned to the same tank, this fish will start to race between the lights as soon as the effects of the anaesthetic (MS222) begin to wear off. The recovering fish appears to be completely distracted by the training régime (Wardle and Kanwisher, 1974). If however, a feeding tank-adapted, but untrained fish, is treated in the same way, this fish will retire to a corner to hide when recovering, shows distress colour patterns and will not feed. In other experiments, the same species of fish were trained to cruise around the circumference of the circular tank following a moving light pattern. A trained fish could be caught from the group in the channel treated and returned to join its fellows with no apparent disturbance to feeding or behaviour (Wardle and Kanwisher, 1974; Pitcher et al., 1977). Introduction of an untrained unfamiliar fish to the channel from a resting feeding stock would lead to quite different unsuccessful results. From these examples, it is clear that certain carefully planned régimes can work well if the experimenter is prepared to attend to the detail and understand the characters of the species with which he is working.

V. REFERENCES

Batty, R. S. and Wardle, C. S. (1979). Restoration of glycogen from lactic acid in the anaerobic swimming muscle of plaice *Pleuronectes platessa* L. *Journal of Fish Biology* **15**, 509–519.

Black, E. C., Robertson, A. C. and Parker, R. R. (1961). Some aspects of carbohydrate metabolism in fish. *In* "Comparative Physiology of Carbohydrate Metabolism in Heterothermic Animals" (A. W. Martin, ed.), pp. 89–122. University of Washington Press, Seattle.

Blaxter, J. H. S. (1975). Reared and wild fish—how do they compare? *In* "10th European Symposium on Marine Biology, Ostend, Belgium", Vol. 1. 11–26.

Blaxter, J. H. S. and Holliday, F. G. T. (1958). Herring (*Clupea harengus* L.) in aquaria. II Feeding. *Marine Research* **6**, 1–22.

Blaxter, J. H. S. and Holliday, F. G. T. (1963). The behaviour and physiology of herring and other clupeids. *In* "Advances in Marine Biology Vol. 1." (F. S. Russell, ed.), Academic Press, London and New York.

Brett, J. R. (1958). Implications and assessments of environmental stress. *In* "The Investigation of Fish Power Problems"—H. R. MacMillan lectures in fisheries (P. A. Larkin, ed.), pp. 69–83. University of British Columbia.

Brett, J. R. (1972). The metabolic demand for oxygen in fish, particularly salmonids, and a comparison with other vertebrates. *Respiration Physiology* **14**, 151–170.

Brett, J. R. and Glass, N. R. (1973). Metabolic rates and critical swimming speeds of Sockeye salmon (*Oncorhynchus nerka*) in relation to size and temperature. *Journal of the Fisheries Research Board of Canada* **30**, 379–387.

Cannon, W. B. (1911). The stimulation of adrenal secretion by emotional excitement. *Proceedings of the American Fisheries Society* **50**, 226.

Chester Jones, I., Chan, D. K. O., Henderson, I. W. and Ball, J. N. (1969). The adrenocortical steroids, adrenocorticotropin and the corpuscles of Stannius. *In* "Fish Physiology: 2" (W. S. Hoar and D. J. Randall, eds.), 322–376. Academic Press, London and New York.

Elmhirst, R. (1908). The keeping of young herring alive in captivity. *Nature London* **79**, 38.

Kleerekoper, H., Matis, J., Gensler, P. and Maynards, P. (1974). Exploratory behaviour of Goldfish (*Carassius auratus*). *Animal Behaviour* **22**, 124–132.

Martin, R. D. (1976). Stress and reproduction in captivity. *In* "The Zoological Society of London, 1826–1976 and beyond" (Professor Lord Zuckerman, ed.). *Symposium of the Zoological Society of London* **40**, 306–311.

Mazeaud, M. M., Mazeaud, F. and Donaldson, E. M. (1977). Primary and secondary effects of stress in fish: Some new data with a general review. *Transactions of the American Fisheries Society* **106**, 201–212.

Mezhnin, F. I. (1978). The interrenal and suprarenal glands and Stannius bodies of the guppy, *Lebistes reticulatus*, under conditions of extreme stress. *Journal of Ichthylogy* **18**, 611–632.

Parrish, B. B., Blaxter, J. H. S. and Holliday, F. G. T. (1958). Herring (*Clupea harengus* L.) in aquaria. I. Establishment. *Marine Research* **5**, 1–11.

Pfeiffer, W. (1977). The distribution of fright reaction and alarm substance cells in fishes. *Copeia* **1977**, 653–665.

Pitcher, R. J., Partridge, B. L. and Wardle, C. S. (1976). A blind fish can school. *Science* **194**, 964–965.

Priede, I. G. (1978) Behavioural and physiological rhythms of fish in their natural environment, as indicated by ultrasonic telemetry of heart rate. *In* "Rhythmic Activity of Fishes" (J. E. Thorpe, ed.). Academic Press, London and New York.

Selye, H. (1936). A syndrome produced by diverse nocuous agents. *Nature, London* **138**, 32.

Selye, H. (1950). "The physiology and pathology of exposure to stress. A treatise based on the concepts of the general-adaptation syndrome and the diseases of adaptation". Acta Inc. Montreal.

Snyder, R. L. (1975). Behavioural stress in captive animals. *In* "Research in Zoos and Aquariums", pp. 41–76. Washington, National Academy of Science.

Soivio, A., Nyholm, K and Huhti, M. (1977). Effects of anaesthesia with MS222, neutralised MS222 and benzocaine on the blood constituents of rainbow trout, *Salmo gairdneri*. *Journal of Fish Biology* **10**, 91–101.

Stevens, E. D. (1972). Some aspects of gas exchange in tuna. *Journal of Experimental Biology* **56**, 809–823.

Strange, R. J., Schreck, C. B. and Golden, J. T. (1977). Corticoid stress responses to handling and temperature in salmonids. *Transactions of the American Fisheries Society* **106**, 213–218.

Verheijen, F. J. (1953). Laboratory experiments with herring, *Clupea harengus*. *Experimentia* **9**, 193.

Wardle, C. S. (1968). Physiological response of fish to capture and captivity. *Report of the Challenger Society* **3**, 37–38.

Wardle, C. S. (1978). Non-release of lactic acid from anaerobic swimming muscle of plaice, *Pleuronectes platessa* L.: A stress reaction. *Journal of Experimental Biology* **77**, 141–155.

Wardle, C. S. and Kanwisher, J. W. (1974). The significance of heart rate in free swimming cod, *Gadus morhua*: Some observations with ultra-sonic tags. *Marine Behavioural Physiology* **2**, 311–324.

Wydoski, R. S., Wedemeyer, G. A. and Nelson, N. C. (1976). Physiological response to hooking stress in Hatchery and wild rainbow trout (*Salmo gairdneri*). *Transactions of the American Fisheries Society* **105**, 601–606.

Appendix

Charles Robb

Marine Laboratory, Aberdeen, Scotland

UNITS AND THEIR CONVERSION

INTERNATIONAL SYSTEM OF UNITS

The Système Internationale d'Unités, SI Units, consists of seven base units from which derived units are formed.

The Base Units

Standard quantity	SI unit	Symbol
length	metre	m
mass	kilogram	kg
time	second	s
electric current	ampere	A
thermodynamic current	kelvin	K
amount of substance	mole	mol
luminous intensity	candela	cd

SI prefixes, symbols and multiplication factors

Prefix	Symbol	Factor	
tera	T	10^{12}	1,000,000,000,000
giga	G	10^{9}	1,000,000,000
mega	M	10^{6}	1,000,000
kilo	k	10^{3}	1,000
hecto	h	10^{2}	100
deca	da	10^{1}	10
deci	d	10^{-1}	0.1
centi	c	10^{-2}	0.01
milli	m	10^{-3}	0.001
micro	μ	10^{-6}	0.000,001
nano	n	10^{-9}	0.000,000,001
pico	p	10^{-12}	0.000,000,000,001
femto	f	10^{-15}	0.000,000,000,000,001
atto	a	10^{-18}	0.000,000,000,000,000,001

SI derived units

Quantity	SI Unit Name	Symbol
area	square metre	m^2
volume	cubic metre	m^3
speed, velocity	metre per second	m/s^{-1}
acceleration	metre per second squared	m/s^{-2}
wave number	1 per metre	m^{-1}
density, mass density	kilogram per cubic metre	$kg\ m^{-3}$
current density	ampere per square metre	$A\ m^{-2}$
magnetizing force, magnetic field strength (H)	ampere per metre	$A\ m^{-1}$
concentration	mole per cubic metre	$mol\ m^{-3}$
specific volume	cubic metre per kilogram	$m^3\ kg^{-1}$
luminance	candela per square metre	$cd\ m^{-2}$

SI supplementary units

Quantity	Name	Symbol
plane angle	radian	rad
solid angle	steradian	sr
angular velocity	radian per second	$rad\ s^{-1}$
angular acceleration	radian per second squared	$rad\ s^{-2}$
radiant intensity	watt per steradian	$W\ sr^{-1}$
radiance	watt per square metre steradian	$W\ m^{-2}\ sr^{-1}$

UK AND US UNITS OF VOLUME AND CAPACITY OF LIQUID

UK units of fluid measure

Symbol	Unit	Metric Equivalent
UK fl oz	1 fluid ounce = 8 fluid drachms	$= 28.4131\ cm^3$
UK gill	1 gill = 5 fluid ounces	$= 0.142\ 065\ dm^3$
UK pt	1 pint = 4 gills (= 20 fluid ounces)	$= 0.568\ 261\ dm^3$
UK qt	1 quart = 2 pints	$= 1.136\ 52\ dm^3$
UK gal	1 gallon = 4 quarts (= 160 fluid ounces)	$= 4.546\ 09\ dm^3$

US units of fluid measure

Symbol	Unit	Metric Equivalent
US fl oz	1 US fluid ounce = 8 fluid drams	29.573 5 cm^3
gi	1 US gill = 4 fluid ounces	= 0.118 294 dm^3
liq pt	1 US liquid pint = 4 gills (= 16 fluid ounces)	0.473 176 dm^3
liq qt	1 US liquid quart = 2 liquid pints	= 0.946 353 dm^3
US gal	1 US gallon = 4 liquid quarts (= 128 fluid ounces)	= 3.785 41 dm^3
bbl	1 US barrel (for petroleum) = 42 gallons	= 158.987 dm^3

UK and US units of volume

The UK and US units of volume are based on traditional UK and US units of length, defined for the UK by the Weights and Measures Act, 1963.

Symbol	Unit	Metric Equivalent
yd^3	1 cubic yard = 27 cubic feet	= 0.764 555 m^3
ft^3	1 cubic foot = 1728 cubic inches	= 0.028 3168 m^3
in^3	1 cubic inch	= 1.638 71 × 10^{-5} m^3

Relationship between UK and US units of capacity for fluid

1 UK fluid ounce = 0.960 760 US fluid ounce
1 UK gill = 1.200 95 US gill
1 UK pint = 1.200 95 US liquid pint
1 UK quart = 1.200 95 US liquid quart
1 UK gallon = 1.200 95 US gallon

1 US fluid ounce = 1.040 84 UK fluid ounce
1 US gill = 0.832 674 UK gill
1 US liquid pint = 0.832 674 UK pint
1 US liquid quart = 0.832 674 UK quart
1 US gallon = 0.832 674 UK gallon

SI derived units with special names

Quantity	SI Unit Name	Symbol	Expression in terms of other units	Expression in terms of SI base units
frequency	hertz	Hz		s^{-1}
force	newton	N		$m\ kg\ s^{-2}$
pressure, stress	pascal	Pa	$N\ m^{-2}$	$m^{-1}\ kg\ s^{-2}$
energy, work, quantity of heat	joule	J	$N\ m$	$m^2\ kg\ s^{-2}$
power, radiant flux	watt	W	$J\ s^{-1}$	$m^2\ kg\ s^{-3}$
quantity of electricity, electric charge	coulomb	C		$s\ A$
electrical potential, potential difference, electromotive force	volt	V	$W\ A^{-1}$	$m^2\ kg\ s^{-3}\ A^{-1}$
capacitance	farad	F	$C\ V^{-1}$	$m^{-2}\ kg^{-1}\ s^4\ A^2$
electric resistance	ohm	Ω	$V\ A^{-1}$	$m^2\ kg\ s^{-3}\ A^{-2}$
conductance	siemens	S	$A\ V^{-1}$	$m^{-2}\ kg^{-1}\ s^3\ A^2$
magnetic flux	weber	Wb	$V\ s$	$m^2\ kg\ s^{-2}\ A^{-1}$
magnetic flux density, magnetic induction, magnetic field	tesla	T	$Wb\ m^{-2}$	$kg\ s^{-2}\ A^{-1}$
inductance	henry	H	$Wb\ A^{-1}$	$m^2\ kg\ s^{-2}\ A^{-2}$
luminous flux	lumen	lm		$cd\ sr^a$
illuminance	lux	lx	$lm\ m^{-2}$	$m^{-2}\ cd\ sr^a$
activity (ionizing radiations)	becquerel	Bq		s^{-1}
absorbed dose	gray	Gy	$J\ kg^{-1}$	$m^2\ s^{-2}$
dynamic viscosity	pascal second	Pa s		$m^{-1}\ kg\ s^{-1}$
moment of force	metre newton	N m		$m^2\ kg\ s^{-2}$
surface tension	newton per metre	$N\ m^{-1}$		$kg\ s^{-2}$
heat flux density, irradiance	watt per square metre	$W\ m^{-2}$		$kg\ s^{-3}$

SI derived units with special names—*continued*

Quantity	SI Unit Name	Symbol	Expression in terms of other units	Expression in terms of SI base units
heat capacity, entropy	joule per kelvin	$J\ K^{-1}$		$m^2\ kg\ s^{-2}\ K^{-1}$
specific heat capacity, specific entropy	joule per kilogram kelvin	$J\ kg^{-1}\ K^{-1}$		$m^2\ s^{-2}\ K^{-1}$
specific energy	joule per kilogram	$J\ kg^{-1}$		$m^2\ s^{-2}$
thermal conductivity	watt per metre kelvin	$W\ m^{-1}\ K^{-1}$		$m\ kg\ s^{-3}\ K^{-1}$
energy density	joule per cubic metre	$J\ m^{-3}$		$m^{-1}\ kg\ s^{-2}$
electric field strength	volt per metre	$V\ m^{-1}$		$m\ kg\ s^{-3}\ A^{-1}$
electric charge density	coulomb per cubic metre	$C\ m^{-3}$		$m^{-3}\ s\ A$
electric displacement, electric flux density	coulomb per square metre	$C\ m^{-2}$		$m^{-2}\ s\ A$
permittivity	farad per metre	$F\ m^{-1}$		$m^{-3}\ kg^{-1}\ s^4\ A^2$
permeability	henry per metre	$H\ m^{-1}$		$m\ kg\ s^{-2}\ A^{-2}$
molar energy	joule per mole	$J\ mol^{-1}$		$m^2\ kg\ s^{-2}\ mol^{-1}$
molar entropy, molar heat capacity	joule per mole kelvin	$J\ mol^{-1}\ K^{-1}$		$m^2\ kg\ s^{-2}\ K^{-1}\ mol^{-1}$
exposure (ionizing radiations)	coulomb per kilogram	$C\ kg^{-1}$		$kg^{-1}\ s\ A$
absorbed dose rate	gray per second	$Gy\ s^{-1}$		$m^2\ s^{-3}$

Unit conversion table

To convert	Into	Multiply by
acres	square metres	4046.8
atmospheres	centimetres of mercury	76.0
atmospheres	feet of water	33.90
atmospheres	kilograms/square centimetre	1.033
atmospheres	newtons/square metre or pascals	101325.0
bars	atmospheres	9.870×10^{-7}
bars	kilograms/square metre	1.020×10^4
bars	newtons/square metre or pascals	10^5
centigrade	fahrenheit	$(C^{\circ} \times 9/5) + 32$
centigrade	celsius	1.0
centigrade	kelvin	$(C^{\circ} + 273.15)$
centimetres	feet	3.281×10^{-2}
centimetres	inches	0.3937
centimetres of mercury	atmospheres	0.01316
centimetres of mercury	feet of water	0.4461
centimetres of mercury	kilograms/square metre	136.0
centimetres/second	feet/minute	1.969
centimetres/second	feet/second	0.03281
centimetres/second	metres/minute	0.6
centimetres/second	miles/hour	0.02237
cubic centimetres	cubic feet	3.531×10^{-5}
cubic centimetres	cubic inches	6.102×10^{-2}
cubic centimetres	cubic metres	1×10^{-6}
cubic centimetres	gallons (UK)	2.199×10^{-4}
cubic centimetres	gallons (US liquid)	2.642×10^{-4}
cubic centimetres	litres	1×10^{-3}
cubic feet	cubic centimetres	2.832×10^4
cubic feet	cubic metres	0.02832
cubic feet	gallons (UK)	6.229
cubic feet	gallons (US liquid)	7.481
cubic feet	litres	28.32
cubic feet/minute	cubic centimetres/second	472
cubic feet/minute	gallons (UK)/second	0.1038
cubic feet/minute	gallons (US)/second	0.1247
cubic feet/minute	litres/second	0.4720
cubic inches	cubic centimetres	16.39
cubic inches	cubic metres	1.639×10^{-5}
cubic inches	cubic yards	2.143×10^{-5}
cubic inches	gallons (UK)	3.604×10^{-3}
cubic inches	gallons (US liquid)	4.329×10^{-3}
cubic inches	litres	1.639×10^{-2}
cubic metres	cubic centimetres	1×10^6

Unit conversion table—*continued*

To convert	Into	Multiply by
cubic metres	gallons (UK)	219.9
cubic metres	gallons (US)	264.2
cubic metres	litres	1×10^3
cubic yards	gallons (UK)	168.2
cubic yards	gallons (US)	202.0
cubic yards	litres	764.6
cubic yards/minute	gallons/second	3.367
cubic yards/minute	litres/second	12.74
cycles/second	hertz	1.0
degrees (angle)	radians	1.745×10^{-2}
dynes	joules/metre	1×10^{-5}
dynes	kilogram	1.02×10^{-6}
dynes/square centimetre	bars	1×10^{-6}
feet	centimetres	30.48
feet	kilometres	30.048×10^{-4}
feet	metres	3.048×10^{-1}
feet	millimetres	3.048×10^2
feet of water	atmospheres	2.95×10^{-2}
feet of water	inches of mercury	0.8826
feet of water	kilograms/square metre	3.048×10^{-2}
feet/minute	centimetre/second	0.508
feet/minute	kilometre/hour	0.01829
feet/minute	metres/minute	0.3048
feet/second	centimetre/second	30.48
feet/second	kilometre/hour	1.097
feet/second	metres/minute	18.29
gallons (UK)	cubic centimetres	4546
gallons (US)	cubic centimetres	3785
gallons (UK)	cubic feet	0.1605
gallons (US)	cubic feet	0.1337
gallons (UK)	cubic inches	277.4
gallons (US)	cubic inches	231.0
gallons (UK)	cubic metres	4.546×10^{-3}
gallons (US)	cubic metres	3.785×10^{-3}
gallons (UK)	cubic yards	5.944×10^{-3}
gallons (US)	cubic yards	4.951×10^{-3}
gallons (UK)	litres	4.546
gallons (US)	litres	3.785
gallons/minute (UK)	cubic feet/second	2.675×10^{-3}
gallons/minute (US)	cubic feet/second	2.228×10^{-3}
gallons/minute (UK)	litres/second	0.07577
gallons/minute (US)	litres/second	0.06308

Unit conversion table—*continued*

To convert	Into	Multiply by
gallons/minute (UK)	cubic feet/hour	9.63000
gallons/minute (US)	cubic feet/hour	8.0208
gallons (US)	gallons (UK)	0.832674
gallons (UK)	gallons (US)	1.20095
grams	dynes	980.7
grams	joules/metre	9.807×10^{-3}
grams	pounds	2.205×10^{-3}
grams/litre	parts/million	1000
grams/square centimetre	pounds/square foot	2.0481
hours	days	4.167×10^{-2}
inches	centimetres	2.54
inches	metres	2.54×10^{-2}
inches of mercury	atmospheres	0.03342
inches of mercury	feet of water	1.133
inches of mercury	kilogram/square metre	345.3
inches of mercury	kilogram/square centimetre	3.453×10^{-2}
inches of water (at 4°C)	atmospheres	2.458×10^{-3}
inches of water (at 4°C)	inches of mercury	7.355×10^{-2}
inches of water (at 4°C)	kilograms/square metre	25.40
joules	BTU	9.486×10^{-4}
joules	kilogram–calories	2.389×10^{-4}
kilograms	dynes	980,665
kilograms	joules/metre (newtons)	9.807
kilogram–calories	joules	4,186.0
kilogram/square metre	atmospheres	9.678×10^{-5}
kilogram/square metre	bars	98.07×10^{-6}
kilogram/square metre	feet of water	3.281×10^{-3}
kilogram/square metre	inches of mercury	2.896×10^{-3}
kilometres	yards	1093.6
litres	cubic centimetres	1×10^{3}
litres	cubic feet	0.03531
litres	cubic metres	1×10^{-3}
litres	gallons (UK)	0.219969
litres	gallons (US)	0.2642
litres/minute	cubic feet/second	5.885×10^{-4}
litres/minute	gallons/second (UK)	3.666×10^{-3}
litres/minute	gallons/second (US)	4.403×10^{-3}
metres	feet	3.2808
metres	inches	39.37
metres	miles (nautical)	5.396×10^{-4}
metres	miles (statute)	6.214×10^{-4}
metres	yards	1.094

Unit conversion table—*continued*

To convert	Into	Multiply by
metres/minute	centimetre/second	1.667
metres/minute	kilometres/hour	0.06
metres/second	kilometres/hour	3.6
metres/second	kilometres/minute	0.06
miles (nautical)	metres	1,852
miles (nautical)	miles (statute)	1.1508
miles (statute)	metres	1,609.0
miles (statute)	miles (nautical)	0.8684
miles/hour	kilometres/hour	1.6093
milligrams/litre	parts/million	1.0
millimetres	microns	1×10^3
million gallons/day (UK)	cubic feet/second	1.8576
million gallons/day (US)	cubic feet/second	1.5474
newtons	dynes	1×10^5
pints (UK)	cubic centimetres	568.3
pints (UK)	cubic inches	34.677
pints (UK)	cubic metres	5.683×10^{-4}
pints (UK)	cubic yards	7.433×10^{-4}
pints (UK)	gallons (UK)	0.125
pints (liquid US)	cubic centimetres	473.2
pints (liquid US)	cubic inches	28.875
pints (liquid US)	cubic metres	4.732×10^{-4}
pints (liquid US)	cubic yards	6.189×10^{-4}
pints (liquid US)	gallons (US)	0.125
pints (liquid US)	litres	0.4732
pounds of water	gallons (UK)	0.0998
pounds of water	gallons (US)	0.1198
pounds/cubic inch	kilograms/cubic metre	2.768×10^4
pounds/square foot	atmospheres	4.725×10^{-4}
pounds/square foot	feet of water	0.01602
pounds/square foot	inches of mercury	0.01414
pounds/square foot	kilogram/square metre	4.882
pounds/square inch	atmospheres	0.06804
pounds/square inch	feet of water	2.307
pounds/square inch	inches of mercury	2.306
pounds/square inch	kilogram/square metre	703.1
square feet	square centimetres	929
square feet	square metres	0.0929
square feet	square millimetres	9.29×10^4
square inches	square centimetres	6.452
square inches	square millimetres	645.2
square miles	square kilometres	2.59

Unit conversion table—*continued*

To convert	Into	Multiply by
square yards	square centimetres	8361
square yards	square metres	0.8361
square yards	square millimetres	8.361×10^5
tons (long) UK	kilograms	1016
tons (metric)	kilograms	1000
tons (short) US	kilograms	907.2
tons (short) US	tons (metric)	0.9078
yards	centimetres	91.44
yards	kilometres	9.144×10^{-4}
yards	metres	0.9144
yards	miles (nautical)	4.934×10^{-4}
yards	miles (statute)	5.682×10^{-4}
yards	millimetres	914.4

Appendix

Temperature conversion formulae and tables
To convert centigrade to fahrenheit: multiply by 9, divide the product by 5 and add 32

$$[(9 \times T) \div 5] + 32$$

To convert fahrenheit to centigrade: subtract 32, multiply by 5 and divide by 9

$$[(T - 32) \times 5] \div 9$$

T is the temperature to be converted.

°C	T	°F	°C	T	°F	°C	T	°F
− 40	− 40	− 40	− 18.3	− 1	30.2	3.3	38	100.4
− 39.4	− 39	− 38.2	− 17.8	0	32	3.9	39	102.2
− 38.9	− 38	− 36.4	− 17.2	1	33.8	4.4	40	104.0
− 38.3	− 37	− 34.6	− 16.7	2	35.6	5.0	41	105.8
− 37.8	− 36	− 32.8	− 16.1	3	37.4	5.6	42	107.6
− 37.2	− 35	− 31.0	− 15.6	4	39.2	6.1	43	109.4
− 36.7	− 34	− 29.2	− 15.0	5	41.0	6.7	44	111.2
− 36.1	− 33	− 27.4	− 14.4	6	42.8	7.2	45	113.0
− 35.6	− 32	− 25.6	− 13.9	7	44.6	7.8	46	114.8
− 35.0	− 31	23.8	− 13.3	8	46.4	8.3	47	116.6
− 34.4	− 30	− 22.0	− 12.8	9	48.2	8.9	48	118.4
− 33.9	− 29	− 20.2	− 12.2	10	50.0	9.4	49	120.2
− 33.3	− 28	− 18.4	− 11.7	11	51.8	10.0	50	122.0
− 32.8	− 27	− 16.6	− 11.1	12	53.6	10.6	51	123.8
− 32.2	− 26	− 14.8	− 10.6	13	55.4	11.1	52	125.6
− 31.7	− 25	− 13.0	− 10.0	14	57.2	11.7	53	127.4
− 31.1	− 24	− 11.2	− 9.4	15	59.0	12.2	54	129.2
− 30.6	− 23	− 9.4	− 8.9	16	60.8	12.8	55	131.0
− 30.0	− 22	− 7.6	− 8.3	17	62.6	13.3	56	132.8
− 29.4	− 21	− 5.8	− 7.8	18	64.4	13.9	57	134.6
− 28.9	− 20	− 4.0	− 7.2	19	66.2	14.4	58	136.4
− 28.3	− 19	− 2.2	− 6.7	20	68.0	15.0	59	138.2
− 27.8	− 18	− 0.4	− 6.1	21	69.8	15.6	60	140.0
− 27.2	− 17	1.4	− 5.6	22	71.6	16.1	61	141.8
− 26.7	− 16	3.2	− 5.0	23	73.4	16.7	62	143.6
− 26.1	− 15	5.0	− 4.4	24	75.2	17.2	63	145.4
− 25.6	− 14	6.8	− 3.9	25	77.0	17.8	64	147.2
− 25.0	− 13	8.6	− 3.3	26	78.8	18.3	65	149.0
− 24.4	− 12	10.4	− 2.8	27	80.6	18.9	66	150.8
− 23.9	− 11	12.2	− 2.2	28	82.4	19.4	67	152.6
− 23.3	− 10	14.0	− 1.7	29	84.2	20.0	68	154.4
− 22.8	− 9	15.8	− 1.1	30	86.0	20.6	69	156.2
− 22.2	− 8	17.6	− 0.6	31	87.8	21.1	70	158.0
− 21.7	− 7	19.4	0	32	89.6	21.7	71	159.8
− 21.1	− 6	21.2	0.6	33	91.4	22.2	72	161.6
− 20.6	− 5	23.0	1.1	34	93.2	22.8	73	163.4
− 20.0	− 4	24.8	1.7	35	95.0	23.3	74	165.2
− 19.4	− 3	26.6	2.2	36	96.8	23.9	75	167.0
− 18.9	− 2	28.4	2.8	37	98.6	24.4	76	168.8

Temperature conversion formulae and tables—*continued*

°C	T	°F	°C	T	°F	°C	T	°F
25.0	77	170.6	50.6	123	253.4	75.6	168	334.4
25.6	78	172.4	51.1	124	255.2	76.1	169	336.2
26.1	79	174.2	51.7	125	257.0	76.7	170	338.0
26.7	80	176.0	52.2	126	258.8	77.2	171	339.8
27.2	81	177.8	52.8	127	260.6	77.8	172	341.6
27.8	82	179.6	53.3	128	262.4	78.3	173	343.4
28.3	83	181.4	53.9	129	264.2	78.9	174	345.2
28.9	84	183.2	54.4	130	266.0	79.4	175	347.0
29.4	85	185.0	55.0	131	267.8	80.0	176	348.8
30.0	86	186.8	55.6	132	269.6	80.6	177	350.6
30.6	87	188.6	56.1	133	271.4	81.1	178	352.4
31.1	88	190.4	56.7	134	273.2	81.7	179	354.2
31.7	89	192.2	57.2	135	275.0	82.2	180	356.0
32.2	90	194.0	57.8	136	276.8	82.8	181	357.8
32.8	91	195.8	58.3	137	278.6	83.3	182	359.6
33.3	92	197.6	58.9	138	280.4	83.9	183	361.4
33.9	93	199.4	59.4	139	282.2	84.4	184	363.2
34.4	94	201.2	60.0	140	284.0	85.0	185	365.0
35.0	95	203.0	60.6	141	285.8	85.6	186	366.8
35.6	96	204.8	61.1	142	287.6	86.1	187	368.6
36.1	97	206.6	61.7	143	289.4	86.7	188	370.4
36.7	98	208.4	62.2	144	291.2	87.2	189	372.2
37.2	99	210.2	62.8	145	293.0	87.8	190	374.0
37.8	100	212.0	63.3	146	294.8	88.3	191	375.8
38.3	101	213.8	63.9	147	296.6	88.9	192	377.6
38.9	102	215.6	64.4	148	298.4	89.4	193	379.4
39.4	103	217.4	65.0	149	300.2	90.0	194	381.2
40.0	104	219.2	65.6	150	302.0	90.6	195	383.0
40.6	105	221.0	66.1	151	303.8	91.1	196	384.8
41.1	106	222.8	66.7	152	305.6	91.7	197	386.6
41.7	107	224.6	67.2	153	307.4	92.2	198	388.4
42.2	108	226.4	67.8	154	309.2	92.8	199	390.2
42.8	109	228.2	68.3	155	311.0	93.3	200	392.0
43.3	110	230.0	68.9	156	312.8	93.9	201	393.8
43.9	111	231.8	69.4	157	314.6	94.4	202	395.6
44.4	112	233.6	70.0	158	316.4	95.0	203	397.4
45.0	113	235.4	70.6	159	318.2	95.6	204	399.2
45.6	114	237.2	71.1	160	320.0	96.1	205	401.0
46.1	115	239.0	71.7	161	321.8	96.7	206	402.8
46.7	116	240.8	72.2	162	323.6	97.2	207	404.6
47.2	117	242.6	72.8	163	325.4	97.8	208	406.4
47.8	118	244.4	73.3	164	327.2	98.3	209	408.2
48.3	119	246.2	73.9	165	329.0	98.9	210	410.0
48.9	120	248.0	74.4	166	330.8	99.4	211	411.8
49.4	121	249.8	75.0	167	332.6	100.0	212	413.6
50.0	122	251.6						

SALINITY AND OXYGEN

The relationship between salinity and chlorinity

Chlorinity (Cl) is the quantity of chlorine (grams) in 1 kilogram of sea water. Chlorinity is expressed in parts per thousand and is used as an index of the amount of salt in a volume of water.

Chlorinity $Cl\%_{oo}$ = Salinity $S\%_{oo} \times 1.80655^{-1}$

Chlorosity (Cl/litre) is the product of the quantity of chlorine (grams) in 1 litre of sea water at $20°C$ or some other stated temperature $_{(t)}$ and the density of the sea water at the same temperature.

Chlorsity $Cl_{(t)} \%_{oo}$ = density $_{(t)} \times$ Chlorinity $Cl^{oo}\%$

Salinity (S) is defined as the total amount of solid material in grams in 1 kilogram of sea water and is expressed in parts per thousand.

Salinity $S\%_{oo}$ = $1.80655 \times$ Chlorinity $Cl\%_{oo}$

Dissolved oxygen levels in water

Physiologists often measure oxygen levels in terms of partial pressures. That is in millimetres of mercury (mm Hg). The partial pressure of oxygen dissolved in water at equilibrium with the atmosphere is equal to the partial pressure of the gas in the atmosphere and is given by the formulae.

$$P_{O2} = (P_b - P_{H2O(T)}) \times 0.209$$

Where T is the temperature:
   P_{O2} is the partial pressure of oxygen
   P_b is the barometric pressure
   0.209 is the oxygen volume fraction in air
   $P_{H2O(T)}$ is the vapour pressure of water at a particular temperature.

In the aquarium, an estimate of the concentration of oxygen is generally required in milligram/litre (mg/l). The output of most oxygen electrodes is proportional to the partial pressure of oxygen rather than the concentration and herein lies a pitfall. Oxygen electrodes must be calibrated in air-saturated solutions of water of known salinity at known temperatures and pressures. Any subsequent change in these parameters must be allowed for.

Oxygen solubility tables

The oxygen saturation data given in the following tables are given with reference to an atmosphere of 20.95% oxygen and 100% relative humidity at an atmospheric pressure of 760 mm Hg. The oxygen solubility is expressed in cm^3/dm^3 or ml/litre, to convert to mg/dm^3 or mg/l multiply the cm^3/dm^3 values by the factor 1.428 (temperature in degrees celsius).

	Salinity				Parts per thousand	
Temperature	0.0	1.0	2.0	3.0	4.0	5.0
0.0	10.22	10.15	10.08	10.01	9.94	9.87
1.0	9.94	9.87	9.80	9.74	9.67	9.60
2.0	9.67	9.60	9.54	9.47	9.41	9.35
3.0	9.41	9.35	9.28	9.22	9.16	9.10
4.0	9.16	9.10	9.04	8.98	8.92	8.86
5.0	8.93	8.87	8.81	8.75	8.70	8.64
6.0	8.70	8.65	8.59	8.53	8.48	8.42
7.0	8.49	8.43	8.38	8.32	8.27	8.22
8.0	8.28	8.23	8.17	8.12	8.07	8.02
9.0	8.08	8.03	7.98	7.93	7.88	7.83
10.0	7.89	7.84	7.79	7.74	7.69	7.64
11.0	7.71	7.66	7.61	7.56	7.52	7.47
12.0	7.53	7.49	7.44	7.39	7.35	7.30
13.0	7.37	7.32	7.27	7.23	7.18	7.14
14.0	7.20	7.16	7.12	7.07	7.03	6.98
15.0	7.05	7.00	6.96	6.92	6.88	6.84
16.0	6.90	6.86	6.81	6.77	6.73	6.69
17.0	6.75	6.71	6.67	6.63	6.59	6.55
18.0	6.61	6.58	6.54	6.50	6.46	6.42
19.0	6.48	6.44	6.40	6.37	6.33	6.29
20.0	6.35	6.31	6.28	6.24	6.20	6.17
21.0	6.23	6.19	6.15	6.12	6.08	6.05
22.0	6.11	6.07	6.04	6.00	5.97	5.93
23.0	5.99	5.96	5.92	5.89	5.85	5.82
24.0	5.88	5.84	5.81	5.78	5.74	5.71
25.0	5.77	5.74	5.70	5.67	5.64	5.61
26.0	5.66	5.63	5.60	5.57	5.54	5.51
27.0	5.56	5.53	5.50	5.47	5.44	5.41
28.0	5.46	5.43	5.40	5.37	5.34	5.31
29.0	5.37	5.34	5.31	5.28	5.25	5.22
30.0	5.28	5.25	5.22	5.19	5.16	5.13
31.0	5.19	5.16	5.13	5.10	5.07	5.05
32.0	5.10	5.07	5.04	5.02	4.99	4.96
33.0	5.01	4.99	4.96	4.93	4.91	4.88
34.0	4.93	4.91	4.88	4.85	4.83	4.80
35.0	4.85	4.83	4.80	4.78	4.75	4.73

Oxygen solubility tables—*continued*

Temperature	Salinity 6.0	7.0	8.0	Parts per thousand 9.0	10.0	11.0
0.0	9.81	9.74	9.67	9.61	9.54	9.48
1.0	9.54	9.48	9.41	9.35	9.28	9.22
2.0	9.28	9.22	9.16	9.10	9.04	8.98
3.0	9.04	8.98	8.92	8.86	8.80	8.74
4.0	8.81	8.75	8.69	8.63	8.57	8.52
5.0	8.58	8.53	8.47	8.41	8.36	8.30
6.0	8.37	8.31	8.26	8.20	8.15	8.10
7.0	8.16	8.11	8.06	8.00	7.95	7.90
8.0	7.97	7.91	7.86	7.81	7.76	7.71
9.0	7.78	7.73	7.68	7.63	7.58	7.53
10.0	7.60	7.55	7.50	7.45	7.41	7.36
11.0	7.42	7.38	7.33	7.28	7.24	7.19
12.0	7.26	7.21	7.17	7.12	7.08	7.03
13.0	7.10	7.05	7.01	6.96	6.92	6.88
14.0	6.94	6.90	6.86	6.81	6.77	6.73
15.0	6.79	6.75	6.71	6.67	6.63	6.59
16.0	6.65	6.61	6.57	6.53	6.49	6.45
17.0	6.51	6.47	6.44	6.40	6.36	6.32
18.0	6.38	6.34	6.31	6.27	6.23	6.19
19.0	6.25	6.22	6.18	6.14	6.11	6.07
20.0	6.13	6.09	6.06	6.02	5.99	5.95
21.0	6.01	5.98	5.94	5.91	5.87	5.84
22.0	5.90	5.86	5.83	5.79	5.76	5.73
23.0	5.79	5.75	5.72	5.69	5.65	5.62
24.0	5.68	5.65	5.61	5.58	5.55	5.52
25.0	5.58	5.54	5.51	5.48	5.45	5.42
26.0	5.48	5.44	5.41	5.38	5.35	5.32
27.0	5.38	5.35	5.32	5.29	5.26	5.23
28.0	5.28	5.25	5.23	5.20	5.17	5.14
29.0	5.19	5.16	5.14	5.11	5.08	5.05
30.0	5.10	5.08	5.05	5.02	4.99	4.97
31.0	5.02	4.99	4.96	4.94	4.91	4.88
32.0	4.94	4.91	4.88	4.86	4.83	4.80
33.0	4.86	4.83	4.80	4.78	4.75	4.73
34.0	4.78	4.75	4.73	4.70	4.68	4.65
35.0	4.70	4.68	4.65	4.63	4.60	4.58

Oxygen solubility tables—*continued*

	Salinity			Parts per thousand		
Temperature	12.0	13.0	14.0	15.0	16.0	17.0
0.0	9.41	9.35	9.29	9.22	9.16	9.10
1.0	9.16	9.10	9.04	8.97	8.91	8.85
2.0	8.92	8.86	8.80	8.74	8.68	8.62
3.0	8.68	8.63	8.57	8.51	8.45	8.40
4.0	8.46	8.41	8.35	8.29	8.24	8.19
5.0	8.25	8.19	8.14	8.09	8.03	7.98
6.0	8.05	7.99	7.94	7.89	7.84	7.79
7.0	7.85	7.80	7.75	7.70	7.65	7.60
8.0	7.66	7.61	7.57	7.52	7.47	7.42
9.0	7.48	7.44	7.39	7.34	7.30	7.25
10.0	7.31	7.27	7.22	7.17	7.13	7.08
11.0	7.15	7.10	7.06	7.01	6.97	6.93
12.0	6.99	6.95	6.90	6.86	6.82	6.77
13.0	6.84	6.79	6.75	6.71	6.67	6.63
14.0	6.69	6.65	6.61	6.57	6.53	6.49
15.0	6.55	6.51	6.47	6.43	6.39	6.35
16.0	6.41	6.37	6.34	6.30	6.26	6.22
17.0	6.28	6.24	6.21	6.17	6.13	6.10
18.0	6.16	6.12	6.08	6.05	6.01	5.97
19.0	6.03	6.00	5.96	5.93	5.89	5.86
20.0	5.92	5.88	5.85	5.81	5.78	5.74
21.0	5.80	5.77	5.74	5.70	5.67	5.64
22.0	5.69	5.66	5.63	5.60	5.56	5.53
23.0	5.59	5.56	5.52	5.49	5.46	5.43
24.0	5.49	5.46	5.42	5.39	5.36	5.33
25.0	5.39	5.36	5.33	5.30	5.27	5.24
26.0	5.29	5.26	5.23	5.20	5.17	5.14
27.0	5.20	5.17	5.14	5.11	5.08	5.06
28.0	5.11	5.08	5.05	5.03	5.00	4.97
29.0	5.02	5.00	4.97	4.94	4.91	4.89
30.0	4.94	4.91	4.89	4.86	4.83	4.81
31.0	4.86	4.83	4.80	4.78	4.75	4.73
32.0	4.78	4.75	4.73	4.70	4.68	4.65
33.0	4.70	4.68	4.65	4.63	4.60	4.58
34.0	4.63	4.60	4.58	4.55	4.53	4.50
35.0	4.55	4.53	4.51	4.48	4.46	4.43

Oxygen solubility tables—*continued*

	Salinity			Parts per thousand		
Temperature	18.0	19.0	20.0	21.0	22.0	23.0
0.0	9.04	8.97	8.91	8.85	8.79	8.73
1.0	8.79	8.73	8.68	8.62	8.56	8.50
2.0	8.56	8.51	8.45	8.39	8.34	8.28
3.0	8.34	8.29	8.23	8.18	8.12	8.07
4.0	8.13	8.08	8.02	7.97	7.92	7.87
5.0	7.93	7.88	7.83	7.77	7.72	7.67
6.0	7.74	7.69	7.64	7.59	7.54	7.49
7.0	7.55	7.50	7.45	7.40	7.36	7.31
8.0	7.37	7.33	7.28	7.23	7.19	7.14
9.0	7.20	7.16	7.11	7.07	7.02	6.98
10.0	7.04	6.99	6.95	6.91	6.86	6.82
11.0	6.88	6.84	6.80	6.75	6.71	6.67
12.0	6.73	6.69	6.65	6.61	6.56	6.52
13.0	6.59	6.55	6.50	6.46	6.42	6.38
14.0	6.45	6.41	6.37	6.33	6.29	6.25
15.0	6.31	6.27	6.24	6.20	6.16	6.12
16.0	6.18	6.15	6.11	6.07	6.03	6.00
17.0	6.06	6.02	5.99	5.95	5.91	5.88
18.0	5.94	5.90	5.87	5.83	5.80	5.76
19.0	5.82	5.79	5.75	5.72	5.69	5.65
20.0	5.71	5.68	5.64	5.61	5.58	5.54
21.0	5.60	5.57	5.54	5.51	5.47	5.44
22.0	5.50	5.47	5.44	5.40	5.37	5.34
23.0	5.40	5.37	5.34	5.31	5.28	5.24
24.0	5.30	5.27	5.24	5.21	5.18	5.15
25.0	5.21	5.18	5.15	5.12	5.09	5.06
26.0	5.12	5.09	5.06	5.03	5.00	4.97
27.0	5.03	5.00	4.97	4.94	4.92	4.89
28.0	4.94	4.91	4.89	4.86	4.83	4.81
29.0	4.86	4.83	4.81	4.78	4.75	4.73
30.0	4.78	4.75	4.73	4.70	4.68	4.65
31.0	4.70	4.68	4.65	4.62	4.60	4.57
32.0	4.63	4.60	4.58	4.55	4.53	4.50
33.0	4.55	4.53	4.50	4.48	4.46	4.43
34.0	4.48	4.46	4.43	4.41	4.39	4.36
35.0	4.41	4.39	4.36	4.34	4.32	4.30

Oxygen solubility tables—*continued*

	Salinity			Parts per thousand		
Temperature	24.0	25.0	26.0	27.0	28.0	29.0
0.0	8.67	8.61	8.56	8.50	8.44	8.38
1.0	8.44	8.39	8.33	8.27	8.22	8.16
2.0	8.22	8.17	8.11	8.06	8.01	7.95
3.0	8.01	7.96	7.91	7.86	7.80	7.75
4.0	7.81	7.76	7.71	7.66	7.61	7.56
5.0	7.62	7.57	7.52	7.47	7.42	7.37
6.0	7.44	7.39	7.34	7.29	7.25	7.20
7.0	7.26	7.22	7.17	7.12	7.08	7.03
8.0	7.09	7.05	7.00	6.96	6.91	6.87
9.0	6.93	6.89	6.84	6.80	6.76	6.71
10.0	6.78	6.73	6.69	6.65	6.61	6.56
11.0	6.63	6.58	6.54	6.50	6.46	6.42
12.0	6.48	6.44	6.40	6.36	6.32	6.28
13.0	6.34	6.31	6.27	6.23	6.19	6.15
14.0	6.21	6.17	6.14	6.10	6.06	6.02
15.0	6.08	6.05	6.01	5.97	5.94	5.90
16.0	5.96	5.93	5.89	5.85	5.82	5.78
17.0	5.84	5.81	5.77	5.74	5.70	5.67
18.0	5.73	5.69	5.66	5.63	5.59	5.56
19.0	5.62	5.59	5.55	5.52	5.49	5.45
20.0	5.51	5.48	5.45	5.42	5.38	5.35
21.0	5.41	5.38	5.35	5.32	5.28	5.25
22.0	5.31	5.28	5.25	5.22	5.19	5.16
23.0	5.21	5.18	5.15	5.12	5.10	5.07
24.0	5.12	5.09	5.06	5.03	5.01	4.98
25.0	5.03	5.00	4.98	4.95	4.92	4.89
26.0	4.95	4.92	4.89	4.86	4.83	4.81
27.0	4.86	4.83	4.81	4.78	4.75	4.73
28.0	4.78	4.75	4.73	4.70	4.67	4.65
29.0	4.70	4.67	4.65	4.62	4.60	4.57
30.0	4.62	4.60	4.57	4.55	4.52	4.50
31.0	4.55	4.53	4.50	4.48	4.45	4.43
32.0	4.48	4.45	4.43	4.41	4.38	4.36
33.0	4.41	4.38	4.36	4.34	4.31	4.29
34.0	4.34	4.32	4.29	4.27	4.25	4.23
35.0	4.27	4.25	4.23	4.21	4.18	4.16

Oxygen solubility tables—*continued*

	Salinity			Parts per thousand		
Temperature	30.0	31.0	32.0	33.0	34.0	35.0
0.0	8.32	8.27	8.21	8.16	8.10	8.05
1.0	8.11	8.05	8.00	7.94	7.89	7.84
2.0	7.90	7.85	7.79	7.74	7.69	7.64
3.0	7.70	7.65	7.60	7.55	7.50	7.45
4.0	7.51	7.46	7.41	7.36	7.31	7.26
5.0	7.33	7.28	7.23	7.18	7.14	7.09
6.0	7.15	7.11	7.06	7.01	6.97	6.92
7.0	6.98	6.94	6.89	6.85	6.81	6.76
8.0	6.82	6.78	6.74	6.69	6.65	6.61
9.0	6.67	6.63	6.59	6.54	6.50	6.46
10.0	6.52	6.48	6.44	6.40	6.36	6.32
11.0	6.38	6.34	6.30	6.26	6.22	6.18
12.0	6.24	6.21	6.17	6.13	6.09	6.05
13.0	6.11	6.07	6.04	6.00	5.96	5.93
14.0	5.99	5.95	5.91	5.88	5.84	5.80
15.0	5.87	5.83	5.79	5.76	5.72	5.69
16.0	5.75	5.71	5.68	5.64	5.61	5.58
17.0	5.64	5.60	5.57	5.53	5.50	5.47
18.0	5.53	5.49	5.46	5.43	5.40	5.36
19.0	5.42	5.39	5.36	5.33	5.29	5.26
20.0	5.32	5.29	5.26	5.23	5.20	5.17
21.0	5.22	5.19	5.16	5.13	5.10	5.07
22.0	5.13	5.10	5.07	5.04	5.01	4.98
23.0	5.04	5.01	4.98	4.95	4.92	4.89
24.0	4.95	4.92	4.89	4.86	4.84	4.81
25.0	4.86	4.84	4.81	4.78	4.75	4.73
26.0	4.78	4.75	4.73	4.70	4.67	4.65
27.0	4.70	4.67	4.65	4.62	4.60	4.57
28.0	4.62	4.60	4.57	4.55	4.52	4.50
29.0	4.55	4.52	4.50	4.47	4.45	4.42
30.0	4.47	4.45	4.43	4.40	4.38	4.35
31.0	4.40	4.38	4.36	4.33	4.31	4.28
32.0	4.33	4.31	4.29	4.26	4.24	4.22
33.0	4.27	4.24	4.22	4.20	4.18	4.15
34.0	4.20	4.18	4.16	4.14	4.11	4.09
35.0	4.14	4.12	4.10	4.07	4.05	4.03

Oxygen solubility tables—*continued*

	Salinity			*Parts per thousand*		
Temperature	36.0	37.0	38.0	39.0	40.0	41.0
0.0	7.99	7.94	7.88	7.83	7.77	7.72
1.0	7.78	7.73	7.68	7.63	7.58	7.52
2.0	7.59	7.53	7.48	7.43	7.38	7.33
3.0	7.40	7.35	7.30	7.25	7.20	7.15
4.0	7.22	7.17	7.12	7.07	7.03	6.98
5.0	7.04	7.00	6.95	6.90	6.86	6.81
6.0	6.88	6.83	6.79	6.74	6.70	6.66
7.0	6.72	6.67	6.63	6.59	6.55	6.50
8.0	6.57	6.52	6.48	6.44	6.40	6.36
9.0	6.42	6.38	6.34	6.30	6.26	6.22
10.0	6.28	6.24	6.20	6.16	6.12	6.08
11.0	6.14	6.10	6.07	6.03	5.99	5.95
12.0	6.01	5.98	5.94	5.90	5.87	5.83
13.0	5.89	5.85	5.82	5.78	5.74	5.71
14.0	5.77	5.73	5.70	5.66	5.63	5.59
15.0	5.65	5.62	5.58	5.55	5.52	5.48
16.0	5.54	5.51	5.48	5.44	5.41	5.38
17.0	5.43	5.40	5.37	5.34	5.31	5.27
18.0	5.33	5.30	5.27	5.24	5.21	5.17
19.0	5.23	5.20	5.17	5.14	5.11	5.08
20.0	5.14	5.10	5.07	5.05	5.02	4.99
21.0	5.04	5.01	4.98	4.95	4.93	4.90
22.0	4.95	4.92	4.89	4.87	4.84	4.81
23.0	4.87	4.84	4.81	4.78	4.75	4.73
24.0	4.78	4.75	4.73	4.70	4.67	4.65
25.0	4.70	4.67	4.65	4.62	4.59	4.57
26.0	4.62	4.59	4.57	4.54	4.52	4.49
27.0	4.54	4.52	4.49	4.47	4.44	4.42
28.0	4.47	4.45	4.42	4.40	4.37	4.35
29.0	4.40	4.37	4.35	4.33	4.30	4.28
30.0	4.33	4.31	4.28	4.26	4.24	4.21
31.0	4.26	4.24	4.22	4.19	4.17	4.15
32.0	4.20	4.17	4.15	4.13	4.11	4.08
33.0	4.13	4.11	4.09	4.07	4.04	4.02
34.0	4.07	4.05	4.03	4.01	3.98	3.96
35.0	4.01	3.99	3.97	3.95	3.93	3.91

Subject Index

A